FROM RUSSIA TO USSR

A Narrative and Documentary History

Union of Soviet Socialist Republics

CONTRIBUTORS

Carol Horgan
Newton North High School
Newton, Massachusetts

Kendall Read Richardson
Needham High School
Needham, Massachusetts

Joan Sindall-Uspensky
Cambridge Friends School
Cambridge, Massachusetts

James J. Valin
Canton High School
Canton, Massachusetts

FROM RUSSIA TO USSR

A Narrative and Documentary History

Janet G. Vaillant

Harvard University
Cambridge, Massachusetts

John Richards II

Phillips Academy
Andover, Massachusetts

Longman

New York & London

To Our Children

CONTENTS

MAPS

Note: Throughout the text, certain words or terms requiring explanation or definition are designated by a "dagger" and will be found in the Glossary with appropriate description.

PREFACE

FROM RUSSIA TO USSR is the result of our efforts to find materials to bring the world of Russia and the Soviet Union to our students. Many are the primary sources, eyewitness accounts and literary works available to the specialist, but often they are inaccessible to the classroom teacher. This book presents a carefully chosen selection of such readings, together with a brief text that provides the essentials of Russian and Soviet history and geography, and a description of how the Soviet system works today.

FROM RUSSIA TO USSR is truly a collaborative project. The teachers who contributed to it met in workshops organized by Janet Vaillant under the auspices of the Soviet and East European Language and Area Center program at Harvard. They decided to meet periodically to share materials that they had found useful in their classes. From those meetings has grown this book. Everyone contributed to all of its parts. John Richards II and Kendall Richardson wrote the text and selected readings for Chapter One; James Valin and Joan Sindall-Uspensky performed the same tasks for Chapter Two. John Richards wrote the text of Chapters Three and Four and put together the readings for Chapter Four; Janet Vaillant put together readings for Chapters Three, Five, and Six, and wrote the text of Chapters Five and Six. Carol Horgan undertook the job of getting permissions. Joan Sindall-Uspensky oversaw the illustrations. Horgan, Richards, and Vaillant edited and checked the whole.

Selecting readings from the wealth of material was a difficult task. We collected many good readings that we could not use without letting the book grow far too long, and shortened others drastically for the same reason. Our standard for choice was that a reading should help bring history to life, and should be useful in the classroom. We highly recommend further reading in the works from which we have drawn excerpts. One omission deserves mention. Marx is not here. We decided that his work is readily available elsewhere, and wanted to make available readings to which teachers and students might not otherwise have access.

There is a technical matter that bedevils anyone who writes on Russian subjects: the transliteration of Russian names into English. We have chosen to use the forms most familiar to American readers rather than to follow one of the several schools of scholarly transliteration. Hence Tolstoy, rather than Tolstoi or Tolstoj. When our sources have used spellings that differ from ours, we have left them as they appeared in the original reading.

Many people have advised and commented on this work. It is even more true than usual that none of them is responsible for the final form of the text. Experts on the early history of Rus' do not agree on any single interpretation of that period, nor is there any consensus on how best to characterize the Soviet Union today. Nonetheless, we have benefited greatly from the willingness of many scholars connected with Harvard's Russian Research Center to guide us through the thickets of interpretation towards clear generalizations. The book is certainly the better for their help, though most of them would have been happier had we made fewer generalizations and more qualifications. Then, however, we would have had a much longer text. For errors that remain we, of course, are responsible. For reading and commenting on parts of this book, we thank Mark Beissinger, William C. Brumfield, William Fuller, Catherine Jones, Aleksandr Nekrich, Mikhail Tsypkin, and Kirill Uspensky. Professor Brumfield also generously allowed us to use three of his photographs. To Lubomyr Hajda goes special thanks for help and encouragement throughout. Student readers, too, have kept us on course. James Aiken, Peter Gefteas, Stephen Love, William Shea, and William Swanson, Jr. read some chapters in progress, as did students at Canton, Newton North, and Needham High Schools, Phillips Academy, Andover, and the Cambridge Friends School. We are grateful to our respective schools for their encouragement of our work. Ellen Lapenson has been our typist and general aid. We have also benefited from the support of the U.S. Department of Education for the Soviet and East European Language and Area Center program at Harvard and from the Russian Research Center which has provided an ever congenial and stimulating atmosphere. To our editor, Marguerite Davis, of the Independent School Press, we owe a great debt for bearing with the special trials and tribulations of such a complicated group project.

We would also like to thank our spouses — Betty, Jane, Henry, Kirill, and Wendy.

FROM RUSSIA TO USSR

A Narrative and Documentary History

Chapter One

The Soviet Union: Geography

FACT: The country we often refer to as Russia is properly called the Union of Soviet Socialist Republics. This has been its name since 1922.

There is no country called Russia today. Russia is a name that refers to the prerevolutionary regime of the Tsars, which was overthrown in 1917. The Revolution of 1917 created a new state, which was formally named the Union of Soviet Socialist Republics six years later. Today the Soviet Union is a federal state that includes fifteen Union Republics, of which by far the largest is the Russian Republic (to be precise, the Russian Soviet Federated Socialist Republic, or RSFSR). This Republic stretches all the way from the Baltic and Black Seas in the west to the Pacific Ocean in the east, and is peopled chiefly by Russians, who are the largest single ethnic group in the Soviet Union. Fourteen other national groups have their own Union Republics as well, while the many other smaller ethnic groups have defined regions within one of the Republics.

To better understand the history of this country, we should first examine the land it occupies. As with other countries, Russia's history has been greatly affected by its geography: its landscape, climate, vegetation, resources, and other natural features. In many respects, the geography of the USSR is both unique and dramatic, and has thus provided an appropriate setting for a history that is also unique and dramatic. A glance at any map will suffice to illustrate the most obvious geographical characteristic of this country: its size.

SIZE

FACT: The Soviet Union with 8.6 million square miles is larger than the United States and Canada combined.

FACT: The Soviet Union spans eleven time zones compared to just four for the continental United States. When it is 7 p.m. in Moscow, it is 6 a.m. the following day in Uelen, a village on the Bering Strait. As with the British Empire of old, it is true to say that the sun never sets on the Soviet Union.

FACT: It is virtually the same distance from Moscow to Vladivostok as it is from Moscow to New York City.

FACT: Should you attempt to walk around the borders of the USSR, you would travel 37,250 miles. That is the equivalent of walking around the globe at the Equator 1½ times. Of this distance, nearly 27,000 miles comprises coastline, leaving over 10,000 miles of frontiers shared with twelve other countries.

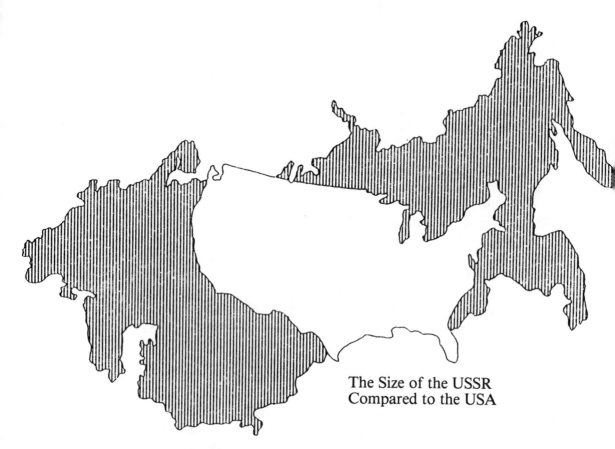

The Size of the USSR
Compared to the USA

As suggested by these facts, the Soviet Union is immense. For the leaders of the Soviet Union, however, their country's size is a mixed blessing. On the one hand, it provides ample living space for an expanding population. It also increases the probability of having an abundance of natural resources to support that population. On the other hand, the vast distances confront Soviet leaders with great challenges, such as giving diverse and scattered peoples the sense that they belong to one country. A large country is hard to govern, communications within it become expensive, and most especially, its lengthy frontiers create staggering defense problems. For example, the Soviet Union's relationships with the twelve nations with whom it shares borders have not always been good. Nonetheless the Soviet Union's status today as a superpower rests, at least in part, on its great size.

LOCATION

FACT: One part of the Soviet Union lies in Europe; the other part is in Asia. Its westernmost point is further west than Warsaw, Poland. Its easternmost point, Big Diomede Island in the Bering Strait, is a scant 3½ miles from Little Diomede Island, which is part of our state of Alaska.

This fact illustrates a unique feature of the USSR. It is the world's only country to occupy a sizable portion of two continents. The line that geographers use to separate Europe from Asia is an invented one. From the north, it runs southward along the Ural Mountains to the Caspian Sea, westward to the Black Sea, and then southwestward through the Bosporus and Dardanelles. Europe lies to the west of the Urals; Asia lies to the east.

This location has posed a dilemma for the Russian and Soviet leaders. Their people have been adjacent to but not really a part of the great Chinese civilization to the East, the Islamic Middle East to the South, and Christian Europe to the West. In the course of their history, the Russians and Soviets have interacted with and borrowed from all three of these great cultures. Today's Soviet leaders must come to terms with the fact that theirs is a country that is both European *and* Asian, with vital interests in both areas. How they deal with this East-West orientation is strongly influenced by the fact that, while a large percentage of their citizens are Slavic and live in Europe, most of their territory lies in Asia and contains a predominantly non-Slavic population.

Another important aspect of the geography of the Soviet Union is its northern location.

FACT: 99.5% of the people in the United States and Canada live south of 54° North Latitude—the latitude of Edmonton, Alberta. However, 75% of the USSR's population lives *north* of 54° North Latitude.

FACT: Moscow, the USSR's capital city of 8 million, is on the same latitude as the southern end of Hudson Bay in Canada. The 3.5 million residents of Leningrad are at almost the same latitude as the Americans living in Skagway, Alaska.

FACT: Sochi, a favorite Soviet Black Sea resort, is farther north than Boston, Massachusetts.

The extreme northern location of the USSR has significant effects on its climate, as does the size of the landmass it occupies.

CLIMATE: TEMPERATURE AND PRECIPITATION

FACT: The mean January temperature in Verkhoyansk, a small city in eastern Siberia, is -56°F. A temperature of -126°F. was once recorded there.

FACT: Another Siberian city, Yakutsk, has a mean January temperature of -46°F., and a mean July temperature of 66°F. Yakutsk has recorded temperatures as low as -84°F. and as high as 102°F.—a span of 186 degrees.

FACT: Batumi and Lenkoran are two communities in the South Caucasus that have an annual rainfall of 95.6″ and 49.3″, respectively. The rest of the USSR has an annual precipitation of 24" or less. On the whole, it is a dry country.

FACT: Of the total precipitation in any given year, 62% of the runoff flows into the Arctic Ocean, and is therefore relatively useless.

At first glance, these facts may appear to be mere trivia, but they have serious implications. They tell us a great deal about how geography, and climate in particular, continues to have a major impact on the Soviet people and their economy. First, much of the Soviet Union is subject to great ranges of temperature. The USSR occupies a very extensive landmass with no large bodies of water to modify temperature extremes. Thus, much of Siberia can be blisteringly hot in the summer and frigidly cold in the winter. (See Reading 2) The Soviet Union has what geographers call a high latitude continental climate.

A location farther north on the globe than most of the United States means more than longer winters and shorter summers. It means that growing seasons are shorter as well. And that in turn means potentially serious problems in providing enough food for a large and growing population.

A high latitude continental climate also is likely to mean marginal amounts of rainfall for sustaining agriculture. This, too, affects food production, and sometimes causes grain and meat shortages, a problem not only for the consumer but for the economic planners as well. The Soviet government sees to it that basic food prices are kept artificially low for the consumer, but subsidizing the consumer creates a strain on the government's budget. While there is no denying that some of the USSR's agricultural problems result from inefficiency, mismanagement, and poor incentives, it is also true that the USSR's location and climate will continue to limit the Soviet Union's ability to feed itself.

The Soviet Union's high latitude climate has other effects as well. The Soviets must devote great energy and resources to such elementary tasks as keeping warm and removing mountains of snow from their streets. Today, Americans are sensitive to the high cost of the energy needed to heat and light homes and factories, and the same is certainly true for the Soviets.

Finally, those bone-chilling temperatures cited above point to yet another way in which the USSR's high latitude climate has had a negative impact on the Soviets and their economy. This, the world's largest country, a country with 27,000 miles of coastline, has remarkably few major ports. Leningrad, the second-largest city in the USSR, is one of these, but because it is so far north it is icebound for most of the winter. The same is true of Archangel, located even farther north on the White Sea, and of Vladivostok, the chief Soviet port in the Far East. Ironically Murmansk, the farthest north of all the major Soviet ports, is ice-free, thanks to the influence of the Gulf Stream. It is far from the country's industry and population centers, however. Ports on the Black Sea such as Sebastopol and Odessa are also ice-free, but do not have direct access to the major oceans, depending for such access on Turkey, which controls the Straits (Bosporus and Dardanelles).

TOPOGRAPHY

FACT: Mount Communism is the highest mountain in the Soviet Union. At 24,250 feet, it is higher than any mountain in Europe, Africa, or the Western Hemisphere.

FACT: To the east and the west of the Ural Mountains lie two vast plains. On the eastern side of the Urals is the West Siberian Plain. At no point does this plain ever rise higher than 1,000 feet above sea level. It is the world's largest area of level land.

A close examination of a physical map of the USSR reveals several significant topographic facts, among them the location of the mountains of the Soviet Union. The entire country can be visualized as a gigantic amphitheatre facing north toward the Arctic Ocean. The only high mountains in the Soviet Union are along its southern border, running in an arc from near the Bering Strait southerly and then westerly, eventually tapering off in the relatively low Carpathians of east central Europe. In the center of this arc the Soviet mountains are very high indeed, and close to the still higher peaks of Tibet, Nepal, and Kashmir. The eastern end of these mountains prevents moisture from the Pacific from penetrating into the interior, and the high mountains in the south prevent warm air currents from the Indian Ocean from reaching the USSR. There are, however, no mountains in the northern USSR to shield the interior from the icy blasts of the Arctic. The Urals are the only chain of mountains in the interior, and they are no barrier to the Arctic winds. Even if Nature had turned them around by 90°, they would not form much of a barrier; they are low mountains with an average elevation of only 2,000 - 2,500 feet.

This absence of natural boundaries, except in the south, has also created security problems for the Russians, especially in the west. No river or mountain range separates the Russians from their Polish or German neighbors, and over the vast plain that stretches from central Russia through Poland and Germany, tragedy has repeatedly struck the Russians: the Napoleonic invasion of 1812, and those of the Germans in 1915 and 1941. In these times of national peril, the country's vast size and devastating winters ultimately became assets in thwarting their enemies. Nonetheless, in terms of topography, the country remains vulnerable.

FACT: Two of the world's five longest rivers, the Yenisey and the Ob'-Irtysh, are in the USSR. They are 3,700 and 3,500 miles respectively. Both flow north to the Arctic Ocean.

FACT: Virtually all of the USSR's rivers flow in a north-south or a south-north direction. The Amur River in Siberia is a notable exception. Its course is generally west to east and, for much of its length, it forms the boundary between the USSR and the People's Republic of China.

Log rafts on the Volga River.

The Soviet Union is a land of rivers. It is estimated that there are more than 100,000 rivers. Traditionally, these rivers have been widely used for transportation, but they have two drawbacks. The first is the fact that the rivers are frozen for much of the year. The passenger vessels plying the Volga don't begin their season until Lenin's birthday on April 22nd. The other drawback has been noted: with the primary need for transportation and communication being east-west, rivers which flow north-south are only moderately useful.

SOIL AND VEGETATION

FACT: 47% of the land of the USSR is permanently frozen. Even in summer, only the top few inches thaw. This is called the permafrost zone.

FACT: Forests cover 50% of the USSR's land area.

FACT: Swamps and marshes occupy 20% of that land area.

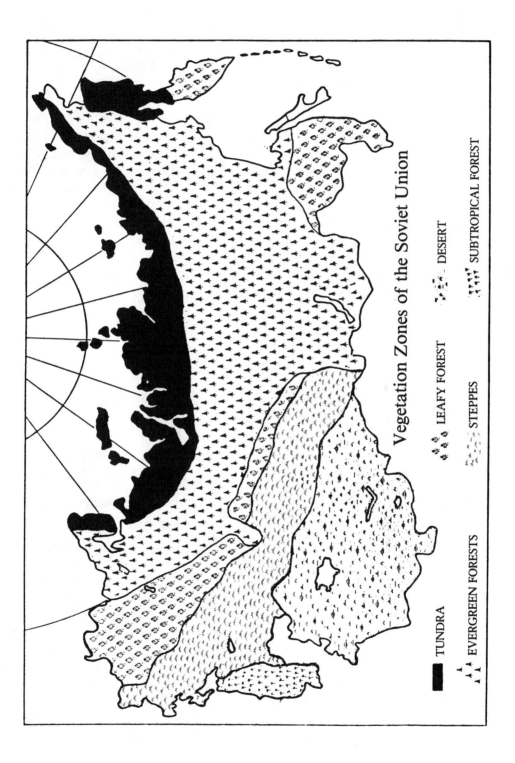

Vegetation Zones of the Soviet Union

TUNDRA

EVERGREEN FORESTS

LEAFY FOREST

STEPPES

DESERT

SUBTROPICAL FOREST

FACT: 17% of the USSR's area consists of semi-arid lands and deserts.

FACT: Only 10.7% of the total area of the USSR is arable land.

Note: Percentages do not total 100% because zones of topography and vegetation overlap. Some of the forested region is within the permafrost zone, while the swamps and marshes are a part of the northern forest region.

The Soviet Union has several belts of vegetation, from tundra† in the north to deserts in the south. But even in the areas that are frost-free for a sufficient number of days each year to cultivate crops, much of the land receives too little moisture to sustain good harvests. When the forests have been partially cleared for cultivation, the soil is acidic and infertile. Such acidic soil is called *podzol*. In the steppe† region in the southwestern USSR, the *chernozem* or "black earth" is exceedingly rich, but here the soil does not receive sufficient precipitation. Throughout Russian history, there has been an average of one poor harvest in every three, causing shortages or famine. In the years 1979-1982, the Soviets experienced four consecutive years of serious grain shortfalls, in large part due to drought. This forced them to import grain from Canada, Argentina, Australia and the United States.

NATURAL RESOURCES

FACT: The USSR is virtually self-sufficient in terms of raw materials. Two exceptions are rubber and quinine.

FACT: The Soviet Union possesses the world's largest timber reserves.

FACT: In 1979, the Soviet Union led the world in the production of oil and coal. It regularly produces 20% of the world's petroleum and 25% of its natural gas.

FACT: 90% of the USSR's coal reserves are located east of the Urals. 75% of the population and 80% of the industry are located west of the Urals.

Although the production of foodstuffs remains a serious problem for the USSR, the fact that it is nearly self-sufficient in most raw materials is unquestionably a source of strength. For centuries, the Russians have depended on the abundant supply of timber for building and as a source of energy. Much of this timber comes from the extensive northern forest, known as the *taiga*, which consists largely of softwood trees such as spruce and fir. In addition to its timber resources, the Soviet Union is in an enviable position as the world's leading producer of petroleum and the possessor of huge reserves of natural gas. Many of the Soviet Union's natural resources are in inaccessible areas, however, and are difficult to extract from the ground. This is particularly true of the permafrost regions. Here the subsoil is always frozen at an average depth of eighteen inches below the surface. The topsoil constitutes an "active layer" that is subject to

Soviet Industrial Resources

thaw during warm seasons. The alternation of this active layer between frost and bog creates extremely severe challenges to miners and construction crews. Projects such as the Baikal-Amur Mainline (BAM) railroad and the natural gas pipeline from Siberia to central and western Europe therefore require complex engineering solutions. The potential for self-sufficiency in natural resources is difficult to reach because of these climatic considerations.

HUMAN RESOURCES

FACT: As of 1983, the USSR's population exceeded 271,000,000— compared to the 262,400,000 registered in the last census in 1979.

FACT: Only the People's Republic of China and India outrank the USSR in size of population.

FACT: 53.4% of the Soviet Union's population is female.

FACT: 64% of the USSR's citizens now live in urban areas. In 1926 only 18% of the population lived in urban areas.

FACT: There are over 100 officially recognized nationalities in the Soviet Union—22 of which have a population in excess of one million.

FACT: 52% of the USSR's population is ethnically Russian.

As these facts suggest, the human resources of the Soviet Union are interesting in a number of ways. Although the USSR has the world's third largest population, a population which is growing steadily, it remains very low in terms of population density. The Soviet Union is, for example, only 4% as dense in population as the state of Massachusetts, with immense stretches of land still virtually unpopulated, especially in the north and east.

The population is also shifting. Perhaps most noticeable is the shift from the countryside to the city during the past fifty years, but there is also an "eastward movement" somewhat comparable to the "westward movement" in the United States during the nineteenth century. The population of Siberia began to increase dramatically toward the end of that century, and this increase has continued throughout the twentieth century, particularly as the Soviet leadership has promoted the location of new industry in the regions east of the Urals. Today Siberia has eight cities with a population of over 500,000, and another forty with a population of over 100,000. (See Reading 3) Nevertheless, 75% of the USSR's population still lives west of the Urals.

The fact that females greatly outnumber males stems from the ravages of the two world wars, especially the second. Demographers believe that this imbalance is likely to remain for several more generations.

Of greater concern to the current Soviet leadership is the fact that, while the population as a whole is growing, it is the non-Russian (and non-Slavic) groups that are increasing most rapidly. For example, between the censuses of 1959 and 1979, the Tadzhiks and Uzbeks of Central Asia increased at six times the rate of the Russians. If this trend continues, as appears likely, the Russians will soon no longer be a majority of the total population. This could make it more difficult for the Russians to maintain the near-monopoly of political power that they have held and continue to hold today. Beyond this is the question of the loyalty of these minority nationalities, a question which came to the surface when Soviet troops crossed into Afghanistan in 1979. Many of these troops were Muslims from Central Asia, and their commanders soon discovered that they were excessively sympathetic to their fellow Muslims of Afghanistan. Entire units of the Red Army in Afghanistan had to be replaced by more reliable, non-Islamic Soviet troops.

Of all the characteristics of the Soviet population today, it is its diversity that is perhaps most striking. That population includes over 137 million Russians, who speak a Slavic language and have an Orthodox Christian religious tradition, but it also includes over a hundred other peoples who speak other

Bukhara, the Citadel, Uzbekistan. *Photo Source: William Craft Brumfield*

tongues and worship other gods. (See Reading 4) Many of these are small in number: the 1979 census listed only 1,510 Eskimos, for example. Yet for all these peoples, their own cultural heritage is a source of pride, while for the Soviet leadership the multitude of cultural traditions constitutes a considerable challenge as they attempt to encourage loyalty to the Soviet Union as a whole. The relationship between the Soviet leadership and the national minorities will be taken up in more detail in Chapter Six.

The Soviet Union has been called a land of extremes. It includes flat plains and high mountains, glaciers and deserts, places that are hot and places that are very cold. Over the centuries, its people have had to cope with these extremes. Geographical conditions have made it difficult to earn a living from the land, and to feed a constantly growing population. Natural resources other than foodstuffs are abundant but often difficult to extract. Perhaps most important of all, the flatness of the land and the absence of natural boundaries have created security problems and a deep-seated fear of invasion. The history of Russia and the Soviet Union has been greatly affected by all of these geographical influences.

The following books were helpful in writing this chapter:

Brown, A., Fennell, J., Kaser, M., and Willetts, H.T., editors, *The Cambridge Encyclopedia of Russia and the Soviet Union,* New York: Cambridge University Press, 1982.

Dewdney, J.C., *USSR in Maps,* New York: Holmes and Meyer, 1982.

East, W.G., *The Soviet Union,* 2nd Ed., New York: van Nostrand, 1976.

Symons, L., editor, *The Soviet Union: A Systematic Geography,* New York: Barnes and Noble, 1983.

Whiting, K.R., *The Soviet Union Today,* New York: Praeger, 1962.

For students who are interested, we recommend further reading in the sources from which we have taken excerpts, as well as the following works:

Blum, D., *Russia: The Land and People of the Soviet Union,* New York: Harry Abrahams, 1980.
This large and lavish volume contains fine color illustrations which vividly convey a visual image of the Soviet land and its peoples.

Konigsberger, H., *Along the Roads of the New Russia,* New York: Farrar, Straus and Giroux, 1968.
A readable account of everyday life in the Soviet Union by a Dutch-American who traveled through that country in an old Italian army truck.

McDowell, B., *Journey Across Russia: The Soviet Union Today,* Washington: The National Geographic Society, 1977.
The combination of McDowell's text and Conger's photographs makes this a fine, albeit impressionistic account of many aspects of Soviet life and culture. The authors had access to most parts of the USSR, in return for which the Soviet authorities approved McDowell's text.

Soloukin, V., *A Walk in Rural Russia,* Miskin, S., translator, New York: E.P. Dutton, 1967.
This is an unusual account of the adventures of a Russian poet and his wife, who spent the summer of 1956 on a walking tour of the woods, bicycle-paths, and tiny villages of the historic region around Vladimir and Suzdal.

Spring, N., *Roaming Russia, Siberia, and Middle Asia,* Seattle: The Salisbury Press, 1973.
A photographic essay, in which the reader is treated to remarkable views of countryside, architectural monuments, and historic sites.

St. George, G., *Siberia and the New Frontier,* New York: David McKay, 1969.
Although its statistics are by now somewhat dated, this book is still valuable for its careful description and analysis of the vast territory of Siberia and its inhabitants.

Readings

Chapter One

List of Readings

1. Impressions of an Early Visitor

The dramatic nature of Russian geography seems to have long impressed visiting Westerners. One of the earliest of these visitors was the Englishman Richard Chancellor, who visited what was then known as Muscovy in the mid-sixteenth century. This is from his account of that visit.

Muscovy, which hath the name also of Russia the white, is a very large and spacious country, every way bounded with diverse nations. Towards the south and the east it is compassed with Tatary; the northern side of it stretcheth to the Scythian Ocean [Arctic Ocean]; upon the west part border the Lapps, a rude and savage nation living in woods, whose language is not known to any other people. Next unto these, more towards the south, is Sweden, then Finland, then Livonia, and last of all Lithuania. This country of Muscovy hath also very many and great rivers in it and is marish [marshy] ground in many places; and as for the rivers, the greatest and most famous among all the rest is that which the Russes in their own tongue call Volga, but others know it by the name of Rha... Besides these rivers are also in Muscovy certain lakes and pools. The lakes breed fish by celestial influence... The whole country is plain and champion [flat], and few hills in it; and towards the north it hath very large and spacious woods wherein is great store of fir trees, a wood very necessary and fit for the building of houses. There are also wild beasts bred in those woods, as buffs, bears, and black wolves... The north parts of the country are reported to be cold that the very ice or water which distilleth out of the moist wood which they lay upon the fire is presently congealed and frozen, the diversity growing suddenly to be so great, that in one and the self-same firebrand a man shall see both fire and ice. When the winter doth once begin there, it doth still more and more increase by a perpetuity of cold; neither doth that cold slake until the force of the sunbeams doth dissolve the cold and make glad the earth returning to it again. Our mariners which we left in the ship in the meantime to keep it, in their going up only from their cabins to the hatches had their breath oftentimes so suddenly taken away that they eftsoons [soon afterward] fell down as men very near dead, so great is the sharpness of that cold climate....

Abridged from "The Voyage of Richard Chancellor," in Lloyd Berry and Robert Crummey, editors, *Rude and Barbarous Kingdom: Russia in the Accounts of Sixteenth Century English Voyagers,* Madison, Wisconsin, 1968.

2. Impressions of a Modern Visitor

The geography of the Soviet Union continues to impress foreign visitors. Wright Miller, an English journalist, lived in the Soviet Union between 1934 and 1961, and recorded his impressions of the Russian winter and the summer forest.

WINTER

...One must begin with the winter, the greedy exhausting winter which, as the peasants used to say, "has a belly on him like a priest." The priest brought forth nothing from the land, but he planted himself at peasant tables and expected to eat his fill. And winter, bringing forth nothing, planted himself across Russia as the great waster and consumer — eating away the hardwon hoards of grain and cabbage, of cucumbers salted in the pickling pond and firewood stacked in the frozen passageway, making lean the wolves who pulled down horses and cattle, wasting the fat of the hibernating bear, and wasting away the patience, the energies, the imaginations and the very breath of human beings in the stale air of the huts where they huddled round the earthen stove.

And still in fifty thousand Soviet villages, and in Soviet cities under the wail of factory sirens and the hoot of American-style locomotives winter is the greatest waster and consumer, wearying body and soul for more than half the year.

In Moscow the frost begins in late September and continues without a respite until April; the last scattering of snow may fall upon the May Day celebrations. Yet the severest part of the winter, the time of twenty or more degrees of frost (-20 °C), is a period of no more than a couple of months as a rule in the Moscow region. It is the chilly monotony of the four, five, or six months of lesser cold which makes the season so hard to bear.

The crows on the Kremlin are the first sign, the host of gray-headed Russian crows which flock in from the countryside to roost among the spires and gilded bulbs until the spring. Every branch is bare already, and out in the fields only an occasional dandelion still shines among the dry stalks. Then one morning these last flowering things have crystallized, as it were, into ice overnight, and for six and a half or seven months there is no green thing but the dark fir trees. The noon-day sun may still strike warm for a few weeks, but until mid-April there is not even a bud to keep the memory of fresh green alive.

November is a black month of icy rain and sleet, and one longs to see the first snow. It comes but it does not stay, and traditionally it should fall and

Abridged from Wright Miller, *Russians as People,* New York, 1960.

melt again three times before it comes for good. In a mild winter it may not stay until December, and the wait is dreary. But when it comes at last the whole city seems warmed into life with the sparkle of the new dry snow, the cushioning of traffic noises and softening of echoes, and the cozy little rise in temperature which follows a snowfall. For a short while it seems as though one had entered on a more benign season instead of a grimmer one, and strangers exchange remarks as though it were spring — 'It's here! It has come!'

But the sparkling vision doesn't last. A grey pall hangs far too often over Moscow; there is no changeable seaborne weather here. There are long, still grey spells and long, still, blue spells, but few — mercifully few — gusty intervals. One misses the lively air of Western Europe, yet if the winds were to blow as they do at home, life out of doors would be impossible in winter. And so the grey pall hangs and hangs for weeks without descending in snow again, the white crests on walls sink to a city drabness, and even the sugar-caps on the Kremlin towers turn dull as the sheet of cloud above them. In the streets snow is soon trodden into slabs and knobs of dirty ice, and one must walk gingerly everywhere, keeping an eye open for little boys who dash through the crowds at top speed, striking sparks as they cross bare patches of flag-stone on their single skate tied up with string.

Slipping and stumbling one goes, and the winter eats up armies of labour to keep city roads useable. In the most important avenues bulldozers attack the snow at once, pushing it into great heaps to slip down the sewer manholes which are left open and unguarded. In lesser streets and yards, the house-porters ...stack up banks of snow until by the end of winter there is barely room for a car to pass. If no more snow falls for a long time, drab bands of sweepers attack the city ice with pick and shovel and pneumatic drill. The points at tram and railway junctions must be kept clear day and night, and this work, like so much unskilled work in Russia, is done by women. Muffled in padded clothes and grasping iron stakes in their clumsy gauntlets, they stand bowed and patient witnesses to the incubus of the winter.

In the worst weather it is so cold that it seems to burn. You launch yourself out of double doors into the street and you gasp. You narrow your shrinking nostrils to give your lungs a chance to get acclimatized, but you gasp again and go on gasping. Ears are well covered against frostbite, but eyebrows and moustache grow icicles in bunches, and sweat runs from under your fur cap and freezes on your temples. Presently a tickle, and the longer hairs of your nostrils have become rigid with ice. Another moment, surely, and the whole nostril will freeze over: in a panic you warm your nose with your glove, but the nostrils do not freeze, and you go on warming your nose and stinging cheeks with your glove, and you go on gasping. Half an hour's walk gives you the exercise of an ordinary afternoon, the only relief is the warm blast from the exhaust of a passing lorry; it is impossible, you think, to bear it all for long, but you can and do....

So, a bundle on two bundled legs, one must go shuffling and stumping through the city winter, scheming to avoid waiting in the open air, banging in and out of double swinging doors and treble swinging doors, leaving everywhere a trail of steaming breath and sweat, queuing always to park your coat, hat, scarf, gloves, and galoshes, and queuing half an hour to get them out again... Sometimes the outside air can be allowed into rooms for a little while through the...little inset double window, but the foreigner, tempted by a milder spell, who reopens his whole inner window will get not only a room which may take a day to heat up again but an outer window which will stay frosted over by his own rash breath for the rest of the season....

It is dark, too, for so long. Moscow's daylight is an hour less than London's in mid-winter, while further north there are only a few hours of whitish day around lunchtime.

It is long and dark and dull, but winter in the towns is tolerable so long as there is wood for heating, or so long as one is connected to the underground heating system....

But out in the villages... life in winter is more its grim and ancient self. The open country is an icy white desolation. White mist — a crystalline veil of air-suspended ice — hangs in the near distance, and only a mile from the villages you would be swallowed up in a swirling white world. There is not a stir in the silent air, but your eyes dazzle at the particles and they seem to swirl. The steely air gnaws and bites at your cheeks, a stiffening of frost aches at the corners of your eyes, and presently out of the padded silence the lightest of winds stirs the surface of the snow, lifting spicules [needlelike crystals] of ices into white wisps and trails, and suddenly it whips one of these across your face like a razor-slash. You turn your back only to meet a stinging slash from the other quarter, and if you must stay out in these conditions your ear-flaps, peak-flap, high fur collar, and a gloved hand together will seem a feeble shield. And this is but the lightest of winds. Every illusion you may have had about enduring Russian cold is undone by wind, and a five-mile-an-hour breeze has a grip like an iron mask. Twice that speed is already a blizzard. Windy weather is frostbite weather, and with ten degrees or more of frost, and a moving air, one must watch out for the white, bloodless patches or, in the ghoulish phrase of the medical book, "Spontaneous amputation may supervene"....

Russians are connoisseurs of cold. There is always some place further inland, they allege, where the cold is more intense but drier and therefore more bearable. Kuibyshevites in Moscow complain of the miserable fifteen or twenty degrees of Moscow frost compared with their sparkling Volga cold, but Siberians in Kuibyshev shiver uneasily at the local thirty or forty degrees and boast of the really stimulating sixties and seventies of their home. Further into the interior of the great land mass the snow is not deeper; there is in fact less of it, there is more sun, and the air is drier and more crackling. In the strange uninhabited region of the north Caspian the snow is a mere sprinkling upon the surface of the brown earth, and one wonders to feel such iron cold....

THE SUMMER FOREST

It was a poetic walk at first — to be making one's way in the silent summer forest without habitation and without another traveller. The dead-straight avenue drew one deeper and deeper into a vegetable silence that was almost unbroken. A squirrel ran across, a jay creaked once or twice, and then all again was a continuity, a silent procession towards the cupful of light balanced on top of the infinitely far-off pines. Imperceptibly the avenue closed in, the gloom grew deeper and the track became faint, but the direction remained. The direction remained but all unnoticed the track grew fainter still, and then there was no track at all and only the merest impression of a direction — an impression left perhaps by beasts but not by men, or not by men for many years past. It seemed to lead, if it led at all, through gloomy, threatening jungle, down into a great basin of dead and leaning trees, still overshadowed by standing giants above... The sun was quite shut out, and one peered nervously at every breath and crackle in the dark underforest of spikes....

There was no other track. One could but stumble through the dead forest, snapping off branches and repeatedly deceived by the ghostliness of light ahead. After a long time the daylight opened on a melancholy clearing — yet no man's clearing but a waste of lichened rocks patched with heather and juniper, and the forest soon closed in again. Another rocky waste followed, of the same ancient, sad appearance, ... and it led indeed to a tumbled stone barrier shrouded in thorns. But this was wild rock, and beyond it only juniper and the dismal firs once more ... One did not need to believe in trolls or spirits of the woods in order to feel that one was treading among the work of strange dead hands, malevolent hands surely because so meaningless in what they had left — the paths that always ended in a silent thicket, the rock which was never the wall or gravestone or gatepost that it appeared at first to be; as one drew closer one always knew the rock could never have been any of these things and yet it must have been something, something neither of nature nor of conscious man, as disorienting as the shape in a surrealist painting. The silence was harder to bear than the cries of strange birds or the lumbering of animals would have been, and for two dark hours I tramped with an ever-growing uneasiness that night would find me still caught in this patternless web....

3. Life in the New Siberia

Siberia is a vast, harsh land that commands the devoted loyalty of its peoples, draws the careful attention of economic planners, and beckons those with a spirit of adventure. It is today one of the fastest growing sections of the Soviet Union. Farley Mowat, a Canadian, traveled and wrote about Siberia with the knowledge and affection of a person familiar with similar landscapes in his own country.

...In spring and summer the Siberian forest is known as the Blue Taiga, because of the smokey blue-green hue imparted to it by the dominant larch trees. After the first frosts, it becomes the Golden Taiga as the larch needles take on the color of honey amber. In September the endless roll of the larch forest begins to glow with a lambent light, given texture by black swaths of pines and defined by the slim white lines of birches.

We drove to a parklike stretch of pines. Nikolai armed me with a double-barreled twelve-gauge gun, and we formed a skirmish line under his direction and set out to hunt for supper.

A heavy, wet snow began falling, and we had not gone fifty yards before we were absorbed into a timeless void. Nikolai came over to join me, and as we moved together into the depths of his inner world, I recalled some lines from one of his poems.

> *The taiga is a universe without an end*
> *Those that live within it are the stars.*
> *Bright stars are the eyes of the beasts*
> *And of the men who walk with the beasts.*
> *The space between the stars is infinite*
> *For the taiga is a universe without an end.*

This is a true poem. The map of Siberia can give no real concept of the immensity of that land. The taiga alone can give the sensation of illimitable space and distance. It is a somewhat daunting feeling, and it makes men walk softly and speak in subdued tones....

CHERNYCHEVSKY

The town was born in 1960 on the banks of the Vilyui about a hundred miles northeast of Mirny and soon became the home of some twelve thousand people engaged in building a most unusual hydroelectric project.

We drove to it through rolling taiga on a newly built road, hard-topped

Abridged from Farley Mowat, *The Siberians,* Boston, 1970.

by nature with glare ice. The skating rink surface did not seem to trouble our driver. Siberians do not bother spreading salt or sand on icy roads, nor are the tires of their vehicles equipped with special treads. Survival depends solely on the driver's skill.

We reached the deep and shadowed Vilyui valley and turned along it. Suddenly our view of the dark gorge was shuttered by a towering gray shape. Although recognizable as a dam — and a mighty one — it was quite unlike any of the great dams I had ever seen. Instead of the usual shining walls of white concrete lifting in precise lunar curves, here was a jumble of huge rock fragments rearing skyward in such apparent confusion that at first glance it seemed as if a natural cataclysm had stoppered the gorge.

The Vilyui dam is two hundred feet high, a third of a mile long, and built almost entirely of materials found in the immediate vicinity of the site. No concrete was used in the main construction. The cement which binds rocks, clay and gravel into a unified whole capable of withstanding the pressure of a reservoir three hundred and twenty miles long is natural too. It is eternal frost. The dam is a staggering demonstration of how Siberian builders have learned to collaborate with a primordial force which they once thought of as their mortal enemy.

The leader of the Vilyui dam builders was a graying, rather ordinary-looking man, a bit pudgy but with clear eyes and an expression as relaxed and amiable as his manner. Gavriel Bijanov had spent thirty years building power dams, but he looked as if he might have spent those years as a gentle schoolteacher.

He met me at the door of the big log building that serves as construction headquarters, and in lieu of the cool handshake I had received in Mirny, he hugged me hard.

"Welcome!" he said. "In 1962 I visited your country and traveled in your North — now I am happy to be the host to Canadian friends!"

The key people of his staff had gathered to meet us in the usual conference room. All save Gavriel seemed very young. Most were men but there were several women among them. Most were of European extraction but there were a number of Siberian natives. Gavriel's second-in-command, Nikolai Atlasov, was Evenki.* We were greeted with the kind of warmth I had come to accept as characteristic of all Siberians.

These people were unregenerate enthusiasts and each was determined that I should hear every detail of the story of Chernychevsky. Gavriel's attempts to quieten them were the half-hearted attempts of a proud father in the presence of his precocious offspring. Nothing could wait. I had to hear everything and see everything immediately — if not sooner.

---

*Evenk: One of the minority nationalities of the USSR. The Evenki are semi-nomadic hunters and herders, widely scattered across Siberia.

I listened for two hours straight until someone leaped to his feet and insisted we go and look at the dam itself. No matter that it was pitch dark outside and the temperature was 24° below zero. Off we went, slipping and slithering along the unfinished crest of the huge structure. Gavriel suggested that we might knock off for a little supper; but the chief of the powerhouse, Ivan Drobishev, pleaded with us at least to take a glimpse into his house of wizardry tunneled into the solid rock beneath our feet. The glimpse took an hour, and even then he was loathe to let us go....

A young woman in charge of social planning for the North [explained its appeal]:

"Human beings must have challenge! That is understood by any thinking person; and we know the best challenge is the one which is the most natural. If men do not have such challenge they find it in unnatural ways — perhaps in a fierce competition for power or money; perhaps in internal struggles that tear a society apart; perhaps in external struggles that become bloody wars. We know all this, you see; and so we have deliberately offered to our people — particularly the young — the challenge of the North, which is a challenge of nature. They have responded with enthusiasm. It is not good to give people security of body alone...we must also make a valid and good purpose for life. Those who go North find such a purpose."

It was early recognized that Northern development on a big scale required careful planning, but until the end of the Stalin era the planning was rather haphazard and sometimes bungled. Stalin was a Georgian and apparently never had the feel of the North. Under Khrushchev things were different. Tremendous efforts and vast sums of money went into planning and into research to back the plans. At the same time tens of thousands of scientists flooded out over Siberia to conduct the most intensive surveys and to compile the most complete inventory of resources ever undertaken by any nation. This resulted in the discovery of nearly every important raw material required by modern technology and, to the perturbation of some Western powers, it assured the Soviet Union of internal self-sufficiency in raw resources, if it proved possible for them to develop these resources on an economically realistic basis. And that was the rub. No country, communist or capitalist, can remain healthy if the things it purchases with its labor or its money are worth less than what it cost to get them. However, the Russians found sound economic methods for developing their Northern resources while at the same time turning an almost empty wilderness into a suitable habitat for modern man....

[The Director of a big project explained the challenge of the North]:

"I believe you know better than I that your country, Canada, has an even bigger proportion of Northern lands than the Soviet Union. So why, may I ask, are you ignoring it as a place for men to work and live and build new cities? Why do you treat it as a distant colony to be exploited but not to be occupied? Well, perhaps you will someday see it differently — if you have not already lost it to your big southern neighbor.

"We think of the North as a land to be lived in. *We* do not go north just to fill our pockets. We are making it a part of our whole nation — and the North is making a new kind of men and women out of us."...

[A dam was built on the Vilyui River to generate hydroelectric power for the region.]

As the work force began blasting a power canal and turbine hall out of the frozen granite (making use of the debris to begin pushing rock wings for the dam out from the canyon walls), a new difficulty appeared. The frozen bedrock which had seemed sturdy enough to support almost any weight, was found to be underlain by a cracked strata full of ice lenses which could easily be deformed by the great weight of the dam and so lead to its collapse.

The solution to this was to increase vastly the breadth of the dam at its base and so spread the load over a much greater area — a solution which meant *trebling* the amount of rock fill that had to be blasted and trucked to the site.

The solving of each problem seemed only to lead to new and worse difficulties. As the riverbed was blasted, in mid-winter, to form a foundation trench, it was discovered that even the upper layers of bedrock were cracked. Although they were cemented together by permafrost, there was the likelihood that the weight of the dam would temporarily generate enough pressure to melt the ice and so again threaten the entire structure. The solution this time was to design a tunnel which would run along the basement rock through the full length of the dam and from which workers could inject cement grout under very high pressure into the fissures as the ice melted. It was estimated that this local melting process would continue for at least six years until permafrost had seeped back through the underlying rock and reasserted its sovereignty.

The bulk of the dam was to be of stone, but the inner core was to be a water-impervious mixture of clay, sand and fine gravel. The core was designed to contain the water of the reservoir while the thick layers of rock around it would act as ballast to keep the core in place and to insulate it from summer heat and from the warmth of the water in the reservoir. The real strength of the dam was to be provided by the Vilyui winter, which would freeze the core into one monolithic block.

Material for the core was found five miles from the site but, of course, it was solidly frozen. The clays and sands had to be thawed, thin layer by thin layer, under the summer suns, then scraped into great, flat-topped mounds for storage. In order to keep these mounds from freezing when winter came, electric heating rods were inserted into them in a rectangular pattern and connected to a series of diesel generators.

The core material had to be hauled to the dam site and placed in position during the coldest months of the year — the colder the better, from Gavriel's point of view.

"We did not like to place core material unless the temperature was at least 30° below zero. We had to be sure it would freeze absolutely solidly. The rods in the storage mounds raised the temperature of the material just high enough so it could be loaded on trucks, driven at top speed to the dam, dumped, spread and compacted before it turned to icy stone. At temperatures of 60° below, we had trouble with it. It insisted on freezing too fast. We fixed that by building big mobile flame throwers and also by saturating it with very high concentrations of salt water.''

"At 60° below you surely must have had trouble with your workers too," I said. "Did you use flame throwers and brine on them as well?"

Gavriel laughed. "No, they had something better. They called it Spirit Vilyui and I am not sure how it was made. They tell about one fellow who dropped a two-liter bottle of it on the frozen ground outside his house one cold winter night. The next morning there was a mudhole there a meter in diameter and, when they tried to find how deep it was, they couldn't get a probe long enough to reach the bottom.

"We had the toughest and best-humored crowd of people in the Soviet Union. Most were just youngsters. They came from all over. There was an Azerbaijanian from Baku who had never even seen snow before. He had a wonderful voice and you could hear him singing all over the dam site. He would sing curses upon the ice and snow so they sounded as beautiful as love songs — but the words were the worst I've ever heard. At least once a week he'd roar that he was going home on the next plane. But, you know, he is still here. Even the women — and there were a lot of them — mostly held out. The wives did not have to work, but most of them did and a lot worked right on the dam alongside the men. I really don't know what kept people here, unless it was some special kind of Russian stubbornness. Perhaps, though, they shared our feelings. Here was a job most people in the South said couldn't be done; but it had to be done if the North was going to develop the way we felt it should.''

By midwinter of 1965-1966, the builders were ready to close the gap in the center of the dam. It was one of the worst winters on record in central Siberia, and working conditions were appalling. Nevertheless, the task was completed a few weeks before the spring breakup unleashed the terrific Vilyui floods. The films taken at the time show thousands of people standing silent on the edge of the canyon watching the waters rise behind the dam. There are no scenes of cheering or flag waving, no bands, no rockets in the air. I asked one of the engineers why there was so little apparent excitement.

"It is difficult to explain. Instead of feeling like cheering, most of us felt closer to tears. It was not a feeling of victory so much as a feeling we had lost something — the thing we had done together, so many thousands of us; the life we had led together in this isolated little world buried in the taiga . . . it was coming to an end. Perhaps we would find it again in some other place, building some other dam, but here in Chernychevsky, the great times when we felt like giants and lived so closely with one another, and relied so much upon one another that we were all brothers and sisters, that time was running out....''

4. Peoples of the USSR

The USSR is comprised of many peoples in addition to the ethnic Russians. While there are over one hundred distinct nationality groupings, the following table is limited to those nationalities with over a million people; even here, the ethnic variety is obvious. (The prize for being the smallest nationality according to the census of 1979 goes to the Negidal—all 504 of them in a northern corner of the USSR.) Note in particular the diversity of languages spoken.

Nationality	Population	% of total	Language Family
Russians	137,397,089	52.42	Slavic
Ukrainians	42,347,387	16.16	Slavic
Uzbeks	12,455,978	4.75	Turkic
Belorussians	9,462,715	3.61	Slavic
Kazakhs	6,556,442	2.50	Turkic
Tatars	6,317,468	2.41	Turkic
Azerbaidzhanis	5,477,330	2.09	Turkic
Armenians	4,151,241	1.58	Armenian
Georgians	3,570,504	1.36	Caucasian
Moldavians	2,968,224	1.13	Romance
Tadzhiks	2,897,697	1.11	Iranian
Lithuanians	2,850,905	1.09	Baltic
Turkmen	2,027,913	0.77	Turkic
Germans	1,936,214	0.74	Germanic
Kirgiz	1,906,271	0.73	Turkic
Jews	1,810,876	0.69	various
Chuvash	1,751,366	0.67	Turkic
Daghestani peoples	1,656,676	0.63	mostly Caucasian
Latvians	1,439,037	0.55	Baltic
Bashkirs	1,371,452	0.52	Turkic
Mordvinians	1,191,765	0.45	Finnic
Poles	1,150,991	0.44	Slavic
Estonians	1,019,851	0.39	Finnic

From Lubomyr Hajda, "Ethnic Groups According to the 1979 Census." 1981.

Chapter Two

The Elements of Old Russian Culture

The Soviet Union is a political entity that came into existence as the result of the Russian Revolution of 1917. It is a new state, but it inherited most of its territory and many of its traditions from the Russian Empire and Old Russia. This is the reason that historians begin the history of the Soviet Union by talking about the Russians. In Old Russia, as the period before the reign of Peter the Great (1689-1725) is known, a number of enduring features of Russian culture first made their appearance. In this chapter, we shall examine the origins of Rus' and some elements of Old Russian culture, specifically the adoption of Orthodox Christianity, the impact of the Mongol invasions, the traditions of the Muscovite court, and the culture of the Russian village.

THE FOUNDATIONS OF KIEVAN RUS'

Inquiries into the origins of Russian culture often begin by examining the cultural patterns of tenth and eleventh century Kiev. Kiev, a city on the Dnieper River, was the most important center in an area that was divided at the time into a number of principalities. These principalities did not form a single state and did not have any central administration or common institutions. They were, however, all ruled by princes from the same family. They shared the Orthodox religion, and all developed a written literature in the Church Slavonic language. For these reasons, historians refer to these principalities collectively as Kievan Rus'. Although the Russian state actually emerged after the fall of Kiev, and to its north in the dense forests around Moscow, Muscovite Russia claimed the heritage of the civilization of Kiev and the other cities that formed the realm of Rus'. Today most historians consider that the heritage of Kiev rightly belongs to several nationalities, not only to the Russians, but also to the Belorussians and Ukrainians.

FACT: The traceable history of Kiev, Novgorod, and the other cities of Rus' begins with the Viking presence in the ninth century.

FACT: Viking expansion in this period was not limited to Rus'. England, France, Sicily and North America were among the other places touched by these adventurous people.

Before the recording of history, Slavic tribes from Central Europe had settled along the river trade routes in the western area of what today is the Soviet Union. One of these major water roads stretched from the Baltic Sea, along the Dnieper River, to the Black Sea and on to Constantinople, the capital of the

ARCTIC OCEAN

FINNS

SWEDEN

Novgorod

Ilmen R.

Volga R.

Duna R.

BALTIC SEA

Moscow

Don R.

KUMENS

Kievan Rus'

POLAND

Donets R.

Kiev

Dnieper R.

Dniester R.

KHAZARS

HUNGARY

Pruth R.

Danube R.

BLACK SEA

BULGARIA

Constantinople

BYZANTINE EMPIRE

Kievan Rus' in the Eleventh Century

Byzantine Empire. In the ninth and tenth centuries, the Vikings, whom the Slavs called the Varangians, plied these rivers to exchange the products of the North — slaves, amber, furs, wax, and honey — for the products of the East — spices and fabrics. Varangian trade with Constantinople proved so profitable that the Varangians were determined to control these river routes. To establish their control over the region, they erected a series of fortified sites along the rivers that led from the Baltic Sea to the Black Sea. By the beginning of the tenth century, the Varangians had established rule over the native Slav population and given their name, "Rus'," to the territory centered at Kiev.

FACT: The name Russia comes from "Rus'," the name originally given to the Varangians who entered the area of Novgorod and Kiev in the ninth and tenth centuries.

Varangian and Slav cooperated in commerce, culture, and war. The Varangian ruler's retinue, or *druzhina,* consisted mostly of Varangian warriors, but Slavs were not excluded.

FACT: A *druzhinik* was a member of the prince's household. In eleventh and twelfth century military tales, he is a hero of great valor and skilled horsemanship. The *druzhina* was a small, efficient cavalry. It has been said that the Kievan princes maintained huge stud farms to breed horses, fined heavily anyone who injured a horse, and when a prince died, his favorite horse often was buried with him.

The developments and events of this vigorous period were recorded in chronicles, or annals, which are the only written records for this early history. They tell us that late in the ninth century the trading town of Novgorod in the northwest was troubled by disputes and that the people invited a Varangian ruler to settle there to restore order. This man, Rurik, and his successors united several towns into a realm which included Kiev. (See Reading 1) Kiev eventually became the largest and most important city in Rus'.

FACT: Conclusive evidence that Rurik existed is lacking. He is a great mythic figure. He has been identified with Roric of Jutland, a Dane, born in 800 A.D., whose father was an ally of the Holy Roman Emperor Charlemagne.

The Primary Chronicle is the earliest and most literary of the chronicles. Begun about 1040 and continued through 1118, it contains entries about important happenings in Kievan Rus' from the year 852. The chronicle writers, all of whom were monks, stressed certain themes such as the need for the princes to live together harmoniously and the importance of Kievan Rus' in the Christian world. The Primary Chronicle has served as a basis for two later historical traditions, that of the north (Russia), and that of the South (Ukraine). The main Russian chronicles of the later period are those of Novgorod and Moscow. The authors of the Moscow Chronicle incorporated the Primary Chronicle as preface, thereby implying that Moscow was the true successor to Kiev, and that Moscow's princes were Kiev's heirs.

THE ADOPTION OF ORTHODOX CHRISTIANITY

The adoption of Christianity in 988 was the greatest single event of this early period. It is recorded in the Primary Chronicle and reverberates throughout it. The chronicler tells us that Prince Vladimir of Kiev (980-1015), a descendant of Rurik, decided that his realm must have a proper religion. He saw several possibilities at the time. He might choose Islam, which had been carried to Central Asia by Arab armies and to the Upper Volga by Arab traders, or Judaism, which had been embraced by the Khazars, a Turkic people on the lower Volga. He might also choose the Christianity of the Germans to the West, or that of the Greeks to the South at Constantinople.* He consulted his advisors and decided to send emissaries to visit each area to see for themselves the rituals of each group. When his emissaries returned, they recommended against Judaism, which appeared stigmatized by the Jews' expulsion from the Biblical lands, against Catholicism which seemed too austere in its observance, and against Islam, which demanded abstention from alcohol. (See Reading 2)

FACT: Vladimir is reported to have said "Drinking is the joy of the Rus'. We cannot exist without that pleasure."

The emissaries expressed a profound admiration for the splendor and pageantry of the Byzantine Orthodox Church. After attending an Orthodox service, they declared, "We knew not whether we were in heaven or on earth." Vladimir decided to be baptized into the Orthodox Christian faith and ordered that all his people should be baptized or risk his displeasure. Whether or not this legend is accurate, it illustrates two things. First of all, the people of Kievan Rus' in the late tenth century did not feel fully part of any one of the culture areas marked by the great religions of the time. It also illustrates that the Orthodox Church from the beginning was a state church tied to the will of the prince. The notion of a division between Church and State that became so important in Western Europe never developed in the Byzantine Empire, nor later in Russia.

In the eleventh and twelfth centuries, the city of Kiev became the center

---

*Although the Western and Eastern branches of the Christian Church had not yet split into two separate churches, already the practices of the Germans to the west and Greeks to the south differed considerably from one another. About seventy years after Kiev adopted Christianity, in 1054, this division in the church was formalized. Thereafter there was a Western, Catholic church, centered at Rome, and an Eastern, Orthodox church, centered at Constantinople, which was the official religion of the Byzantine Empire.

of a rich Christian culture. Imitation of Byzantine Orthodox ritual and tradition was important in the cities where it was cherished by the upper classes, but for most of the rural Slavs, Orthodox practices and beliefs blended with pagan folkways. The early Slavs had worshipped the sun, the wind, fire, and other natural elements, and believed their rivers and forests to be populated with spirits. Now, for example, Perun, the Slavic deity of fire and thunder, was merged with the Biblical prophet Elijah whose fiery chariot was prefigured by the famous Firebird of Slavic mythology.

Orthodox churchmen in Kiev borrowed Byzantine literary forms to express their new faith. Epic poems, military tales and sermons were used to entertain, instruct, and glorify God and His princes. An early Christian writer proclaimed:

> Now hear with the power of your understanding!
> Thus hear, Slavic people!
> Hear the Word which feeds human souls.
> The Word which strengthens the heart and mind.
> This Word ready for the knowledge of God.

But, in fact, Kievan Rus' adopted Orthodox Christianity in its own way. There was great emphasis on ritual, chant, vestments, processions, and blessed icons in beautiful churches, all of which served to elevate and transfix the beholder. Although Kiev soon produced a vibrant Christian culture with numerous holy men and saints, it did not fully take part in the great theological and intellectual life of the Byzantine Empire. The church used the Slavonic language primarily as a liturgical language in its services rather than to wrestle with religious or political ideas.

FACT: The Greek alphabet and language were not introduced with Orthodoxy. Two great missionaries, Cyril and Methodius, had already given the Slavs an alphabet — the Cyrillic alphabet and a written language, Slavonic, based on their vernacular language. Not knowing Greek or Latin, literate Slavs were not able to read philosophy or scientific works written in these languages.

When Vladimir adopted Orthodoxy as the official religion of his realm, he sent for craftsmen from Constantinople to construct and decorate great churches. In this way, the icon, a venerated image of a saint painted on wood, came to Kievan Rus'. Just as the Orthodox Church was an earthly reflection of heaven, the icons were a sacred reflection of the saint, the Mother of God, or Christ himself, to whom the faithful prayed. Legends surround miracle-working icons that helped to drive off enemies, icons of St. George, the patron saint of the army, were frequently taken into battle. As late as 1914, Tsar Nicholas II used an icon to bless his troops departing for World War I. Icons were placed also in a corner of a peasant's hut and, even today, some Russians continue to have an icon corner in their homes.

The Cyrillic Alphabet

The Russians still use the Cyrillic alphabet. They have spread the use of this alphabet among Soviet peoples, who in the past had no written language, and also to those who previously used other alphabets. For example, the Soviet Moldavians, whose language is virtually indistinguishable from that of the Romanians, traditionally used the Roman alphabet, as do the Romanians. The Soviets changed this. The result, of course, is to drive a wedge between similar peoples who live on opposite sides of the Soviet border.

First steps in Reading Russian

1. Russian Consonants that look and sound like English.

5	6	7
Б	б	b
К	к	k
М	м	m
Т	т	t
З	з	z

2. Russian Consonants that look different from English.

5	6	7
Д	д	d
Ф	ф	f
Г	г	g
Л	л	l
Н	н	n
П	п	p
Р	р	r
С	с	s
В	в	v
Й	й	y

3. Russian Consonants that have no English equivalent.

5	6	8
Ч	ч	ch
Х	х	kh
Ш	ш	sh
Щ	щ	shch
Ц	ц	ts
Ж	ж	zh
	ь	soft sign

4. The Russian Vowels.

5	6	8
А	а	ah
Я	я	yah
Э	э	eh
Е	е	yeh
Ы	ы	ih
И	и	i (ee)
О	о	oh
Ё	ё	yo
У	у	u (oo)
Ю	ю	yu

1. Russian Consonants that look and sound like English.
2. Russian Consonants that look different from English.
3. Russian Consonants that have no English equivalent.
4. The Russian Vowels.
5. Russian Capital Letter.
6. Russian Small Letter.
7. English Letter.
8. Sound.

FACT: Icon painters prayed continuously as they painted the holy images. It was a devotional as well as an artistic act. They sought to portray the supernatural rather than the human qualities of the subject, and to copy original icons without allowing their individuality to show in their work. For this reason, the icon remains little changed in style since early times.

By the second half of the eleventh century, Christianity was established, and Kiev flourished under the rule of Yaroslav the Wise (1019-1054). Kiev was an important center of Christian art and learning. A magnificent cathedral dedicated to Saint Sophia (Holy Wisdom) was built, as well as several other churches and monasteries.

FACT: The Kievan prince wanted to build an enormous cathedral, Saint Sophia, on the model of the great church of Saint Sophia in Constantinople, then the largest church in the world. The builders did not know how to construct a single large dome, similar to that on the Byzantine church, so they created a new style characterized by the presence of many small domes.

Christian education also flourished and Yaroslav the Wise created a great library in the Cathedral of Saint Sophia. Generous works of charity became the sign of a great prince.

FACT: Anna, daughter of Yaroslav, married King Henry I of France. She seems to have been the only lay person in the French court who could write. She also spoke three languages. Members of the Kievan royal family also married into the ruling houses of the Byzantine Empire, England, Germany, Norway, Poland, and Hungary. Connections with Kievan Rus' were important to Western European rulers.

FACT: Some historians think that Kiev was larger than Paris and twice the size of London in the eleventh century. They estimate its population at 80,000.

This early period was also characterized by vigorous trading, a growing concern about princely feuding, and a real sense of being God's chosen in the Orthodox faith. Kiev, Novgorod and smaller towns such as Chernigov*, Galich*, Rostov and Riazan, linked to Kiev by trade and culture, were centers of a proud tradition. Life in these cities bustled with activity. In Novgorod busy markets resounded with the haggling of merchants and tradesmen over prices and with discussions of politics, especially the merits of their princes. (See Reading 3) The peal of the *veche* bell in Novgorod was a summons to participa-

*These towns are today in the Soviet Ukraine. The Russians call them Chernigov and Galich; the Ukrainians call them Chernihiv and Halych.

The Russian Onion Dome

The exact origin of the "onion dome" which typifies most Russian churches is not known. One theory is that the flat Byzantine dome, seen on the now-destroyed Cathedral of Saint Sophia in Kiev (illus. a), was ill-suited to the heavy snows of the Russian north. Two smaller churches (b and c) illustrate the Russian architects' adaptation to their climate. The Cathedral of the Assumption in the Moscow Kremlin (d) displays five domes, a style popular in the later Moscow period. The Church of the Ascension in Kolomenskoye (e), built to commemorate the birth of Ivan the Terrible, rises from a low base into a brick spire called a "tent." The tent spire and rounded domes combine to create the most famous of all Russian buildings: the Church of the Intercession in Moscow (f), popularly known as St. Basil's. Finally, the development of the baroque style of architecture from the West is strikingly evident in the Church of the Intercession at Fili (g).

(a) 1037   (b) 1165   (c) 1198

(d) 1475   (e) 1532

(f) 1555   (g) 1693

tion in the vital questions of the day. The *veche* or town meeting was the place where events of significance were announced and important issues were debated. The potential for the development of popular self-rule in these towns, especially in Novgorod, appeared to exist. However, subsequent events, namely the Mongol invasions and the rise of Moscow, put an end to it.

A major weakness of the Kievan political system was its practice of princely inheritance. Each son inherited a share of his father's estate. The prince of Kiev assigned his sons and younger brothers to rule different towns on the basis of seniority. The older son usually received a larger town, the younger received a smaller town. This led to jealousies and power struggles that plagued Rus'.

These princely rivalries prevented the development of a strong monarchy or a unified state. No feeling based on a spirit of common interest and cooperation took root in this loosely-organized realm. In fact, the princes feuded continually, and with such bitterness that they were unable even to unite against outside invaders. The chronic disunity allowed the Polovtsians, horsemen from the East, and later the Mongols, to overrun the southern region, and sack the cities of Rus'. In the face of impending disaster, some of the Slavs fled to the forests of the North. The way of life that developed in this northern forest combined with Orthodox traditions to become a new culture. A small town in the forest emerged as its center: Moscow. Kiev did not provide the sole basis for this new Russian culture, but its Orthodox Christianity, Slavonic literary language, and the dynasty of Rurik were important elements in the building of a new Russian state.

THE IMPACT OF THE MONGOLS

The disintegration of Rus' actually began in the second half of the twelfth century. The Polovtsians, nomads of Turkic origin, entered the southern steppe regions and interfered with the flow of Kiev's trade with the Byzantine Empire. These invaders demanded tribute from the Kievan princes, occasionally pillaged Kievan towns, and frequently took captives. Military response to the invaders was feeble. The epic *Tale of Igor's Campaign* tells of the desperate effort of Prince Igor of Novgorod-Seversk, a town on the southeastern frontier of Rus', to expel these invaders, and the failure of his brother princes to aid his effort. The epic leaves the reader with a sense of foreboding and impending disaster. (See Reading 4)

Fifty years after Igor's defeat, Kiev and other towns of Rus' fell under the Mongol yoke. In 1223, the Mongols, united under Genghis Khan, entered the area, but at his death returned to Mongolia. A decade later, the Tatars, as these Mongols were called by the Slavs, returned under Genghis Khan's grandson Batu. This time, the Tatars stayed and held the Russian lands for more than two centuries, from 1237-1460. The sacking of towns and Tatar brutalities forced submission to the khan's will. The Mongols stripped the people of their portable wealth — jewels, gold, fur, and livestock. Land was the only thing of value that the Mongols could not carry away. (See Reading 5)

Although the Tatar khan was the supreme ruler — the Tsar as the Slavs called him — local political life was never completely stifled, only controlled and altered by Tatar rule. Indeed, as the Mongol empire itself gradually weakened, native institutions re-emerged with great vigor. The local princes and the Tatars cooperated in curbing and controlling the cities that had, before, existed with a great deal of independence. The landed estate became increasingly important as city life declined, and ownership of the land became the most important source of power. Eventually the Moscow prince emerged as Grand Prince of all Russia, combining his rights as the owner of a vast domain and his authority as ruler.

Moscow's power developed in part because the Moscow princes observed and copied the methods by which the Tatars established central autocratic rule in their lands. The Tatars were especially efficient in tax-collecting, census-taking, and military recruitment. They imposed a payment of tribute, custom duties, fees and tolls at all stages of the transportation of goods, and taxes on the sale of livestock. The collection, recording, and management of this money was well organized.

FACT: The Russian terms *kazna* (treasury) and *kaznachei* (treasurer) are of Tatar origin and indicate that this office and position were created after the Mongol pattern.

Moscow's princes secured the right to collect taxes for the Mongols. Competition to possess the *iarlyk,* the Tatar authorization to collect taxes, was intense among rival princes. Moscow's continuous success in holding the *iarlyk* was a crucial factor in its emergence as ruler of Russia.

The Russians also copied the military organization of the Mongols. Though they first met the Mongols as enemies, the Russians later served in the Mongol armies and campaigned with them. The Muscovite army of the sixteenth century followed the Mongol setup of divisions with five units: a big center unit, a right arm, a left arm, an advance guard, and a rear guard. They employed the Mongol tactic of enveloping the enemy on both flanks and copied the style of Mongol armor and weapons.

Mongol innovation included the recruitment of troops for regular intervals of service. In Kievan times, the rural population was not subject to conscription. The Mongol invasion changed this. A system of military conscription including the rural population was established. Furthermore, the prince created a new privileged group, the *dvoriane,* made up of military servitors who were granted land and position on condition that they serve him. They gradually displaced the powerful independent companions of the prince as his main source of support. This relationship whereby the *dvoriane* held land and position only so long as they served the prince was an important factor in the development of princely power.

The collaboration between Moscow's prince and the Mongol khan resulted in the emergence of new institutions that formed the basis for a large, immensely powerful state. Perhaps the greatest consequence of the period of Mongol domination was the growing centralization of power by this new state, Moscow.

THE TRADITIONS OF THE MUSCOVITE COURT

The prince of Moscow gradually united all Russia under his authority and assumed the titles of Autocrat† and Tsar. His right to collect taxes on behalf of the Mongols was a key factor in this rise to power. Both Ivan III "the Great" (1462-1505) and Ivan IV "the Terrible" (1533-1584) ruled with an absolute authority using techniques of control learned from the Mongols.

FACT: Ivan IV was officially crowned Tsar in 1547. He used the title Autocrat in the sense of a ruler absolutely supreme in the affairs of his country. The title Tsar was borrowed from the Byzantines. Russians called the Byzantine emperor Tsar or Caesar, applied the title to the Mongol khan, and later took it for themselves.

Ivan III and his grandson Ivan IV wore the cap of Vladimir Monomakh, a crown said to have been given to this early Kievan prince by the Byzantine emperor, as a symbol of power.

FACT: The cap of Vladimir Monomakh is actually a masterpiece of early fourteenth century Central Asian art. It was probably given to Ivan I (1325-1341) by the Mongol Khan, Uzbeg.

Ivan III's marriage to Sophia Paleologus, a niece of the last Byzantine emperor, gave added strength to the Russian Tsars' later claim that Moscow was the rightful heir of the Byzantine Empire as the center of Orthodox Christianity. Moscow princes began to view Orthodoxy as the one, true Christian faith and Moscow as its citadel.

FACT: The Ottoman Turks destroyed the Byzantine Empire. The city of Constantinople fell to the Turks in 1453. The Turks later renamed the city Istanbul.

FACT: Moscow claimed to be the "Third Rome." Rome had fallen into the Catholic heresy and Constantinople, the "Second Rome," had been overrun by the Turks. Early in the sixteenth century, the monk Philotheos wrote: "Listen and attend pious Tsar, that all Christian empires are gathered in your single one, that two Romes have fallen, and the third one stands, and a fourth one there shall not be."

The Muscovite court continued the traditions of the Mongols in the conduct of diplomacy. These were often very different from the customs of Western Europe. The Russians, like the Mongols, viewed ambassadors as guests who had to be provided with free transportation, lodging, food, drink, and security. Europeans sent to the Muscovite court were kept under constant surveillance. European ambassadors were also expected to offer appropriate gifts to the Tsar and in audience with the Tsar they were expected to surrender their swords. Russian ambassadors to Europe were often indignant that they had to pay for their own maintenance. Moscow's familiarity with Mongol protocol made relations with the East more successful than its relations with the West and created a favorable situation for Russian eastward expansion.

FACT: Some Turkic peoples of Central Asia considered Moscow a successor state to the Mongol Golden Horde. They called the Russians the White Horde and the Tsar, White Tsar.

In fifteenth and sixteenth century Moscow, a new concept of society and its relation to the ruler was introduced. All classes were required to serve the ruler. If a person served and pleased the Tsar, he was rewarded with land and men to work it. If he displeased the Tsar, his land was taken away. As a result, even the most privileged of the *dvoriane* were totally dependent on the Tsar for their economic position, as well as their political influence. The Tsar then used these men who were dependent on him to crush the power of the formerly independent princes and nobles.

It was important to both Tsar and landowner that there be adequate labor for the landed estates. Since land was abundant and labor scarce, this posed a problem. A peasant who did not like his situation could simply move away. To insure a steady, permanent labor force on the estates, a means had to be found to prevent the free movement of peasants. The state established the legal institution of serfdom.† Laws were introduced that bound peasants to an owner and to the land. Peasants could not move away without the landlord's permission, and had to render him services. In effect, the landlord could do whatever he liked with these peasants, now called serfs.

FACT: The process of enserfment of the peasants was a long one. Serfdom was institutionalized in the Code of Laws of 1649. In contrast, by that date in France and England, the last obligations and restrictions on the peasantry were being removed.

By the end of his reign, Ivan IV had succeeded in establishing an autocracy. The formerly independent princes and nobles had become permanent servitors of the Tsar. Peasants were increasingly bound to the land as serfs. Military and administrative service became a requirement for the *dvoriane;* serfdom, taxation, and conscription became the burden of the people. Resistance to these new measures was crushed, often with the use of force.

The Tsar not only increased his power over his own subjects but he also expanded his authority over his neighbors. This was a long process, with ups and downs, beginning in the Mongol period and continuing through the sixteenth century. Moscow's princes began to demand that they be called *gosudar* (sovereign) by the other Russian princes. In 1487, Ivan III backed up his demand that the Novgorodians recognize him as *gosudar* by sending his troops to Novgorod. So ended this town's long history of independence.

FACT: The removal of Novgorod's famous *veche* bell to Moscow in 1487 was a powerful symbol of Moscow's ascendancy. It also symbolized the end of Novgorod's rule by its town council.

Moscow benefited also from a delineated succession policy. The Muscovite succession remained in one family, with power passing from father to oldest son. This principle replaced the earlier practice of Rus' that viewed the realm as the collective property of the ruling dynasty and all its members. Thus Moscow could consolidate its gains. (See Reading 6)

With the death of Ivan IV's feeble-minded son and heir, Feodor, in 1598, the Rurikid dynasty came to an end. Russians of that time could not conceive of how the realm could continue without a prince of the blood of Rurik. Feodor's death plunged Russia into the Time of Troubles (1598-1613), a prolonged period of dynastic rivalry, social upheaval, and foreign intervention. A series of individuals fought for Moscow's vacant throne: Boris Godunov, a regent appointed in Feodor's reign; Vasili Shuiski, a member of an aristocratic Moscow family; and pretenders supported by Polish Catholic armies. Chaos reigned. Famine and the flight of people to the frontiers worsened the sorrows and suffering of Russia. It seemed that the state would not survive. The Time of Troubles was a period of trial and partial disintegration. (See Readings 7 and 10)

Yet, the Time of Troubles also precipitated the building of a great empire. Russia emerged from this cataclysmic episode under a new dynasty, the Romanovs, who ruled without interruption from 1613 to 1917. The new Russian state continued its attachment to many of the traditions and cultural patterns of the past: Orthodox Christianity, autocracy, serfdom, and the relatively self-contained life of the village.

THE TRADITIONS OF THE RUSSIAN VILLAGE

The northern forests were the home of the Russians throughout the formative period of both their state and their culture. By the fifteenth century, Moscow had become a center of Orthodox Slav civilization. This was a cold and remote frontier cut off from Constantinople and also from Western Europe.

FACT: In the course of the fourteenth century, mention of Rus' vanished from French literature. Byzantine writers made the distinction between "distant" or "great" Rus', later Russia, and "near" or "little" Rus', later the Ukraine.

The homeland of the Russians was poor and inhospitable. Great forests covered a land that had poor soil, bad drainage and impassable swamps. Winters were long, dark, and bitterly cold. Summers were short and unpredictable. The Russians learned how to survive in these harsh surroundings. From the forest, the peasant took logs for his hut, wax for his candles, bark for his shoes, fur for his clothing, moss for his floors, and pine boughs for his bed. The forest also provided mushrooms, berries, and honey. As the Russians spread throughout the forest, they developed a remarkably durable and adaptive culture marked by the qualities of caution, determination, and endurance.

For most peasants, the world began and ended at the edge of their village. Given the vast distances and difficulties of transportation, each village was isolated from the next, and had to be virtually self-sufficient. Like many agricultural peoples who have had to survive in small settlements scattered throughout a harsh natural terrain, the Russians developed a village organization based on the extended family and the principle of shared resources.

FACT: Individual Russians, even today, include the name of their father in their full name. This is their patronymic. The children of Ivan, for example, are called Feodor *Ivanovich* (Fedor, son of Ivan), and Maria *Ivanovna* (Maria, daughter of Ivan).

FACT: The Russian words for country *(rodina)* and people *(narod)* have the same root as the word for birth *(rod)*; the words for native land *(otechestvo)* and land ownership *(otchina)* have the same root as the word father *(otets)*.

FACT: The Russian peasant spoke of "Mother Russia" thinking of it less as a political entity than a common mother *(matushka)* and its ruler less a prince than a common father *(batiushka)*. Many peasants thought of the Tsar as a father who would help them "if only he knew how they suffered," at the hands of the landlords and tax collectors.

The overpowering objective of the peasant village (commune†), was physical survival. Until the nineteenth century, land was relatively plentiful, and was considered the property of the group, not the individual. Each individual received a share of the land for his own use. Periodically the land was redivided so that workers and land were equitably matched. As the commune was held jointly responsible for its obligations to the outside world, including the payment of taxes to landlord and state, and the provision of young men for the Tsar's army, the group as a whole had an interest in the work habits and behavior of each of its members. If someone did not do his work, he could not contribute his share to the group's well-being, nor help pay its taxes. (See Reading 8)

A meeting of the village elders.

A village council resolved all local issues. It was made up of household heads and a village elder, who discussed issues freely and tried to reach consensus. Unanimity and cooperation were important, for with the margin of survival so slight, failure of the village to work together could be life-threatening. Individual differences and self-assertion had to give way once the council had reached a decision. Thus, the culture of the Russian village was characterized by an effort to avoid risk, and to maintain unanimity and order. The central importance of shared living in the extended family and commune shaped the traditions of village Russia. This way of life had taken shape by the middle of the sixteenth century. It changed remarkably little right up to the beginning of the twentieth century. Villages such as these formed the world of nearly eighty per cent of the Russian people until the time of the First World War and the Revolution of 1917.

FACT: The Russian word for village, *mir,* is also the word for "world" and for "peace."

The Russian peasant lived in a hut called an *izba*. Until the early twentieth century, it was made of wood. Nowadays brick sometimes replaces the logs, and families are then far better protected from fires. Although there were some differences in *izba* design between northern and southern regions, the construction was essentially uniform. The huts in the south tended to be quite small, approximately fifteen feet by twenty-four feet. In the north, the huge trees made it possible for the hut to be considerably larger. Many of the log huts in the north display intricate carving around window frames, shutters, and along the roof ridge. All this carving was done with a simple axe. Birds and animals were popular designs. Huts in the south tended to be painted.

About one-fourth of the space in the *izba* was devoted to the stove. To live through the winter without freezing to death, the peasants made the stove the center of their lives. It was made from clay or brick, and provided many other services as well as warmth. On it clothes were dried, bread was baked, and food was cooked for the family. The stove protected the animals, too, during the long, harsh winter, and the warmest bed in the hut was across its top. Until the end of the nineteenth century, many huts had no chimney, and the smoke went out through the door, or through a hole in the roof. When a family moved to a different house, coals from the old stove were brought to start a fire in the new stove, and when a bride left her family's house, she took with her a piece of clay from the stove to protect her in her new home.

Today, even in modern apartments, the kitchen is the gathering place for friends, and the stove symbolically retains its central importance. Hospitality among the Russian people has been and remains especially important, and to be invited to sit near the stove is a gesture of acceptance and of friendship. People often shared their food from a common bowl. A character in a story by the contemporary writer Alexander Solzhenitsyn expresses unfamiliarity with another person when he says: "Why should I trust *you*? We haven't eaten cabbage soup from the same bowl."

Certain objects in the *izba* were particularly important. In the corner diagonally opposite the stove, the family would place its icon, usually on a shelf with a small oil lamp suspended before it. In the north of Russia, an axe would certainly be hung on the wall, for the task of clearing the forest was a never-ending struggle against the encroaching trees which threatened the family's tiny, life-supporting field of crops. The north Russian became extremely adept at using the axe. The famous wooden churches in the area around Lake Onega were all built using no other tool than an axe. In old peasant families, the father of a newborn baby cut the umbilical cord with his axe. This time-honored tradition was his only participation in the delivery.

In the south, an axe was not needed to fell trees, but the grasses of the *steppe* had to be cut. For this purpose, a long-handled scythe was used, and at harvest time groups of peasants could be seen against the horizon swaying rhythmically to and fro as they cut through the fields.

Church of the Dormition, Nikulino, 1599. *Photo Source: William Craft Brumfield*

Folklore and mythology, military tales and events recorded in the chronicles, the ritual of the Church, and seasonal observances formed the fabric of early Russian culture. From earliest pre-Christian times, birth, marriage and death, spring, summer, fall and winter created cycles which the Russian peasant celebrated with an awareness and reverence of nature. These celebrations were later supplemented and solemnized by the glorious rituals of the Church.

Many of the early peasant traditions continue to this day. In earliest times, for example, a midwife was called for the birth of a child, and she served a special "christening porridge" to all those present at the feast that celebrated the birth. Nowadays, although most children are born in hospitals (with no midwife in attendance), the father is still obliged to eat some porridge which is over-salted, while friends and family joke and tease him. At the time of a marriage, decorated trees are put in the house of the bride and groom. They symbolize virginity, and represent a custom that goes back for centuries. In some areas today, obstacles are placed in the road when the bride and groom make their way to register their marriage. Although now done in a joking way, this tradition goes back to ancient times when the bride's party set up poles in the road, and the groom's party could pass only if they offered wine or food as gifts.

Story-telling is also an old custom in Russia. The dark forest seemed to be inhabited by spirits and creatures, and gradually such popular figures as the witch Baba Yaga, the beautiful maiden Fair Vasilissa, the Snow Maiden, and the Firebird found their way into folk tales that have inspired Russian authors and composers for centuries. Evenings in the *izba* were spent telling tales around the stove, and in the winter a whole village would sometimes crowd into the largest hut to listen to the local story teller. Folk tales entertained people from all levels of society. (See Reading 9)

FACT: Ivan the Terrible kept three blind story tellers in his court who took turns helping him to fall asleep.

FACT: In his childhood, Count Leo Tolstoy, author of *War and Peace,* listened to a serf his grandfather had bought for his story-telling ability. Later in his life, Tolstoy wrote a collection of fairy tales for the children of the serfs on his estate.

Farmers everywhere are keenly aware of the seasons, and of any changes in the weather. Russians are no exception, and many holidays are closely related to the change of season and to the Christian liturgical observances that mark them. Christmas was the first major winter holiday. In pre-Christian times, there had probably been a holiday celebrating the winter solstice, the time of the rebirth of the sun. To celebrate the birth of Christ, the family gathered on Christmas Eve for a joyous and peaceful meal. A cross, the symbol of the Christ, formed from all kinds of grains, was placed on the table under the cloth. The grains symbolized fertility. The peasant dreaded infertility in crops, livestock or offspring: fertility meant life, and life meant continuation. The head of the house prayed for health in the coming year for all family members as well as for the family's livestock.

The second winter festival, *Maslenitsa,* was a carnival time before the seven-week fast of Lent. During Lent, preparation for spring work was completed. Lent ends on Easter Eve, and the Russian people then celebrated the greatest feast of all: the Resurrection of Christ. Trinity Week, in the late spring, mirrored the festival at Yuletide, but instead of a fir tree as the central decoration, a birch tree became the focus symbolizing reanimated nature. Birch boughs decorated the *izba,* and the village planted a strong, young birch for new life and continuity.

Russian village traditions provided a meaningful pattern of order for the peasant to counterbalance grave threats, both natural and political, from the outside world. Faced with famine, disease, invasion, and countless repressions, the Russian peasant nevertheless could rejoice in the birth of a son, the marriage of a daughter, or the coming of spring. These traditions endured because they represented some continuity in the midst of often drastic change.

Many formidable changes took place in Rus' and in Russia between the ninth and seventeenth centuries. Some were violent and destructive, others were positive and constructive. Despite these upheavals, the peasant's attachment to the land, to the family, to God, and to the Tsar created a system of attitudes and values that continued up to the beginning of the twentieth century.

The following books were helpful in writing this chapter:

Billington, J., *The Icon and the Axe,* New York: Knopf, 1966.

Dunn, S. and E., *The Peasants of Central Russia,* New York: Holt, Rinehart and Winston, 1967.

Rice, T.T., *A Concise History of Russian Art,* New York: Praeger, 1963.

Vernadsky, G., *Origins of Russia,* Oxford: The Clarendon Press, 1959.

Vernadsky, G. *et al, A Sourcebook for Russian History from Early Times to 1914* (3 vols.), New Haven: Yale University Press, 1972.

For students who are interested, we recommend further reading in the sources from which we have taken excerpts, as well as the following works:

Berry, L. and Crummey, R., *Rude and Barbarous Kingdom,* Madison: University of Wisconsin Press, 1968.
See Chapter One reading. This is a collection of colorful accounts of sixteenth century English explorers and merchants who visited Russia.

Brumfield, W.C., *Gold in Azure: One Thousand Years of Russian Architecture,* Boston: David R. Godine, 1983.
Beautiful photographs by the author, accompanied by a scholarly text for those who want to know more.

Downing, C., *Russian Tales and Legends,* New York: Oxford University Press, 1978.
An attractive, well-selected, and well-edited collection.

Massie, S., *Land of the Firebird,* New York: Simon and Schuster, 1980.
A wonderfully readable yet authoritative narrative history of Russia's cultural heritage, with colorful attention to its art and music, manners and morals, pastimes and celebrations.

Voyce, A., *Art and Architecture of Medieval Russia,* Norman: University of Oklahoma Press, 1977.
One of the few books on this subject that covers its subject in an interesting manner.

Readings

Chapter Two

List of Readings

A note to the reader: You are about to enter a new area where you will encounter many unfamiliar names. Do not be alarmed. The purpose of these readings from the early Chronicles is to give you a sense of the atmosphere, the flavor of what is being described. You do not need to remember all the names.

1. The Arrival of Rurik

All people have a story to tell of their origins. What follows is the story of the beginning of Rus'. It is the first written account we have.

...6367 (859).* The Varangians from beyond the sea imposed tribute upon the Chuds, the Slavs, the Merians, the Ves, and the Krivichians. But the Khazars imposed it upon the Polyanians, the Severians, and the Vyatichians, and collected a squirrel-skin and a beaver-skin from each hearth.

6368-6370 (860-862). The tributaries of the Varangians drove them back beyond the sea and, refusing them further tribute, set out to govern themselves. There was no law among them, but tribe rose against tribe. Discord thus ensued among them, and they began to war one against another. They said to themselves, "Let us seek a prince who may rule over us, and judge us according to the law." They accordingly went overseas to the Varangian Russes: these particular Varangians were known as Russes, just as some are called Swedes, and others Normans, Angles, and Goths, for they were thus named. On account of these Varangians, the district of Novgorod became known as the land of Rus. The present inhabitants of Novgorod are descended from the Varangian race, but aforetime they were Slavs....

2. The Baptism of Vladimir

...6495 (987). Vladimir summoned together his vassals and the city-elders, and said to them, "Behold, the Bulgarians [Bulgars who lived on Volga River] came before me urging me to accept their religion. Then came the Germans and praised their own faith; and after them came the Jews. Finally the Greeks appeared, criticizing all other faiths but commending their own, and they spoke at length, telling the history of the whole world from its beginning. Their words were artful, and it was wondrous to listen and pleasant to hear them."...

The vassals and the elders replied, "You know, oh Prince, that no man

---

*The early Slavs dated their history from the Biblical creation. Thus, the year 859 in our calendar was the year 6367 in theirs.

Abridged from "The Primary Chronicle," Samuel Cross, translator, *Harvard Studies in Philology and Literature,* Vol. XII, Cambridge, 1930.

Ibid.

condemns his own possessions, but praises them instead. If you desire to make certain, you have servants at your disposal. Send them to inquire about the ritual of each and how he worships God.''

Their counsel pleased the prince and all the people, so that they chose good and wise men to the number of ten, and directed them to go first among the Bulgarians and inspect their faith. The emissaries went their way, and when they arrived at their destination they beheld the disgraceful actions of the Bulgarians and their worship in the mosque; then they returned to their own country. Vladimir then instructed them to go likewise among the Germans, and examine their faith, and finally to visit the Greeks. They thus went into Germany, and after viewing the German ceremonial, they proceeded to Tsargrad [Constantinople], where they appeared before the Emperor. He inquired on what mission they had come, and they reported to him all that had occurred. When the Emperor heard their words, he rejoiced, and did them great honor on that very day.

On the morrow, the Emperor sent a message to the Patriarch to inform him that a Russian delegation had arrived to examine the Greek faith, and directed him to prepare the church and the clergy, and to array himself in his sacerdotal robes, so that the Russes might behold the glory of the God of the Greeks. When the Patriarch received these commands, he bade the clergy assemble, and they performed the customary rites. They burned incense, and the choirs sang hymns. The Emperor accompanied the Russes to the church, and placed them in a wide space, calling their attention to the beauty of the edifice, the chanting, and the offices of the archpriest and the ministry of the deacons, while he explained to them the worship of his God. The Russes were astonished...and in their wonder praised the Greek ceremonial. Then the Emperors Basil and Constantine invited the envoys to their presence, and said, ''Go hence to your native country,'' and thus dismissed them with valuable presents and great honor.

Thus they returned to their own country, and the Prince called together his vassals and the elders. Vladimir then announced the return of the envoys who had been sent out, and suggested that their report be heard. He thus commanded them to speak out before his vassals. The envoys reported, ''When we journeyed among the Bulgarians, we beheld how they worship in their temple, called a mosque, while they stand ungirt. The Bulgarian bows, sits down, looks hither and thither like one possessed, and there is no happiness among them, but instead only sorrow and a dreadful stench. Their religion is not good. Then we went among the Germans, and saw them performing many ceremonies in their temples; but we beheld no glory there. Then we went on to Greece, and the Greeks led us to the edifices where they worship their God, and we knew not whether we were in heaven or on earth. For on earth there is no such splendor or such beauty, and we are at a loss how to describe it. We only know that God dwells there among men, and their service is fairer than the ceremonies of other nations. For we cannot forget that beauty.''...

3. Life in Novgorod

Novgorod occupies a unique place in Russia's early history. The town prospered as a trading center in the ninth century. Its bold democracy inspired the wrath of Moscow's rulers. Ivan the Terrible crushed Novgorodian liberties brutally in 1570. The city is famous today for its restored medieval architecture. The weather is frequently mentioned in this chronicle as commerce was central to medieval Novgorod's prosperity.

...6636 (1128) This was a cruel year: the people ate lime leaves, birchbark; they ground wood pulp and mixed it with husks and straw; and some ate buttercups, moss, and horseflesh. And the corpses of those who had fallen from starvation were in the streets, the marketplace, the road, and everywhere. And they hired men to carry the dead out of town, for the stench was poisoning the air. Sorrow and misery befell all. Fathers and mothers would give their children as gifts to merchants or put them to death. And many people went to other lands. Thus a blight was brought upon our lands for our sins. And this year the water of the river Volkhov was very high, and it carried away many houses.

6651 (1143) All this autumn was rainy; from Our Lady's Day of Nativity until the winter solstice it was warm and wet. The water was very high in the river Volkhov, and it carried away hay and wood. The lake froze, and there was great coldness in the night. And the wind broke up the ice and carried it into the river Volkhov, where it broke the bridge and carried away four of the bridge piles.

6664 (1156) The Novgorodians expelled Sudilo, the *posadnik* [elected high official] of the city, and he died five days later. And they gave the position of *posadnik* to Yakun Miroslavovich. In the same spring, on April 21st, Archbishop Nifont passed away. Before he died he went to Kiev to oppose the *metropolitan* bishop [head of Orthodox Church], but many people say that he went to Constantinople after having plundered the Cathedral (St. Sophia in Kiev). They say many things about him, but it is their sin for doing so. We should remember that he was the one who embellished the Cathedral (St. Sophia of Novgorod), who decorated the porches, who made the icon case, and who adorned the church on the outside. He also built the Church of the Holy Savior in Pskov and the Church of St. Clement in Ladoga. I believe that God, because of our sins, did not desire that we should have his grave for our consolation and so he sent him to Kiev, where he died. And he was buried in the Crypt Monastery....

6665 (1157) There was malice among the people, and they rose against Prince Mstislav Yurievich and began to drive him from Novgorod, but the merchants took up arms for him. And brother quarreled with brother. The bridge over the river Volkhov was seized. Guards took their stand on either side of the town gates, and it nearly came to the shedding of blood between them.

Abridged from Serge A. Zenkovsky, editor and translator, *Medieval Russia's Epics, Chronicles, and Tales,* New York, 1963.

In the spring Prince George died at Kiev, and the people of Kiev set Iziaslav Davidovich on the throne. In the same year Andrew, Abbot of the Church of the Holy Mother of God, died. And Alexis was appointed in his place. And in the fall the weather was fearsome with thunder and lightning, and on November 7th, at five in the night, there was hail of the size of apples.

4. The Lay of Igor's Campaign

The author of "The Lay of Igor's Campaign" is unknown. However, Prince Igor was a well-known historical personality. The "lay" (from the French lai *or lyrical poem) tells of the defeat of Igor and his escape from the Kumans, a nomadic tribe of Turkic origin who entered southern Russia in 1185. The poem is filled with omens as well as with admonitions to the grand princes of the Kievan period to cease fighting among themselves.*

• •

THE OMENS

Then Prince Igor set his foot in the golden stirrup
and rode into the open prairie.
The sun barred his way with darkness
and night, moaning with tempest, awoke the birds.
The whistling of the beasts arose.
And the Div* arose and from the treetops it cried,
enjoining unknown lands to listen:
    the land of the Volga,
    the land on the Azov Sea,
    the land at the river Sula,
    the city of Surozh,
    the city of Kerson,
    and you, the idol of the city of Tmutorokan.

The Kumans hastened by untrodden ways
to the Great river Don.
Their carts squeak at midnight,
one may say, as dispersed swans.
Igor leads his warriors to the river Don.
The birds in the forests of oak portend his misfortune.
The wolves conjure the tempest in the ravines.
The screeching eagles call the beasts to the feast of bones.
Foxes bark at scarlet shields.
O Russian land! You are already far beyond the hills.

*Div: a deity in the form of a bird (a cross between an owl and a peacock) that represented foreboding for the Russians.

Ibid.

THE FIRST DAY OF BATTLE: THE RUSSIANS ARE VICTORIOUS

Evening is slow to fade into night.
The glow of dusk disappeared.
Mist enveloped the prairie.
The song of the nightingale died out.

The daws began to caw.
Russian warriors barred the wide prairie
with their scarlet shields.
They seek honor for themselves
and glory for their prince.

Early in the morning of Friday
the Russians trampled the infidel Kuman armies,
and, spreading like arrows over the prairie,
they galloped away with beautiful Kuman maidens.
And with them they took:
  golds and brocades,
  and precious velvets.
With cloaks and coats and fur mantles
and with all kinds of Kuman finery
they began to bridge their way over the swamps and marshes.
The scarlet banner,
the white gonfalon,
the scarlet panache, and
the silver lance
were taken to brave Igor,
son of Sviatoslav.

Brave Oleg's clan slumbers in the prairie.
They have flown far away.
They were born to be offended
  neither by the falcon,
  nor by the gyrfalcon,
  nor by you, the black raven,
  the infidel Kuman.
Khan Gza flees like a gray wolf.
Khan Konchak shows him the way to the great river Don.

THE SECOND DAY OF BATTLE: THE VICTORY OF THE KUMANS

Very early on the second morn
a bloody dawn announced the day.
Black clouds arrive from the sea
and want to envelop the four suns.
Blue lightning shows through the clouds.
There is to be a mighty thundering.
The rain of arrows will come from the great river Don.
Here, on the river Kaiala,

close to the great river Don,
lances will be broken
and swords will be dulled on Kuman helmets.
O Russian land! You are already far beyond the hills.

Here the winds, grandsons of god Stribog,
blow the arrows from the sea
against Igor's brave regiments.
The earth groans.
The rivers become turbid.
Dust covers the prairie.
The pennants announce:
   "The Kumans have come from the river Don
   and from the sea.
   They encircle the Russian regiments from all sides."
The devil's children bar the prairie with their battle cries.
The brave Russians bar it with their scarlet shields....

5. The Sack of Riazan

The Mongol or Tatar invasion under the leader Batu Khan visited great devastation upon the Russian people. Riazan, a city on the Kievan frontier between the lower Volga and the Don, was the first town to be razed. The towns of Old Russia were forced to accept Mongol overlordship: over two hundred years of the "Tatar Yoke."

...The accursed Batu began the conquest of the land of Riazan, and soon approached the city of Riazan itself. They encircled the city and fought without surcease for five days. Batu changed his regiments frequently, replacing them with fresh troops, while the citizens of Riazan fought without relief. And many citizens were killed and others wounded. Still others were exhausted by their great efforts and their wounds. On the dawn of the sixth day the pagan warriors began to storm the city, some with firebrands, some with battering rams, and others with countless scaling ladders for ascending the walls of the city. And they took the city of Riazan on the 21st day of December. And the Tatars came to the Cathedral of the Assumption of the Blessed Virgin, and they cut to pieces the Great Princess Agrippina, her daughters-in-law, and other princesses. They burned to death the bishops and the priests and put the torch to the holy church. And the Tatars cut down many people, including women and children. Still

Ibid.

others were drowned in the river. And they killed without exception all monks and priests. And they burned this holy city with all its beauty and wealth, and they captured the relatives of the Riazan princes, the princes of Kiev and Chernigov. And churches of God were destroyed, and much blood was spilled on the holy altars. And not one man remained alive in the city. All were dead. All had drunk the same bitter cup to the dregs. And there was not even anyone to mourn the dead. Neither father nor mother could mourn their dead children, nor the children their fathers or mothers. Nor could a brother mourn the death of his brother, nor relatives their relatives. All were dead. And this happened for our sins.

Seeing this terrible letting of Christian blood, the heart of godless Batu became even more hardened, and he marched against the cities of Suzdal and Vladimir, intending to conquer all Russian lands, to uproot the Christian faith, and to destroy the churches of God. At that time a Riazan lord, Eupaty Kolovrat, who was in Chernigov at the time of the destruction of the city of Riazan, heard of Batu's invasion. He left Chernigov with a small force and hurried to Riazan. When he came to the land of Riazan he saw it devastated and the cities destroyed, the rulers killed, and the people dead. And he rushed to the city of Riazan and found it destroyed, the rulers killed, and the people slaughtered. Some of them were cut down, while others were burned, and still others were drowned. And Eupaty wept with great sorrow and his heart became angry. He gathered a small force of seventeen hundred men who had been preserved by God outside the city. And they hurriedly pursued the godless emperor. And with difficulty they caught up with him in the principality of Suzdal, and suddenly fell upon his camp. And there began a battle without mercy, and confusion reigned. And the Tatars lost their heads from fear as Eupaty fought so fiercely that his sword became dull, and, taking a sword from a fallen Tatar, he would cut them down with their own swords. The Tatars thought that the Russians had risen from the dead, and Eupaty was riding through the ranks of the Tatar regiments so bravely that Batu himself became frightened.... [Euphaty Kolovrat's brave but unsuccessful defense of the Russian lands won him the respect of Batu Khan.]

6. The Tsar and His Powers

Adam Olearius, a seventeenth century German visitor to Moscow, described the autocratic traditions of the Moscow court. Although he viewed the court of the early Romanovs, his account is accurate in its description and applicable to the earlier period under Ivan IV as well.

The Russian system of government is what the political thinkers call 'a dominating and despotic monarchy.' After he inherits the crown, the Tsar, or Grand Prince, alone rules the whole country; all his subjects, the noblemen and princes as well as the common people, townsmen, and peasants, are his serfs and slaves, whom he treats as the master of the house does his servants. This mode of rule is very like that which Aristotle describes in the following words: 'There is also another kind of monarchy, found in the kingdoms of some of the barbarian peoples, which stands closest of all to tyranny.' If one keeps in mind the basic distinction between a legitimate and a tyrannical order, that the first subserves the welfare of the subjects and the second the personal wants of the sovereign, then the Russian government must be considered closely related to tyranny.

In addressing the Tsar the magnates must unashamedly not only write their names in the diminutive form, but also call themselves slaves, and they are treated as such. Formerly the *gosti* [merchants] and magnates who were supposed to turn out at public audiences in sumptuous dress, were beaten on the bare back with the knout, like slaves, if they failed to appear without good reason. Now, however, they get off with a two- or three-day confinement in prison, depending upon [the influence of] their patrons and intercessors at court.

They call the Grand Prince, their ruler, 'Tsar' or 'His Tsarist Majesty,' and some trace the title's origin to the word Caesar. Like the Holy Roman Emperor, he has an imperial coat of arms and a seal depicting a two-headed eagle with its wings hanging downward. Formerly one crown was shown above the eagle's head, but now there are three, to represent in addition to the Russian realm, the two Tartar kingdoms of Astrakhan and Kazan. On the eagle's breast hangs a shield showing a horseman plunging a spear into a dragon. This eagle was first introduced by the tyrant Ivan Vasilevich [Ivan IV, The Terrible], for his glorification, for he prided himself on being descended from the Roman emperors. The Tsar's interpreters and some of the German merchants call him 'Emperor.'...

The Russians exalt their Tsar very highly, pronouncing his name with the greatest reverence at assemblies, and they fear him exceedingly, even more than

Reprinted from Samuel H. Baron, editor and translator, *The Travels of Olearius in Seventeenth Century Russia,* Stanford, 1967.

God...Beginning very early, they teach their children to speak of His Tsarist Majesty as of God, and to consider him equally lofty. Thus they often say, 'God and the Grand Prince [alone] know that.' The same idea is expressed in others of their bywords: they speak of appearing before the Grand Prince as 'seeing his bright eyes.' To demonstrate their great humility and sense of duty, they say that everything they have belongs not so much to them as to God and the Grand Prince. They came to use such expressions partly in consequence of the violent acts perpetrated by the tyrant Ivan Vasilevich and partly because they and their property indeed are in that condition. So that they might remain tranquil in slavery and terror, they are forbidden, on pain of corporal punishment, to travel out of the country on their own initiative [for they might then] tell [their countrymen] of the free institutions that exist in foreign lands. Likewise, no merchant may cross the border and carry on trade abroad without the Tsar's permission....

Ten years ago, through the special favour of the Grand Prince, the old German translator Hans Helmes (who died at the age of 97) was allowed to send his son, who had been born in Moscow, to a German university to study medicine; [the son was expected] afterwards to serve the Tsar. He was so successful that he obtained the medical degree with great honor, and at Oxford University in England was considered almost a marvel. But once having escaped from Muscovite slavery, he had no wish to return. Later the Novgorod merchant Petr Miklyayev, an intelligent and knowledgeable man who was ambassador to our country a year ago and who then asked me to instruct his son in Latin and German, was unable to obtain permission [for his son to leave] from either the Patriarch or the Grand Prince.

The present Grand Prince is a very pious ruler who, like his father, does not wish a single one of his peasants to be impoverished. If one of them, whether a *boyar's* serf or his own, is stricken by misfortune as a result of a bad harvest or some other untoward occurrence, the *prikaz* [government department] to whose jurisdiction he is subject gives him assistance and, in general, keeps an eye on his activity so that he may recover, pay his debt, and fulfill his obligations to the authorities. And if someone is sent in disgrace to Siberia for having abused his Majesty or for some other serious offence — which seldom happens nowadays — even this disfavour is mitigated by providing the exile with a tolerable livelihood, in keeping with his personal condition and worth. Magnates are given money, scribes positions in the chancelleries of Siberian cities;...soldiers are given places as soldiers, which yield an annual salary and a decent living. The most oppressive aspect for most of them is that they are banished from His Majesty's countenance and deprived of the right to see his bright eyes. Moreover, there have been instances in which such disgrace worked a great advantage, namely when the exiles' professions or trades were more fruitfully pursued [in Siberia] than in Moscow; some prospered so well that, if they had their wives and children with them, they did not wish to return to Moscow even when released.

The Tsar is understandably concerned about his majesty and quality, and enjoys the rights of majesty as other monarchs and absolute rulers do. He is not subject to the law and may, as he desires and deems fit, publish and establish laws and orders. These are accepted and fulfilled by all, whatever their station, without any contradiction...they have a proverb: "One may not alter the word of God and the Tsar, but must obey it without fail."

The Grand Prince appoints and removes officials, and even expels and executes them as he pleases. Thus they have precisely the same customs that, according to the prophet Daniel, prevailed in the reign of Nebuchadnezzar [King of Babylon] who slew, had beaten, elevated, or humbled whomsoever he wished.

7. The Time of Troubles

In the Time of Troubles, dynastic conflict led to the emergence of rivals for the throne: the Godunovs, the Romanovs, and the Shuiskys were contending families. Other pretenders appeared claiming, in turn, to be Dmitri, a son of Ivan IV who had been viciously eliminated early in this troubled period. This reading details events in the episode of the first False Dmitri's appearance. He claimed that he had survived the attack in his boyhood and returned in his manhood to claim his rightful position with the support of Polish armies. This account presents the idea of a threat from the West, an idea that preoccupies Russia to this day.

...In the year 7113 (1605) a certain monk, whose name was Gregory and who was a scion of the Otrepiev family, and who had been an addict of occult books and other evils, left Russia and went to the Polish Kingdom. Living there, he began to write subversive proclamations, sending them to all parts of Russia, in which he declared that he was the real Dmitry, son of the tsar. He would go from city to city, hiding himself and causing disturbances among the people of both realms. Then he was joined by fugitives from western Russian and Polish cities, by serfs whose time had arrived according to the will of the evil spirit, and by one village after another, and by one city after another, and finally all were tempted. However, his scheme was evident to many. Yet, what a great amount of evil did they cause! And until this day Russia is unable to be rid of this yoke. He and his followers in evil have done so many base deeds in Russia that no one could describe them all, even if he wrote for many years. In two years this unfrocked monk Gregory succeeded in winning over one-quarter of the entire universe, the entirety of Europe; and even the Pope of Rome wrote

Abridged from Serge A. Zenkovsky, editor and translator, *Medieval Russia's Epics, Chronicles and Tales*, New York, 1963.

on his behalf to the entire West, presenting Gregory as an exile from his fatherland. And the Pope ordered the Polish king, Sigismund III, to start a campaign against Russia in order to take revenge for the impostor. Gregory joined the Catholics, that eternal enemy of Christians, and he gave them a written promise that he would bring entire Russia under the blessing of the *Antichrist,* † thus delivering all Russians to eternal death through the abomination of the Catholic Communion. And he would have done this, if the Lord hadn't overthrown his evil design....

This enemy, the defrocked monk, plotted with the heretics [the Poles] to massacre the Russian people of all ranks, beginning with the courtiers and ending with common officers. And he intended to have a great celebration with the shooting of artillery in the Pond Field at the Sretensk Gate. And when the people went to this celebration, then he would order the gate to be closed and all would be slain.

But this base plot did not come to fruition because two days before the celebration was to have taken place,...this accursed man died an evil death, having reigned for one year. He used to say of himself that he was thirty-four years of age, but his friends, the demons, didn't give him many more years of life....

After his death, the people of Moscow gave themselves to drinking in their joy, instead of rendering thanks to God. And everyone bragged about his deeds in murdering the impostor, Pseudo-Dmitry, and all boasted about their courage. But the people forgot to give thanks through prayer in the Church of the Holy Virgin for this most glorious victory....

8. The Russian Peasant Community

The culture of the Russian village changed little from the sixteenth century until the beginning of the twentieth. Although Professor Keenan writes here about the sixteenth century village, he also describes the ageless struggle of the Russian peasant. The chapter on geography in this book pointed out the harsh conditions under which a farmer had to grow his crop. This reading further explains the Russian's resistance to taking risks, and the importance of maintaining a collective rather than an individual direction. Professor Keenan's work draws on T. Shanin, The Awkward Class, *and Shanin's sources.*

...In most agricultural communities, like the Russian, isolated from trade and the stabilizing influences of neighboring units — the line between prosperity and disaster, for the group as well as the household unit, is a thin and shifting one. One man's field is flooded, another's is not. One family's cow goes dry, another's does not; one couple has four healthy sons, another is barren, and so on. Different cultures develop different institutionalized means of dealing with the fragility and unpredictability of life. In the Russian village these means of self-preservation can, in narrative fashion be described as follows:

Let us take two new households, Ivan's and Fedor's, both of which contain four healthy individuals (the two adults and two sons in Ivan's case, a son and daughter in Fedor's), have equal and adequate amounts of land, and one horse each. Now for reasons that will become clear in a moment, it is in the village's interest to keep each of these households, individuals, and horses just as productive as possible, that is to match up labor and land and draft power. Thus as Ivan's sons grow, his household will be allotted or acquire more land, will acquire or be loaned draft power, and so on. Ivan will prosper. As he moves up on the economic scale, however, the village will begin to exert certain downward forces on him. He will be required to take in the widow or orphan of a neighbor or the village cripple. He will be expected to bear the expense of the major local feast, and so on. Thus a real ceiling will be placed on his socio-economic movement — he will be kept, as it were, within the orbit of the particles revolving around the nucleus of that village.

Fedor's case might be different. His son dies, and he and his wife and daughter are unable to cultivate their allotment of land, which is correspondingly reduced. His mare foals, but then his house burns and Fedor is killed. Disaster threatens his wife and daughter. But here again the village steps in, because arable land, and useful labor, and two horses are of vital interest to the

Abridged from Edward L. Keenan, "Russian Political Culture," 1975.

whole community. Fedor's widow, if still of child-bearing age, will be married, along with one horse and some of the land, to an able-bodied man who has no wife and no horse and no land, as will the daughter — also with a horse and land. Thus a kind of floor is also imposed, and upward forces are brought to bear which keep these unfortunate individuals alive, within the village, and within the productive nexus of the common survival pattern.

Now these all seem to be reasonable arrangements, but of course the question arises of the wishes and motivations of the individuals and family units concerned, and the sanctions applied in case, for example, Ivan doesn't *want* to take in waifs and widows, and wants instead to become rich, or Fedor's daughter or wife doesn't want to marry the hired hand being provided, but wants to enter a nunnery. In extreme cases, of course, the villagers can beat them to death or, in Ivan's case, let loose the red rooster (i.e., burn his house down), but such extreme measures are usually not necessary because this system of reciprocating mechanisms *is* a system and its virtues and sanctions are known to every member of the culture. Given the chanciness and suddenness of fortune and famine in such conditions, all adult members of such a village will have experienced the benefits of both the "ceiling" and the "floor" in their own lifetime — perhaps in their own family, and will understand the importance of the village organization as the warrant of their own future viability. Under normal circumstances they will not only acquiesce, but will force others to do so in their own interest.

Thus the overpowering objective of the peasant village organization — an objective developed over centuries of unchanging subsistence agriculture, an objective whose imperatives created a tight nucleus bound by immense forces of both cohesion and fission — was survival, economic, biological and social survival. Not justice, as the Slavophiles† and many city-bred ethnographers thought, not material improvement or the accumulation of wealth, not the "preservation of a way of life," but the preservation of life itself, human life, the life of vital stock, the life of life-giving field cultures. And the smallest political unit of peasant life was not the individual (who was unviable in this environment), and not the nuclear family (which, in its extended form, was marginally viable, but too vulnerable to disease or sudden calamity), but the village, to whose interests all others were subordinated. And the primary mode of decision-making of such a collective was minimization of risk, of the danger of the interruption of life through any of the calamities that could come upon an isolated, technologically primitive, necessarily self-sufficient and by consequence vulnerable community. If innovation offered a short-term improvement of the standard of living at the cost of an increased risk of possible calamity, it was rejected. If the interests of an individual reduced the basic viability of the group, they were denied. When faced with danger, the village would hunker down — or pick up and move on — rather than change.

9. The Maiden Tsar

The roots of Russian folk tales can be traced back to pagan mythology.
The tales have been popular at all levels of society. The Maiden Tsar *introduces*
the Firebird and the witch, Baba Yaga, who flies through the sky in a mortar and
pestle, two important characters in many Russian folk tales.

In a certain land, in a certain kingdom, there was a merchant whose
wife died, leaving him with an only son, Ivan. He put this son in charge of a
tutor, and after some time took another wife; and since Ivan, the merchant's
son, was now of age and very handsome, his stepmother fell in love with him.
One day Ivan went with his tutor to fish in the sea on a small raft; suddenly
they saw thirty ships making toward them. On these ships sailed the Maiden
Tsar with thirty other maidens, all her foster sisters. When the ships came close
to the raft, all thirty of them dropped anchor. Ivan and his tutor were invited
aboard the best ship, where the Maiden Tsar and her thirty foster sisters received them; she told Ivan that she loved him passionately and had come from afar
to see him. So they were betrothed.

The Maiden Tsar told the merchant's son to return to the same place the
following day, said farewell to him, and sailed away. Ivan returned home and
went to sleep. The stepmother led the tutor into her room, made him drunk,
and began to question him as to what had happened to him and Ivan at sea.
The tutor told her everything. Upon hearing his story, she gave him a pin and
said: "Tomorrow, when the ships begin to sail toward you, stick this pin into
Ivan's tunic." The tutor promised to carry out her order.

Next morning Ivan arose and went fishing. As soon as his tutor beheld
the ships sailing in the distance, he stuck the pin into Ivan's tunic. "Ah, I feel
so sleepy," said the merchant's son. "Listen, tutor, I will take a nap now, and
when the ships come close, please rouse me." "Very well, of course I will rouse
you," said the tutor. The ships sailed close to the raft and cast anchor; the
Maiden Tsar sent for Ivan, asking him to hasten to her; but he was sound
asleep. The servants began to shake him, pinch him, and nudge him. All in
vain—they could not awaken him, so they left him.

The Maiden Tsar told the tutor to bring Ivan to the same place on the
following day, then ordered her crews to lift anchor and set sail. As soon as the
ships sailed away, the tutor pulled out the pin, and Ivan awoke, jumped up,
and began to call to the Maiden Tsar to return. But she was far away then and
could not hear him. He went home sad and aggrieved. His stepmother took the

From Alexander Afanas'ev, *Russian Fairy Tales,* translated by Norbert Guterman,
New York, 1975.

tutor into her room, made him drunk, questioned him about everything that had happened, and told him to stick the pin through Ivan's tunic again the next day. The next day Ivan again went fishing, again slept all the time, and did not see the Maiden Tsar; she left word that he should come again.

On the third day he again went fishing with his tutor. They came to the old place, and beheld the ships sailing at a distance, and the tutor straightway stuck in his pin, and Ivan fell sound asleep. The ships sailed close and dropped anchor; the Maiden Tsar sent for her betrothed to come aboard her ship. The servants tried in every possible way to rouse him, but no matter what they did, they could not waken him. The Maiden Tsar learned of the stepmother's ruse and the tutor's treason, and wrote to Ivan telling him to cut off the tutor's head, and, if he loved his betrothed, to come and find her beyond thrice nine lands in the thrice tenth kingdom.

The ships had no sooner set sail and put out to sea than the tutor pulled the pin from Ivan's garment; he awoke and began to bemoan his loss of the Maiden Tsar; but she was far away and could not hear him. The tutor gave him her letter; Ivan read it, drew out his sharp saber, and cut off the wicked tutor's head. Then he sailed hurriedly to the shore, went home, said farewell to his father, and set out to find the thrice tenth kingdom.

He journeyed onward, straight ahead, a long time or a short time—for speedily a tale is spun, but with less speed a deed is done—and finally came to a little hut; it stood in the open field, turning on chicken legs. He entered and found Baba Yaga the Bony-legged. "Fie, fie," she said, "the Russian smell was never heard of nor caught sight of here, but now it has come by itself. Are you here of your own free will or by compulsion, my good youth?" "Largely of my own free will, and twice as much by compulsion! Do you know, Baba Yaga, where lies the thrice tenth kingdom?" "No, I do not," she said, and told him to go to her second sister; she might know.

Ivan thanked her and went on farther; he walked and walked, a long distance or a short distance, a long time or a short time, and finally came to a little hut exactly like the first and there too found a Baba Yaga. "Fie, fie," she said, "the Russian smell was never heard of nor caught sight of here, but now it has come by itself. Are you here of your own free will or by compulsion, my good youth?" "Largely of my own free will, and twice as much by compulsion! Do you know, Baba Yaga, where lies the thrice tenth kingdom?" "No, I do not," she said, and told him to stop at her youngest sister's; she might know. "If she gets angry at you," she added, "and wants to devour you, take three horns from her and ask her permission to blow them; blow the first one softly, the second louder, and the third still louder." Ivan thanked the Baba Yaga and went on farther.

He walked and walked, a long distance or a short distance, a long time or a short time, and finally beheld a little hut standing in the open field and turning upon chicken legs; he entered it and found another Baba Yaga. "Fie,

fie, the Russian smell was never heard of nor caught sight of here, and now it has come by itself," she said, and ran to whet her teeth, for she intended to eat her uninvited guest. Ivan begged her to give him three horns: he blew one softly, the second louder, and the third still louder. Suddenly birds of all kinds swarmed about him, among them the firebird. "Sit upon me quickly," said the firebird, "and we shall fly wherever you want; if you don't come with me, the Baba Yaga will devour you." Ivan had no sooner sat himself upon the bird's back than the Baba Yaga rushed in, seized the firebird by the tail, and plucked a large handful of feathers from it.

The firebird flew with Ivan on its back; for a long time it soared in the skies, till finally it came to the broad sea. "Now, Ivan, merchant's son, the thrice tenth land lies beyond this sea. I am not strong enough to carry you to the other shore; get there as best you can." Ivan climbed down from the firebird, thanked it, and walked along the shore.

He walked and walked till he came to a little hut; he entered it, and was met by an old woman who gave him meat and drink and asked him whither he was going and why he was traveling so far. He told her that he was going to the thrice tenth kingdom to find the Maiden Tsar, his betrothed. "Ah," said the old woman, "she no longer loves you; if she gets hold of you, she will tear you to shreds; her love is stored away in a remote place." "Then how can I get it?" "Wait a bit! My daughter lives at the Maiden Tsar's palace and she is coming to visit me today; we may learn something from her." Then the old woman turned Ivan into a pin and stuck the pin into the wall; at night her daughter flew in. Her mother asked her whether she knew where the Maiden Tsar's love was stored away. "I do not know," said the daughter, and promised to find out from the Maiden Tsar herself. The next day she again visited her mother and told her: "On this side of the ocean there stands an oak; in the oak there is a coffer; in the coffer there is a hare; in the hare there is a duck; in the duck there is an egg; and in the egg lies the Maiden Tsar's love."

Ivan took some bread and set out for the place she had described. He found the oak and removed the coffer from it; then he removed the hare from the coffer; the duck from the hare, and the egg from the duck. He returned with the egg to the old woman. A few days later came the old woman's birthday; she invited the Maiden Tsar with the thirty other maidens, her foster sisters, to her house; she baked the egg, dressed Ivan the merchant's son in splendid raiment, and hid him.

At midday, the Maiden Tsar and the thirty other maidens flew into the house, sat down to table, and began to dine; after dinner the old woman served them each an egg, and to the Maiden Tsar she served the egg that Ivan had found. The Maiden Tsar ate of it and at once conceived a passionate love for Ivan the merchant's son. The old woman brought him out of his hiding place. How much joy there was, how much merriment! The Maiden Tsar left with her betrothed, the merchant's son, for her own kingdom; they married and began to live happily and to prosper.

10. Seventeenth Century Moscow

Peter the Great's succession to the throne ushered in major changes in Russian history. This account is based on English travelers' descriptions of life in Moscow on the eve of Peter's accession. It emphasizes how alien Muscovy seemed to the cultivated Englishman.

...The secular and religious life of old Moscow was closely intertwined, Byzantine survivals and influences being distinguishable even up to the end of the seventeenth century. Every ceremony, every national or court celebration was primarily religious in form. Straightforward religious festivals, of St. Simeon 'bringer in of the New Year', of St. Peter the Thaumaturge, of the blessing of the water at the feast of the Epiphany and of Christmas and other more familiar anniversaries were, of course, commemorated with elaborate and picturesque ritual and closed with ample banquets. The Tsar himself, surrounded by his chamberlains and court dignitaries, took as important a part as the Patriarch of Moscow and his deans, priests and deacons. But functions outside the calendar of the church were apt to assume an equally religious form. The declaration of a war or the celebration of a victory would be the occasion for a solemn service at which the Tsar would eat the holy bread and partake of the 'cup of the Mother of God' before regaling the court, moved sometimes to tears by the fervour of the Tsar's or the Patriarch's address, with red and white mead and vodka.

The *boyars*† lived in the closest personal contact with the Tsar. The Tsar's position was very much nearer to that of the 'head of a family' than has since been the case with a monarch. Every morning the gentry and nobility had to assemble at the court and were received in order, according to the minute gradations of precedence on which the life of the court was hung. What seem the most trivial requests had to be made to the Tsar in person—such as permission to leave Moscow for a week-end to go to a christening. The Tsar dined in public with his whole court and after the usual siesta the rest of the day was given over to business, each public office having its allotted day for attention.

The principle and prerogatives of seniority were extended beyond the dreams of the English public school. A *boyar* spent a large part of his life standing on his dignity. Quarrels as to who should sit above whom at the Tsar's table were carried to extraordinary lengths and a member of one family would resort to any expedient rather than yield precedence to a member of another.

Anything more rigidly conservative than the old *boyar* circles would be impossible to imagine. The family—which counted for everything and the individual for nothing—was run on patriarchal and sternly monastic lines. The head of a family was the bourgeois lord-and-master carried to a fantastic

From Christopher Marsden, *Palmyra of the North: The First Days of St. Petersburg,* London, 1942.

degree of authority. Complete obedience to the father was demanded of all, including the wife and everyone who dwelt under the master's roof. Every hour of the day had its appointed prayers and the simplest domestic business was accompanied by religious obeisances. That extraordinary document, the *Domostroi* [guide to household behavior] of the Archimandrite Silvester, minister of Ivan IV, with its recipes for food and drink, its instructions about clothes, furniture, servants, women and domestic utensils, shows very clearly the narrowness, the detail, and at the same time the licence, as regards drunkenness or wife-beating (don't use a 'staff tipped with iron', says the Archimandrite), of the religious regulations according to which life had to be lived.

Intellectual life and discussion were entirely lacking. Illiterate, and fettered hand and foot by the most absurd religious bigotry, the Russian was incapable of grasping the difference between the essential and the unessential or, as we see it, between true right and wrong. His penal legislation, farcically unjust, is a case in point. The pettiest details of ritual or tradition assumed for him prodigious importance; change of any kind he considered *ipso facto* sinful and anything foreign was automatically an abomination. He lived in a thick fog of ignorance, bias and superstition, unenlightened by any effort on the part of church or of government.

Intense puritanism marched hand in hand with uncontrolled vice. Singing, card or chess-playing, games and sports of all kinds—the common, harmless amusements of any people—were forbidden as inventions of the Prince of Devils; the universal drunkenness and wife-beating were accepted as a matter of course. The common people had no recreations. And apart from the cruel organized bullying of jesters—the dwarfs, imbeciles, negroes and freaks who were kept by every *boyar* family—heavy drinking was the only amusement of the nobility, and banquets, which always began with an edifying religious service, invariably ended as orgies. Travellers were disgusted by the drunkenness and general bestiality of the Muscovites. It was nothing to see women and children, let alone priests, reeling about in the streets and suddenly falling dead drunk. Their ordinary manners were those of savages. Their behaviour, especially towards women, on their rare appearances outside Russia, led to diplomatic remonstrances. Filthily dirty, clad in long, cumbersome garments which prevented all free movement, with their unkempt hair down to their shoulders and matted beards, they behaved hoggishly at table, dipping their black and greasy fingers indiscriminately into plates and dishes, always eating too much and drinking noisily and greedily out of unwashed vessels.

Yet they lived in a state of pointless asceticism. Their houses were furnished with only the barest benches and tables; they were always dark, as a room lit by more than ten tallow dips was considered extravagantly lighted, and their only ornaments were a few religious icons. Visitors were impressed by the richness and oriental strangeness of the *boyars'* dress at court, but these vestments were only assumed on very solemn occasions and their ordinary attire was the simple girdled caftan. Their food, though all too abundant, was of the simplest—'gross meats and stinking fish'; mead and raw spirit their only drink.

The position of their women was deplorable. Ignorant and uneducated, they were regarded as domestic, barely human and permanently immature creatures, whose chastity would in some mysterious way be tainted by any appearance in public. Their duties in the household were arduous but went unnoticed—unless a mistake was made, when the master, with certain small limitations (he was enjoined not 'to humiliate unduly by flogging before men'), was entitled to inflict upon his wife what form of corporal punishment he thought fit. 'Yet three or four years ago,' wrote Collins in 1671, 'a merchant beat his wife as long as he was able, with a whip two inches about, and then caused her to put on a smock dipt in brandy three or four times distilled, which he set on fire, and so the poor creature perished miserably in the flames. And yet what is more strange, none prosecuted her death: for in this case they have no penal law for killing of a wife or slave, if it happen upon correction. Some of these barbarians will tie up their wives by the hair of the head, and whip them stark naked.' Within the *terem* [secluded women's area], which was a cross between a fortress and a nunnery, the women spent their days in seclusion while their lords roistered, only appearing, with great formality and timid obeisance, before some distinguished guest to whom the master of the house wished to show special hospitality by displaying his collection. Any journeys they made, such as to church (where special sections were reserved for them) were undertaken in heavily closed carriages or litters. They themselves wore the *fata* [veil] over their faces. To all intents and purposes the Orthodox Russian woman of the seventeenth century was as completely veiled and segregated as her Moslem sister. Indeed the whole outlook on the female sex was entirely Oriental, for the beauty of a woman was placed in her fatness, a neat waist being thought ugly, so that slender girls would have to, as an outraged Englishman put it, 'on purpose to fatten themselves, lie abed all day long drinking Russian brandy (which will fatten extremely), then sleep, and afterwards drink again, like swine designed to make bacon.' Moreover they stained their teeth black—at a time when Louis XIV was on the throne of France!...

The light of the Renaissance had by now illuminated almost every corner of western and northern Europe. The Turk held his oppressive sway in the south-east. But Muscovy, cut off until the middle of the seventeenth century from any contact with Europe, illiterate, without culture other than the religious veneer which the now forgotten Byzantine Empire had long ago superimposed upon its Asiatic inheritance, lay in darkness, wallowing in the sordid slough of superstition....

Chapter Three

Imperial Russia

In 1721, Tsar Peter I accepted a new title for himself and his successors: "Father of the Fatherland, Emperor of All Russia." The new title, conferred upon one of Russia's most able and dynamic rulers, effectively symbolized the beginning of a new era in Russian history, generally known as The Imperial Period. This era lasted for approximately two hundred years, until it ended abruptly and violently in 1917. Imperial Russia retained many of the institutions and traditions of Old Russia, but there were profound changes as well. Through continued expansion, many non-Russians were incorporated into the Russian state, transforming that state into an empire. A new capital on Russia's western border, St. Petersburg, replaced the historic capital, Moscow. In the latter part of the Imperial Period, Russia not only became considerably more urban and industrialized but also came into much closer contact with the European countries to the west than it ever had before. Increased contact led to greater exposure to European ideas and practices. Because these tended to be very different from those of Russia, they had a dramatic impact. To some Russians, "joining" Europe and borrowing from its more advanced societies seemed a positive way to strengthen Russia. Others opposed such borrowing, because they did not want Russia's basic identity changed. The resulting tension, between the need for reform and the fear of what reform might bring, never resolved itself, and ultimately contributed to the downfall of the Russian empire.

WESTERNIZATION: PETER THE GREAT

By the end of the seventeenth century, Russia had already become a huge and potentially powerful state. Compared to the European states to its west, however, it was less developed economically, culturally, and technologically. Had Russia been able to remain isolated, this might not have mattered, but isolation was impossible. In wars with neighboring states, Russian armies usually lost. For Russia to be able to compete effectively with these other states, a major transformation was necessary. This was difficult to accomplish, however, for most Russians, suspicious of anything new and different, clung to traditional ways. In the latter half of the seventeenth century, a number of farsighted Russian leaders recognized the need for major changes, but none before Peter the

Great had the vision, power, or energy to bring these changes about. Peter possessed all of these qualities, and undertook to transform Russian society to its very foundations. As a result, his long reign (1689-1725) is still regarded as a watershed in Russian history.

FACT: Peter the Great was one of the largest rulers in history, standing nearly seven feet tall. He was powerfully built, as well.

Peter was also interesting and impressive in other ways. Born in a hut, he developed an early fondness for soldiering, boats, drinking, and women. He loved parties and enjoyed playing practical jokes. And he had tremendous curiosity. Contact with foreigners in Moscow's "German Quarter"† sparked his fascination for the West. He decided to take a two-year "fact-finding" tour, called "The Grand Embassy," through Europe in 1697-98. During this trip, Peter deliberately traveled incognito, avoiding ceremony and concentrating on learning. His particular interest lay in technical subjects, so he concentrated on such areas as shipbuilding, munitions, printing, and medicine, but his curiosity extended to many diverse fields. In short, during the trip, which included Prussia, Holland, England, and the Hapsburg Empire, he attempted to absorb as much of Europe as possible.

On his return, Peter immediately began to institute changes in almost every aspect of Russian life. These changes were not so much part of a grand design as they were measures to meet the needs of the day. Primary among these was the need for military reform. War had been commonplace in Russian history before Peter, and he continued the tradition.

FACT: Russia was at war in every year of Peter's reign but one (1725).

Peter inherited a long and indecisive conflict with the Turks, and he also initiated a campaign against Sweden, in the hope of gaining territory on the Baltic Sea. Charles XII of Sweden proved to be a formidable adversary, soundly defeating Peter's army at Narva, near the Baltic, in 1701. Peter responded to this challenge by rebuilding the Russian army. He introduced conscription (for life), created a professional officer class, and ordered the development of new weapons, from bayonets to heavy artillery.

FACT: On orders from Peter, thousands of bells from Russian churches were melted down and made into cannons and cannonballs.

To Peter, cannons were a more vital need than bells, the military more important than the church. By 1720, Peter's army numbered more than 200,000 regular troops, the largest and one of the most effective fighting forces in Europe. Peter's navy, which he built practically from scratch, included 48 ships of the line, 750 auxiliary vessels, and 28,000 sailors. It was larger than the navies of Sweden and Denmark combined, and became an imposing presence on the Baltic Sea.

Peter's military reforms paid off. Leading his troops himself, he defeated Charles and the Swedes in the key battle of Poltava, in the Ukraine, in 1709. During this conflict, Russia obtained territory on the Baltic coast roughly equivalent to modern Latvia and Estonia, and decisively ended Swedish domination of the Baltic Sea area. Above all, the Poltava victory marked the emergence of Russia as a military power to be reckoned with in Europe.

Peter realized that to make Russia a powerful military state, he had to develop its economy and create a better, more enlightened administration. To achieve these goals and galvanize Russia's energies, he saw that he must play a very active role. Peter was everywhere, a human dynamo exhorting, bullying, leading by example. He introduced sweeping governmental changes, using West European models. A Senate was created, to supervise affairs when he was away at war. With advice from the German philosopher Leibnitz, Peter established twelve "colleges," prototypes of later ministries, to handle specialized functions such as finance, foreign affairs, and trade and industry. At his directive, the government took steps to stimulate the economy and produce increased revenue. New industries were created. Foreign trade increased by 400% during Peter's reign. He introduced new taxes, including a head or "soul" tax on the entire lower class. By 1724 the revenue collected was 5½ times what it had been in 1680.

Peter left very few areas untouched.

FACT: Peter decreed that all Russian men were to shave their beards, or be fined.

Since Frenchmen and Englishmen of the time did not wear beards, these became for Peter a symbol of backwardness, unacceptable in Russia. To facilitate learning from the West, Peter decided that Russians must learn and speak German or Dutch. Later, these gave way to French as the favored court language. He also believed that the Orthodox Church promoted tradition and superstition, so he placed it under the control of the Holy Synod, a secular office. Peter changed, or tried to change, everything: dress, social customs, the calendar, the language. Among his most dramatic creations was a new capital city, to symbolize the new Russia he was trying to construct. Starting in 1703, this new city, St. Petersburg, was built at the mouth of the Neva River, on the Baltic shore. (See Reading 1) In this location, the new capital became a "Window on the West" for Russia, providing easy access to Europe via the Baltic Sea. To this day, St. Petersburg (now Leningrad) looks very much like a European city, a northern Venice with its network of canals.

FACT: St. Petersburg was built by the forced labor of huge numbers of serfs, who worked under frightful hardships. Some 30,000 died in the process, mostly of disease. This led to a saying that it was "a city built on bones."

This use of forced labor was typical of Peter's methods. He believed that the transformation of Russia would not occur by itself. It would result only from command and compulsion. In attempting to westernize and modernize his country, Peter thus reinforced one of the oldest and strongest of Russian traditions, the principle of autocracy.

Even an autocrat such as Peter could not accomplish everything by himself, and so he turned to the gentry for assistance. This group had long been required to serve the state, but this obligation was now increased and formalized by the establishment of a "Table of Ranks." It set out a hierarchy of government positions in which promotion was based chiefly on merit. Portions of the gentry thus became not only beardless speakers of German, but even more dependent on the state than they had been in the seventeenth century, their rank determined by the quality of their service.

Peter's reforms were impressive, but at the same time they were both incomplete and controversial. They were incomplete in that they only really affected those members of the upper classes who lived in or near St. Petersburg. The peasants, who comprised the overwhelming majority of the population, were largely untouched, and continued to live much as before. They became known as "The Dark People" to the new, westernized gentry, who viewed them as ignorant, superstitious, and backward. Peter's reforms thus created a schism, or divison, in Russian society that grew wider as time went on.

Peter's reforms were controversial as well. Some Russians acknowledged their necessity, but most resented them. The gentry was angry at having to change its lifestyle. Peasants resented the crushing new tax burden, military conscription, and forced labor. Many Orthodox Christians opposed Peter's attempt to secularize their Church; they called him the Antichrist. (See Reading 2)

FACT: Among the most violent opponents of Peter's programs were the "Old Believers," a group of conservative Christians, and among their sympathizers was Peter's own son Alexis, who was condemned to death in part for refusing to submit to his father's will on church reform.

For many Russians, the new capital symbolized all that was bad with Peter's Russia. It was Western, secular, and soulless, "a city where all is stone, not only the houses but the trees and the inhabitants." It stood in direct contrast to Moscow, which had been largely built of wood, like the peasant huts of rural Russia. The differing views on Peter's reforms became an open debate in the nineteenth century, and lasted for the duration of the Imperial Period. (See Reading 3)

CULTURE AND EXPANSION: CATHERINE THE GREAT

Following Peter's death in 1725, Russia entered a period of considerable political instability. Of the "autocrats" on the throne during the next thirty-seven years, one was a boy of eleven, one an infant, one mentally unbalanced, and two were empresses whose abilities were modest and whose interests were not primarily political. (See Reading 4) This weakness at the top permitted the gentry to flourish. They acquired large amounts of land and new privileges, and threw off unwanted obligations. In 1762, the resurgence of the gentry reached a high point when Tsar Peter III rescinded the requirement that gentry serve the state. Thereafter, state service by the gentry was rendered voluntarily and in the expectation of reward. Whereas Peter the Great had kept the gentry under his tight control, his successors increasingly used a different tactic, buying the gentry off, and rewarding their particular favorites handsomely.

In 1762, an unusually able and forceful woman gained the throne, Catherine II, also known as Catherine the Great. Holding power until her death thirty-four years later, she restored much of the stability that had been missing since Peter the Great's death.

FACT: Catherine's real name was Sophia. She was neither Romanov nor Russian. Born and raised in Germany, she married the future Tsar Peter III in 1745, and took a Russian name. In 1762, she instigated a coup d'etat against the current Tsar, her husband, during which he was murdered.

In many respects, Catherine was like Peter the Great. She possessed great intelligence, a strong will, boundless energy, and a natural sense of how to rule. A passionate and clever woman, she was able to turn her romances to the advantage of the state.

FACT: Catherine once wrote, "The trouble is, my heart is loath to remain even one hour without love." She had many lovers, of whom several were distinguished statesmen.

Like Peter, Catherine admired Western Europe. But whereas Peter had a practical nature and was chiefly interested in importing Western technology, Catherine's interests were more cultural and intellectual. Shipbuilding had fascinated Peter; ideas fascinated Catherine. The eighteenth century was the period of the Enlightenment in Europe, a period which stressed the expansion of knowledge and the application of reason to the solution of social problems. Catherine fancied herself an enlightened ruler, and set about to initiate enlightened programs. Her aim was, as she said, "to do good...to bring happiness, freedom, and well-being to my subjects." In this spirit, she initiated a reform of local government, encouraged the development of medicine, patronized the arts and sciences, and established a Legislative Commission to codify the country's laws. With her encouragement, the ideas of the European Enlighten-

A view of Moscow in the eighteenth century, with the Kremlin on the right and the Moscow River on the left.

A street scene in eighteenth century St. Petersburg, showing the Western-style architecture which contrasts markedly with the Russian-style of Moscow at the same time.

ment gradually made their way into Russia, influencing at least the upper reaches of society. The publication of books increased dramatically.

FACT: During Peter the Great's reign, 600 books were published in Russia. Between 1775 and 1800, a comparable period of time, 7500 were published.

These books were not written in the archaic and restrictive Church Slavonic language, but in a new, secular Russian language that emerged gradually during the eighteenth century. One of the pioneers of the new language was Michael Lomonosov, who wrote the first Russian grammar in 1755. Lomonosov, whom the poet Alexander Pushkin later dubbed "the first Russian university," was both a literary figure and a pioneer in various scientific fields. He conducted notable research in chemistry, was the first to observe the atmosphere of Venus, and performed experiments in electricity similar to those of Benjamin Franklin, with whom he corresponded.

The eighteenth century was the "golden age" of St. Petersburg, which, under Catherine and her predecessor, Empress Elizabeth, became a city of extraordinary beauty and culture, and very different in style from Moscow. That city is still dominated by architectural masterpieces of the period, notably the magnificent Winter Palace on the shore of the Neva River. The pastel colors and lavish decorations of these creations, all by Western architects, continue to this day to bear witness to the opulence and extravagance of Russian court society at the time.

Unfortunately, there was a lack of real substance under the outward display.

FACT: To impress Catherine and two visiting monarchs on a grand tour through southern Russia in 1787, her minister and favorite, Gregory Potemkin, is alleged to have created displays consisting of stage fronts, which appeared at a distance to be actual buildings and communities and which thus gave the impression of real economic progress in the area. These displays gave rise to the expression "Potemkin villages," denoting sham and deceit. Historians now dispute the validity of this story, but it suggests an important reality.

The fact is that Catherine's good intentions were not matched by her achievements in bringing "freedom, happiness, and well-being" to her people, most of whom were still peasants. Most Russian peasants were serfs, living in villages that had not changed since the sixteenth century. Unlike the American slave of the same period, the Russian serf and his family lived in their own house and had access to a small amount of land which they could work after the obligation to the landlord had been satisfied. Still, the serf's conditions were often little better than slavery, and royal edicts put them increasingly at the landlords' mercy. The landlords rarely acted in brutal fashion, but they interfered constantly in the daily lives of their serfs. As the ones who worked the land, the serfs felt that they should have title to it, and they resented having to support the landlord who stood in their way, controlled their future, and appeared to contribute little to the betterment of society as a whole. Like people close to the soil anywhere, the Russian peasant was conservative in outlook, wary of outsiders, and skeptical of new-fangled ideas and practices. Since most Russians were peasants until the early twentieth century, the influence of the rural background is still strong among today's Russians.

Generally, the Russian peasant accepted his lot in a fatalistic manner, evading obligations when possible and resorting to drink as an escape. *Volia,* the Russian word for will or wish, expressed the peasant dream of freedom. A Russian writer, Vissarion Belinsky, explained this dream in the 1830s.

> Our people understand freedom as *volia,* and *volia* for it [our people] means to make mischief. The liberated Russian nation would not head for the parliament but would run for the tavern to drink liquor, smash glasses, and hang the *dvoriane* (landlords) who shave their beards and wear a frock-coat....

Belinsky is here suggesting that there was an anarchic streak in Russians. For them, freedom was the opportunity to do whatever they wanted. They had no concept of freedom as responsible self-rule.

Periodically, the Russian peasants, in the spirit of *volia,* rose up in a massive revolt. Such a revolt occurred in 1773, during Catherine's reign. Led by the Cossack Emilian Pugachev, this great rebellion began in the Urals and spread very quickly, fanned by peasant unrest. Soon it encompassed much of Russia east of Moscow. Pugachev was betrayed by one of his followers, however, and his forces fell to the better-organized army of Catherine. Pugachev was taken to Moscow in a cage and executed.

Catherine was shaken by the Pugachev revolt. This threat to the established order convinced her that the gentry was correct in distrusting the "Dark People," and that what was needed most in Russia was not reform but crackdown. She dissolved the Legislative Commission, reasserted her autocratic power, and turned increasingly to the gentry for support in return for favors. In 1785, her Charter of the Nobility confirmed the gentry's freedom from state service and granted freedom from taxation. It also gave the gentry the exclusive right to buy and sell both land and the serfs living on such land. When the author Alexander Radishchev pointed out the evils of serfdom in his *Journey from St. Petersburg to Moscow* in 1790, he incurred the great displeasure of Catherine. She first sentenced him to death but later changed the sentence to a ten-year Siberian exile.

Catherine's policies contributed greatly to the crystallization of the Russian social system, in which the gentry evaded political responsibilities while re-

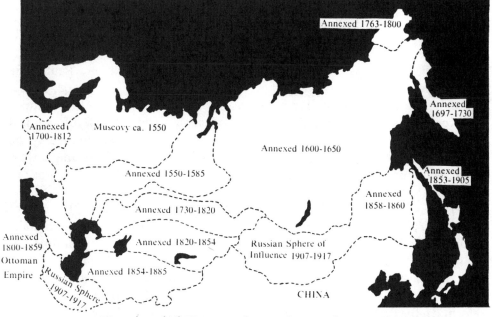

Annexed 1763-1800

Annexed
1697-1730

Annexed
1700-1812

Muscovy ca. 1550

Annexed 1600-1650

Annexed
1853-1905

Annexed 1550-1585

Annexed
1858-1860

Annexed 1730-1820

Annexed
1800-1859

Annexed 1820-1854

Russian Sphere of
Influence 1907-1917

Ottoman
Empire

*Russian Sphere
1907-1917*

Annexed 1854-1885

CHINA

Territorial Expansion of Russia, 1550-1917

taining and increasing their privileges. The masses of peasants continued to work the land hard, pay taxes, support the landlords, and lead a very meager existence.

In domestic affairs, Catherine's record is mixed, but in foreign affairs her successes were considerable. During her reign, Russia gained more new territory than in any reign since Ivan IV in the sixteenth century, and most of this territory contained people who were not ethnic Russians. Peter the Great had ended the threat to Russia from Sweden, and Catherine did the same in the case of two other long-term rivals, the Ottoman Empire and Poland. In two wars against the Ottoman Turks, Catherine forced them to cede much of the northern coast of the Black Sea, including the Crimean Peninsula. Russia also received the right to send merchant ships through the Turkish-held Straits, the Bosporus and Dardanelles. Russia now had ports that were ice-free and close to the major grain-producing regions of the country.

Catherine's second foreign policy success involved Poland. Between 1772 and 1795, a relatively weak Poland was partitioned three times by three stronger neighbors, Austria, Prussia, and Russia. From this, Russia gained an immense amount of territory in the south and west, including Belorussia and the Ukraine. Russian territory now extended into the heart of central Europe for the first time. In the long run, however, these gains produced a mixed blessing. The Poles never accepted the partitions and posed a constant threat of revolt. Also, the partitions brought Russia face to face with another expanding state, and future enemy, Prussia.

REFORM AND REACTION : ALEXANDER I AND NICHOLAS I

The nineteenth century was a year old when a new Tsar, Alexander I, came to the throne, as the result of a coup d'etat against his father, Paul. The early years of this century were ones of great promise for Russia politically, economically, militarily, and diplomatically. By the middle of the century, however, the situation had changed considerably. The promise of political reform gave way to the reality of reaction. Economic progress was limited by the continued existence of serfdom, and military and diplomatic triumph were replaced by embarrassing defeat. In 1801, however, the mood in Russia was optimistic. The new Tsar's accession was a cause for rejoicing.

Alexander I (1801-25) has been called "the enigmatic Tsar" because of his equivocal and unpredictable nature. Having been raised by an emotionally disturbed father (Paul) and an overpowering and possessive grandmother (Catherine the Great), he learned early to hide his real thoughts and to trust no one. But Catherine had selected French tutors for the young Alexander, and as he came to the throne, he seemed genuinely committed to the principle of reform. In the first decade of his reign, he relaxed travel restrictions and censorship, and granted amnesty to thousands who had been unjustly exiled by Paul. He created a Council of State to assist him with legislation, streamlined the ministries, and established a civil service exam to improve the quality of the bureaucracy.

Most important, Alexander dared to question the principle of autocracy, something no Tsar had done before.

FACT: Alexander was interested in the idea of constitutional government, and corresponded with Thomas Jefferson about the United States Constitution.

In 1809 Alexander asked a very able minister, Michael Speransky, to draw up a constitution for Russia. Speransky produced a noteworthy document that called for a separation of powers, local self-government, and a national legislative assembly, or *duma*. Had Speransky's plan been implemented, it could have made Russia one of Europe's more progressive states.

This did not occur, however. Progressive as he might have appeared at first, Alexander was, like Catherine, an autocrat at heart. Just as Pugachev's rebellion had influenced Catherine to cease her reform efforts, so events in Europe now convinced Alexander that major reforms were unwise. In France, another absolute monarch, the Bourbon King Louis XVI, had been forcibly overthrown in 1789, and the French revolutionaries were encouraging other peoples of Europe to revolt for "liberty, equality, and fraternity." This became a real threat to Russia when the ambitious French general Napoleon Bonaparte invaded Russia with 600,000 troops in 1812.

FACT: Napoleon's "Grande Armée" was initially successful, getting all the way to Moscow. He found the city abandoned and burned by the Russians. With winter approaching and his supply lines overextended, he was forced to retreat. Harrassed by Russian forces and plagued by hunger and frostbite, the French army fell apart. Only one-tenth of its number left Russia alive. It was an epic and popular victory for Russia, later to be justly celebrated in word (Tolstoy's novel *War and Peace)* and music (Tchaikovsky's "1812 Overture").

This triumph brought Alexander great prestige, but it also marked the end of his career as reformer. Fearful of future revolutions and Napoleons, he thereafter pursued a reactionary policy. Speransky was sent to Siberia, his constitution consigned to the scrap-heap, and Alexander turned for advice to a mystic, the Baroness von Krudener, and an unpleasant, hated minister, Count Arakcheev.

Realizing that they could not look to the Tsar for political reform, other Russians decided to take the initiative. Young army officers, who had come into contact with the radical ideas of the French Revolution after pursuing the French armies back to France in 1814, formed secret societies to press for political change. Similar radical groups were springing up in other European countries, which encouraged these Russian radicals. This early underground movement culminated in the Decembrist Revolt of 1825. When Alexander died on December 14, the Decembrist leaders organized a protest against the new Tsar, Nicholas, who was reputed to be an extreme reactionary. On the same day, some 3000 rebels gathered on the Senate Square in St. Petersburg.

FACT: The Decembrist Revolt was one of history's least eventful rebellions. The rebels killed the military governor of St. Petersburg when he attempted to negotiate with them but otherwise their only action was to stand in place for five hours, in full battle array and in sub-zero temperature, until at dusk they were dispersed by loyal troops and their leaders arrested.

Despite its uneventfulness, the Decembrist Revolt was a blatant challenge to Nicholas's authority. He arrested and dealt harshly with the ringleaders. Moreover, this event confirmed Nicholas's belief in order and discipline.

FACT: Since childhood, Nicholas had a fondness for soldiering and the military. He delighted in the details of army regulations and uniforms. A French visitor, the Marquis de Custine, said of Nicholas, "The Tsar of Russia is a military chief and each of his days is a day of battle." (See Reading 5)

As a result, his thirty-year reign (1825-55) was marked by a militaristic atmosphere and a preoccupation with the danger of subversion. He imposed strict censorship, created a highly efficient secret police (The Third Section), conducted endless investigations, and made certain that no political opposition could develop. In short, Nicholas, the "Iron Tsar," was a model despot. Whereas Peter the Great had used his autocratic power to change Russia, Nicholas used his to freeze Russia politically and socially for three decades.

Although the Decembrists had failed to provoke change, these martyrs of 1825 inspired others to oppose the regime. New groups drawn from the *intelligentsia,* began a revolutionary movement which eventually succeeded in overthrowing Tsardom in 1917. The Russian term *intelligentsia* has a very specific meaning in the context of nineteenth century Russian history. It signifies a small group of educated, thinking persons who were alienated from society and particularly from the Tsarist regime, and who saw it as their duty to oppose that regime. Since open political opposition was not possible, this group had to use other means. Starting in the 1830s, a few of these *intelligents* began writing philosophical treatises. In these, they agonized over what one of them termed "the accursed questions," by which they meant questions that had no easy or definite answers: questions of right and wrong, truth and justice, freedom and responsibility. At a time when English and French philosophers were becoming increasingly concerned with the material world, Russian thinkers followed the lead of German romantic philosophers into the world of metaphysics, prophecy, and other forms of abstraction. Like so many Russian thinkers before and after them, they were especially fascinated by the question of Russia's place in history. (See Reading 6)

Some of these early *intelligents* came to be called "Westerners," because they believed that Russia's best hope for the future was to follow the lead of Peter the Great and become more like the countries of Western Europe. They admired West European constitutions, their increasingly productive economies, and the emphasis they placed on the individual in society. Others, known as "Slavophiles," disagreed. They believed that Russia had its own greatness and uniqueness. They further suggested that Russia should develop its own culture and in so doing provide inspiration and leadership for the entire world in the future. Whereas the Westerners admired the technological progress and the rational attitude characteristic of the West at the time, the Slavophiles felt that the Occident, as they often called the West, was becoming increasingly soulless and incapable of the kind of spiritual life necessary to keep a society alive and vital. They believed that Russia had not only the material resources necessary for a position of world leadership, but an intangible inner strength, symbolized by the *muzhik* or peasant, whom the Slavophile writers adopted as their hero. Both groups opposed the Tsarist regime, however. The Tsar was insufficiently western for the Westerners and insufficiently Russian for the Slavophiles. Both groups also found the oppressiveness of the regime, and the lack of freedom to express themselves, intolerable. Throughout the 1840s and 50s, they confined their opposition to carefully guarded philosophical speculation. They wrote letters to one another, expounding their views, and joined in discussion groups. Both their numbers and their output remained small and they had no influence whatsoever among the vast majority of Russian people. Still, these *intelligents* are important as the initiators of a tradition of opposition that persisted until the Tsarist regime was overthrown in 1917.

There was limited progress in the Russian economy during the reigns of Alexander and Nicholas. By 1860 Russia had 3000 factories, double the number in 1800, but still far fewer than most West European countries. In 1837 the first Russian railroad began operation, between St. Petersburg and nearby Tsarskoye Selo, and in 1851 the Moscow-St. Petersburg line was opened.

FACT: This line, still in use today, is one of the straightest in the world. The legend is that Nicholas settled a dispute over the proper route by taking out a ruler and drawing a straight line on a map. The railroad was built under the supervision of an American engineer, George Washington Whistler.

Boatmen on the Volga River, a familiar scene throughout the Imperial Period. From a painting by Ilya Repin (1844-1930).

By 1860, Russian exports had increased in value from 75 to 230 million rubles, while imports had risen from 52 to 200 million. Despite these impressive gains, the Russian economy during the first half of the nineteenth century continued to be severely hampered by its inability to increase agricultural productivity.

FACT: In Medieval Europe, one seed sown yielded an average of three seeds at harvest time. The result of this low yield was a low standard of living. By 1850 in Western Europe, the average yield had increased dramatically, to a 1:10 ratio, permitting a larger, non-agricultural population to exist. In Russia, the yield remained at about 1:3 throughout most of the nineteenth century.

Many Russians believed that serfdom was largely responsible for this low productivity, and was also morally wrong. Even Nicholas I recognized this; in a meeting of the State Council in 1842, he said "There is no doubt that serfdom, as it exists at present in our land, is an evil, palpable and obvious to all." But this did not necessarily mean that serfdom should be abolished. Nicholas continued, "But to touch it now would be a still more disastrous evil... the Pugachev rebellion proved how far popular rage can go." Throughout his reign, Nicholas was worried about the effects of peasant *volia,* and with good reason: during his reign there were over 700 officially recorded disturbances caused by serfs. He also worried about another violent reaction, from the landlords, if he were to emancipate the serfs. Hence serfdom continued, agricultural output remained low, and the Russian economy lagged. (See Readings 7, 9, and 10)

Russian foreign policy during the first half of the nineteenth century followed the same pattern. Its early success and promise gave way to failure. After defeating Napoleon in 1812, Russia gained a prominent position in European affairs. Alexander participated actively in the international settlement that ended the Napoleonic Wars in 1815, and thereafter both he and Nicholas took seriously their role as "gendarme of Europe."† In this role, they were prepared to combat outbreaks of revolution wherever they might occur on the continent. For a time, this policy was successful, but by 1848 too many revolts were occurring throughout Europe for the gendarme to quell completely.

Russia continued to expand, too, during this time. In fact, Russians could be found in a variety of surprising places.

FACT: In 1812 Russian explorers, venturing south from their base in Alaska, still a Russian territory, founded Fort Ross in California. They established a base in Hawaii in 1820. The next year, a Russian expedition seeking a southern route to Eastern Siberia discovered Antarctica in the process, naming it "Alexander I Land."

The principal direction of Russian expansion was to the south and east, into the Caucasus, Central Asia, and remote Siberia. This expansion began to worry other, more powerful states. England, in particular, viewed Russian expansionism as a threat to her mercantile interests in the Near East, and later in the Middle East and Far East as well. With support from France, England sent an expeditionary force to the Crimean Peninsula in the Black Sea in 1854. Once again, Russia was back on the defensive, invaded by two strong industrialized powers intent on putting the Russian bear back in his lair. The Crimean War, which lasted for two years, was mismanaged on both sides, but the essential fact was that the Russian Empire, with a population of 67 million, could not defeat, on its own soil, an invading force of 70,000.

Russian Settlements in North America

FACT: During the Crimean War, it took longer for supplies to reach the Russian armies from Moscow than it took for supplies to reach the British and French armies from London and Paris.

After a lengthy siege, the English and French captured the major fortress of Sebastopol, and the Russians sued for peace. In less than two generations, the triumph over Napoleon had given way to embarrassing defeat. Once again, Russia had fallen behind other European countries, most obviously England and France, which by this time were well on their way to becoming modern industrial powers. Nicholas I died during the Crimean War, and it was clear that his successor faced a major challenge.

REFORM AND REACTION : ALEXANDER II AND III

The Crimean War demonstrated once again the close relationship between foreign and domestic policy in Russia. An expansionist foreign policy had led to war, and economic backwardness and inefficiency had caused defeat. This Crimean humiliation showed dramatically the need for reform. In the second half of the nineteenth century, Russia repeated the same pattern of reform and reaction that had characterized the reigns of Alexander I and Nicholas I. The need for a complete overhaul was great, but the Tsars' desire to preserve the autocracy and the established order was greater. Faced with the more complex challenges of an industrializing world, the Tsars of the later nineteenth century hesitated, and then abandoned the policy of reform. Russia thus remained relatively backward, and conflicts resulting from continued expansionism turned into defeats. So the cycle was repeated, and as it became more and more apparent that the regime could not or would not break the cycle, the opposition gathered momentum. By 1900 the situation was approaching the crisis stage.

Alexander II (1855-81) was trained for his role from birth, and inherited his father Nicholas's belief in autocracy and fondness for militarism. He was also a realist, however, and understood the need for drastic action to strengthen his country and restore its competitive position. He further understood that if he did not take the lead in making the necessary changes, these changes were likely to occur anyway. "It is better," he said to the Russian nobility in 1856, "to abolish serfdom from above rather than await the time when it will begin to abolish itself from below." Once again, the memory of Pugachev was clear.

Alexander II emancipated the serfs in 1861, despite opposition from most of the landlords, who saw their privileged position severely threatened.

FACT: By this peaceful legal process over 50 million serfs received their freedom. At about the same time, some 4 million black slaves were being freed in the United States, as the result of a violent civil war.

Unfortunately, the emancipation process was fatally flawed. The serfs were free as far as they themselves, their families, and their households were concerned. Only about one-third of the land to which they felt entitled was made available to them, however, and it was not free. To buy land, they had to borrow money from the state, to be repaid in installments over forty-nine years. The *mir,* the village community, was collectively responsible for these redemption payments, so individual peasants could not leave the *mir* until all payments had been made. The peasants became disillusioned, a disillusionment that grew as the population increased and their living conditions failed to improve during the remainder of the century.

Alexander was not prepared to establish any sort of legislative assembly on a national scale in Russia, but in 1864 he did institute assemblies, called *zemstvos,* at the local level. These gave propertied Russians a chance to elect representatives who controlled certain local affairs. While limited in scope and authority, these *zemstvos* accomplished much in the fields of education and health, founding schools and hospitals, and seemed to be a training ground for a future representative government at the national level.

Alexander's reforms, which earned him widespread praise and the unofficial title of "Tsar Liberator," did not save him from the increasingly radical opposition. In 1866, a young school dropout named Karakozov attempted to assassinate the Tsar.

FACT: Dmitri Karakozov's attempt to assassinate Alexander II in 1866 was the first such attempt on that Tsar's life, but it was far from the last: in the following fifteen years, there were no fewer than nine additional attempts, and in 1881 the final attempt was successful.

By this time, a new generation of *intelligents* had appeared. Not satisfied with the philosophizing of the earlier Westerners and Slavophiles, these "new men" or *raznochintsy* (literally "men of diverse rank") were seldom of aristocratic birth, and they tended to be far more impatient than their predecessors. They are often referred to as "men of the sixties," in contrast to the previous generation, the "men of the forties." Not able to rely on inherited income to finance their writing, they scraped by, living on the fringes of society. They raised immediate and practical issues, in a direct and blunt manner. They believed that art, literature, and philosophy were useful only if they served a worthy social purpose. There had been enough talk. What was needed now was action. They urged that the old customs and traditions be rejected, the slate wiped clean, and society placed in a position from which it could start afresh.

The attitude of this group is portrayed by the figure of Bazarov in Ivan Turgenev's great novel *Fathers and Sons* (1862). Bazarov, an arrogant, materialistic youth, holds the lifestyle and values of the older generation in contempt. He is a "nihilist," one who wishes to destroy the past (a term, based on the Latin word *nihil,* meaning "nothing" and first used by Turgenev in this work). Though Turgenev intended Bazarov as a caricature, many young radicals of the time took him as their hero. (See Reading 11)

FACT: Most of the "New Men" (and women) of the 1860s and 70s were very young. Nicholas Chernyshevsky was a dedicated revolutionary by age 27, but he was old in comparison with his associate Nicholas Dobrolyubov, who was only 22 when he began writing for the radical journal *The Contemporary.* When Dmitri Pisarev was arrested and jailed in 1862, he was also 22. Pyotr Zaichnevsky was but 19 when he wrote the incendiary pamphlet "Young Russia," Sergei Nechaev 21 when he authored his "Revolutionary Catechism," and Nicholas Rysakov was barely 18 when he was hanged for his part in the assassination of Alexander II.

Life was not easy for these young revolutionaries. Most were imprisoned, exiled, or otherwise harassed, and many died young, often in obscurity. Their determination was strong, however, and they persevered.

Karakozov's assassination attempt, as well as other outbreaks of violence and the increase of radical thought and writing, prompted Alexander gradually to de-emphasize his program of reform and introduce certain reactionary measures. The 1870s saw greater discipline introduced in schools and universities, new restrictions placed on the press, and the tightening of judicial processes. The new radicals, unsatisfied with Alexander's reforms, were undeterred by his reaction. It only made them more determined to pursue their goal. Most of the radicals had little idea yet of what should replace the hated autocracy, but that did not matter. The immediate task was to overthrow the Tsar, and to that task they devoted their entire will and energy. After a pause in the early 1870s, a new wave of revolutionary activity broke out in 1878, begun by the shooting of General Feodor Trepov, the military governor of St. Petersburg.

FACT: Trepov was shot by Vera Zasulich, a young revolutionary, who fired one shot, wounding him, while he was sitting at his desk. Despite clear and overwhelming evidence of her guilt, she was acquitted by a sympathetic jury at her trial — largely because Trepov was a very unpopular authority figure.

Vera Zasulich belonged to The People's Will, a revolutionary organization, which in 1879 mounted an all-out campaign of terror against the regime. Not only was it responsible for eight of the assassination attempts on Alexander, including the successful one, but similar and often successful attempts on the lives of prominent Tsarist officials. Because of the highly centralized nature of the Russian government, a few assassinations of key officials could wreak havoc. Very rarely in history has such a small group of terrorists caused such disruption. (See Reading 12)

FACT: The People's Will developed a variety of schemes to make it appear to have a large membership and substantial resources and support. The total membership during its five-year existence was only forty-four.

While this and other revolutionary groups benefited from the lack of sympathy for the Tsarist regime among many Russians, the chief reasons for its success were its highly disciplined organization, the thoroughness of its planning, the boldness of its actions and the complete dedication of its members. That so much could be accomplished by a small group with these attributes was carefully noted by one who was shortly to become a revolutionary, Vladimir Ilyich Lenin.

The assassination of Alexander by a bomb in 1881 was a great triumph

After a number of unsuccessful attempts, the revolutionary organization known as The People's Will succeeded in assassinating Tsar Alexander II in 1881. The five key conspirators were arrested and hanged. In this picture, they are receiving the last rites of the Church before their execution.

for The People's Will, but the crackdown that followed not only broke up that organization, but eliminated revolutionary activity and terror from Russia, with a very few exceptions, for twenty years.

FACT: The five who were directly responsible for the Tsar's brutal death were hanged before a crowd of 80,000 in the last public execution to be held in Russia.

The effect of the assassination was much the same as that of the Decembrist Revolt fifty-six years before. The next Tsar, Alexander III (1881-1894), pursued a policy of reaction much like that of Nicholas I.

FACT: Alexander III's nickname was "the bull." At six feet six, he was the largest Tsar since Peter the Great. Stubborn, awkward, and direct, he once responded to a dancing partner's thank-you by saying, "Why can't you be honest? It was just a duty neither of us could have relished. I have ruined your slippers and you have made me nearly sick with the scent you use."

Alexander's reign was generally peaceful, but it was a "peace of the graveyard." He instituted no new political reforms, and attempted to undo reforms of the past. Wary of domestic disorder and suspicious of anything foreign, he established a new security police, the *Okhrana*, to combat subversion. A law of 1881 gave these government officials the authority to declare a state of emergency when they believed public order to be threatened. Armed with this authority, these officials could arrest, imprison, and exile individuals upon suspicion. (See Reading 13) They could also confiscate property, suppress publications, and close schools. These measures foreshadowed the widespread use of the security police by the Soviet state of the twentieth century. There was a resurgence of pogroms against the Empire's Jewish population. Anti-semitism was not uncommon in Europe at this time, but was particularly strong in Russia. While Alexander himself was opposed to anti-Jewish pogroms, he did institute a campaign to spread the Orthodox religion and to Russify† the peoples of the Empire. In these policies, Alexander was encouraged by the most reactionary of all nineteenth century Russian statesmen, Constantine Pobedonostsev, Procurator of the Holy Synod. Pobedonostsev, a man of brilliant intellect, who was tutor to both Alexander and his successor, Nicholas II, once remarked that parliamentary institutions were "the great lie of our age." He is also alleged to have said that the solution to the Jewish Question was to have one-third convert to Orthodoxy, one-third emigrate, and one-third die.

Not all of Alexander's advisors were as reactionary, however. Sergei Witte, Minister of Finance, was a political conservative who opposed the idea of popular limitations on government. Unlike Pobedonostsev, however, he believed that Russia and the Tsarist regime could benefit from industrialization. He argued that this would enable Russia to compete more effectively with the industrialized states of Europe, and at the same time would create a prosperous middle class to provide greater economic and political support for the regime. To this end, Witte instituted many ambitious projects: the stabilization of finance based on the import of foreign capital, the construction of the Trans-Siberian Railroad to assist in opening up Siberia, and the development of mining and manufacturing. Indeed, under Witte, the pace of Russian industrialization picked up dramatically. (See Reading 14)

FACT: During the 1890s, Russian industry grew by an average of 8% per year. Russian railroads increased in length by 40% between 1881 and 1894, and doubled again between 1894 and 1905. This growth was greatly facilitated by foreign capital, which by 1900 totalled 900 million rubles.

Territorial expansion continued to be a key element of Russian policy during the second half of the nineteenth century, as it had been since the time of Peter the Great. This was the period of Great Power empires: while Britain and France and others scrambled to divide up Africa, and the United States looked greedily at the Caribbean and the Pacific, Russia continued its pressure on adjacent lands, particularly the Black Sea area and the Balkan Peninsula. This was justified by an aggressive Pan-Slav + ideology, as Russia claimed to be the protector of its fellow Slavs in southeastern Europe. When contained by a gathering of European powers in Berlin in 1878, Russia turned its attention to Central Asia and the Far East. Alexander III, and especially his successor Nicholas II, believed that success in these foreign endeavors could restore Russian pride, inspire patriotism, and help the Russian people to forget their domestic grievances. (See Reading 15) This was not to be, however. After Alexander's death in 1894, these adventures led to conflict with the English in Central Asia, and, more seriously, with the Japanese in the Far East. The latter conflict had grave consequences for Alexander's successor, Nicholas II.

RUSSIAN CULTURE TO 1917

Before turning to the reign of the last Tsar and the end of the Russian empire, a brief review of cultural developments in Russia during the nineteenth and early twentieth century is in order. This period witnessed a sustained outburst of creative energy in many fields. In contrast to the previous century, when much of the cultural activity in Russia imitated that of Western Europe, nineteenth century art, music and literature focused on native Russian themes. In all three fields, works of great distinction were produced, with Russian literature in particular gaining a worldwide reputation.

The so-called "Golden Age" of Russian literature began with the poet Alexander Pushkin (1799-1837). He and the other authors of the nineteenth century tended to dwell on the most basic and universal of subjects: the nature of man and the problems between the individual and society. The tragic hero of Pushkin's long poem *Eugene Onegin* has difficulty finding a useful place for himself; he feels superfluous. Given a society in which political involvement on the part of individuals was not possible, it is not surprising that this theme of "the superfluous man" reappears in literature throughout the century. Another common theme is that of conflict between generations, portrayed dramatically in Turgenev's *Fathers and Sons*. Few nineteenth century authors offered solutions for these issues, though Leo Tolstoy (1828-1910) openly condemned the growing materialism he witnessed, and advocated a return to the good, simple life close to the soil. Other important writers of the "Golden Age" were Mikhail Lermontov, Nikolai Gogol, and Fyodor Dostoevsky.

At the same time, artists and composers were extolling Russian themes in art and music. Painters like Ilya Repin brought to life individuals and groups from every level and every corner of Russian society. A small group of composers during the latter half of the century created a national school of music, using folk songs and legends to dramatize the Russian past. From this school came many notable works, such as Mussorgsky's opera *Boris Godunov* and Borodin's *Prince Igor*.

The twentieth century ushered in a new era in Russian culture, with an emphasis on experimentation and bold new forms. In literature, the period 1900-1917 was called the "Silver Age." In contrast to the more realistic approach of the earlier period, the authors of the "Silver Age" emphasized impressions and symbols to convey their messages. The leading prose writers of the early twentieth century were Anton Chekhov, Andrei Bely, and Maxim Gorky, while Alexander Blok was the most prominent poet. Experimentation also characterized the arts of this period. Painters like Kandinsky, Chagall, and Malevich shocked viewers with their revolutionary canvasses.

FACT: The world's first totally abstract painting was Russian: Malevich's "Black Square" of 1902.

Composers such as Scriabin and Stravinsky produced similar shock waves in the music world, as did Stanislavsky in drama and Diaghilev in ballet.

FACT: These *avant-garde*† Russian authors and artists not only produced startling and puzzling works, but also defied convention in the way they lived and dressed. The poet Mayakovsky carried a wooden spoon in his lapel, while his friend and associate David Burliuk had "I am Burliuk" painted on his forehead.

In their fascination with radical forms, these artists helped create a climate for political and social revolution. When such a revolution came, in 1917, many of them supported it wholeheartedly. Ironically, this same revolution soon thereafter put an end to artistic experimentation in Russia.

THE DECLINE AND FALL OF IMPERIAL RUSSIA: NICHOLAS II

When Nicholas II succeeded his father, Alexander III, in 1894, he faced a variety of serious new challenges. The world, including Russia, was fast becoming urbanized and industrialized. Russian agriculture was stagnant. Diplomatic tensions were increasing in Europe. After a lull in the 1880s, opposition groups were once again clamoring for change. The situation required a ruler able and willing to take decisive action, a new Peter the Great. Unfortunately, Nicholas was no Peter. A worthy individual and devout family man, he was a weak and ineffectual emperor. He was conscientious and highly patriotic, but lacked both vision and flexibility.

FACT: Shy and insecure as a youth, Nicholas was tempted to renounce the throne. He always felt ill-prepared to accept the responsibilities, and once remarked to a foreign ambassador that he would much rather have been a sailor.

Nicholas relied heavily on reactionary advisors throughout his reign, and came increasingly under the influence of his narrow-minded and stubborn wife, Alexandra, to whom he was devoted. Worst of all, Nicholas and Alexandra allowed an ignorant and corrupt peasant named Rasputin into their court, and he gradually became a power behind the throne, to the great detriment of them, their dynasty, and their country.

FACT: Nicholas and Alexandra had a son, Alexis, who was heir to the throne and who suffered from acute hemophilia, or internal bleeding. Rasputin, posing as a holy man and healer, convinced Alexandra that he could stop the bleeding attacks and ease the boy's suffering. She came to trust him completely, first in private matters and eventually in everything, including government policy.

The first few years of Nicholas' reign were quiet and peaceful, but the challenges facing Russia soon changed that. Domestic trouble stemmed from three sources, one of which was the peasantry. Contrary to hopes and expectations, the condition of the Russian peasant grew worse after the emancipation of 1861. Tied to the *mir,* without incentive to improve farming techniques, saddled with redemption payments and taxes, and short of land due to steady population growth, the peasants led a marginal existence and became increasingly bitter. When periodic droughts occurred, as in 1891-92, they brought terrible famine.

FACT: The population of Russia increased from 73 million in 1861 to over 125 million by 1900. Of these, 75% were peasants. Calculations show that 28% of the peasantry could not support themselves from the land in 1861, and that by 1900 this figure had risen to 52%.

A second trouble area was that of the industrial workers, who by 1900 numbered approximately two million. They were concentrated in large, recently constructed factories in St. Petersburg, Moscow, and the Don River basin, and so easily formed sizeable and closely-knit groups. Workers led an existence even more miserable than that of the peasants. Poorly paid, housed in crowded and filthy slums, their death rate was the highest among industrial workers of all countries. Although they were prohibited from organizing in unions, they went on strike with increasing frequency. (See Reading 16)

FACT: Serious strikes began in the 1890s, and increased dramatically in the early years of the twentieth century. In 1910 there were 226 strikes, involving 46,000 workers. Three years later the totals had escalated to 2,400 strikes staged by 887,000 workers.

A final source of trouble lay in the middle class, which began to emerge in Russia only in the latter part of the nineteenth century. Capitalist businessmen remained largely uninvolved in political concerns, but this was not true of the professional groups. Lawyers, teachers, journalists and doctors began to take greater and greater interest in politics. Very often their liberal inclinations led them to join the opposition, which began to organize during the 1890s. The more moderate founded the Union of Liberation in 1902, and a political party, the Constitutional Democrats or "Cadets," in 1905. The more radical opted for parties that called for revolution. One of these was the Socialist Revolutionary (SR) Party of 1901, which believed that the peasants could be the agents of revolution, and which advocated terrorism. The SRs became the largest and most popular radical party in Russia prior to 1917.

Other radicals turned to Marxism. Karl Marx, a nineteenth century German philosopher, had explained the causes of social inequity and suffering in *The Communist Manifesto* (1848). He suggested that a proper understanding and application of the laws of history would result in a world where hunger and poverty would be unknown, and all men would be equal. In Marx's view, once capitalism had led to the industrialization of society, the working class (proletariat) would rise up against the capitalist factory owners who were exploiting them. In a violent, revolutionary class war, the proletariat would overthrow the capitalists and establish first a dictatorship of the proletariat and later a true communist, or classless, society. History thus proceeded in stages: capitalist industrialization had to be fully developed before a working class revolution could take place.

Marx's description of the evils of capitalism was vivid, and seemed validated by the experience of Russian workers. His accuracy and appeal in this one area suggested that he might well be correct, too, in saying that capitalism was doomed and that revolutionary change for the better was inevitable. No other creed of the time offered such assurance. It is not surprising that many who favored revolution found Marxism attractive.

One of those who embraced Marxism was Vladimir Ilyich Ulyanov, better known by his revolutionary name Lenin. Product of a respectable gentry family, Lenin first studied law, but later turned to radical politics, and ultimately to Marxism, in the late 1880s. He soon adopted Marxism completely, involving himself in Marxist discussion groups and the movement to found a Marxist political party in Russia. In 1895, these activities got him arrested, and, for the first and last time in his life, he was a political prisoner, confined to a small cell in a St. Petersburg jail for fourteen months. While this was his only incarceration, he did spend much time in exile, first in Siberia (1897-1900), then in Western Europe.

FACT: Lenin became the dominant figure in Russian revolutionary activity prior to 1917 despite the fact that, between 1894, when he began his revolutionary career, and 1917, he was in Russia for a total of less than two years.

For Lenin, however, jail and exile simply meant time to refine and promulgate his revolutionary ideology. When he emerged from Siberian exile in 1900, he already had a clear notion of what needed to be done, and he spent the next four years trying to convert fellow Russian Marxists to his way of thinking.

Lenin's views, as they emerged in his writings after 1900, reflected both his strong commitment to Marxism and his impatience for revolution in Russia. He noted, correctly, that in the half-century since Marx had written the *Communist Manifesto,* there had been no revolution of the sort Marx had predicted. He also noted that members of the working class throughout Europe had become generally satisfied with trade unions as a means of improving their lot. His impatience led him to produce a modification of orthodox Marxist theory by introducing the concept of a revolutionary party. Lenin argued that a tightly-organized party of professional revolutionaries, drawn from the *intelligentsia,* was necessary to lead the workers toward the revolution. Without such leadership, the workers would act "spontaneously," and seek only the material improvements that could be obtained through trade union activity. The party's task was to develop the "consciousness" of the workers, so that they would rise above their search for material benefits, understand the need for revolution, and work actively to bring it about. (See Reading 17)

Lenin brought his ideas to the attention of the Marxist Social Democratic (SD) Party at the Second Party Congress, held first in Brussels and then London in 1903. His model of the revolutionary party became the basis of his Bolshevik faction, and this model remains the basis of the Communist Party today.

FACT: At the Second Congress of the Russian Social Democratic Party in 1903, the intransigent Lenin caused a split in the Party. Lenin christened his faction "Bolsheviks" (majority-men) and his opponents "Mensheviks" (minority-men), despite the fact that he held a majority only briefly, and by a very slim margin. The name stuck, even though in the years to come his Bolsheviks were a small minority within the S.D. Party ranks. The preemption of the term Bolshevik was typical of Lenin's political skill.

From the beginning of his reign, Tsar Nicholas had preferred to live in the calm world of his court. He had little awareness of what was going on outside that world, and so didn't realize that his empire was in deep trouble as the twentieth century began. Strikes, peasant disturbances, and student demonstrations were becoming more frequent. The SRs and SDs called ever more loudly for revolution, and the SRs began an assassination campaign that included over three hundred attempts and eliminated a number of high-level officials between 1902 and 1905. On top of all this, Russia's adventuristic foreign policy in eastern Siberia led to war with Japan in 1904.

In this conflict, fought on land in Manchuria and on far eastern waters, the Russian empire was beaten by a country a fraction of its size. Two Russian

"Demonstration." A drawing by Boris Kustodiev depicting a typical city scene during the revolutionary year 1905, when the working class first demonstrated in mass protests against the Tsarist regime.

fleets were destroyed, and their armies fared little better. The consequent embarrassment was greater than in the Crimean War, since now Russia's defeat was at the hands of a non-European state, Japan, which had until recently been undeveloped, and which was considered by many Russians to be inferior.

FACT: Nicholas, who had nearly been murdered while on a state visit to Japan in 1892, when he was still Crown Prince, referred to the Japanese as "little short-tailed monkeys" and did little to hide his belief that they were an inferior race.

In 1905 trouble spread from the battlefields of the Far East to the streets of Moscow and St. Petersburg. On January 22, 1905, the people of St. Petersburg made their first major protest against the miserable conditions in which they lived and worked, and against the lack of political freedom. Led by Father George Gapon, an Orthodox priest, thousands of St. Petersburg workers and their families marched peacefully to the Winter Palace to present petitions to Nicholas. Unjustifiably alarmed, the palace guard fired on the crowd to disperse them, and by the end of "Bloody Sunday" over a hundred were dead and some 3,000 wounded. This event had two significant results: there were new martyrs for the revolutionary cause, and the common peoples' long-cherished faith in the Tsar as a benevolent father-figure was largely destroyed. For years, ordinary Russians had viewed the Tsar as their protector against evil landlords and bureaucrats, but increasingly they now realized that the Tsar himself was largely to blame for their troubles.

Throughout 1905, demonstrations occurred across Russia. Peasants rose and burned their landlords' houses, young radicals assassinated a number of public figures, the sailors of the battleship "Potemkin" mutinied on the Black Sea (See Reading 18) and workers went out in a series of strikes which culminated in a general strike in October. At the last moment, Nicholas issued the October Manifesto, promising a constitution, an elected state *duma* (parliament), and civil liberties for all. Although the Tsar later reneged on many of the promises made in the Manifesto, he temporarily satisfied the moderate politicians. The main reason that the Tsar survived the events of 1905, however, was that those who sought to overthrow him had no effective leader, and as a result the multiple outbreaks by workers, peasants, the national minorities, and the military were not in synchronization. Twelve years later, this would not be the case.

From 1905 to 1917, Russia appeared at first glance to be a legitimate constitutional monarchy. (See Reading 19) Certainly the autocracy had been modified. The *duma* turned out to be little more than window-dressing, however. It was ineffective as an arena for radical political opposition to voice itself, particularly after the electoral laws were modified in 1907 to increase the voting power of the conservative elements in society. More important, the executive branch was not responsible to it. This period also saw a continuation of the police repression that had existed under Alexander III. The head policeman this time was the extremely able Prime Minister Stolypin, whose policy of "pacification" included summary courts-martial, severe sentences, and countless regulations limiting the civil rights granted in 1905.

FACT: The term "Stolypin's necktie" was created; this was the noose used in the many executions of political radicals.

This repression made life very difficult for the revolutionary parties which, after seeing their hopes first raised and then all but destroyed in 1905, were forced back into exile. There, while the Marxists awaited the expected international revolution, they contemplated the future of their own country with considerable gloom.

FACT: This gloom lasted until 1917. In January of that year Lenin said, "I do not believe that we of the older generation will live to see the revolution..."

The pessimism of the revolutionaries stemmed from the fact that, in many respects, the years 1905-14 were good for Russia and its ruler. Stolypin was a perceptive statesman. As Witte had focused on the need to develop Russian industry in the previous decade, Stolypin now attempted to solve the serious problems that continued to haunt agriculture and the rural population. He abolished redemption payments, dissolved the *mirs,* consolidated landholdings, and encouraged the emergence of a new class of strong, independent peasant landowners. He reasoned that a prosperous peasantry would have a stake in the *status quo,* and not lean toward rebellion, as the impoverished peasantry had done in 1905. In one sense, this process was quite successful. Despite great peasant resistance, by 1917 almost half the peasant households in European Russia were independent and on the road to prosperity. On the other hand, this process forced many peasants off the land and into the cities, to be exploited by factory owners.

In other areas, too, there was progress. The *zemstvos* played an increasingly important role in local affairs. Industrialization was given greater priority. A national system of education was established, and literacy became a national goal.

There is continued debate among historians about these last years of Imperial Russia. Some argue that Russia's progress between 1905 and 1914 was real and substantial, and that the Tsarist regime might well have survived and flourished had it not been for the crisis presented by World War I. Others argue that the regime had a terminal disease and that World War I simply hastened an end that was inevitable. This debate probably will never be settled. Suffice it to say that while things were looking quite good for Russia as late as 1913, the

Nicholas II blesses the troops. Russian soldiers kneel in homage to the Tsar, at the outbreak of World War I. Nicholas sanctifies the occasion by carrying a holy icon; bearing an icon into battle was a Russian tradition dating back many centuries.

outbreak of war in the following year was far more of a trauma than the regime could bear. Russia was not equipped politically, economically, or militarily to fight a lengthy conflict against Germany, the continent's most heavily industrialized and best-armed power. It was ironic that Russia's aggressive Pan-Slav foreign policy in the Balkan peninsula after 1908 helped to precipitate the outbreak of war in August, 1914. In this war, which turned out to last much longer than anyone expected, the Russians were the first to mobilize and the first to cross into enemy territory on a large scale.

Russia's initial enthusiasm and success didn't last long. By 1915, the tide had turned, and on the German front the Tsarist armies began a retreat which never ended. The Romanov dynasty had survived military humiliation in the Crimea in 1855, and again — just barely — in the recent Japanese war. This time it could not. Military defeat was accompanied by growing restiveness among the civilian population, for whom the war crystallized and brought to a head all their long-standing grievances. Symbolic of the disastrous state of affairs in Tsardom was the continued presence at court of Rasputin. Hoping that his removal might improve the situation and permit the survival of the *status quo,* a group of Russian aristocrats murdered Rasputin in December, 1916. (See Reading 20) By then, it was much too late. The end of the Russian Empire occurred, in violent fashion, three months thereafter.

Since the reign of Peter the Great, Russia had tried to cope with a modernizing world. Peter had started a process of domestic transformation in order to catch up with the West, but both he and his successors shied away from some of the most necessary changes. When reform did occur, it was fitful, halfhearted, and insufficient. Russia never became capable of competing with the more advanced nations, particularly in the wars that were the inevitable result of its own expansionistic policy. To the very end, Imperial Russia remained a backward autocracy, unsuited to a world of industrialism and political freedom, and unsuited, too, for the leading role it wanted to play in world affairs.

The following books were helpful in writing this chapter:

Crankshaw, E., *The Shadow of the Winter Palace,* New York: The Viking Press, 1976.

Kohn, H., editor, *The Mind of Modern Russia,* New York: Harper and Row, 1962.

Pipes, R., *Russia Under the Old Regime,* New York: Scribner's, 1974.

Riasanovsky, N., *A History of Russia,* 3rd ed., New York: Oxford University Press, 1977.

Szamuely, T., *The Russian Tradition,* New York: McGraw Hill, 1974.

Ulam, A., *The Bolsheviks,* New York: Collier Books, 1965.

For students who are interested, we recommend further reading in the sources from which we have taken excerpts, as well as the following works:

Bergamini, J.D., *The Tragic Dynasty,* New York: G.P. Putnam's Sons, 1969.
One of several recent accounts of the Romanovs, with many fascinating anecdotes.

Maclean, F., *Holy Russia,* London: Century Publishing Co., 1982.
Readable narrative history of Russia by well-known British traveler-writer.

Massie, R.K., *Nicholas and Alexandra,* New York: Alfred A. Knopf, 1978.
Well-researched and colorful account of the reign of the last Tsar.

Massie, R.K., *Peter the Great,* New York: Alfred A. Knopf, 1980.
A similar treatment of Russia's first emperor.

Massie, S., *The Land of the Firebird*
See Chapter Two bibliography.

Salisbury, H., *Black Night, White Snow,* Garden City: Doubleday & Co., 1978.
A narrative history of the 1905-17 period in Russia by a *New York Times* journalist with much knowledge of Russia. Anecdotal and fast-paced.

Ulam, A., *In the Name of the People,* New York: Viking Press, 1977.
A fascinating history of the radical revolutionaries of mid-nineteenth century Russia.

Readings

Chapter Three

List of Readings

1. The Building of St. Petersburg

This reading describes the building of St. Petersburg. It illustrates the degree to which the city took shape as a result of Peter's strong will, with little attention paid to the price in human suffering.

...Activity was increased to fever pitch. Encampments, larger than the city itself, swelled to absorb the incoming labour. The work went on winter and summer, day and night, in the face of every obstacle. The privations and setbacks which the workers endured were appalling. Disastrous floods constantly overwhelmed the low-lying islands, and in 1705 the whole city was several feet deep in water. As late as 1721 the Neva was still not controlled; in that year all the streets of St. Petersburg were navigable and Peter was nearly drowned in the Nevsky Prospekt.† Fire, too—an almost weekly occurrence—played its sinister part. In 1710 all the chief emporiums of the city—the original *Gostinny Dvor* or Bazaar— with hundreds of wood and canvas shops were destroyed in one night. Wolves roamed the streets after dark: even in 1715 a woman was devoured in broad daylight not far from Menshikov's house. There was as yet little at St. Petersburg to attract the people of Moscow. One of Peter's jesters gloomily described the position of the new city in these words: 'On one side the sea, on the other sorrow, on the third moss, on the fourth a sigh.'

But in 1710 all the members of the Imperial family moved to the new city, together with all government institutions still remaining in Moscow. The same year a *ukase* [proclamation] was issued demanding forty thousand workmen a year, together with their essential tools, to be sent from the provinces. A little later Peter also ordered two thousand thieves and robbers, and all who had been deported or banished, to be sent to the Neva. Then he forbade the erection, owing to the shortage of masons, of any stone buildings in any part of the empire outside St. Petersburg, under penalty of banishment to Siberia and of confiscation of property, while every boat or cart entering the city had to bring a certain quantity of unhewn stones, as stone was sadly lacking in these marshy wastes. It was also forbidden to cut wood on the islands, and, to economize fuel, no one was allowed to heat his bath-house more than once a week. The city was populated by force. All officials, nobles and landowners possessing not less than thirty families of peasant serfs were obliged to settle in St. Petersburg and build houses for themselves, of stone, brick, *pise*† or wood according to their means: those who owned five hundred peasants had to raise a stone house of two stories,

Abridged from Christopher Marsden, *Palmyra of the North: The First Days of St. Petersburg,* London, 1942.

while the poorer ones often found themselves obliged to club together to build one. Such *ukases* continued to be issued. In 1712 came this decree:

I. One thousand of the best families of the nobility, etc., are required to build houses of beams, with lath and plaster, in the old English style, along the bank of the Neva from the Imperial palace to the point opposite Nyenskantz.

II. Five hundred of the best known merchant families and five hundred traders less distinguished, must build for themselves wooden houses on the other side of the river, opposite to the dwellings of the nobility, until the government can provide them with stone houses and shops.

III. Two thousand artisans of every kind—painters, tailors, joiners, blacksmiths, etc.—must settle themselves on the same side of the river, right up to Nyenskantz.

The haste with which these dwellings must have been put up is reflected later on in the dilapidated state of the city under Peter's successors; they often did not even stand up to the first winters after the erection and rich banquets in the new houses were spoiled by cracking walls, gaping floors and leaky roofs. They were built with groans and curses both from the wretched labourers and the unwilling occupants, who still saw only evil in every idea and action of the heretical tsar. Nevertheless, in 1712 Peter announced that Sankt Piterburkh [St. Petersburg] was to be the Imperial capital....

But already building had been progressing elsewhere than on the two original islands—on the adjacent Isle of Buffaloes, afterwards called Vasilievsky Ostrov, also on the northern bank of the Neva; and on the left bank of the river, opposite Vasilievsky Ostrov, where the Admiralty had been built. There was of course no bridge, not even a pontoon, linking the islands. The twenty boats, manned by ignorant peasants, which were used as ferries were a severe menace to the population. Many people, including such important personages as the Polish Minister, a Major General and one of the tsar's First Physicians, lost their lives in the hazardous transit. On Vasilievsky Ostrov, Peter later wished to have a town on the model of Amsterdam, planted with rows of trees and intersected by navigable canals, and to make this the official centre of his maritime city. Work was begun on the canals, but circumstances eventually made it clear that it would have to be upon the left bank of the river that the life of the city must revolve. As there were no bridges, and as the Neva, at the time of the first ice and again when it breaks, is almost untraversable, the northern islands were virtually cut off from the rest of Russia. Many important buildings, to be sure, were to appear on Vasilievsky Ostrov in Peter's reign and afterwards, as we shall see; but the subsequent history of the city is that of a withdrawal to the mainland—and in the first place to the environs of the Admiralty.

Ten years, then, after the foundation of the city, and with some five hundred houses built, the active influences at work on its architecture are all Germanic: Trezzini and his pupils, Italian and Russian, working in the German-Dutch style of Baltic baroque, and the followers of Schluter—Mattarnovy (who inherited Schluter's plans and models), Schadel, Schwertfeger, Forster and Braunstein—in the equally Dutch-influenced North German manner.

2. Resistance to Peter: Ruthless Razoring

Peter the Great's reforms affected dress and appearance, as well as the organization of his government. Many Russians were particularly disturbed by the order that they must go clean shaven, as they felt to cut their beards was an offense against God. John Perry, the English author of this account, served as an engineer in Peter's service from 1698 to 1712.

...It had been the manner of the Russes, like the Patriarchs of old, to wear long beards hanging down upon their bosoms, which they comb'd out with pride, and kept smooth and fine, without one hair to be diminish'd....The Czar, therefore, to reform this foolish custom, and to make them look like other Europeans, ordered a tax to be laid, on all gentlemen, merchants, and others of his subjects (excepting the priests and common peasants, or slaves) that they should each of them pay a hundred rubles per annum, for the wearing of their beards, and that even the common people should pay a copeck [100 copecks make up one ruble] at the entrance of the gates of any of the towns or cities of Russia....This was look'd upon to be little less than a sin in the Czar, a breach of their religion, and held to be a great grievance for sometime, as more particularly by being brought in by the strangers. But the women liking their husbands and sweethearts the better, they are now for the most part, pretty well reconciled to the practice.

It is most certain, that the Russes had a kind of religious respect and veneration for their beards; and so much the more, because they differed herein from strangers, which was back'd by the humours of the priests....and which nothing but the absolute authority of the Czar, and the terror of having them (in his merry humour) pull'd out by the roots, or sometimes taken so rough off, that some of the skin went with them, could ever have prevailed with the Russes to have parted with their beards. On this occasion there were letters drop'd about the streets, sealed and directed to His Czarish Majesty, which charged him with tyranny and heathenism....

About this time the Czar came down to Veronize, where I was then on service, and a great many of my men that had worn their beards all their lives, were now obliged to part with them, amongst which, one of the first that I met with just coming from the hands of the barber, was an old Russ carpenter that had been with me at Camishinka, who was a very good workman with his hatchet, and whom I always had a friendship for. I jested a little with him on this occasion, telling him that he was become a young man, and asked him what he had done with his beard? Upon which he put his hand in his bosom and pull'd it out, and shew'd it to me: farther telling me, that when he came home, he would lay it up to have it put in his coffin and buried along with him, that he might be able to give an account of it to St. Nicholas, when he came to the other world; and that all his brothers (meaning his fellow-workmen, who had been shaved that day) had taken the same care....

Abridged from Peter Putnam, editor, *Seven Britons in Imperial Russia, 1698-1812,* Princeton, 1952.

3.   Alexander Pushkin: The Bronze Horseman

Alexander Pushkin (1799-1837) is considered one of the greatest Russian poets. Of him, a critic of the 1860s wrote, "In his verse, the living Russian language was made known to us for the first time," and after the Revolution, Lunacharsky, the Soviet Commissar for Public Enlightenment in the 1920s, wrote, "Pushkin was the Russian Adam." Pushkin was the grandson of an African, an Abyssinian who was adopted and educated by Peter the Great. He met a tragic young death in a duel. This poem, The Bronze Horseman, *is based on a real flood in St. Petersburg and expresses well the ambivalence Pushkin and other patriotic Russians felt towards the titanic figure of Peter the Great. The bronze horseman of its title, is the huge statue of Peter that today still looks out over the River Neva. It was raised by an admiring Catherine the Great.*

PROLOGUE

Upon a shore of desolate waves
Stood *he*, with lofty musings grave,
And gazed afar. Before him spreading
Rolled the broad river, empty save
For one lone skiff stream-downward heading.
Strewn on the marshy, moss-grown bank,
Rare huts, the Finn's poor shelter, shrank,
Black smudges from the fog protruding;
Beyond, dark forest ramparts drank
The shrouded sun's rays and stood brooding
And murmuring all about.

                               He thought:
"Here, Swede, beware—soon by our labor
Here a new city shall be wrought,
Defiance to the haughty neighbor.
Here we at Nature's own behest
Shall break a window to the West.
Stand planted on the ocean level;
Here flags of foreign nations all
By waters new to them will call,
And unencumbered we shall revel."

A century passed, and there shone forth
From swamps and gloomy forest prison,
Crown gem and marvel of the North,
The proud young city newly risen.
Where Finnish fisherman before,

Abridged from Walter Arndt, editor and translator, *Alexander Pushkin: Collected Narrative and Lyrical Poetry,* Ann Arbor, 1984.

Harsh Nature's wretched waif, was plying,
Forlorn upon that shallow shore,
His trade, with brittle net-gear trying
Uncharted tides—now bustling banks
Stand serried in well-ordered ranks
Of palaces and towers; converging
From the four corners of the earth,
Sails press to seek the opulent berth,
To anchorage in squadrons merging;
Neva is cased in granite clean,
Atop its waters bridges hover,
Between its channels, gardens cover
The river isles with darkling green.
Outshone, old Moscow had to render
The younger sister pride of place,
As by a new queen's fresh-blown splendor
In purple fades Her Dowager Grace.

I love you, work of Peter's warrant,
I love your stern and comely face,
The broad Neva's majestic current,
Her bankments' granite carapace,
The patterns laced by iron railing,
And of your meditative night
The lucent dusk, the moonless paling;
When in my room I read and write
Lampless, and street on street stand dreaming,
Vast luminous gulfs, and, slimly gleaming,
The Admiralty's needle bright;
And rather than let darkness smother
The lustrous heavens' golden light,
One twilight glow speeds on the other
To grant but half an hour to night.

I love your winter's fierce embraces
That leave the air all chilled and hushed,
The sleighs by broad Neva, girls' faces
More brightly than the roses flushed,
The ballroom's sparkle, noise, and chatter.

● ●

Thrive, Peter's city, flaunt your beauty,
Stand like unshaken Russian fast,
Till floods and storms from chafing duty
May turn to peace with you at last;
The very tides of Finland's deep
Their long-pent rancor then may bury,
And cease with feckless spite to harry
Tsar Peter's everlasting sleep.

● ●

[The poet then recounts the sad story of Eugene, whose wife-to-be perished in a flood. Tormented by the discovery of her death, Eugene dreams that he is pursued by the Bronze Horseman. This Peter has no sympathy for the hardships his city has caused the common people like Eugene.]

Eugene's heart shrank. His mind unclouding
In dread, he knew the place again
Where the great flood had sported then,
Where those rapacious waves were crowding
And round about him raged and spun—
That square, the lions, and him—the one
Who, bronzen countenance upslanted
Into the dusk aloft, sat still,
The one by whose portentous will
The city by the sea was planted...
How awesome in the gloom he rides!
What thought upon his brow resides!

His charger with what fiery mettle,
His form with what dark strength endowed!
Where will you gallop, charger proud,
Where next your plunging hoofbeats settle?
Oh, Destiny's great potentate!
Was it not thus, a towering idol
Hard by the chasm, with iron bridle
You reared up Russia to her fate?

• •

The dread Tsar's face,
With instantaneous fury burning,
It seemed to him, was slowly turning...
Across these empty spaces bound,
Behind his back he heard resound,
Like thunderclouds in rumbling anger,
The deep reverberating clangor
Of pounding hoofs that shook the ground.
And in the moonlight's pallid glamor
Rides high upon his charging brute,
One hand stretched out, 'mid echoing clamor
The Bronzen Horseman in pursuit.
And all through that long night, no matter
What road the frantic wretch might take,
There still would pound with ponderous clatter
The Bronzen Horseman in his wake.

4.   Anna's Ice Palace

The Empress Anna (1730-40) amused herself with lavish, costly enter-tainments: fireworks, the creation of ice mountains for sliding on the frozen river Neva, and one of her masterpieces, the ice palace here described.

...The winter of 1739-40 was unusually cold, and the scientists of the Academy embarked on a programme of experiments to test the properties of ice that was available in such abundance. Knowing this, a court Chamberlain called Alexander Tatishchev thought of combining it with a new entertainment for the court — building a palace of ice on which artists and artisans as well as scientists could exercise their skills. In the end it turned out to be a setting for another of the Empress's macabre jokes....

The Prince [Golitsyn]...was in his forties now and long since a widower. But the Empress insisted that he should take another wife. Indeed she chose one for him — Avdotaya Ivanovna, nicknamed 'Bujenina' after Anna's favourite dish — roast pork done in a sauce of onions, vinegar and spices. Avdotaya was of Kalmyk origin, extremely ugly and wanted desperately to find a husband. The Empress not only answered her prayers but agreed to pay for the wedding, deciding that it should be made the greatest comic spectacle ever seen in Russia.

A rocket whistled into the air and exploded with a loud report above the city. Within seconds a whole sheaf of rockets was set loose; fountains of coloured fire began to flame, catherine wheels to circle madly. All St. Petersburg was lit up in brilliant flashes of light. The New Year 1740 had arrived.

The Empress attended the usual round of functions, but her own special comedy was due to be staged a few days later. Already the city was alive with ex-citement and despite the bitter cold, large crowds gathered on the frozen river, hoping to catch a glimpse of what the hundreds of craftsmen were up to con-cealed behind thick lines of guarding troops.

Then one morning a huge and astonishing procession formed up in the streets. Goats, pigs, cows, camels, dogs and reindeer were seen harnessed to various strange vehicles each of which contained a representative pair from each of the 'Barbarous Races' in the Empire. There were Lapps and Kirghiz, Tunguses and Tatars, Bashkirs and Finns — each couple in 'national dress'. But the cen-trepiece was an elephant with an iron cage on its back. The cage contained Golit-syn and his unlovely bride.

To the accompaniment of cymbals, bells and the occasional roaring of an angry beast, the procession passed the Palace and eventually arrived at Ernest Biron's covered riding school, where a banquet had been prepared for the captive bridal pair and their guests. By the Empress's express command each couple was

Abridged from P. Longworth, *The Three Empresses,* London, 1972.

served with its own traditional dishes — including such culinary delights as reindeer meat, horse-flesh and fermented mare's milk. There was entertainment too. A poet named Tredyakovski declaimed an ode composed specially for the occasion entitled: 'Greetings to the Bridal Pair of Fools', and each pair of guests was made to dance its own 'national dance' for the amusement of the onlookers. Then the procession formed up again to accompany the bride and groom to their home for the night — the palace made of ice.

No other material had been used in its construction — walls and steps, baroque balustrades, cornices and columns, even the decorative figurines and window-panes were made of ice. So was the furniture — a huge four-poster bridal bed, chairs, tables, chandeliers, a clock, a commode, a set of playing cards, with the markings coloured in, and a statue of a Cupid. Outside there were other marvels of engineering and the sculptor's art — flowers and trees complete with perching birds, ice cannon which fired real charges, a pair of dolphins which breathed out flames of fire (thanks to a device inside which pumped out naptha), and a life-sized model of an elephant equipped with a machine to squirt out water to a height of two hundred and fifty feet. Everything had been done to excite the eye and astonish the imagination — and all at a cost of only thirty thousand roubles.

The Empress accompanied the bridal pair inside, saw them undressed and laid upon their bed of ice. Then she withdrew. From her bedroom she had an excellent view of the Ice Palace, and next morning she saw Golitsyn and his wife emerge apparently none the worse for their experience. The stove installed inside their chilly bedroom, as the scientists of the Academy took careful note, had proved effective....

5.   A Frenchman's View of Autocracy

The Marquis de Custine was a French aristocrat and opponent of the French Revolution who traveled to Russia in 1839. He expected to find much to admire in the strong government of the Tsar. What he actually found was something quite different. Here he describes his reaction to the city of St. Petersburg and the man responsible for its construction. The translator of this selection, Phyllis Penn Kohler, was the wife of the American Ambassador to the USSR after World War II. She undertook this translation because she and her friends were struck by the similarity of de Custine's Russia to what they saw in Stalin's day.

I had my pockets full of letters of recommendation which had been given to me in Paris, in part by the Russian ambassador himself, as well as by other equally well-known persons; but as they were sealed I had been afraid to leave

Abridged from Phyllis Penn Kohler, editor and translator, *Journey For Our Time: The Russian Journals of the Marquis de Custine,* Chicago, 1951.

them in my portfolio; consequently, I buttoned my coat when I saw the police approaching. They let me pass without searching my person, but when I had to unpack all my trunks before the customs officers, these new enemies undertook the most minute examination of my effects, particularly the books. After being subjected to an interminable examination, all of my books were confiscated—always with the most extreme politeness, but with no regard for my protests. They also took from me two sets of traveler's pistols and an old travel clock. I tried in vain to understand and explain to myself why this latter object should have been subject to confiscation. Everything taken from me was later returned, as they had assured me it would be, but not without a great deal of annoyance and lengthy discussions. Accordingly, I repeat what the Russian gentlemen said: Russia is the country of useless formalities....

...However shocked one may be by the stupid imitations that ruin the appearance of Petersburg, one cannot contemplate it without a sort of admiration for this city raised from the sea at the command of a man, which, in order to survive must fight against periodic inundation by ice and permanent inundation by water. It is the result of an immense force of will, and, if one does not admire it, one fears it—which is almost to respect it.

The highly overrated, famous statue of Peter the Great was the first thing to attract my attention; it seemed to me to have a singularly disagreeable effect; placed on its rock by Catherine, with this inscription—rather conceited in its apparent simplicity—"To Peter I Catherine II." This figure of a man on a horse is neither ancient nor modern; it is a Roman of the time of Louis XV. (See Reading 3)

I stopped for a moment in front of the scaffolding of a building already famous in Europe, in spite of the fact that it is not finished. This will be the Church of Saint Isaac. Finally, I saw the facade of the new Winter Palace, another prodigious product of the will of a man applied to aligning the strength of men against the laws of nature. The goal was attained, for in one year this palace rose up out of its ashes. I believe it is the largest palace in existence. It is the equivalent of the Louvre and the Tuileries combined.

In order to finish the work in the period specified by the Emperor, unprecedented efforts were required. The interior construction was continued during the bitterest cold of winter. Six thousand laborers were continually at work; a considerable number died each day, but, as the victims were instantly replaced by other champions who filled their places, to perish in their turn in this inglorious gap, the losses were not apparent. And the only purpose of so much sacrifice was to satisfy the caprice of a man! With naturally civilized people, that is to say of an old civilization, men's lives are risked only for common interests whose gravity is recognized by the majority. But how many generations of sovereigns have been corrupted by the example of Peter I!

During freezes of fifteen to twenty degrees below zero, six thousand obscure martyrs, martyrs without merit, martyrs of an involuntary obedience — for this virtue is innate and forced in the Russians — were shut up in rooms heated to eighty-six degrees in order to dry the walls more quickly. Thus these wretches on entering and leaving this abode of death — now become, thanks to their sacrifice, the home of vanity, magnificence and pleasure — underwent a difference in temperature of 100 to 108 degrees.

Work in the mines of the Urals is less injurious to life; however, the laborers employed in Petersburg were not malefactors. I have been told that the unfortunate ones who painted the interior of the hottest rooms were obliged to put a kind of ice cap on their heads in order to keep their senses under the boiling temperature they were condemned to endure while they were working.

If one wished to disgust us with art, gilt, luxury, and with all the pomp of courts, one could not choose a more efficacious means. Nevertheless, the sovereign was called "Father" by men sacrificed in such great numbers under his eyes and for the satisfaction of sheer imperial vanity.

I feel ill at ease in Petersburg since I have seen this palace and heard what it cost in human lives. I guarantee the authenticity of the details; they were given to me by people who are neither spies nor scornful Russians.

The millions spent on Versailles fed as many French workers' families as these twelve months of the Winter Palace killed Slav serfs; but, by means of this sacrifice, the command of the Emperor accomplished miracles and the completed palace, to the general satisfaction, is to be inaugurated by the festivals of a marriage. A prince can be popular without attaching a high price to human life. Nothing colossal is obtained without pain; but when a man is himself both the nation and the government he should impose upon himself the law of employing the great resources of the machine he operates only for the attainment of an end worthy of the effort....

An absolute sovereign is wrong to say that he is in a hurry; he should, above all, fear the zeal of his subjects who can use the word of the master, innocent in appearance, like a sword to bring about miracles, but at the cost of an army of slaves! It is great, it is too great; God and mankind will finish by taking vengeance for these inhuman wonders. It is imprudent, to say the least, for a prince to rate satisfaction of vanity at so high a price; but the renown that they gain abroad is more important to the Russian princes than anything else — more important than the reality of power — for in that they are acting in the sense of public opinion; furthermore, nothing can discredit authority with a people for whom obedience has become a condition of life. Some peoples have worshiped light; the Russians worship eclipse. How can their eyes ever be opened?

I do not say that their political system produces nothing good; I say only that it produces at too high a cost.

It is not only now that foreigners are astonished by the love of these people for slavery;...

[De Custine recalls that in the sixteenth century a German traveler had written about the power of the Tsar and the obedience of his subjects. He comments tnat the same situation still seems true at the time of his visit in the early nineteenth century, and quotes the German traveler]:

"He (the Czar) speaks and everything is done: the life, the fortune of the laity and of the clergy, of the nobility and of the citizens, all depend on his supreme will. He has no opposition, and everything in him appears just — as in the Divinity — for the Russians are pursuaded that the Great Prince is the executor of celestial decrees. Thus, God and the Prince willed it; God and the Prince know best, such are the ordinary expressions among them; nothing equals their zeal for his service.

"I do not know whether it is the character of the Russian nation which has formed such autocrats or whether the autocrats themselves have given this character to the nation."...

It seems to me, however, that the influence is reciprocal — the Russian government would never have been established anywhere other than in Russia, nor would the Russians have become what they are under a different government.

Today you will hear, in Paris or in Russia, any number of Russians become ecstatic over the miraculous effects of the word of the Emperor; and, while they are priding themselves on the results, not one will be moved to pity by the means employed. The word of the Czar has the power to create, they say. Yes, it brings stones to life, but in doing so it kills men. Despite this small reservation, all Russians are proud of the ability to say to us: "You see, in your country one deliberates three years over the means of rebuilding a theater, whereas our Emperor builds the biggest palace in the world in one year." This childish triumph does not seem to them too dearly paid for by the death of some paltry thousands of workers sacrificed to this regal impatience, to this imperial fantasy, which becomes, to use a fashionable plural, one of the national glories. As for me, however, being French, I see in this only inhuman pedantry. But from one end of this vast Empire to the other, not a single protest is raised against these orgies of absolute sovereignty.

— People and government — here all is harmony. The Russians would not give up the miracles of will of which they are witnesses, accomplices, and victims, if it were a question of bringing back to life all the slaves they have cost. All the same, the thing that surprises me is not that a man, steeped in self-idolatry, a man ascribed as all-powerful by sixty million men, or so-called men, undertakes and brings to conclusions such things; it is that among the voices which recount these accomplishments to the glory of this one man, not one separates itself from the chorus to protest in the name of humanity against the miracles of autocracy. It can be said of the Russians, great and small — they are intoxicated with slavery....

6.   Mikhail Lermontov: Prediction

Throughout the nineteenth century, a number of writers made gloomy predictions about what lay ahead for Russia. This is one of the most dire, the work of M. Lermontov, who was an extraordinarily gifted writer, and who himself died young. He lived from 1814-1841.

> The day will come, for Russia that dark day
> When the Tsar's diadem will fall, and they,
> Rabble who loved him once, will love no more
> And many will subsist on death and gore.
> Downtrodden law no shelter will provide
> For child or guiltless woman. Plague will ride
> From stinking corpses through the grief-struck
> Land where fluttering rags from cottages demand
> Help none can give. And famine's gnawing pangs
> Will grip the countryside with ruthless fangs.
> Dawn on the streams will shed a crimson light.
> And then will be revealed the Man of might
> Whom thou wilt know, and thou wilt understand
> Wherefore a shining blade is in his hand.
> Sorrow will be thy lot, grief melt thine eyes
> And he will laugh at all thy tears and sighs.

7.   Leo Tolstoy: A Morning of a Landed Proprietor

Leo Tolstoy (1828-1910) was one of the finest and most enduring of the world's great writers. Best known for his novels War and Peace *and* Anna Karenina, *he also wrote simple stories and fairy tales for children and the peasants on his estate. In this selection, he portays the world of the landed estate, and the attitudes of peasant and landlord toward their world and each other: the suspiciousness and stubborn conservatism of the peasant and the ineffectual good will of a well-meaning young landlord.*

Prince Nekhlyudov was nineteen years old when he came from the Third Course of the university to pass his vacation on his estate, and remained there by himself all summer. In the autumn he wrote in his unformed childish hand to his aunt, Countess Byeloryetski, who, in his opinion, was his best friend and the most brilliant woman in the world. The letter was in French, and ran as follows:

Abridged from Leo Tolstoy, *Childhood, Boyhood, Youth, The Incursion, A Landed Proprietor, The Cossacks, Sevastopol,* Leo Wiener, editor and translator, Boston, 1904.

From Nicolas Berdyaev, *The Origin of Russian Communism,* Ann Arbor, 1960.

"Dear Aunty: — I have made a resolution on which the fate of my whole life must depend. I will leave the university in order to devote myself to country life, because I feel that I was born for it. For God's sake, dear aunty, do not laugh at me! You will say that I am young; and, indeed, I may still be a child, but this does not prevent me from feeling what my calling is, and from wishing to do good, and loving it.

"As I have written you before, I found affairs in an indescribable disorder. Wishing to straighten them out, and to understand them, I discovered that the main evil lay in the most pitiable, poverty-stricken condition of the peasants, and that the evil was such that it could be mended by labour and patience alone. If you could only see two of my peasants, Davyd and Ivan, and the lives which they lead with their families, I am sure that the mere sight of these unfortunates would convince you more than all I might say to explain my intention to you.

"Is it not my sacred and direct duty to care for the welfare of these seven hundred men, for whom I shall be held responsible before God? Is it not a sin to abandon them to the arbitrariness of rude elders and managers, for plans of enjoyment and ambition? And why should I look in another sphere for opportunities of being useful and doing good, when such a noble, brilliant, and immediate duty is open to me?

"I feel myself capable of being a good landed proprietor; and, in order to be one, as I understand this word, one needs neither a university diploma, nor ranks [bureaucratic hierarchy], which you are so anxious I should obtain. Dear aunty, make no ambitious plans for me! Accustom yourself to the thought that I have chosen an entirely different path, which is, nevertheless, good, and which, I feel, will bring me happiness. I have thought much, very much, about my future duty, have written out rules for my actions, and, if God will only grant me life and strength, shall succeed in my undertaking.

"Do not show this letter to my brother Vasya. I am afraid of his ridicule; he is in the habit of directing me, and I of submitting to him. Vanya will understand my intention, even though he may not approve of it.".…

[Nekhlyudov returns to his estate and visits his peasants.]

Nekhlyudov walked into the hut. The uneven, grimy walls were in the kitchen corner covered with all kinds of rags and clothes, while the corner of honour was literally red with cockroaches that swarmed about the images and benches. In the middle of this black, ill-smelling, eighteen-foot hut there was a large crack in the ceiling, and although supports were put in two places, the ceiling was so bent that it threatened to fall down any minute.

"Yes, the hut is in a very bad shape," said the master, gazing at the face of Churis, who, it seemed, did not wish to begin a conversation about this matter.

"It will kill us, and the children, too," the old woman kept saying, in a tearful voice, leaning against the oven under the hanging beds.

"Don't talk!" sternly spoke Churis, and, turning to the master, with a light, barely perceptible smile, which had formed itself under his quivering moustache, he said: "I am at a loss, your Grace, what to do with this hut. I have braced it and mended it, but all in vain."

"How are we to pass a winter in it? Oh, oh, oh!" said the woman.

"Now, if I could put in a few braces and fix a new strut," her husband interrupted her, with a calm, business-like expression, "and change one rafter, we might be able to get through another winter. We might be able to live here, only it will be all cut up by the braces; and if anybody should touch it, not a thing would be left alive; but it might do, as long as it stands and holds together," he concluded, evidently satisfied with his argument.

Nekhlyudov was annoyed and pained because Churis had come to such a state without having asked his aid before, whereas he had not once since his arrival refused the peasants anything, and had requested that everybody should come to him directly if they needed anything. He was even vexed at the peasant, angrily shrugged his shoulders, and frowned; but the sight of wretchedness about him, and Churis's calm and self-satisfied countenance amidst this wretchedness, changed his vexation into a melancholy, hopeless feeling.

"Now, Ivan, why did you not tell me before?" he remarked reproachfully, sitting down on a dirty, crooked bench.

"I did not dare to, your Grace," answered Churis, with the same scarcely perceptible smile, shuffling his black, bare feet on the uneven dirt floor; but he said it so boldly and quietly that it was hard to believe that he had been afraid to approach the master.

"We are peasants: how dare we —" began the woman, sobbing.

"Stop your prattling," Churis again turned to her.

"You cannot live in this hut, that is impossible!" said Nekhlyudov, after a moment's silence. "This is what we will do, my friend —"

"I am listening, sir," Churis interrupted him.

"Have you seen the stone huts, with the hollow walls, that I have had built in the new hamlet?"

"Of course I have, sir," replied Churis, showing his good white teeth in his smile. "We marvelled a great deal as they were building them, — wonderful huts! The boys made sport of them, saying that the hollow walls were storehouses, to keep rats away. Fine huts!" he concluded, with an expression of sarcastic incredulity, shaking his head. "Regular jails!"

"Yes, excellent huts, dry and warm, and not so likely to take fire," retorted the master, with a frown on his youthful face, obviously dissatisfied with the peasant's sarcasm.

"No question about that, your Grace, fine huts."

"Now, one of those huts is all ready. It is a thirty-foot hut, with vestibules and a storeroom, ready for occupancy. I will let you have it at your price; you will pay me when you can," said the master, with a self-satisfied smile, which he could not keep back, at the thought that he was doing a good act. "You will break down your old hut," he continued; "it will do yet for a barn. We will transfer the outhouses in some way. There is excellent water there. I will cut a garden for you out of the cleared ground, and also will lay out a piece of land for you in three parcels. You will be happy there. Well, are you not satisfied?'' asked Nekhlyudov, when he noticed that the moment he mentioned changing quarters Churis stood in complete immobility and, without a smile, gazed at the floor.

"It is your Grace's will," he answered, without lifting his eyes.

The old woman moved forward, as if touched to the quick, and was about to say something, but her husband anticipated her.

"It is your Grace's will," he repeated, firmly, and at the same time humbly, looking at his master, and shaking his hair, "but it will not do for us to live in the new hamlet."

"Why?"

"No, your Grace! We are badly off here, but if you transfer us there, we shan't stay peasants long. What kind of peasants can we be there? It is impossible to live there, saving your Grace!"

"Why not?"

"We shall be completely ruined, your Grace!"

"But why is it impossible to live there?"

"What life will it be? You judge for yourself: the place has never been inhabited; the quality of the water is unknown; there is no place to drive the cattle to. Our hemp plots have been manured here since time immemorial, but how is it there? Why, there is nothing but barrenness there. Neither fences, nor kilns, nor sheds, — nothing. We shall be ruined, your Grace, if you insist upon our going there, completely ruined! It is a new place, an unknown place —" he repeated, with a melancholy, but firm, shake of his head.

Nekhlyudov began to prove to the peasant that the transfer would be very profitable to him, that fences and sheds would be put up, that the water was good there, and so forth; but Churis' dull silence embarrassed him, and he felt that he was not saying what he ought to. Churis did not reply; but when the master grew silent, he remarked, with a light smile, that it would be best to settle the old domestic servants and Aleshka the fool in that hamlet, to keep a watch on the grain.

"Now that would be excellent," he remarked, and smiled again. "It is a useless affair, your Grace!"

"What of it if it is an uninhabited place?" Nekhlyudov expatiated, patiently. "Here was once an uninhabited place, and people are living in it now. And so you had better settle there in a lucky hour — Yes, you had better settle there —"

"But, your Grace, there is no comparison!" Churis answered with animation, as if afraid that the master might have taken his final resolution. "Here is a cheery place, a gay place, and we are used to it, and to the road, and the pond, where the women wash the clothes and the cattle go to water; and all our peasant surroundings have been here since time immemorial, — the threshing-floor, the garden, and the willows that my parents have set out. My grandfather and father have given their souls to God here, and I ask nothing else, your Grace, but to be able to end my days here. If it should be your favor to mend the hut, we shall be greatly obliged to your Grace; if not, we shall manage to end our days in the old hut. Let us pray to the Lord all our days," he continued, making low obeisances. "Drive us not from our nest, sir."

While Churis was speaking, ever louder and louder sobs were heard under the beds, in the place where his wife stood, and when her husband pronounced the word "sir," his wife suddenly rushed out and, weeping, threw herself down at the master's feet:

"Do not ruin us, benefactor! You are our father, you are our mother! What business have we to move? We are old and lonely people. Both God and you —" She burst out in tears.

Nekhlyudov jumped up from his seat, and wanted to raise the old woman, but she struck the earth floor with a certain voluptuousness of despair, and pushed away the master's hand.

"What are you doing? Get up, please! If you do not wish, you do not have to," he said, waving his hands, and retreating to the door.

When Nekhlyudov seated himself again on the bench, and silence reigned in the hut, interrupted only by the blubbering of the old woman, who had again removed herself to her place under the beds, and was there wiping off her tears with the sleeve of her shirt, the young proprietor comprehended what meaning the dilapidated wretched hut, the broken well with the dirty puddle, the rotting stables and barns, and the split willows that could be seen through the crooked window, had for Churis and his wife, and a heavy, melancholy feeling came over him, and he was embarrassed.

"Why did you not say at the meeting of last week that you needed a hut? I do not know now how to help you. I told you all at the first meeting that I was settled in the estate, and that I meant to devote my life to you; that I was prepared to deprive myself of everything in order to see you contented and happy, — and I vow before God that I will keep my word," said the youthful proprietor, unconscious of the fact that such ebullitions were unable to gain the confidence of any man, least of all a Russian, who loves not words but deeds, and who is averse to the expression of feelings, however beautiful.

The simple-hearted young man was so happy in the sentiment which he was experiencing that he could not help pouring it out.

Churis bent his head sideways and blinking slowly, listened with forced attention to his master as to a man who must be listened to, though he may say things that are not very agreeable and have not the least reference to the listener.

"But I cannot give everybody all they ask of me. If I did not refuse anybody who asks me for timber, I should soon be left with none myself, and would be unable to give to him who is really in need of it. That is why I have put aside a part of the forest to be used for mending the peasant buildings, and have turned it over to the Commune. That forest is no longer mine, but yours, the peasants', and I have no say about it, but the Commune controls it as it sees fit. Come this evening to the meeting; I will tell the Commune of your need: if it resolves to give you a new hut, it is well, but I have no forest. I am anxious to help you with all my heart; but if you do not want to move, the Commune will have to arrange it for you, and not I. Do you understand me?''

"We are very well satisfied with your favour," answered the embarrassed Churis. "If you will deign to let me have a little timber for the outbuildings, I will manage one way or other. The Commune? Well, we know —''

"No, you had better come.''

"Your servant, sir. I shall be there. Why should I not go? Only I will not ask the Commune for anything."...

Nekhlyudov had long known, not by hearsay, nor trusting the words of others, but by experience, all the extreme wretchedness of his peasants; but all that reality was so incompatible with his education, his turn of mind, and manner of life, that he involuntarily forgot the truth; and every time when he was reminded of it in a vivid and palpable manner, as now, his heart felt intolerably heavy and sad, as though he were tormented by the recollection of some unatoned crime which he had committed.

"Why are you so poor?" he said, involuntarily expressing his thought.

"What else are we to be, your Grace, if not poor? You know yourself what kind of soil we have: clay and clumps, and we must have angered God, for since the cholera we have had very poor crops of grain. The meadows and fields have grown less; some have been taken into the estate, others have been directly attached to the manorial fields. I am all alone and old. I would gladly try to do something, but I have no strength. My old woman is sick, and every year she bears a girl; they have to be fed. I am working hard all by myself, and there are seven souls in the house. It is a sin before God our Lord, but I often think it would be well if he took some of them away as soon as possible. It would be easier for me and for them too, it would be better than to suffer here —''

"Oh, oh!" the woman sighed aloud, as though confirming her husband's words.

"Here is my whole help," continued Churis, pointing to a flaxen-haired, shaggy boy of some seven years, with an immense belly, who, softly creaking the door, had just entered timidly, and, morosely fixing his wondering eyes upon the master, with both his hands was holding on to his father's shirt. "Here is my entire help," continued Churis, in a sonorous voice, passing his rough hand through his child's hair. "It will be a while before he will be able to do anything, and in the meantime the work is above my strength."...

"I shall wait for the little fellow to grow up. If it is your will, excuse him from school; for a few days ago the village scribe came and said that your Grace wanted him to come to school. Do excuse him: what mind can he have, your Grace? He is too young, and has not much sense yet."

"No; this, my friend, must be," said the master. "Your boy can comprehend, it is time for him to study. I am saying it for your own good. You judge yourself: when he grows up, and becomes a householder, he will know how to read and write, and he will read in church, — everything will go well with you, with God's aid," said Nekhlyudov, trying to express himself as clearly as possible, and, at the same time, blushing and stammering.

"No doubt, your Grace, you do not wish us any harm; but there is nobody at home; my wife and I have to work in the manorial field, and, small though he is, he helps us some, by driving the cattle home, and taking the horses to water. As little as he is, he is a peasant all the same," and Churis, smiling, took hold of his boy's nose between his thick fingers, and cleaned it.

"Still, send him when he is at home, and has time, — do you hear? — without fail."

Churis drew a deep sigh, and did not reply....

"Where are these dreams?" now thought the youth, as he approached his house after his visits. "It is now more than a year that I have been seeking happiness upon this road, and what have I found? It is true, at times I feel that I might be satisfied with myself, but it is a kind of dry, mental satisfaction. Yes and no, I am simply dissatisfied with myself! I am dissatisfied because I have found no happiness here, and yet I wish, I passionately wish for happiness. I have not experienced enjoyment, and have already cut off from me everything which gives it. Why? For what? Who has been better off for it? My aunt was right when she said that it is easier to find happiness than to give it to others.

"Have my peasants grown richer? Have they been morally educated and developed? Not in the least. They are not better off, but I feel worse with every day. If I only saw any success in my undertaking, if I saw gratitude — but no, I see the perverted routine, vice, suspicion, helplessness.

"I am wasting in vain the best years of my life," he thought....

8. Nikolai Gogol: Nevsky Avenue

Not all Russians lived in the country during the nineteenth century. Nikolai Gogol (1809-1852), another of Russia's great nineteenth century prose writers, abhorred what he saw as the nightmare of modern city life. Gogol, best known for his long novel Dead Souls, *was a master of satire, fantasy, and the grotesque. This description of the finest street in St. Petersburg, Nevsky Prospect, or Nevsky Avenue as it is called here, illustrates his love of the odd detail and satirical style, and also provides a glimpse of the cosmopolitan life of the Russian capital during the reign of Nicholas I, the second quarter of the nineteenth century. Many Russian writers used St. Petersburg as a symbol for what was at best cosmopolitan, and at worst, alien to Russia.*

...There is nothing finer than Nevsky Avenue, not in St. Petersburg at any rate; for in St. Petersburg it is everything. And, indeed, is there anything more

Abridged from Nikolai Gogol, "The Overcoat," David Magarshack, translator, *Tales of Good and Evil*, New York, 1956.

gay, more brilliant, more resplendent than this beautiful street of our capital? I am sure that not one of her anaemic inhabitants, not one of her innumerable Civil Servants, would exchange Nevsky Avenue for all the treasures in the world. Not only the young man of twenty-five, the young gallant with the beautiful moustache and the immaculate morning coat, but the man with white hair sprouting on his chin and a head as smooth as a billiard ball, yes, even he is enthralled with Nevsky Avenue. And the ladies…Oh, for the ladies Nevsky Avenue is a thing of even greater delight! But is there anyone who does not feel thrilled and delighted with it? The gay carriages, the handsome men, the beautiful women — all lend it a carnival air, an air that you can almost inhale the moment you set foot on Nevsky Avenue! Even if you have some very important business, you are quite certain to forget all about it as soon as you are there. This is the only place in town where you meet people who are not there on business, people who have not been driven there either by necessity or by their passion for making money, which seems to have the whole of St. Petersburg in its grip. It really does seem that the man you meet on Nevsky Avenue is less of an egoist than the man you meet on any other street where want and greed and avarice can be read on the faces of all who walk or drive in carriages or cabs. Nevsky Avenue is the main communication centre of the whole of St. Petersburg. Anyone living in the Petersburg or Vyborg district who has not seen a friend on the Sands or the Moscow Tollgate for years can be sure to meet him here. No directory or information bureau will supply such correct information as Nevsky Avenue. All-powerful Nevsky Avenue! The only place in St. Petersburg where a poor man can combine a stroll with entertainment. How spotlessly clean are its pavements swept and, good gracious, how many feet leave their marks on them! Here is the footprint left by the clumsy, dirty boot of an ex-army private, under whose weight the very granite seems to crack; and here is one left by the miniature, light as a feather, little shoe of the delightful young creature who turns her pretty head towards the glittering shop-window as the sun-flower turns to the sun; and here is the sharp scratch left by the rattling sabre of some ambitious lieutenant — everything leaves its imprint of great power or great weakness upon it. What a rapid phantasmagoria passes over it in a single day! What changes does it not undergo in only twenty-four hours!

Let us begin with the early morning when all St. Petersburg is filled with the smell of hot, freshly baked bread and is crowded with old women in tattered clothes who besiege the churches and appeal for alms to the compassionate passers-by. At this time Nevsky Avenue is deserted: the stout shopkeepers and their assistants are still asleep in their fine linen shirts, or are lathering their noble cheeks, or drinking coffee; beggars gather at the doors of the pastry-cooks' shops where the sleepy Ganymede*, who the day before flew about like a fly with the cups of chocolate, crawls out without a cravat [tie] and flings some stale pastries

*Ganymede: Beautiful youth, cupbearer to the gods in Greek mythology.

and other leavings at them. Workmen are trudging through the streets: occcasionally the avenue is crossed by Russian peasants, hurrying to their work in boots soiled with lime which not all the water of the Yekaterinsky Canal, famous for its cleanness, could wash off. At this time it is not proper for ladies to take a walk, for the Russian workman and peasant love to express themselves in vigorous language that is not even heard on the stage. Sometimes a sleepy Civil Servant will walk along with a brief-case under his arm, if the way to his office lies across Nevsky Avenue. It can indeed be stated without fear of contradiction that at this time, that is to say, until twelve o'clock, Nevsky Avenue does not serve as a goal for anyone, but is merely a means to an end: it is gradually filled with people who have their own occupations, their own worries, their own disappointments, and who are not thinking about it at all. The Russian peasant is talking about the few coppers he earns; old men and women wave their hands about or talk to themselves, sometimes with picturesque gestures, but no one listens to them or even laughs at them except perhaps the boys in brightly coloured smocks who streak along Nevsky Avenue with empty bottles or mended boots. At this time you can please yourself about your dress. You can wear a workman's cap instead of a hat, and even if your collar were to stick out of your cravat no one would notice it....

At twelve o'clock Nevsky Avenue is invaded by tutors and governesses of all nationalities and their charges in cambric collars. English Johnsons and French Coques walk arm in arm with the young gentlemen entrusted to their parental care and explain to them with an air of grave decorum that the signboards over the shops are put there to tell people what they can find inside the shops. Governesses, pale misses, and rosy-cheeked mademoiselles walk statelily behind slender and fidgety young girls, telling them to raise a shoulder a little higher and to walk straighter. In short, at this time Nevsky Avenue is a pedagogic Nevsky Avenue. But the nearer it gets to two o'clock in the afternoon, the fewer do the numbers of tutors, governesses, and children grow, until finally they are crowded out by their loving fathers who walk arm in arm with their highly-strung wives in gorgeous, bright dresses of every imaginable hue. These are by and by joined by people who have by that time finished all their important domestic engagements, such as talking to their doctors about the weather and the small pimple that suddenly appeared on their nose; or enquiring after the health of their horses and the children, who, incidentally, seem always to be showing great promise; or reading in the papers the notices and important announcements of the arrivals and departures; or, lastly, drinking a cup of tea or coffee. They are soon joined by those upon whom enviable fate has bestowed the blessed calling of officials on special duties as well as by those who serve in the Foreign Office and who are particularly distinguished by their fine manners and their noble habits. Dear me, what wonderful appointments and posts there are! How they improve and delight the soul of man! But, alas, I am not in the Civil Service myself and so am deprived of the pleasure of appreciating the exquisite manners of my superiors. Every one you now meet on Nevsky Avenue is a paragon of respectability:

the gentlemen in long frock-coats with their hands in their pockets; the ladies in pink, white and pale blue redingotes and hats. You will meet here a most wonderful assortment of side-whiskers, a unique pair of whiskers, tucked with astonishing and extraordinary art under the cravat, velvety whiskers, satiny whiskers, and whiskers black as sable or coal, the latter, alas, the exclusive property of the gentlemen from the Foreign Office. Providence has denied black whiskers to those serving in any other ministry, and to their great mortification they have to wear red whiskers. Here you come across moustaches so wonderful that neither pen nor brush can do justice to them, moustaches to which the best years of a lifetime have been devoted — the object of long hours of vigil by day and by night; moustaches upon which all the perfumes of Arabia have been lavished, the most exquisite scents and essences, and which have been anointed with the rarest and most precious pomades; moustaches which are wrapped up for the night in the most delicate vellum; moustaches for which their possessors show a most touching affection and which are the envy of all who behold them. Thousands of different sorts of hats, dresses, multicoloured kerchiefs, light as gossamer, to which their owners sometimes remain faithful for two whole days, dazzle every eye on Nevsky Avenue. It looks as if a sea of butterflies have risen from flower stalks and are fluttering in a scintillating cloud above the black beetles of the male sex....

9.   The Peasant's Apology

John Rickman, the teller of this anecdote, spent the years 1916-1918 in Russia where he worked as a physician with the Friends' War Victims Relief Unit. He presents this story as typifying an attitude he found among peasants of that time.

Some time before the Bolsheviks were even heard of in our part of Russia, I was driving at dusk through a village on my way back to hospital when a drunken peasant jumped on to the runners of the sledge and demanded that I should stop and treat his headache. He tried to drag me from the sledge by force, so I put my foot on the pit of his stomach and pushed him into a snowdrift. His manner and the strong language he used when he rose were such that a more exact diagnosis and a more medical treatment of his condition did not seem to be indicated. My driver, remarking that the fellow would have a worse head next morning, whipped up the horses and drove on. The trivial incident passed out of my mind.

One day, months later when the snow had gone, an unusual thing happened. A peasant in the waiting-room of the out-patients asked to be seen *last,* in contrast to the usual clamour to be seen first. When all the other comers had been attended to, the *moujik,* [peasant man] standing rather shyly by the door, said 'Doctor, don't you recognize me?' I looked at him carefully and said I did not,

Abridged from G. Gorer and J. Rickman, *Great Russian Peoples* London, 1949.

then turning to the out-patient register, asked when he had been before and what his trouble was. He said he had never been before and had no ailment, but before proceeding he must know that I recognized him...[He then began his story.]

'Do you remember months ago in the village of ————— a drunken man set upon you as you were driving through and demanded that you should stop?' The scene came back in a flash. 'And do you remember,' I said, smiling, 'the doctor who put his foot in that man's belly and gave a shove? Damn it all, man, we were quits.'

'Now doctor, don't make a joke of it. It's a serious matter.' I thought I must have injured him, so apologized and asked him to tell me all about it.

He then began a long story. He had been drunk and felt sick and thick in the head; so seeing me, he suddenly had the bright idea of demanding an instant cure. But his headache made him angry and he tried to do this by force. He had attacked me and that was wrong. Before he asked my forgiveness, it was necessary that I should know exactly who he was and recall the circumstances. He then very shyly produced a document which ran roughly as follows:

This is to certify that I (here there was a space for my name) have received the apology of _____ _____, of the village of _____, on the (space for the date). And this is also to certify that the elders of the said village of _____, after careful examination are convinced that _____ _____'s apologies are from the heart. (Date, signatures of village elders and crosses of attestation.)

The whole thing seemed fantastic; an apology was in the circumstances odd but understandable, but the certificate seemed all out of proportion. I made up my mind to see the village elders and try to clear the matter up.

A few days later my round lay through that village and I called on several of the elders. They said they had been horrified by the attack on me. I had done them no harm, on the contrary had been diligent for their good, and it was necessary to eradicate the evil disposition which had shown itself amongst them that night. I pointed out that my quite adequate physical defence had prevented injury to me being laid on the man's conscience, and also that I had attended patients in the village after the episode just as before, so they need not fear the loss of my assistance; but that was not the point. They felt the attack to be a stain on the honour of the village. They had reproached him the next day and asked him to apologize. He was defiant in refusal.... Then, since as a group they had not been able to persuade him to apologize, they changed their policy and approached him as individuals. They also got his friends to join in their efforts and for weeks the poor devil was followed wherever he went with reproachful eyes. One day he burst upon them with the news that he would go and apologize. But his manner of saying it did not satisfy them; it was hasty and still somewhat defiant; his heart had not changed. They accepted his consent to apologize as a good sign but not necessarily as an indication of true repentance. Gradually he became more passive and waited patiently to be 'released' by the village elders from the yoke of guilt. He then came to me with their certificate....

They wished me to know that they felt themselves also to be involved in the insult and hence also in the restoration of the honour of the village.

This was their explanation. There were, of course, other reasons for dealing with me in this way. A physician was an object of value to them. They were helplessly dependent on him and his goodwill, and however familiar he might be as a visitor in their homes and at their councils, they *as a group* could not replace or reproduce him because he belonged to a different civilization, that of the metropolis and of international communications. Towards all members of this civilization they looked with abject submission, envy, and sometimes hatred; from the metropolitan civilization came to them tax gatherers, political police (civil order was maintained, as this story shows, by the villagers themselves in a most unbureaucratic way), landlords (for the most part absentee), priests, a few schoolteachers, and a very few doctors. These, one and all, belonged to the metropolis, not to the village. Over all loomed the distant and terrible, revered and incomprehensible figure of the Czar, who, however widely his characteristics ranged over everything Russian, certainly was not 'one of us'....

...This little episode shows something of the way in which the villagers were bound together by ties of love and how they kept the spirit of their community intact. This spirit gave the members strength when they were in accord with it, and they lived in misery and isolation when they broke, in thought or mood, with the opinion and sentiment of their neighbours. The episode also shows how difficult it was for them to include a member of the alien caste in their way of thought and living.

* * * * *

Some of the social history of the next few years is well known. The Bolsheviks came to power and made all things new. The peasants were collectivized, many were forcibly moved to public works, many more were driven by starvation to seek a living in the towns. The new social unit became the factory, and the old village organization ceased to be typical for the Russian people. But its spirit did not die.

Seventeen years passed, and an Intourist [Soviet travel service for foreign visitors] traveller brought back from one of the large new cities a collection of factory wall-newspapers (the placards on which anyone may freely criticize anyone and anything except the essentials of the new regime). Most of the contents related to the factory statistics, how the shock workers were breaking records, sport, the factory theatre, music news, and so forth. Down in a corner (always the same corner of each issue) there was a series of notes which at first glance seemed of the most trivial significance. But their spirit was reminiscent of the village I have mentioned, and heaven knows how many thousand like it. The notes ran somewhat as follows: 'We do not like the way Sonia ——— does her work. She doesn't show the right spirit; she slacks.' Several times was she thus publicly reproved. Later she was said to show signs of adopting the proper attitude. Finally Sonia was declared an enthusiastic worker who had entered truly into the spirit of the Revolution.

On reading this my mind went back to the peasant whose heart was changed by the silent but not harsh pressure of the group; the steps in this re-entry into the community seemed to be remarkably similar in the two cases; in spite of the greatest imaginable change in the economic and political life the behaviour of the group to a wayward member remained the same. The village spirit, the need to feel that everyone was 'one of us', had re-emerged; and I have no doubt that this plays its part in strengthening and consolidating a regime which often seems to us in the West to be based only on force....

10. Alexander Herzen: Thoughts on the Peasant Community

The Russian intelligentsia of the mid-nineteenth century idealized peasant life. For them, the peasant embodied all the virtues of unspoiled rural Russia. Those who favored an egalitarian society even saw in the peasant commune a spontaneous socialism, far in advance of anything Western Europe had to offer. Needless to say, few of them knew much about the hard realities of peasant existence, nor of the mentality Tolstoy depicts in the Morning of the Landed Proprietor *(Reading 7). Alexander Herzen was one of these intelligents, here writing from exile in his periodical "The Bell," smuggled into Russia from London.*

...The Russian peasant has no real knowledge of any form of life but that of the village commune: he understands about rights and duties only when these are tied to the commune and its members. Outside the commune, there are no obligations for him—there is simply violence...The commune has preserved the Russian people from Mongol barbarism, from Imperial civilization, from the Europeanized landowners and from the German bureaucracy: the organic life of the commune has persisted despite all the attempts made on it by authority, badly mauled though it has been at times. By good fortune it has survived right into the period that witnesses the rise of socialism in Europe. For Russia this has been a most happy providence....

The peasants have remained faithful guardians of the national character, which is based on *communism,* i.e., on the regular division of the fields according to the number of workers and the absence of private landownership. . . The Russian people, crushed by slavery and the Government, cannot follow in the

Abridged from Alexander Herzen, "The Bell," Hans Kohn, editor, *Mind of Modern Russia: Historical and Political Thought of Russia's Great Age,* New Jersey, 1955.

footsteps of European nations and repeat their past revolutions. These were revolutions exclusively of the cities, and anything of that nature would instantly fracture the foundations of our communal system. The opposite is the case: the coming revolution will take place on more native ground....

We have none of the Western man's blind prejudices which paralyze and deprive him of half his faculties. Our people's life is based on the village community, with division of the fields, with communistic landownership, with elected administration and equal responsibility for each worker...The only thing that is conservative on our shifting, unsettled soil is the village community—that is, the only thing deserving preservation...I believe, with all my heart and mind, that it is our door on which history is knocking....

The word *Socialism* is unknown to our people, but its meaning is close to the hearts of Russians who have lived for ages in the village community....

11. Ivan Turgenev: The Nihilist

The beliefs of the Nihilists of the early 1860s are difficult to determine precisely, partly because of their essentially negative outlook and partly because they spoke and wrote as individuals, rather than as spokesmen for a cohesive philosophy. Nevertheless, certain facets of their thinking can be deduced from statements made by and about them. For example, a Nihilist named Dmitri Pisarev is said to have once remarked that a good pair of boots was worth more than all the works of Pushkin. The most famous Nihilist of all was probably the radical doctor Bazarov in Fathers and Sons, *a novel by Ivan Turgenev, ironic in that the author clearly intended his portrait of Bazarov to be a caricature. The following reading is a passage from that novel, in which Bazarov is conversing with Pavel Kirsanov, uncle of his friend Arkady. Pavel has just asked Bazarov what he and others like him are up to, and Bazarov replies:*

...''I'll tell you what we're doing. Formerly—not very long ago—we used to say that our officials took bribes, that we had no roads, no commerce, no just courts. . .''

"Well, yes, yes, you are denunciators—it seems that's the term for it. I agree with many of your denunciations, but. . .''

"And then it dawned on us that just to talk on and on about our ulcers wasn't worth the trouble and would only lead to mediocrity and doctrinairism. We observed that our wise men, such as the so-called progressive people and denunciators, are good for nothing, that we spend our time on rot, debating so-called art, meaningless creations, parliamentarianism, jurisprudence, and the devil knows what, when it's a question of our daily bread, when we're being

Abridged from Ivan Turgenev, *Fathers and Sons,* Barbara Makanowitsky, translator, New York, 1959.

choked by the crudest superstitions, when all our businesses are disintegrating apparently only because of a lack of honest people, when the very freedom the government is fussing about would hardly benefit us because our peasant is glad to rob himself solely in order to drink himself into a stupor in the tavern.''

"So," interrupted Pavel, "so: you became convinced of all this and decided not to undertake anything seriously yourselves.''

"And decided not to undertake anything," Bazarov repeated gruffly. He had become suddenly annoyed with himself; why had he talked so unrestrainedly in front of that squire?

"Just curse everything?''

"And just curse.''

"And that's called nihilism?''

"And that's called nihilism," Bazarov repeated again, this time with marked insolence.

Pavel blinked.

"So that's how it is," he said in a strangely calm voice. "Nihilism is supposed to cure all ills, and you are our liberators and heroes. All right. But why do you abuse the others, including even the denunciators? Aren't you merely talking like everyone else?''

"We've other sins, but not that one," Bazarov muttered through his teeth.

"So, then. You do act, is that it? You're preparing to take action?''

Bazarov didn't answer. Pavel shuddered, but immediately got hold of himself.

"Hmmm!. . . To act, to destroy. . .'' he continued. "But how can you destroy without even knowing why?''

"We destroy because we are a force.'' Arkady remarked. . . [Arkady, a young friend of Bazarov, is also Pavel's nephew].

"Bravo! Bravo! Listen, Arkady—that's how young people today should express themselves! When you think of it, how could they fail to follow you! Young people used to have to study. If they didn't want to be considered ignoramuses, they were forced to exert themselves, like it or not. And now all they have to do is say: Everything in the world is rubbish!—and it's in the bag. Young people are delighted. In reality, while they used to be simply blockheads, now they've suddenly become nihilists.''

"And your boasted feeling of personal dignity has failed you," Bazarov remarked phlegmatically, while Arkady boiled with anger, his eyes flashing. "Our argument has gone too far. I believe it would be better to break it off. And I'll be ready to agree with you," he added, standing up, "when you give me just one institution in our contemporary existence, in private or public life, which doesn't deserve complete and merciless annihilation.''...

12. Ivan Turgenev: The Revolutionist's Promise

There are a number of testimonies to the dedication of the young revolutionaries of the 1860s and 1870s. One of the most eloquent is in the form of a prose-poem by Ivan Turgenev, the author of Fathers and Sons, *titled "The Threshold." The heroine of the poem is Sophia Perovskaya, organizer of the plot to assassinate Tsar Alexander II in 1881, and probably Russia's most famous female revolutionary in the nineteenth century. Because of censorship, "The Threshold" did not appear in Turgenev's collected works, but it was published by the underground press of The People's Will in 1883.*

I see a huge building. In its front wall is a narrow door, standing ajar; behind the door spreads a gloomy mist. In front of the high threshold is a girl, a Russian girl.

That opaque mist breathes a glacial chill and a slow, hollow voice comes with an icy draught from the depths of the building.

"O thou, who art desirous of crossing this threshold, dost thou know what is awaiting thee?"

"I know," answered the girl.

"Cold, hunger, mockery, scorn, insult, prison, illness, death itself?"

"I know."

"Ostracism, unrelieved loneliness?"

"I know. I am ready. I can endure every suffering, every blow."

"Not only from thy enemies, but from thy family and friends?"

"Yes. . . from them also."

"Good. Thou art prepared to sacrifice thyself?"

"Yes."

"To sacrifice thyself anonymously? Thou wilt perish, and no one, no one will even know whose memory to revere."

"I need neither gratitude nor compassion. I do not need a name."

"Art thou prepared to commit a crime?"

The girl bowed her head: "For that, too, I am ready."

There was a pause before the voice again took up its questioning.

"Dost thou know," it resumed at last, "that thou mayst lose faith in what thou now believest, that thou mayst come to think that thou hast been mistaken and thrown away thy young life in vain?"

"That, too, I know. And nevertheless I wish to enter."

"Enter!"

The girl crossed the threshold, and a heavy curtain fell behind her.

"Fool!" came the grating voice of someone behind.

"Saint!" was heard from somewhere the reply.

From Ivan Turgenev, *"The Threshold." The Underground Press of the People's Will,* 1883.

13. Siberian Exiles on the Road

The Tsar's secret police arrested many people accused of speaking or working against the autocracy. Both they and regular criminals were sent to work and live in Siberia, sometimes in prisons or labor camps, at other times simply to live there in exile. To get there, they walked in slow-moving caravans, a distance up to 2000 miles. George Kennan (1845-1924) lived in Russia as a young man, and returned there in 1885 to do a report on the Russian prison system. This section of his account gives a glimpse of this special part of the nineteenth century Russian world. It is interesting to compare the communal organization of the prisoners with that of the peasant community. George Kennan is the great-uncle of the diplomat and Soviet scholar of the same name. (See Chapter Six, Reading 14)

...Marching parties of convicts three or four hundred strong leave Tomsk for Irkutsk weekly throughout the whole year, and make the journey of 1040 miles in about three months. *Etapes,* or exile station-houses, stand along the road at intervals of from twenty-five to forty miles....

Each prisoner receives five cents a day in money for his subsistence, and buys food for himself from peasants along the road who make a business of furnishing it. The dress of the exiles in summer consists of a shirt and a pair of trousers of coarse gray linen; square foot-wrappers of the same material in lieu of stockings; low shoes or slippers called *kati;* leather ankle-guards to prevent the leg-fetters from chafing; a visorless Glengarry cap; and a long gray overcoat. The dress of female convicts is the same, except that a petticoat takes the place of the trousers. Women and children who voluntarily accompany relatives to Siberia are permitted to wear their own clothing, and to carry severally as much baggage as can be put into a two-bushel bag. No distinction is made between common convicts and political convicts, except that the latter, if they are nobles or belong to one of the privileged classes, receive seven and a half cents a day for their subsistence instead of five, and are carried in *telegas* [carts] instead of being forced to walk....

Five or six miles from Tomsk the party passed a *chasovnaya,* or roadside shrine, consisting of an open pavilion, in which hung a ghastly wooden effigy of the crucified Christ. Here, as upon our departure from Tomsk, I noticed that two-thirds of the convicts removed their caps, crossed themselves devoutly, and muttered brief supplications. A Russian peasant may be a highway robber or a murderer, but he continues, nevertheless, to cross himself and say his prayers....

Soon after leaving Tomsk, every exile party organizes itself into an *artel,*† or "union," elects a chief or head man known as the *starosta,* and lays the foundation of an *artel* fund by levying an assessment upon each of its members, and

Abridged from George Kennan, "Siberia," *Siberia and the Exile System,* Vol. 1, New York, 1891.

by selling at auction to the highest bidder the privilege of keeping an exile sutler's store or *maidan,* where the prisoners can openly buy tea, sugar, or white bread, and where they can secretly obtain tobacco, playing-cards, and intoxicating liquor. The organization of the party into an *artel* has for its primary object concerted and combined action against the common enemy—the Government. A single convict, regarded as an individual, has neither rights nor means of self-defense. He is completely at the mercy, not only of the higher authorities in the forwarding prisons and the provincial towns, but of every petty officer in the convoy command that escorts him from *etape* to *etape;* and the only way in which he can acquire even a limited power of self-protection is by associating himself with his fellow-convicts in an *artel,* or union. This *artel,* as an organized body, exercises all of its functions in secret, and strives to attain its ends, first, by enforcing solidarity and joint action on the part of all its members, and, secondly, by deceiving, outwitting, or bribing the officers and soldiers with whom it has to deal. It concerts plans of escape; it contrives means of obtaining forbidden articles, such as playing-cards and tobacco; it hires *telegas,* or sleighs, from the peasants along the road, and sells, or grants, to its members the privilege of riding in them for short distances when exhausted; it bribes executioners to flog lightly; it pays soldiers for smuggling intoxicating liquor into the forwarding prisons and *etapes;* and, finally, it sanctions and enforces all contracts and agreements entered into by its convict members. It is, in short, the body politic of the criminal world; and it fills, in the life of the exile, the same place that the *mir,* or commune, fills in the life of the free peasant. Within the limits of its prison environment the power of the *artel* over its members is absolute. It has its own unwritten laws, its own standards of honor and duty, and its own penal code....

The late Colonel Zagarin, inspector of exile transportation for Eastern Siberia, told me that he himself had often made a substantial contribution to the fund of an exile *artel* merely in order to secure from the latter a promise that no attempts to escape should be made within the limits of his jurisdiction. Such promises, he said, were always faithfully observed by the *artel* in its corporate capacity, and were rarely disregarded even by individuals. If, however, an inexperienced "first-timer," tempted by a favorable opportunity, should try to escape, in defiance of the *artel's* prohibition, the veterans of the party, namely, the *brodyags,* would always undertake either to recapture the fugitive, or to bring in some other runaway convict as a substitute, and thus save the honor of the *artel.* He could not remember a single case, he said, in which the *artel* had broken faith. It must not be supposed, however, that the prison commune, in such dealings with the authorities, is actuated by any high or honorable motives. In keeping its promise, in enforcing solidarity, and in punishing disloyalty and disobedience with death, it is merely protecting its own existence and securing what a majority of its members believe to be the greatest good of the greatest number. It has no sentimental regard for truthfulness or faithfulness in the abstract. It simply knows that, at certain times and in certain circumstances, honesty is the best policy, and then it enforces honesty under penalty of death. If however, circumstances so change as to render dishonesty the best policy, then the *artel* sanctions and compels the practice of deception, fraud, untruthfulness, and treachery, under the same tremendous penalty....

As the party, wet, tired, and hungry, approaches one of the little log villages that lie along its route, the *starosta,* or chief of the *artel,* asks the convoy officer to allow them to sing the "begging song" as they pass through the settlement. The desired permission is granted; certain prisoners are designated to receive the expected alms; the convicts all remove their gray caps; and entering the village with a slow, dragging step, as if they hardly had strength enough to crawl along, they begin their mournful appeal for pity.

I shall never forget the emotions roused in me by this song when I heard it for the first time....Suddenly my attention was attracted by a peculiar, low-pitched, quavering sound which came to us from a distance, and which, although made apparently by human voices, did not resemble anything that I had ever before heard. It was not singing, nor chanting, nor wailing for the dead, but a strange blending of all three. It suggested vaguely the confused and commingled sobs, moans, and entreaties of human beings who were being subjected to torture, but whose sufferings were not acute enough to seek expression in shrieks or high-pitched cries. As the sound came nearer we went out into the street in front of the station-house and saw approaching a chained party of about a hundred bare-headed convicts, who, surrounded by a cordon of soldiers, were marching slowly through the settlement, singing the "exiles' begging song." No attempt was made by the singers to pitch their voices in harmony, or to pronounce the words in unison.... Rude artless, and inharmonious as the appeal for pity was, I had never in my life heard anything so mournful and depressing. It seemed to be the half-articulate expression of all the grief, the misery, and the despair that had been felt by generations of human beings in the *étapes,* the forwarding prisons, and the mines.

As the party marched slowly along the muddy street between the lines of gray log houses, children and peasant women appeared at the doors with their hands full of bread, meat, eggs, or other articles of food, which they put into the caps or bags of the three or four shaven-headed convicts who acted as alms-collectors. The jingling of chains and the wailing voices of the exiles grew gradually fainter and fainter as the party passed up the street, and when the sounds finally died away in the distance, and we turned to reenter the post-station, I felt a strange sense of dejection, as if the day had suddenly grown colder, darker, and more dreary, and the cares and sorrows of life more burdensome and oppressive....

14. Sergei Witte: A Proposal for Russia's Industrialization

It is important to remember that not all Russian statesmen were reactionaries. This selection from Witte's secret memorandum of 1899 to Tsar Nicholas II indicates that there were far-sighted top-level bureaucrats who had ambitious plans for modernizing Russia's economy. All too often, however, their projects were never put into effect or were so badly crippled that they did not come to fruition. This particular discussion of industrialization is a reminder that by the last decade of the nineteenth century and the first decade of the twentieth, Tsarist Russia had begun to industrialize and had an economic growth rate that was one of the highest in the world.

...The entire economic structure of the empire has been transformed in the course of the second half of the current century, so that now the market and its price structure represent the collective interest of all private enterprises which constitute our national economy....

The economic relations of Russia with western Europe are fully comparable to the relations of colonial countries with their metropolises. The latter consider their colonies as advantageous markets in which they can freely sell the products of their labor and of their industry and from which they can draw with a powerful hand the raw materials necessary for them. . . . Russia was, and to a considerable extent still is, such a hospitable colony for all industrially developed states, generously providing them with the cheap products of her soil and buying dearly the products of their labor. But there is a radical difference between Russia and a colony: Russia is an independent and strong power. She has the right and the strength not to want to be the eternal handmaiden of states which are more developed economically....

We need capital, knowledge, and the spirit of enterprise. Only these three factors can speed up the creation of a fully independent national industry....

Industry gives birth to capital, capital gives rise to enterprise and love of learning; and knowledge, enterprise, and capital combined create new industries. Such is the eternal cycle of economic life, and by the succession of such turns our national economy moves ahead in the process of its natural growth. In Russia this growth is yet too slow, because there is yet too little industry, capital, and spirit of enterprise. But we cannot be content with the continuation of such slow growth....

The influx of foreign capital is, in the considered opinion of the minister of finance, the sole means by which our industry can speedily furnish our country

Abridged from Theodore H. von Laue, "A Secret Memorandum of Sergei Witte on the Industrialization of Imperial Russia." *Journal of Modern History,* Vol. 26 (March, 1954).

with abundant and cheap goods. . . . Hence the natural riches of the Russian land and the productive energies of its population will be utilized to a considerably greater extent; our economy will begin to work with greater intensity....

If in our present situation we cannot satisfy all our demands from our own resources and have to resort to purchasing abroad, it will be more advantageous for us to buy not finished goods but capital, which is one of the most necessary productive forces, particularly in industry....Foreign capital... works its way into our industry only because it is satisfied wherever it goes with smaller profits than its Russian predecessors. A new hundred million, flowing into the country from abroad during a given year, lowers by the laws of competition the rate of interest of all capital previously invested in Russian industry, which amounts to billions. If the country pays for these new hundred million rubles ten million in dividends, it gains still a considerably larger sum from the lower interest rates for the capital already invested in its economy. As the billions of national capital become cheaper, the prices of all industrial products will also fall considerably. We have at our disposal cheap labor, tremendous natural riches, and only the high price of capital now stands in the way of getting cheap goods. So why not let foreign capital help us to obtain still more cheaply that productive force of which alone we are destitute?...

The import cultural forces thus become an inseparable part of the country itself. Only a disintegrating nation has to fear foreign enslavement....

We cannot possibly count on an adequate growth of our industry out of our own national resources, because our store of capital, knowledge, and the spirit of enterprise is altogether insufficient to provide us with cheap industrial goods.

To obtain cheaper goods, of which the population stands in such urgent need, by a substantial tariff reduction would be too expensive. It would forever deprive the country of the positive results of the protective system, for which a whole generation has made sacrifices; it would upset the industries which we have created with so much effort just when they were ready to repay the nation for its sacrifices.

It would be very dangerous to rely on the competition of foreign goods for the lowering of our prices. But we can attain the same results with the help of the competition of foreign capital, which, by coming into Russia, will help Russian enterprise to promote native industry and speed up the accumulation of native capital....

15. Justification for Imperial Expansion

In 1864, a high Russian official, Prince Alexander Mikhailovich Gorchakov, notified the foreign powers of Russia's occupation of what is now part of the Uzbekistan. His letter, with its talk of savages and their need for peace, as well as its claim that Russia must expand in accordance with its destiny, suggests many parallels with contemporary writings of English and French writers about their duties in their growing empires in Africa and East Asia.

...The situation of Russia in central Asia is similar to that of all civilized states that come into contact with half-savage nomadic tribes without a firm social organization. In such cases, the interests of border security and trade relations always require that the more civilized state have a certain authority over its neighbors, whose wild and unruly customs render them very troublesome. It begins first by curbing raids and pillaging. To put an end to these, it is often compelled to reduce the neighboring tribes to some degree of close subordination. Once this result has been achieved, the latter take on more peaceful habits, but in their turn they are exposed to the attack of tribes living farther off. . . The state therefore must make a choice: either to give up this continuous effort and doom its borders to constant unrest, which would make prosperity, safety, and cultural progress impossible here, or else to advance farther and farther into the heart of the savage lands, where the vast distances, with every step forward, increase the difficulties and hardships it incurs. Such has been the fate of all states placed in a similar situation. The United States of America, France in Africa, Holland in its colonies, England in the East Indies—they all were inevitably driven to choose the path of onward movement, not so much from ambition as from dire necessity, where the greatest difficulty lies in being able to stop....

From A.M. Gorchakov in G. Vernadsky, et al. editors, *A Source Book for Russian History From Early Times to 1917,* Vol. 3, New Haven, 1972.

16. The Worker's Life under the Last Tsar

The conditions in which workers lived in Russia at the end of the nineteenth century were terrible by modern standards, and sound much like those Charles Dickens described in London more than fifty years before. Such conditions seem to be common in the early stages of industrialization. Henri Troyat describes these conditions as seen by a fictional traveler, Russell, who tells here what he saw when he visited a suburb of Moscow with his Russian guide, Paul Egorovitch Sychkin. Karl Marx had theorized that peasants would never organize or overthrow their landlords because they lived in isolation from one another, whereas workers, crowded together, would see that their shared interest lay in getting rid of the capitalistic factory owners. Troyat puts a similar observation into the mouth of Paul Egorovitch Sychkin.

...Whatever his occupation, every worker when engaged received a booklet from his employer, in which the conditions of his employment, the payment of wages, deductions in the form of fines, rents and various liabilities were recorded, and, should the occasion arise, the reason for his dismissal. In brief, it was a sort of professional passport which, together with his official passport, ended by fixing an individual's capabilities and predisposed him to accept his inferior status.

Russell, who thought his own country a century ahead of Russia in social progress, was surprised to learn that the employment of children of less than twelve years and the employment of women at night had been forbidden is Russia...and that in Russia there was a medical service at large factories (of more than 100 workers), and that employers' responsibility in the matter of working accidents was constantly recognized....

[The Russian, Sychkin, explains to Russell how the Russian workers live.]

In your country the workers live where they like and usually quite a long way from the factory. Even when they are settled in dwellings specially built by their employer, they pay rent in exchange. In short, they forget the factory atmosphere when they go home. In Russia, on the contrary, half the workers live gratuitously, either in the workshops themselves or in huge buildings attached to the factories. This is explained by the fact that in Russia the majority of the population is rural and the peasant who comes to town to seek employment is obviously unable to find a room at a low cost. Moreover, in their *izba* they have acquired the habit of living six, eight or ten together in a smoky room. Why should they be more refined now? If you want to understand the life of the Russian worker you must visit a few of these houses exclusively occupied by the workers and their families.

Abridged from Henri Troyat, *Daily Life in Russia Under the Last Tsar,* Malcolm Barnes, translator, London, 1961.

Under the guidance of Paul Egorovitch Sychkin, it did not take Russell long to see that all the large factories were flanked by grey and dejected buildings of several stories, which were simply warehouses of labour. The same architectural style was recognizable in all: they were civilian barracks. Inside, a dark and narrow corridor was flanked by thin plank doors, which opened into dormitories for twenty or thirty workers or into minute rooms *(kamorki)* each sheltering several families. Each family strove to mark off its modest domain in the *kamorka* with hangings made of old pieces of cloth and plaited mats. But these flimsy partitions were not enough to ensure the privacy of couples. The beds (simple plank bunks) touched one another. One chair and one table served ten persons. Men, women and children mingled their voices, odours, illnesses, quarrels and reconciliations. Yet the tenants of a *kamorka* were envied by those who lived in the dormitories. There the bunks stood side by side without the least separation. Often they were placed one above the other, the highest being about two feet below the ceiling. The workers did their washing in the room and dried it on lines strung from wall to wall. A sour odour came from these rags as they dripped upon the muddy floor. The casement windows were clearly too small to permit the ventilation of the premises. In any case, they were carefully nailed up and blocked in.

This kind of dormitory was generally reserved for single men. Nevertheless, Paul Egorovitch Sychkin showed Russell some communal rooms in which, as a result of overpopulation at the factory, women, couples and complete families lived among the bachelors. The beds were separated by wooden partitions fixed to their frames and rising to a height of about three feet six inches. Thus each household had its compartment and the room resembled a stable. According to Sychkin, in certain workers' houses the tenants had on the average only two square yards of space and three or four cubic yards of air per person. And these figures took account only of the number of occupants at a given moment. Now, all the big factories worked continuously, and quite often the same beds were occupied turn and turn about by two workers, one on day shift and the other on night shift. Because of this relief system the dormitory was never empty. In such conditions the quantity of breathable air calculated by Sychkin must be reduced again by half. Appalled by these details, Russell wondered why the Russian worker, himself so badly housed, was not content till he had made his family leave the village to join him.

'It's very simple,' said Paul Egorovitch Sychkin. 'Having left his own people to work in the town, a man soon sees that he doesn't get money enough to keep both himself and those whom he has left in the country. In forcing his wife and children to join him, he reckons that they will be hired at the factory for a fair wage and that their housing will raise no problem. Doubtless to encourage this kind of family migration, the big manufacturers have built such barracks on their factory land. The Russian peasant has a robust constitution. Comfort and hygiene do not interest him. He almost distrusts them. What he wants is a corner in which to lie down on bare boards for not too much money. Now the dormitory is always free of charge, and the *kamorki,* at the very most, are let for a deduction of one per cent of the wage, or virtually nothing, so the worker writes home. His wife and children arrive, and the whole lot pile up in some stifling den, already overcrowded with two families, or in the communal room with worn-out bodies strewn upon their litters all around them. With the help of bits of cardboard and cloth hung from nails, the women try to make a refuge in which to protect themselves against indiscreet glances. But no one pays any attention to them. The men are too worn out during the week and on Sundays most of them are drunk. According to statistics which I have consulted, the proportion of women working in the factories in 1855 was 33 per cent, and today it has risen to 44 per cent. In the textile industries they represent as much as 77 per cent of the staff. We are watching a strange phenomenon. So long as the worker's family lives far away from him in the country, he keeps his ties with the soil and with the patriarchal customs of former times. He returns to the village from time to time in order to share in the work in the fields. He knows that there he has his roof, his friends, his graves, his memories. This nostalgic attraction ends abruptly as soon as our man has been able to make his wife and children come and settle in the great barrack. All are employed in the same factory. They have sold their little shanty. They are no longer peasants. And they are proud of it! Gradually a new class is born, homeless, without regrets and without traditions, who have no possessions of their own and live from day to day, lost in an anonymous mass of people just like themselves. As a result of living so close together, they acquire a vague awareness of their strength. Just consider that at the present moment there are no more than two and a half million workers in Russia for a total population of 129 millions. Nevertheless, one can already speak of a "workers' will," while the Russian peasants, many times more numerous, are far from showing the same cohesion in defending their interests.

17. Vladimir Ilyich Lenin: The Organization of the Party

Lenin published a long pamphlet, What is to be Done? *in 1902. It was a vehement attack on his rivals for leadership of the Marxist workers movement. It also gave his blueprint for party organization, a blueprint closely followed both before and after the revolution of 1917. Lenin emphasizes the need for a small, tightly disciplined, secret, vanguard party† to educate and lead the workers. He also makes a distinction between scientific and democratic socialism,† the first and correct type requiring knowledge, and justifying leadership by an elite. The second, democratic socialism, according to Lenin, grows muddled, acts "spontaneously" and will never accomplish the revolution. This distinction later justified many authoritarian practices of the Bolsheviks. Even today, the term "scientific socialism"† is used as a code word by which the Soviets indicate approval of a Marxist regime. For definitions of words used by Lenin that have a special meaning, consult Glossary.*

Without revolutionary theory there can be no revolutionary movement....

The German workers have for the moment been placed in the vanguard of the proletarian struggle. How long events will allow them to occupy this post of honour cannot be foretold. But let us hope that as long as they occupy it, they will fill it fittingly. This demands redoubled efforts in every field of struggle and agitation. In particular, it will be the duty of the leaders to gain an ever clearer insight into all theoretical questions, to free themselves more and more from the influence of traditional phrases inherited from the old world outlook, and constantly to keep in mind that socialism since it has become a science, demands that it be pursued as a science, i.e., that it be studied. The task will be to spread with increased zeal among the masses of the workers the ever more clarified understanding thus acquired, to knit together ever more firmly the organization both of the party and of the trade unions....

The strength of the present-day movement lies in the awakening of the masses (principally, the industrial proletariat) and its weakness lies in the lack of consciousness and initiative among the revolutionary leaders....

The strikes that followed the famous St. Petersburg industrial war of 1896 assumed a similar general character. Their spread over the whole of Russia clearly showed the depth of the newly awakening popular movement, and if we are to speak of the "spontaneous element" then, of course, it is this strike movement which, first and foremost, must be regarded as spontaneous....

The workers were not [in 1890s], and could not be, conscious of the irreconcilable antagonism of their interests to the whole of the modern political and

Abridged from V.I. Lenin, "What Is To Be Done?" *Collected Works,* Vol. 5, Moscow, 1964.

social system, i.e., theirs was not yet Social-Democratic consciousness. In this sense, the strikes of the nineties, despite the enormous progress they represented as compared with the "revolts," remained a purely spontaneous movement.

We have said that there could not have been Social-Democratic consciousness among the workers. It would have to be brought to them from without. The history of all countries shows that the working class, exclusively by its own effort, is able to develop only trade union consciousness, i.e., the conviction that it is necessary to combine in unions, fight the employers, and strive to compel the government to pass necessary labour legislation, etc. The theory of socialism, however, grew out of the philosophic, historical, and economic theories elaborated by educated representatives of the propertied classes, by intellectuals. By their social status, the founders of modern scientific socialism, Marx and Engels, themselves belonged to the bourgeois† intelligentsia....

Since there can be no talk of an independent ideology formulated by the working masses themselves in the process of their movement, the only choice is—either bourgeois or socialist ideology. There is no middle course (for mankind has not created a "third" ideology, and moreover, in a society torn by class antagonisms there can never be a non-class or an above-class ideology). Hence to belittle the socialist ideology in any way, to turn aside from it in the slightest degree means to strengthen bourgeois ideology....

In order to become a Social-Democrat, the worker must have a clear picture in his mind of the economic nature and the social and political features of the landlord and the priest, the high state official and the peasant, the student and the vagabond; he must know their strong and weak points; he must grasp the meaning of all the catch-words and sophisms by which each class and each stratum camouflages its selfish strivings and its real "inner workings."...

Class political consciousness can be brought to the workers only from without....

[Lenin here describes the vanguard party.]

A small, compact core of the most reliable, experienced, and hardened workers, with responsible representatives in the principal districts and connected by all the rules of strict secrecy with the organization of revolutionaries, can, with the widest support of the masses and without any formal organization, perform all the functions of a trade-union organization, in a manner, moreover, desirable to Social-Democracy. Only in this way can we secure the consolidation and development of a Social-Democratic trade-union movement, despite all the gendarmes [policemen]....

I assert that it is far more difficult to unearth a dozen wise men than a hundred fools. This position I will defend, no matter how much you instigate the masses against me for my "anti-democratic" views, etc. As I have stated repeatedly, by "wise men," in connection with organization, I mean professional revolutionaries, irrespective of whether they have developed from among students or working men, I assert: (1) that no revolutionary movement can endure without a stable organization of leaders maintaining continuity; (2) that the broader the popular mass drawn spontaneously into the struggle, which forms of the basis of the movement and participates in it, the more urgent the need for such an organization, and the more solid this organization must be (for it is much easier for all sorts of demagogues to side-track the more backward sections of the masses); (3) that such an organization must consist chiefly of people profession- ally engaged in revolutionary activities; (4) that in an autocratic state, the more we confine the membership of such an organization to people who are professionally engaged in revolutionary activity and who have been professionally trained in the art of combating the political police, the more difficult it will be to unearth the organization; and (5) the greater will be the number of people from the working class and from the other social classes who will be able to join the movement and perform active work in it....

The active and widespread participation of the masses will not suffer: on the contrary, it will benefit by the fact that a "dozen" experienced revolu- tionaries, trained professionally, no less than the police, will centralize all the secret aspects of the work—the drawing up of leaflets, the working out of approx- imate plans; and the appointing of bodies of leaders for each urban district, for each factory district, and for each educational institution....

Try to fit this picture into the frame of our autocracy! Is it conceivable in Russia for all "who accept the principles of the Party programme and render the Party all possible support" to control every action of the revolutionary working in secret? Is it possible for all to elect one of these revolutionaries to any particular office, when, in the very interests of the work, the revolutionary must conceal his identity from nine out of ten of these "all?" Reflect somewhat over the real mean- ing of the high-sounding phrases...and you will realize that "broad democracy" in Party organization, amidst the gloom of the autocracy and the domination of the gendarmerie, is nothing more than a useless and harmful toy. It is a useless toy because, in point of fact, no revolutionary organization has ever practiced, or could practice, broad democracy, however much it may have desired to do so. It is a harmful toy because any attempt to practice "the broad democratic principle" will simply facilitate the work of the police in carrying out large-scale raids, will perpetuate the prevailing primitiveness, and will divert the thoughts of the prac- tical workers from the serious and pressing task of training themselves to become professional revolutionaries to that of drawing up detailed "paper" rules for elec- tion systems. Only abroad, where very often people with no opportunity for con- ducting really active work gather, could this "playing at democracy" develop here and there, especially in small groups....

18. The Potemkin Mutiny

One of the most dramatic events during the revolutionary year 1905 in Russia was the mutiny of the sailors of the battleship "Potemkin" in The Black Sea in June. The ostensible cause was the sailors' objection to being fed meat that was full of maggots, or worms. In reality, however, the mutiny resulted from all the same problems that affected Russia as a whole: poor living and working conditions, and a weak leadership which appeared to be divided and unable to bring reform. As such, the mutiny was both a symbol and a microcosm of Russian society at the time.

What were a few maggots? It was excellent meat. The ship's senior surgeon, Honorable Counsellor Smirnov, had pronounced it of first quality. There was, he said, no justification for the complaints.

The disturbance which had begun as a murmur at dawn, circulating gently, had then spread and grown in volume and bitterness. Like oilmen at a gusher, the ship's agitators had risen to the occasion and fought to tame these sudden riches to their purpose. It had been their busiest morning since the November uprising at Sevastopol, and by the time the dinner gongs were sounding at midday, they had succeeded in creating an atmosphere of threatening purpose. Mutiny was in the air, bearing down on the battleship Potemkin with the inevitability of a predicted typhoon.

Until that morning of June 27, 1905, Captain Eugene N. Golikov of the Potemkin had every reason to be satisfied with the state of morale in his ship. Compared with many others in the Black Sea Fleet, his crew had seemed free of strong revolutionary elements, and there had been no trouble ashore during the period of the refit she had just completed at Sevastopol. Vice-Admiral Krieger, temporarily commanding in the absence of Admiral Chukhnin, must also have felt confident of the Potemkin's loyalty to have detached her at a time when reports of increasing seditious activity were reaching him from every battleship in the fleet. There had even been rumors of a general mutiny of the Black Sea Fleet, timed to take place during the imminent summer maneuvers; but Captain Golikov, not being of an alarmist nature, had discounted these. With the disastrous Far Eastern war against Japan reaching its closing stages, rumors of every kind were rife in both the services, however distant from the fighting front. The pressure of discontent among the peasants and new factory classes might be rapidly increasing to the point of detonation; that was common knowledge ashore at Sevastopol and in the wardrooms of every unit of the Black Sea Fleet. But Captain Golikov of the Potemkin had no apparent cause for serious anxiety about the loyalty of his crew....

[On June 26, the Potemkin anchored near Odessa. The captain sent a boat to Odessa for provisions. They returned in the evening]...with sacks of flour,

Abridged from R. Hough, *The Potemkin Mutiny,* New York, 1960.

groceries, wine and delicasies for the Potemkin's wardroom. Spread in a row across her little deck were the big carcasses of beef which were destined for the Potemkin's caldrons to be made into the crew's staple diet of meat *borsch*. [soup] There was enough of it to last the cooks until the ship was joined by the rest of the Black Sea Fleet for the summer maneuvers, due to start on July 4. Later in the evening the meat was hoisted aboard the battleship and hung up on the spar deck from hooks.

If decay had already set in, on that evening it was too dark for anyone to observe it; and it was not until the following morning that the attention of a sailor on the four-to-eight watch swabbing down the spar deck was drawn to the carcasses by their evil smell. On closer inspection he saw that the meat was riddled with white maggots, and that they were active. Perhaps it had been spoiled before it had been purchased in Odessa, or exposure to the heat, exceptional even for the Black Sea in June, may have caused it to spoil. Within minutes a small group of men, carrying buckets and swabs and with their sleeves and bell-bottoms rolled up, were standing around the obscene swinging objects. The crowd grew as the word spread down to the crew's quarters and to the mess decks, where the forenoon watch was breakfasting on black bread and tea. When the watches changed there were more than a hundred men in an unorganized protest demonstration, humming with indignation and pushing one another in order to get a close look at the squirming maggots.

The men were shouting their protests when one of the "conductors," or petty officers, hurried along to investigate, and he could recognize certain voices raised above the others among the cries of "It's not fit for pigs," "Let's get the doctor to look at it," "Chuck the stinking stuff overboard." It was evident that the agitators were already hard at work. The men fell back hesitantly at the petty officer's orders, like the big blue flies that had come with the morning sun, but only hovered ready to return with their courage. "All right, but call the doctor," a voice cried out from the back. "Even the Japanese wouldn't feed us with stuff like this."

When news of his crew's disaffection reached Captain Golikov later on the morning of June 27, it is unlikely that he was greatly alarmed. By the standards of the Imperial Russian Navy, and in contrast with his second-in-command and many of his own junior officers, he was a tolerant and even lax commander; and complaints about the food were, after all, common enough in the service. There was no real cause for anxiety yet. From his cabin aft in the Potemkin he sent up a message to his senior surgeon asking him to inspect the carcasses and to report their condition to him.

Surgeon Smirnov, a tall, narrow-faced officer dressed in his full-length coat, carrying the three black stars of his rank on his silver epaulettes, left the wardroom at once and proceeded, accompanied by a petty officer, forward to the spar deck, where a small group of sailors was still gathered. This hard core had refused to disperse, and had already witnessed the arrival and departure of the ship's butchers with sufficient meat for that day's dinner. Smirnov recognized the attitude of unusual defiance and insubordination in the men by the manner in which they glanced at him and only reluctantly allowed him to break through.

"Now what's all this about—what's all this about?" Smirnov demanded of them. He covered what must have been the first traces of fear by bustling officiously and talking loudly as he slipped on his pince-nez and bent down to look at the carcasses. His examination was brief and cursory. "It's excellent meat," he told the petty officer. "Nothing wrong with it. Just a wash with some vinegar, that's all it needs." And he pushed past the men again to report this satisfactory and reassuring news to his captain.

So far as Captain Golikov was concerned the incident was over: it had been no more than a minor flare-up, of the kind that had become unhappily frequent in a fleet cut off from the Far Eastern fighting of the Russo-Japanese War, and demoralized by the news of the defeats in Manchuria and the almost total destruction of the rest of the Imperial Navy. At the same time the men were acutely aware of the great social upheavals that were occuring all over the Empire, from Warsaw to Vladivostok, St. Petersburg to the Crimea....As a precautionary measure, for Surgeon Smirnov had indicated that the men had shown unusual insubordination, he ordered a sentry to be posted on the spar deck with a pencil and paper to take the name of any man who approached the meat. They were easily enough scared, these peasant conscripts, and he was confident that this measure would prevent further trouble.

By midday, the wind had died, the sea was calm, and the sun beat down almost vertically on the empty decks of the battleship. The Potemkin, brilliant in her paintwork, as spotless and outwardly placid as if prepared for a royal review, seemed far removed from acts of violence. There was only one officer aboard who continued to feel concern about the state of unrest of the men. He was Commander Ippolit Giliarovsky, the tough, uncompromising disciplinarian and second-in-command—a young and handsome aristocrat who was the most feared and hated officer in the ship. Giliarovsky made it his business to be more closely acquainted with the real state of morale of the ship's crew than his captain, both by frequent inspections and by regular consultations with certain of the most trusted petty officers. Word had already reached his ears that a dangerous change had come over the men, that the troublemakers aboard the ship had succeeded in converting, at least temporarily, to the cause of the revolution many previously uncommitted crew members. Where pamphlets and persuasion had failed in the weeks past, some stinking carcasses were succeeding.

While his fellow officers answered the "dine-and-wine" call from the wardroom, Giliarovsky made a sudden escorted tour of the mess decks forward to make sure that his anxieties were without foundation. He at once found the men even more uneasy and threatening than he had feared. The place was in a state of uproar, sailors shouting their defiance and beating their eating irons on the mess tables. It appeared as if a major riot might break out at any moment. The caldrons of meat borsch were steaming and ready in the ship's caboose, or galley, but not one among the six hundred or so men present was eating it.

Giliarovsky, still unnoticed by all but a few men, walked rapidly over to the open serving hatches and demanded to know what was going on and why the men were not eating.

"They won't touch their borsch, sir" he was told by Ivan Daniluc, one of the cooks. "They said we ought to throw it overboard—and the rest of the meat as well." He pointed to the nearest table. "You see, sir, they're only eating their bread and water, though they've asked us for tea and butter."

Giliarovsky turned angrily on the men nearest the hatches who had now quieted down under the threat of his proximity, and attempted to make his voice heard above the cries from the rest of the crew. "Silence, do you hear?" he shouted. "What do you think you're doing? This is a disgraceful demonstration. Why don't you eat your borsch?"

Half lost in the confusion of shouts and jeers, Giliarovsky could just make out one or two broken sentences: "Because the meat is stinking!" "Eat it yourself—we'll stick to bread and water."

Seeing that conditions were now out of hand, and being anxious to avoid further humiliation, Giliarovsky departed to consult his captain....

The pace of events on the Potemkin was now rapidly increasing as more and more among both officers and men became aware that a crisis was at hand and acted accordingly. Giliarovsky interrupted Captain Golikov's luncheon, which he was taking in his cabin, and reported on the situation. "Something will have to be done, sir, right away," he told him urgently.

Golikov agreed, but, as a naturally cautious man, he was not in favor of too hasty action. He rang for a messenger and told him to ask both the chief surgeon and his assistant, Dr. Golenko, to report to him at once. Golikov liked to be certain of his facts before finally making a decision. Asked to confirm once again that the meat was fresh and that there was no justification for the men's refusal to eat it, Smirnov had difficulty in controlling his patience. He did not care for his word to be doubted.

"Very well, Doctor, and thank you," the ship's captain said. "Commander Giliarovsky, will you please order the drums to be beaten for roll call on the quarter-deck."

It was one o'clock and time for the afternoon watch to take over, when Captain Eugene Golikov left his cabin for the last time as commander of his ship, and made his way up to the quarter-deck with the officer-of-the-watch, Junior Lieutenant Alexeev, and Commander Giliarovsky. The entire ship's company of some 670 men, with the exception of the other officers who remained in the wardroom, was already assembled aft, in line upon line and along both sides of the stern 12-inch gun turret. They were dressed in their summer uniform of white bell-bottoms, white jumper over blue-and-white striped jersey, and cap with long ribbon tail falling down the back. They looked neat and clean, and but for their mustaches, the Slavic set of their dark features, and short stature, might almost have been the crew of a Royal Navy battleship on the Mediterranean station, or a U.S. warship in the Pacific, awaiting inspection.

They also appeared to have lost entirely their spirit of sedition at the prospect of a general dressing-down from their captain, and their silence and orderly appearance must have reassured Golikov in his confidence in their loyalty as he passed through the gap in the ranks left for him. He was a heavily built man, and he mounted the capstan in the center of the quarter-deck with some difficulty.

From his superior height, Captain Golikov glanced over the close-packed ranks....He was well aware that there was hardly a real seaman among them. Except for the conductors and petty officers and a few long-service men, they were nearly all conscripts, almost illiterate, and crude in their habits, men who had never got their feet wet and who would still be doubled over the soil in Bessarabia or the Ukraine but for the Far Eastern war. They should be treated, he may have decided, sternly, but simply, more as recalcitrant children than as dangerous insurrectionists.

"We have repeatedly told you," he began in a strong voice, "that disorders like these are utterly forbidden in a warship of the Imperial Navy. You don't appear to understand that for stirring up a demonstration you can be strung up on the yard-arm." And he pointed to the mast to underline his threat...Now, men, let us have no more of this nonsense. Whoever is willing to eat the borsch, step forward two paces.

For a moment there was silence and not a man moved. Then slowly, as if impelled forward, a number of the petty officers, and bosuns, and a few of the older men broke ranks. But none followed, and suddenly the silence on the quarterdeck had become more dangerously threatening than the tumult on the mess deck earlier.

"Very well, then," called out Golikov with finality, as if about to act on his threat, "if you won't eat your borsch, there is nothing else for it. I shall seal some of the meat in a bottle for the analysts and report the whole matter to the commander in chief. He shall decide what shall be done with you. You are dismissed." The captain climbed down from the capstan and without another word or a glance at his men hurried off back to his cabin as if fearing pursuit. Lieutenant Alexeev followed at his heels....

The ringleaders could not have asked for a more complete capitulation. But if they were surprised and even caught off their guard by this sudden turn of events, Commander Giliarovsky was horrified. After this victory he knew that the men would be quite uncontrollable and the state of the ship must become anarchic. What could have come over the captain to treat them so leniently? Giliarovsky decided to take the initiative at once before everything was lost. Leaping onto the capstan even before Golikov was out of sight, he called out, "Reform ranks—at attention! Bosun, call out the guard—and bring a tarpaulin."

Only a few among the older men, and the corporals, petty officers, and warrant officers, understood the possible significance of this order. Under old naval disciplinary practice, now long superseded, a ship's commander would call out a firing squad and, to preserve as far as possible the impersonal element to the proceedings, order a sailcloth to be thrown over mutineers before having them shot. Furious as he was, it is unlikely that Giliarovsky had any intention of acting on the threat implied behind his order. Discipline in the Imperial Navy was no more and no less severe than in the British or United States navies, and if rather more individual latitude was allowed to senior officers—in the way of flogging, for example,—Giliarovsky knew that he was limited to ordering a seaman fifteen lashes or a month's imprisonment, and that if he exceeded his powers he would be in serious trouble.

Commander Giliarcvsky was bluffing, there seems little doubt of that, and the first response among the men, after the order had been barked out so loudly that none could fail to hear it, appeared to justify the bluff. Rapidly the word spread around, circulating like ripples from the men who knew that a tarpaulin meant death by shooting, that the ringleaders would soon be facing the firing squad. From amidships came the steady hammer beat of a marching squad; and preceding them came eight corporals in peaked caps carrying at a half trot the heavy tarpaulin. Giliarovsky, tall, imposing, and threatening, stared impassively over the heads of the men and awaited from the capstan the arrival of the firing squad. This action he was taking on his own initiative might be drastic and even dangerous, but he was confident of its efficacy.

It was men like Afanasy Matushenko, Fyodor Mikishkin, and Josef Dymtchenko who had been working all morning to create purpose and direction from the disaffection on the lower decks. Torpedo Quartermaster Matushenko was the supreme revolutionary commander and official Social Democratic leader in the Potemkin, a short, sturdy, vigorous-looking man, with high Slavic cheekbones and with the intent glitter of the zealot in his little dark eyes. There was not a man on the battleship's lower decks who had not witnessed or surrendered to Matushenko's powers of persuasion; and though many might be weary of his continued hectoring and pamphleteering, and others were afraid of his consciousness of power and fanaticism, he was widely respected and recognized as a man of great courage and daring. The converted, Matushenko knew, would follow him anywhere; the rest would follow behind like the simple peasants they were.

Matushenko and his lieutenants now suddenly recognized that the moment had come to touch off the charge that had so fortuitously been laid to their fuse. First the spoiled meat and the surgeon's refusal to condemn it; and now this unexpected threat of violence. If the officers had set out to conspire their own destruction, they could hardly have arranged events more conveniently. Matushenko had to calculate only the moment to strike, and that moment was fast approaching.

"Now we'll try again," began Giliarovsky, seemingly oblivious to the obsessed, ominous air that now hung over the crew as he awaited their decision. "All those prepared to eat the borsch, step forward."

Again there was a moment of uncertainty, and again the almost apologetic step forward by the older men. Giliarovsky waited, still confident that the presence of the armed guard would this time turn the tide. A few more followed, but not more than fifty in all. His patience was fast draining away, faster than the courage of the men.

"So it's mutiny, is it?" he called out in a voice that one listener described as "so strange that one could scarcely recognize it." "All right, we know how to deal with that. If you think there is no discipline in the Navy, then I'll show you how wrong you are. Bosun, bring the ringleaders here."

With two members of the guard, the bosun walked boldly into the tight ranks, arbitrarily selecting a man here, a man there, who was dragged away by the guard until a dozen seamen were grouped in an untidy huddle by the rails.

"Now throw the tarpaulin over them," he ordered the corporals who had been standing by, "and we'll see what the other mutineers have to say." Once again he turned back to the men, and at his third appeal there was an unmistakable note of hysteria in his voice. "Those who will eat their borsch are dismissed. Anyone who remains can see for himself what we do with mutineers in the Navy."

It will never be known whether, at this point, the Potemkin's first officer suddenly recognized that his bluff had been called and that he was committed to ordering the squad to fire, or whether he realized that, like his captain, he would be obliged finally to capitulate. But if he was gripped by uncertainty, the period of agonized indecision was brief. From the rear of the starboard section of men Afanasy Matushenko was edging his way forward, speaking quietly to the men he passed. The other ringleaders followed his example, like beaters edging through standing corn, and the agitation that followed in their train broke up the final semblance of symmetry in the ranks. Ahead was the double line of sailors, at their sides the rifles brilliantly silvered where the sun caught the bayonet blades; beyond stood the manifestation of their fear, sword hanging low at his side, the stars of his rank clear on his shoulders; and beyond again, huddled and poignant beneath the tarpaulin and with only their shuffling feet visible, were the men awaiting execution....

Matushenko now forced his way toward the front ranks with increased determination, pushing the men aside and calling out to the members of the firing squad. "Don't shoot your own comrades—you can't kill your own shipmates! Don't fire, comrades!" The appeal rapidly spread, voice rising above voice.

"Get yourselves rifles and ammunition," came the cries. "We're taking over the ship."

With these words, full-scale mutiny had been irrevocably invoked, and nothing could save the Potemkin and her officers. The undecided were caught up in the sudden flood tide, and even those who were to remain loyal in spirit to authority were swept along. Some seven hundred men were running amok, and only a fusillade could have quelled them.

In those agonized seconds, Commander Giliarovsky must have been well aware of this, and, whatever his earlier intentions may have been, now he shouted directly at the squad to open fire. Like his captain, he had a low opinion of the courage of the men and was confident that the sound of shots alone could break the uprising. But he had underestimated the strength of leadership the ringleaders had acquired. The men were already beyond control; many were racing toward the spar deck and the armory. The squad was resolute only in its refusal to raise its rifles, more fearful of the wrath of the mob than of the unarmed officer still futilely ordering them to shoot.

Now desperate, Giliarovsky leaped down from the capstan and wrenched a rifle from the nearest man. "So you're in on this, too, are you?" he called out to the rest of the blue jackets furiously. "You obey orders or—"

At that moment the first shot rang out, the first bullet sang overhead.

Like any warship, the Potemkin had known only that order which is governed by a strict code of discipline since she had first been commissioned five years before. In no other circumstances is insurrection so sharp in its application, the contrast between restraint and anarchy so appalling in its impact, as on a man-of-war in peacetime, when hundreds of men live packed in their steel shell for no other purpose than to conform to the strict routine of their existence. In the Potemkin the situation was irritated even further by the hot spirit of revolution then infusing the whole nation; hate and despair had found their way down to the lower decks of every vessel in the Black Sea Fleet. No other mutiny in history can have flared up so quickly into flames as searing and uncontrollable as the mutiny in the battleship Potemkin.

Able seaman Gregori Vakulinchuk was the first to return from the armory, where the rifles stood pyramid-stacked, at the end of the gun deck. It had been a frenzied race involving only the most determined men, while many more hovered uncertainly or ran and shouted without purpose, aware only of the confusion that reigned without obvious cause all about them, recognizing intuitively that self-survival depended on remaining neutral for the present.

Vakulinchuk had fired that first shot, but it might have been from a starter's pistol fired high only for effect.

Giliarovsky ran to meet him, shooting with hasty aim and without effect twice across the quarter-deck, and closed with the mutineer near the 12-inch gun turret hatch. Vakulinchuk tried to bring his rifle to bear on the officer, but Giliarovsky got his shot in first, and Vakulinchuk crumpled up, half in and half out of the turret.

Afanasy Matushenko was at the head of a group of armed seamen who came off the spar deck at that moment. He saw the wounded man lying at Giliarovsky's feet. He saw Giliarovsky swing his rifle around, take aim, and fire twice, missing both times; and then heard him calling out, "Drop your rifle—do you hear? Drop your rifle."

"You'll have to kill me first," Matushenko replied. "Get off the ship. It belongs to us now."

Again Giliarovsky raised his rifle, but Matushenko was too quick for him. A single shot rang out and the Potemkin's first officer fell dead to the deck.... [The mutineers shot the gunnery officer next]

It was time to organize the mutiny, to drive out from cover the other officers, and to take formal control of the battleship.

"Come on, comrades, hunt them down," a voice was urging them from the top of the big gun turret. "The ship's not ours yet." And at once the blooded pack was off in full cry, spreading out on the main deck, the spar deck, and the gun deck, down gangways to the lower compartments of the ship, and aft to the wardroom and officer's quarters....

19. The Duma of 1906

This account of the Duma of 1906 conveys the democratic and hopeful spirit of that gathering. The writer of this selection, Bernard Pares, a visiting English historian, was an eyewitness to the events he describes.

He emphasizes here and in other of his writings his view that Russia came very close to developing a constitutional government for itself in the days before the outbreak of World War One. Had the Tsar worked with the Duma, as some of his advisors urged him to do, and not dissolved it, as his strongest advisor, Stolypin, successfully persuaded him to do, the country would have taken an important step towards establishing a representative government with limits on the Tsar's autocratic powers.

...The Duma met on May 10, 1906. The Emperor, who had not visited his capital since the attempt made upon his life in January, 1905, in a firm and vigorous voice expressed his hope that the labours of the Assembly would be conducive to the welfare of Russia....

The Duma now settled down to its work of discussing separate Bills. The family atmosphere, which is so noticeable in Russia, was here peculiarly strong. The Assembly, having complete control of its own house, turned it into something like a vast caravanserai [large inn for caravans]. The beautiful hall soon came to be regarded, even by the peasant members, as a kind of home. The long side lobbies were furnished with great tables covered with green baize, at which peasants and Intelligents sat down indiscriminately to write letters to their families. A constant stream of members was always passing through these rooms; and all congregated from time to time in the great noisy corridor. Here the chief leaders walked up and down arm in arm; and isolated peasants, Russian, Cossack,† or Polish, sat about on the different benches and were quite ready to converse with any stranger. Members and correspondents gathered without distinction at the buffet and in the restaurant, and little groups of acquaintances wandered through the pleasant gardens outside. The building contained its own postal and telegraph office. If the Duma did nothing else, it brought together for the first time representatives of every class and of every interest in Russia. It was

Abridged from Bernard Pares, *Russia and Reform,* London, 1907.

of course far more Imperial than any other European Parliament. It would be difficult to imagine a more picturesque gathering. Each man wore the costume of his class. The country gentry of the Intelligents dressed very simply, but there were Russian priests with long beards and hair, a Roman Catholic bishop in skull-cap lined with red, finely accoutred Cossacks from the Caucasus, Bashkirs and Buryats in strange and tinselled Asiatic dress, Polish peasants in the brilliant and martial costumes of their people, and a whole mass of staid, bearded, and top-booted Russian peasants. Strangers easily obtained admittance; and amongst the most picturesque visitors were the so-called "walking deputies" who were sent by peasant constituents to look after their members, and others who had tramped for hundreds of miles to ask the Duma to settle their private disputes. Groups of members and non-members formed in the corridor to discuss without reticence any question of the moment. Small party conferences, sitting in the committee-rooms, seemed in no way disturbed by passing strangers. Miliukov [leader of Constitutional Democrats—Cadets], in the simple dress of an English country gentleman, walked up and down the corridor receiving the suggestions of various party leaders, which seldom induced him to deviate a yard from the tactics upon which he had determined. One noticed that the Cadets as a body quite failed to get hold of the non-party members. These peasants, who would not sink their individuality in any party formula, expressed the most fresh and interesting opinions of all. Count Heyden [a conservative, far to the right of Miliukov], could often be seen discussing matters with them; he understood them, and they understood him; but Miliukov was hardly ever to be seen talking to a non-party man.

Nearly every newspaper published the fullest reports of the sittings, and these were eagerly devoured in distant villages all over the country....

[Pares continues his account]...If I may trust the common conclusions of peasant members from almost every part of the Empire, only the least enterprising of the peasants were still in favour of the communal system of land tenure, though all wished to retain the Village Society. The most cherished dream of the intelligent peasant was that of personal property in land....

It was now proposed, with the hearty concurrence of the Labour Group, to constitute in the country small committees to investigate the land question in each locality; in other words, the Duma was making a bid to gradually become the Government of the country. The tension between the representatives of the people and the Ministers was too severe to last.... [The Tsar hesitated, undecided as to whether or not he should name a Prime Minister from the most numerous party in the Duma. General Trepov urged this course which would be an important step towards creating a truly parliamentary government.]

At Peterhof† the counsels of General Trepov were opposed by Mr. Stolypin, the only Minister who had followed the later debates in the Duma. Stolypin's view was clear and consistent; he recognized Russia as having passed into a constitutional regime: that is to say, there would always be a Duma to join in the work of legislation; but he refused to concede the principle that the Ministers should, as a matter of course, be selected from the party prevailing in the Assembly. He was against the formation of a Cadet Ministry, because it would be compelled by its pledges to surrender almost all the power of the administrative system in a single day. The Duma was at war with the Government; if the Government would not make way for a Cadet Ministry, the only step left for it was to dissolve the Duma. The discussion of the two views at Peterhof was long; but by the evening of Saturday, July 21, the view of Mr. Stolypin had prevailed, and the Emperor had signed the decree of dissolution [of the Duma]. The decree expressed in no uncertain terms the Emperor's disappointment at what he regarded as the factious spirit of the Duma. It was read out in churches and posted up in public places all over the Empire; Stolypin himself accepted office as the new Prime Minister.

The dissolution of the Duma was the victory of a single strong-minded man.

Russia had reached a new turning-point in the movement for liberation. There was no question that the people, educated by the events of the last few years into an interest in public affairs, were slowly beginning to find their feet in the new world of politics, and that extremes both of reaction and of revolution were becoming more and more distasteful to them; but as there was now no central and controlling formula, the tension became greater, and violence became more and more possible....

20. Felix Youssoupoff: The Murder of Rasputin

By 1916, Rasputin's influence in the court of Nicholas II had grown immensely. In the previous year, the Tsar had left Petrograd to take direct command of Russian armies at the front. His wife, the Tsaritsa Alexandra, was thus in charge of the court. She relied for advice almost completely on the corrupt peasant Rasputin. Late in 1916, a group of prominent men decided that the situation was intolerable, and that it was their duty to save the Russian state by murdering Rasputin. On the night of December 16, the conspirators gathered in Prince Felix Youssoupoff's palace in Petrograd, and while the others waited upstairs, Youssoupoff invited Rasputin to have drinks with him in the dining-room, having previously poisoned some of the wine.

...Time passed. I began to get impatient. I poured out two glasses, one for him [Rasputin], the other for myself. I placed his glass in front of him and began to drink out of my own, thinking that he would follow my example.

"Well, let me try it," said Rasputin, stretching out his hand for the wine. It was not poisoned.

Why I first gave him wine in an unpoisoned glass I am at a loss to explain.

Abridged from Prince Felix Youssoupoff, *The End of Rasputin,* New York, 1927.

He drank it with obvious pleasure. He became animated. "Now give me some Madeira," he said.

I got up to take another glass, but he protested. "Pour it into this one."

I had to give way.

By an apparent accident, however, I soon managed to knock his glass to the floor, where it smashed.

I took advantage of this to pour wine into one of the glasses containing cyanide of potassium.

He drank slowly, taking small sips at a time, just as if he had been a connoisseur.

His face did not change; but from time to time he put his hand to his throat as if he found slight difficulty in swallowing. He got up and moved about the room, and when I asked him whether anything was the matter, "Oh, nothing much," he said, "just an irritation in the throat."

There was a nerve-racking pause.

"That's very good Madeira. Give me some more."

The poison still had no effect.

I took no notice of the glass which he held out to me, but seized another poisoned one from the tray. I poured wine into it, and passed it to him.

He drained it: and still the poison had no effect.

There remained the third and last glass.

He looked at me with a cunning smile. I seemed to hear him say: "You see! you can't do me any harm."

But all of a sudden his expression changed into one of fiendish hatred.

I felt that he knew why I had brought him there, and what I intended to do to him. A mute and deadly conflict seemed to be taking place between us. A strange feeling of numbness took possession of me. My head reeled...I saw nothing...I do not know how long this lasted....

I regained my presence of mind and offered him some tea.

While I was pouring out tea, he got up and paced the room. His eye fell on the guitar.

"Play something," he begged, "I love the way you sing."

He sat and listened attentively at first; but as I continued, his head dropped towards the table. He seemed half-asleep.

The moment I stopped he opened his eyes and looked at me with a calm and sad expression: "Sing another," he said.

Time passed...The hands of the clock pointed to half-past two. This nightmare had lasted over two hours.

Upstairs, too, patience had evidently become exhausted. The sounds from that quarter became pronounced, and I was afraid that my friends would come down.

"What's all that noise?" asked Rasputin.

"Probably it's the guests going away; I'll go and see."

As I entered the study [my friends] rushed towards me with revolvers in their hands. Questions showered on me.

"The poison has had no effect," I said.

"Impossible," exclaimed the Grand Duke. "The dose was amply sufficient."

With great difficulty I persuaded them to leave me to finish with Rasputin alone. They had qualms on my behalf.

But finally I took the Grand Duke's revolver and went down to the dining-room.

Rasputin was sitting at the table, just as I had left him. His head was sunken and he was breathing heavily.

"Are you feeling unwell?" I asked.

"Yes, my head is heavy and my stomach is burning. Give me another glass—that will ease me."

I poured him some Madeira; he drank it at a gulp and at once revived and regained his good spirits. All of a sudden he suggested that we should go to the gypsies. I refused on the ground that it was too late.

I had been watching every one of his movements in the expectation of a fatal issue; and now he was suggesting that we should go to the gypsies! But what amazed me most was that in spite of his instinctive knowledge and insight, he should now be so utterly unconscious of his approaching end.

How could his sharp eyes fail to observe that, clenched in my hand behind my back, was a revolver?

As this thought flashed through my mind, I looked round for some reason or other, and my glance fell on a crystal crucifix. I rose and went up to it.

"What are you doing over there so long?" asked Rasputin.

"I love this cross; it's a very beautiful thing."

"Yes, it's a nice thing. How much did you pay for it?"

He came towards me.

"Grigori Efimovich, you had better look at the crucifix, and say a prayer before it."

Rasputin looked at me in amazement, and with a trace of fear.

I saw a new and unfamiliar expression in his eyes, a touch of gentleness and submission. He came right up to me, looking me full in the face, and he seemed to read in my glance something which he was not expecting. I realised that the supreme moment was at hand.

"God give me strength to end it all," I thought, and I slowly brought the revolver from behind my back. Rasputin was still standing motionless before me, his head turned to the right, and his eyes on the crucifix.

"Where shall I shoot?" I thought. "Through the temple or through the heart?"

A streak of lightning seemed to run through my body. I fired.

There was a roar as from a wild beast, and Rasputin fell heavily backwards on the bear-skin rug.

I heard a noise on the staircase: my friends were hurrying to my aid.

We examined the wound. The bullet had passed through the region of the heart. There could be no doubt about it; he was dead.

We all felt elated, so convinced were we that the events of the night would deliver Russia from ruin and dishonour....

Chapter Four

Russia in Revolution, 1917-28

FACT: The term "Russian Revolution" is misleading. Actually, there were *two* revolutions in Russia during the year 1917. While they are generally known as the February and October Revolutions, the Soviets celebrate them today in March and November.

Not only were there two revolutions in Russia in 1917, but they were very different. The first, a popular revolt which succeeded in toppling the Romanov dynasty, took place during the second week of March, according to our calendar, known as the Gregorian. At the time, however, Russia was still using the old Julian calendar, whose dates were thirteen days behind the Gregorian. (The Soviets changed to the Gregorian in 1918.) Thus the events that we date from March 8, 1917 began, according to the Russian calendar of the time, on February 24. Hence the term "February Revolution."

The following autumn there was another revolution, of a very different sort. The Bolshevik Party, led by Lenin, overthrew the Provisional Government established by the earlier revolution. Our calendar dates this second, Bolshevik revolution on November 6 and 7, but the Julian dated it on October 24 and 25. It is therefore known as the "October Revolution," but celebrated every November 7 in the Soviet Union. As that country's most important holiday, it parallels our Independence Day, though it is celebrated in somewhat different fashion, with strong militaristic overtones. The dates used in this chapter will be according to the Western calendar.

While the Bolsheviks were able to overthrow the Provisional Government in 1917, it was a full decade before they were able to consolidate their position. This decade, 1917-28, was a chaotic one. During it the Bolsheviks had to cope with a devastating civil war, revolts, a bankrupt economy, severe famine, the untimely death of their leader, Lenin, and the question of who would succeed him. Not until 1928, with these issues resolved, could the Bolsheviks, or Communists, as they came to be called, finally consider their position secure.

1917: THE FEBRUARY REVOLUTION

The February Revolution began in the capital city of Petrograd.

FACT: Because "St. Petersburg" sounded German, Russia's capital city was renamed "Petrograd" in 1914, shortly after the outbreak of World War I. ("Burg" is the German suffix for city, "grad" is the Russian.) Today the city is called "Leningrad."

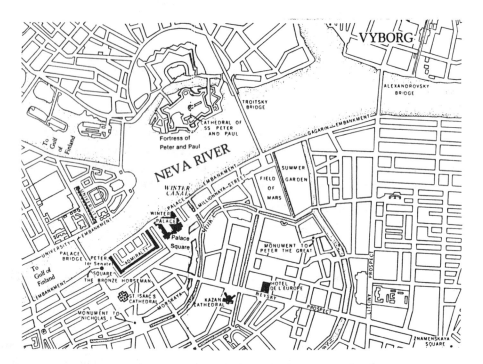

Petrograd at the Time of the Revolution

It erupted quite spontaneously and anonymously at the end of a particularly harsh winter. The participants were not the well-known revolutionary léaders, who were either in jail or exile, but the ordinary people of Petrograd, who were hungry, cold, fed up with the war, and disenchanted with Nicholas II, who seemed unable to remedy the situation.

On March 8, many factory workers went on strike, and began to congregate in the city's streets. (See Readings 1 and 2) In the three following days, more and more joined in, carrying banners calling for "Peace, Land, and Bread." On March 9, the British ambassador cabled London, "Some disorders today, but nothing serious." He could not use these words even one day later, however. By March 10, the disorders had increased, and the city was nearly paralyzed. A general strike was called. Trolleys stopped running. Bread stores closed, as did schools. Nicholas, who was informed of these events while at the front lines with his army, sent a telegram to General Khabalov, who commanded the troops in the city. It read, "I command you to suppress from tomorrow all disorders on the streets of the capital." The Emperor still presumed that a simple order was sufficient to solve such problems.

Unfortunately for him, it wasn't. March 12 proved a turning point when the troops, who were supposed to put an end to the demonstrations, rebelled. These troops were not seasoned soldiers but recently-inducted men who were still civilians at heart, and their sympathies lay with the demonstrators. In 1905, the troops had remained loyal to the Tsar and fired on the Bloody Sunday demonstrators, saving the regime in the process. In 1917, they did not. By the end of the day on March 12, it was really all over. Without the support of the troops, neither government nor Tsar could carry on.

FACT: The Tsar, once Autocrat of All the Russias, ended his reign, and with it the Romanov dynasty, in ignominious fashion. Finally persuaded that he must return to Petrograd to cope with the disturbances, he was prevented from doing so by rebellious railwaymen, and his royal car was shunted to a siding in the city of Pskov. Here on March 15, he was finally persuaded to abdicate, and 304 years of Romanov Tsars came to an end. (See Reading 3)

In Petrograd on March 11, the Duma had appointed a Temporary Committee to act on its behalf during the crisis. This Committee in turn appointed a Provisional Government to carry on the affairs of state until a permanent government could be established. The Provisional Government was an executive group, or cabinet, composed largely of moderate to conservative members, with Alexander Kerensky, a socialist, the only representative of the left wing. The Provisional Government moved swiftly. It granted amnesty to political prisoners, abolished capital punishment, ended all restrictions based on class, creed, or nationality, guaranteed civil rights, instituted an eight-hour working day, and gave labor the right to organize and strike. Finally, it began immediate preparations for the election of a Constituent Assembly, to produce a constitution and permanent government. Unfortunately, these preparations proceeded at a very slow pace. (See Reading 4)

At the same time and in the same building that the Provisional Government was formed, another group also convened. This was the Petrograd Soviet of Workers' Deputies, a body of workers from factory soviets (councils) throughout the city, which had previously appeared briefly in the last months of 1905. This time soldiers were soon added, and it became the Petrograd Soviet of Workers' *and* Soldiers' Deputies: one deputy for approximately 1000 workers, and one for each company of soldiers. The purpose of the Soviet was to represent the interests of the workers and soldiers during this time of change. While the Soviet initially supported the Provisional Government, it did not hesitate to challenge its policies if it did not agree with them. (See Reading 5)

The February Revolution thus produced two political organizations that competed for influence and support. An initial crisis between these two groups developed over control of the armed services. The Soviet feared the army as a potential force for counterrevolution. To decrease this threat, the Soviet, on March 14, issued Order No. 1 to the soldiers and sailors of Petrograd. This Order was designed to reduce the influence of officers in non-combat situations, and to extend the authority of the Soviet to military units through elected political committees of soldiers and sailors within these units. This led to a further breakdown of discipline in an already-demoralized army, which in turn reduced its fighting capability.

The February Revolution resulted in the most autocratic country in the world becoming one of the freest countries in the world, all in the space of a week. Tsardom was gone, and there was the promise of a truly democratic government for the first time in Russian history.

FACT: This great change was accomplished at relatively slight cost: by one reckoning, the February Revolution resulted in only 169 killed and 1,264 wounded.

The significance of these events extended beyond the borders of Russia. Now that Russia was a democracy, the American President Woodrow Wilson found it easier to justify American participation in World War I, with his goal of "making the world safe for democracy." The United States entered that war on April 6, 1917.

1917: FROM MARCH TO NOVEMBER

The sense of freedom felt by Russians following the February Revolution was exhilarating. Political groups proliferated, meetings were held, newspapers and journals appeared in large numbers. At all levels of society and in all parts of the country the current situation was discussed and debated with great enthusiasm and excitement. While there were many variations, the central theme of these discussions was how and how soon the fruits of the Revolution might be enjoyed by all. The peasants wanted land; neither Emancipation nor the Stolypin reforms had achieved this age-old goal. The workers wanted greater control of their factories to obtain better working conditions. They also sought bread, to relieve hunger. The national minorities, i.e., the non-Russian peoples of the Empire, wanted greater autonomy, if not independence. And at least by summer everyone, most particularly the soldiers, wanted an end to the horrors of war.

It soon became apparent that the Provisional Government was not going to satisfy these aspirations. The Provisional Government felt obligated to Russia's allies to continue fighting. It hoped that the new political leadership would produce a surge of patriotism in the army, which would fight harder and increase the chance of victory. On the domestic front, it was reluctant to institute the most significant and most necessary reforms until a permanent, legal government was established. As a practical matter, even when the Provisional Government wished to take decisive action, it could not do so, as the bureaucracy necessary to carry out its orders had broken down almost completely. In addition, the people of Russia were beginning to ignore orders. Finally, as previously noted, the Soviet was quick to challenge the Provisional Government's authority if it felt the interests of the masses were at stake. For all these reasons, the Provisional Government's accomplishments were greatly limited.

As a result, the initial elation that followed the March events gradually gave way to disappointment and bitterness, cynicism and despair, and fear for the future. Angry, frustrated people now began increasingly to take matters into their own hands. An anarchic spirit, which Vissarion Belinsky had called *volia* and which had been long present beneath the surface of Russian life, quickly spread throughout the land. By summer, massive worker strikes and demonstrations were commonplace. The national minorities were on the brink of rebellion. Peasants satisfied their desire for land by simply taking it, chasing out landlords and burning houses in the process. Soldiers, exhausted from combat and anxious to get their share of land, deserted. A genuine social revolution was taking place. (See Reading 6)

Into this extremely complex and challenging situation there had arrived in mid-April a new and dramatic force: Vladimir Ilyich Lenin. Lenin was in Switzerland when the Revolution broke out. He was determined to return to Russia as soon as possible.

FACT: To solve his problem of how to return to Russia and participate in the Revolution, Lenin contemplated a variety of devices, including traveling by airplane (this before the age of commercial airliners), and posing as a deaf-and-dumb Swede. In the end, he accepted a German offer of safe conduct through Germany in a "sealed train" for himself, his wife, Krupskaya, and a number of associates. (See Reading 7)

Upon his arrival at Petrograd's Finland Station on April 16th, Lenin wasted no time in announcing that he sought to change the course of the Revolution. This was an audacious move on his part. A gambler would have hesitated to wager money on Lenin at this point. Out of the country for a full decade, he had returned under circumstances that suggested collaboration with the German enemy. His Bolshevik Party numbered only about 25,000, far less than the other significant parties, and it had very few representatives on the influential Executive Committee of the Petrograd Soviet.

These handicaps did not deter Lenin. Nor did the somewhat mixed reception he received from his fellow Bolshevik leaders upon his arrival. The next day he presented a set of radical propositions concerning the current situation. Known as the April Theses, his ideas contrasted sharply not only with the views held by other parties, but with those of his Bolshevik colleagues as well. He proposed an immediate end to the war; no support, not even temporary, for the capitalist Provisional Government; and nationalization of all land. Every point in this radical document was geared to link the Bolshevik Party with social revolution, and to satisfy popular aspirations. But despite their respect for Lenin, his fellow Bolsheviks found his Theses difficult to accept at first. Most of them were still sufficiently orthodox Marxists to believe that revolution had to proceed in stages, with the ultimate, popular revolution not possible until the capitalists had consolidated their power and industrialized the country. Lenin was not dismayed, however. Never flinching, retreating only when pressure required it, he steadfastly held to his course. The story of 1917 in Russia is the story of how Lenin "beat the odds," first winning over his party, then exhorting the people to support it, and finally guiding it to a position from which it could strike for power.

ТОВ. ЛЕНИН ОЧИЩАЕТ ЗЕМЛЮ ОТ НЕЧИСТИ.

The Communists made widespread use of propaganda from the beginning. During and after the Revolution, "Education Trains" took the Party's message throughout the land (above left). A political cartoonist in 1920 portrayed Lenin sweeping the world, "clearing it of dirt" in the form of capitalists and kings.

Bolshevik strength began to develop in the late Spring. By May, the Party claimed a membership of 79,000. This figure increased to 200,000 by August. When the first All-Russian Congress of Soviets convened in June, the Bolsheviks had over 100 delegates, out of 777, or 12.8% of the seats. While still very much a minority, this figure represented an extraordinary gain since March, a gain which increased at an even greater rate during the summer. The results of city council elections in Petrograd and Moscow tell the story.

Petrograd elections 20 August 1917

Parties	Representatives in old council	Representatives in new council	Total vote
Kadets	47	42	114,485
SRs	54	75	205,666
Mensheviks	40	8	23,552
Bolsheviks	37	67	183,694
Others	22	7	21,982

Moscow elections 1917

Parties	Reps	June Votes	%	Reps	September Votes	%
Kadets	17	108,781	17	30	101,106	26
SRs	58	374,885	58	14	54,374	14
Mensheviks	12	76,407	12	4	15,887	4
Bolsheviks	11	85,409	11	47	198,320	51

By the end of September, the Bolsheviks had an absolute majority in the influential Petrograd Soviet, and were nearing the point at which a seizure of power could be contemplated realistically.

In the meantime, the Provisional Government was struggling. By early May, banners had appeared in the streets of Petrograd with the legend "Down with the Provisional Government!" Faced with increasing unpopularity and pressure from the Soviet, the Provisional Government in May reorganized itself to include more left-wing members. It was at this point that the socialist lawyer Kerensky first emerged as a prominent figure in the government. He was named Minister of War. In a second government shakeup in August he became Prime Minister. But these changes in leadership were not enough. What was needed were new programs, not merely new faces.

During the summer of 1917, two serious crises rocked the Provisional Government. The first of these was a popular uprising in the streets of Petrograd by dissatisfied workers, known as "The July Days." The Provisional Government survived, and cracked down on those responsible. While the Bolsheviks had not initiated these disturbances, they had participated, and to avoid arrest Lenin was forced to flee to Finland, where he remained until October.

FACT: Lenin's escape to Finland was very tricky, and he was almost caught on several occasions. He shaved his beard and took the identity of Konstantin Petrovich Ivanov, workman. One of his hiding-places, before leaving Petrograd, was the home of a worker named Aliluyev, whose daughter later married Joseph Stalin.

The second crisis was quite different, resulting from an attempted coup d'etat by Army Commander-in-Chief Kornilov in September. To combat this threat from the right wing, Prime Minister Kerensky turned for support to the Bolshevik-dominated Petrograd Soviet, and gave its members arms. The Kornilov coup was averted, and the Provisional Government survived, but the incident was a bonanza for the Bolsheviks, who were now not only armed but finding it increasingly easy to pose as champions of the revolutionary cause.

1917: THE OCTOBER REVOLUTION

By October, the political situation in Russia bordered on anarchy. City, countryside, and front line were all out of control, or nearly so, and the Provisional Government was almost completely paralyzed. In this situation, the Bolsheviks, with their disciplined, authoritarian approach to politics, had a great advantage. People increasingly viewed them as the only group that might be able to get something done. Within the Party leadership, however, there was considerable debate over the proper course of action. Some hesitated to take decisive action. Lenin, however, was anxious to move. By the end of September, he was bombarding his colleagues with demands for an armed uprising by the Bolsheviks. At first, the other Bolshevik leaders paid little attention to these demands. Lenin, undaunted, continued his campaign, and as disillusionment with the Provisional Government increased, his position grew stronger. Finally, in a secret, late-night meeting in Petrograd on October 23, Lenin persuaded his Party's Central Committee to vote in favor of an armed uprising. In the following two weeks, the Bolsheviks tightened their hold on the leadership of the Petrograd Soviet and set the date for the coup in early November.

While Lenin continued throughout 1917 to be the force behind every move of the Bolsheviks, another figure emerged during the autumn to assist him by taking charge of the detailed operations of the coup. This was Leon Trotsky, a long-time radical but only recently a Bolshevik, a man with immense organizational ability and effectiveness as an orator.

FACT: Just as Lenin had rushed back to Russia from Switzerland, Trotsky had returned from New York City where he had been working for a Russian emigré newspaper.

In November, 1917, Trotsky both organized and inspired. In particular, he persuaded the soldiers of the Petrograd garrison to defect from the Provisional Government and become politically neutral. So, when Kerensky later called on Government troops to defend the regime, very few responded.

The Bolshevik Revolution began on November 6, and was over within thirty-six hours. Actually, to say that in this short time the Bolsheviks seized power is misleading, since the Provisional Government had effectively disintegrated and there really was no longer any power to be seized. The Bolsheviks filled a power vacuum, and they did so swiftly and easily. (See Readings 8, 9, and 10)

FACT: The events of November 6-7 did little to interrupt the life of the city. Both theaters and movie houses remained open, and their shows went on without interruption. (See Reading 11)

The coup had been called for by Lenin, engineered principally by Lenin and Trotsky, and carried out by the Bolshevik-dominated Military Revolutionary Committee of the Petrograd Soviet. It was accomplished under the slogan "All Power to the Soviets." That the Bolsheviks did not intend to share power with other socialist parties in the Soviet was clearly hinted on November 8, however, when the Congress of Soviets was informed that the new government would *not* be the Soviet's duly elected Central Executive Committee, as was generally expected. Instead, the Bolsheviks established a new governing body, the Council of People's Commissars (SOVNARKOM), made up entirely of Bolsheviks, with Lenin as Chairman. Through the November 6-7 coup, the Soviets became the *nominal* source of political authority in Russia, but in retrospect, it is clear that the Bolsheviks assumed *actual* power for themselves alone. Immediately after the coup, the Bolsheviks began the creation of a system in which the legal organs of government coexisted with a single political party, which dictated policy to the government. This parallelism of government and Party, with the Party calling the shots, continues to this day.

The Bolsheviks came to power committed to a set of theories and principles. As Marxists, they believed in the establishment of an ideal Communist society in which exploitation would be ended and all people would share equally in society's benefits. More immediately, in decrees issued soon after the coup, Lenin committed his Party to securing an immediate end to the war, to distributing land to the peasants, to obtaining greater control of factories by workers, and to permitting greater autonomy for the national minorities. The next few years were to see these goals once again drastically compromised. To some extent, this was due to the very difficult circumstances in which the Bolsheviks found themselves after the October Revolution. (See Reading 12)

FACT: Lenin himself seemed momentarily awed by his success, which catapulted him into "the driver's seat." Said he to Trotsky, "You know, from exile and a life underground, to come suddenly to power...it makes one dizzy."

BOLSHEVIK CONSOLIDATION OF POWER

As of the morning of November 8, the Bolsheviks could be pleased with their success of the previous two days, but in reality the success was precarious, and would remain so for some time. They held only certain portions of one city, and they faced most of the problems that had caused the downfall of both the Tsar and the Provisional Government.

Perhaps the most immediate and serious of these problems was the war against Germany. Lenin realized that if the Revolution was to survive, the war must end, however costly that end might be. Consequently, an armistice was signed in December, and peace negotiations began at the town of Brest-Litovsk. It soon became clear that the Germans would settle only for an extremely harsh treaty, and this caused great debate within the Bolshevik leadership. Once again, Lenin's persistence, bolstered by his threat to resign, produced ultimate agreement with his position. On March 3, 1918, the Bolsheviks signed the Treaty of Brest-Litovsk with Germany, ending hostilities between the two countries. The cost to Russia was great.

FACT: In this treaty, Russia was forced to give up 25% of its territory, including the Ukraine, Finland, Georgia, Poland, and the Baltic States. These lands contained 26% of its population, 27% of its arable land, 26% of its railroads, 33% of its manufacturing industries, 73% of its iron industries, and 75% of its coal and iron mines.

The Germans were not the only problem for the Bolsheviks, however. A domestic problem that faced the Bolsheviks almost immediately was what to do about elections to the Constituent Assembly, already scheduled for late November. The Bolsheviks, not yet daring to interfere with the electoral process, and at the same time hoping for a popular mandate, allowed the elections to be held on November 25.

FACT: In this, the only free national election in Russian and Soviet history, the Bolsheviks received 23.5% of the vote, whereas the Socialist Revolutionaries received 41%.

While hoping for better results, the Bolsheviks were probably not surprised at the outcome. When the Constituent Assembly met in January 1918, the Bolsheviks simply dissolved it by force, branding it counterrevolutionary. (See Reading 14) Many opposition groups emerged to challenge the Bolsheviks

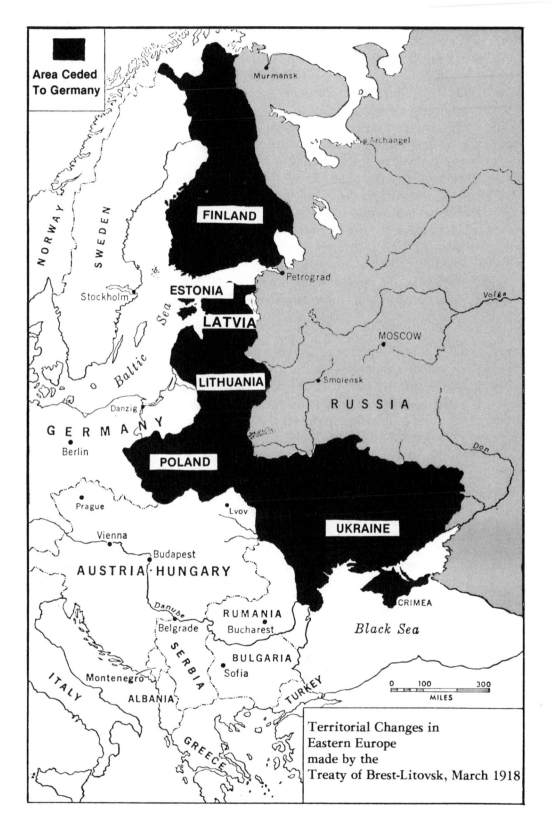

Area Ceded
To Germany

NORWAY

SWEDEN

Murmansk

Archangel

FINLAND

Stockholm

Baltic Sea

ESTONIA

Petrograd

LATVIA

Volga

MOSCOW

LITHUANIA

Smolensk

Danzig

RUSSIA

GERMANY

Berlin

POLAND

Don

Prague

Lvov

UKRAINE

Vienna

Budapest

AUSTRIA-HUNGARY

Danube

RUMANIA

CRIMEA

Belgrade

Bucharest

Black Sea

SERBIA

ITALY

Montenegro

BULGARIA

Sofia

ALBANIA

TURKEY

0   100   300
MILES

GREECE

Territorial Changes in
Eastern Europe
made by the
Treaty of Brest-Litovsk, March 1918

in the six months following the coup. These opponents were originally moderate groups such as the Cadets, who had supported the Provisional Government, and any remaining Tsarists. But as the Bolshevik determination to monopolize power became more and more evident, other left-wing groups were alienated also. While these opposition groups never became unified, they posed a very real threat to the new regime.

To meet this threat, the Bolsheviks issued decrees and took active measures against what they called counterrevolutionary elements. Among these were religious groups, automatically classified as counterrevolutionary. Marx had called religion "the opiate of the people" and attacked it for promoting superstition. The real problem, however, was that religious groups proclaimed allegiance to an authority higher than any on earth. The Bolsheviks, faithful to their atheistic ideology, issued a series of decrees in December, 1917, stripping the Orthodox Church of its economic power and weakening its control over individual followers. At the same time, a decree shut down newspapers judged to be anti-Bolshevik, and another established the CHEKA, a secret police charged specifically with the task of eliminating opposition groups. (See Readings 15 and 16)

FACT: The CHEKA, whose full title was the Extraordinary Commission to Combat Counterrevolution and Sabotage, might be considered the successor to the Tsarist Okhrana, though the Okhrana was very small and inactive compared to the CHEKA. It has been succeeded in turn by a series of organizations over the years that had a similar mission: the GPU, OGPU, NKVD, MVD, KGB.

Their blatant contempt for the outcome of a free election and the willingness of the Bolsheviks to use force illustrated clearly the arbitrary and authoritarian nature of the new regime, and hastened the division of the country into the two factions of the Civil War: The Reds (Bolsheviks) and the Whites (Anti-Bolsheviks).

FACT: There was a third group active in the Civil War, sometimes known as the Greens. These were Cossack and peasant units representing local interests, mostly in the south, who liked neither Reds nor Whites, but hurt the latter more because they were mostly located in White territory.

The Russian Civil War broke out in the late spring of 1918 and lasted through 1920, though an associated campaign by the Bolsheviks against Poland continued for an additional year. The Whites enjoyed superiority in numbers and the support of several foreign powers. The English and the French leaders were angry at the Bolsheviks for having withdrawn Russia from World War I at a critical time, allowing Germany to concentrate all its forces on the western front. Later, Japan and the United States joined England and France, both land-

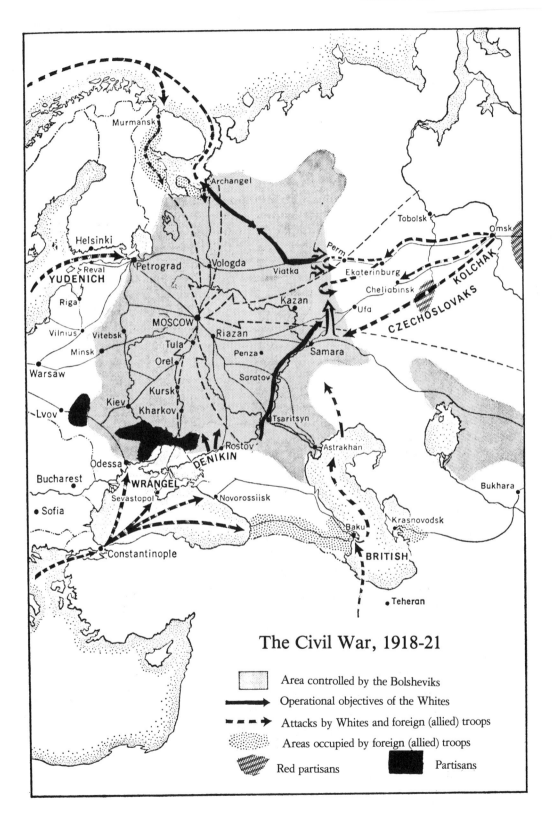

Murmansk

Archangel

Helsinki

Reval
YUDENICH
Petrograd   Vologda   Viatka   Perm
Riga   Ekaterinburg
                                                    Cheliabinsk
Vilnius   Vitebsk   MOSCOW   Kazan   Ufa
Minsk   Tula   Riazan   Penza
Warsaw   Orel   Samara
Kursk   Saratov
Lvov   Kiev
          Kharkov   Tsaritsyn
Odessa   Rostov   Astrakhan
Bucharest   DENIKIN   WRANGEL
Sofia   Sevastopol   Novorossiisk   Bukhara
                                          Krasnovodsk
Constantinople   Baku   BRITISH
                              Teheran

Tobolsk   Omsk
KOLCHAK
CZECHOSLOVAKS

The Civil War, 1918-21

Area controlled by the Bolsheviks

Operational objectives of the Whites

Attacks by Whites and foreign (allied) troops

Areas occupied by foreign (allied) troops

Red partisans

Partisans

ing troops at Vladivostok, and the U.S. also at Murmansk, in 1918. Their purpose was to assist the Whites and to prevent allied supplies from falling into German or Bolshevik hands.

FACT: Fourteen countries intervened in the Russian Civil War. The Japanese force was the largest, at 60,000, and the British second, with 40,000. The United States dispatched about 10,000, mostly to the Far East, through Vladivostok. While helpful to the Whites and openly hostile to the Bolsheviks, these foreign detachments normally avoided actual battle. The intervention was largely ended by 1920, having achieved little or nothing except Bolshevik animosity.

The Civil War was a bitter and bloody struggle. (See Readings 17 and 18) Coming as it did on top of the disastrous conflict of 1914-1918, it wreaked further havoc on an already devastated society. The Bolsheviks finally emerged victorious, because the Whites were handicapped by lack of leadership, unity of purpose, and geographical fragmentation. The Bolsheviks had interior lines and were under the capable leadership of Leon Trotsky, who headed the Red Army, turning it into a well-organized and effective fighting force. In the end, peasant support for the Reds probably tipped the scale. While they disliked many of the Bolshevik policies, they were even more skeptical of the Whites, who represented the old Russia of the landlords.

The United States was among a number of foreign countries that sent troops to Russia during the Civil War. In this photograph, American soldiers are feeding soup to Red soldiers they have captured.

The Bolshevik Party had been, since its inception in 1903, authoritarian in nature, but the challenge of the Civil War and fear of counterrevolution made it more so. Beset by enemies and fearful for their political lives, the Bolsheviks resorted to increasingly extreme measures to protect their fragile position.

Under the CHEKA, a Red Terror was begun during the summer of 1918, with the aim of wiping out enemies of the new regime. Among the victims were former Tsar Nicholas and his family, who were brutally murdered by a local revolutionary group in Ekaterinburg, where they had been sent the previous year. (See Reading 19) The Bolsheviks themselves calculated that, in twenty provinces of European Russia during 1918 and the first half of 1919, over 8,000 people were shot without trial by the CHEKA, and close to 80,000 others arrested without a legal hearing. (See Reading 20) The actual numbers were doubtless much higher. The crackdown on religion and the Orthodox Church continued too. Priests were deprived of voting rights, Church property was confiscated, and many Church leaders, including Patriarch Tikhon, were arrested.

In their economic policy as well, the Bolsheviks cracked down, instituting in 1918 what was called War Communism. Marxism-Leninism taught that, following the overthrow of capitalism, the means of production should be controlled by the state. War Communism sought to achieve this ideological goal by accelerating the transition from a free enterprise economy to a socialist one. There was a pragmatic goal as well, however: to get the stalled economy working again by direct state intervention. To these ends, the Bolsheviks nationalized industries, abolished free trade, requisitioned food from the peasantry by force, and adopted other extreme measures that greatly decreased the freedom of many Russian workers and peasants. In so doing, they incurred increased resistance among these groups. In 1919 alone, 1.7 million peasants deserted the Red Army.

In political affairs the Bolsheviks increased the centralization of authority. The Party's Central Committee, which was in charge of everyday matters and directed Party policy between Party Congresses, continued to exist, but its importance decreased. Increasingly, significant decisions were made by a small group within the Central Committee, and in 1919 this small group was formalized as the Political Bureau (Politburo). In theory, the Politburo was, and still is, a subcommittee responsible to the Central Committee. In actuality, however, it soon became the principal source of political authority, to whose decisions the Central Committee would normally give a rubber stamp approval. Originally numbering eight, the Politburo today contains ten to fifteen members plus half a dozen Candidate (non-voting) members.

FACT: In March 1918, Lenin and the Bolshevik Party abandoned Petrograd, Peter's "Window on the West," in favor of Moscow, the ancient capital, and the Kremlin once again became the center of government.

FACT: In that same month, at the 7th Party Congress, Lenin changed the name of his party from the Russian Social Democratic Workers' Party (Bolshevik) to the Russian Communist Party (Bolshevik). In 1924, it was renamed Communist Party of the Soviet Union (Bolshevik). Finally, in 1949, the bracketed term, "Bolshevik," was dropped from the title.

THE NEW ECONOMIC POLICY

With the Civil War largely over by 1920, Lenin and his Party controlled the country as a whole for the first time. There were still major challenges to be faced, however, and the Communists devoted the following seven years to facing them and consolidating their control.

Among these challenges, the most crucial was that of the economy, which continued to be at a near-standstill, causing opposition to the Communist Party from its own followers. "I am for the Bolsheviks, but against the Communists," was a saying common among peasants in 1919, symbolic of the fact that much of the support Lenin and his colleagues had enjoyed in 1917 had begun to erode shortly thereafter. To many of the ordinary people of Russia, the Bolsheviks were the party that had accomplished a revolution on their behalf, a revolution from which they could expect greater democracy and a higher standard of living. The Communists, who had imposed unpopular political and economic controls, appeared to be an entirely different group. Workers found that they did not receive control of factories, and a Workers' Opposition movement developed in 1919. Peasants resented War Communism and the forced requisitioning of their produce. They responded by sowing fewer crops and hoarding their surpluses, which in turn produced severe food shortages. Famine occurred in 1921-1922, accompanied by epidemics. Deaths from hunger and disease in those two years alone were greater than the total number of Russian battle deaths in World War I and the Civil War.

FACT: The ravages of the famine were so great that the Soviet regime appealed to other countries for help. Despite its anti-Communist stance, the U.S. government responded by organizing The American Relief Administration, under future President Herbert Hoover, in the summer of 1921. This organization distributed food and medical supplies; in August, 1922 alone, it fed more than ten million individuals daily. (See Reading 21)

Peasant revolts broke out, the most notable of which, in the Tambov region of central Russia in 1920, required 50,000 Red Army troops to put down. But the most dramatic protest came in 1921, from the sailors of the huge naval base at Kronstadt in the Gulf of Finland.

The sailors of Kronstadt had been among the most ardent supporters of the Bolshevik Party. By 1921 they had become disillusioned. They deplored what they called "the arbitrary rule of the commissars," by which they meant the growing centralization of government, the lack of participation by the masses in the decision-making process, and harsh government policies toward both workers and peasants. They drew up a manifesto, hoisted the flag of rebellion, and waited for the Moscow regime to accede to their demands. They misjudged that regime. The Tenth Party Congress, which was meeting at the time, authorized force to put down the revolt, and an army was dispatched under Trotsky's leadership. After a bloody siege, the fortress fell.

FACT: Fifteen thousand Kronstadt defenders who surrendered to Trotsky were executed without even the semblance of a trial.

The manner in which the Communist leadership dealt with the Kronstadt Revolt, by claiming that it was the work of reactionary emigrés, was the clearest indication yet that the new regime was no more accountable to the wishes of the Russian people than the Tsarist autocracy had been.

The protests, opposition movements and outright revolts of 1919-1921 led the Communist Party, still very much under Lenin's guiding hand, to institute two new policies, one political and one economic. The political policy was to tighten discipline within the Party and eliminate what was defined as "factionalism," i.e., the right to form political groups within the Party and to challenge Party decisions. At the Tenth Party Congress in 1921, Lenin introduced a resolution "On Party Unity," which dissolved existing factions and prohibited them in the future. This decision was an important step in the development of the monolithic Party that characterized the Stalin period. Hereafter, Party discipline was rigidly enforced. One result was the first large purge, or expulsion, of 200,000 Party members in 1921.

While tightening political control, Lenin recognized the need to loosen up in the economic area, in order to stabilize the economy, increase production, and decrease popular unrest. War Communism was abandoned, and replaced in 1921 by the New Economic Policy (NEP). Forced requisitioning of food was replaced by a tax. In industry, the attempt at total nationalization was also abandoned, and the state retained control only over the "commanding heights" of the economy, i.e., large-scale industry and banking. Free trade was reintroduced, and private enterprise once again tolerated. While a definite retreat from the Communist ideal of public ownership and collectivism, NEP was unquestionably a success economically. By 1928, both the volume of industry and the amount of land under cultivation (but not actual output of grain) exceeded pre-war levels, and a degree of prosperity returned to Soviet Russia. The task of reviving the economy and building a new socialist society appealed to many Russians. Taken together with the relaxation of economic controls, it made the NEP period one of enthusiasm and even excitement in the Soviet Union.

The peasants were not the only ones to whom concessions were made during the early 1920s. In fact, it was generally a period of relaxation, with concessions made to various groups in Soviet society. The national minorities were encouraged to develop educational and cultural institutions. The Orthodox Church, though restricted in many respects, was formally recognized. Private book printing and publishing reappeared. While some literary figures opposed the new regime, others found it possible to come to terms with it, among them such noteworthy writers as Isaac Babel, Eugene Zamiatin, Yuri Olesha, and Vladimir Mayakovsky, the unofficial poet laureate of the regime. New forms in

ЖЕНЩИНА!
УЧИСЬ ГРАМОТЕ!

ЭХ, МАМАНЯ! БЫЛА
БЫ ТЫ ГРАМОТНОЙ,
ПОМОГЛА БЫ МНЕ!

One of the early goals of the Soviet regime was to raise the literacy rate through education. A poster designed to promote this campaign says: "Girl, learn your grammar!" The daughter replies, "Ah, mama! If you were literate, you would've helped me!"

literature, theater, and art appeared, and under the leadership of Sergei Eisenstein and others, Soviet filmmaking gained prominence. In short, it was still possible to engage in cultural experimentation in the Soviet Union in the NEP period.

The regime faced a substantial challenge with regard to the minority nationalities of the former Russian Empire. In 1917, Lenin had called the Tsarist empire "the prison house of nationalities," and promised these peoples greater autonomy, but their efforts at self-determination in the years following the Revolution were opposed by the Communist regime. During the Civil War, Red armies brought the Ukrainians, Transcaucasians and Central Asians under Party control. In December 1922, a federal state was created, the Union of Soviet Socialist Republics.

FACT: The new U.S.S.R. initially included Russia, the Ukraine, Belorussia and Transcaucasia. In 1925, it was joined by the Turkmen and Uzbek, and in 1929 by the Tadzhik Republics of Central Asia. Later,

Transcaucasia was divided into the Armenian, Georgian and Azerbaijan Republics, and six additional republics were created for the total of fifteen which exist today.

In 1924, a constitution for the new state was produced. It guaranteed many freedoms, including the freedom for republics to secede from the Union, but as with many of the rights guaranteed by the Soviet constitution, this one was not exercised.

In addition to the various domestic challenges, the Communists faced serious international challenges after 1917. The Western powers were still openly hostile to the Communists, for being "godless atheists," for withdrawing Russia from World War I, for repudiating Russia's debts to other countries, and for promoting a world-wide Communist revolution through the Comintern, an agency established in 1919 to coordinate and support the activities of Communist parties throughout the world. The Western powers particularly resented the intrusion into their domestic political affairs orchestrated by the Comintern. For their part, the Communist leaders felt hostile toward those powers that had intervened in the Russian Civil War and excluded Soviet Russia from the post-World War I settlements and the League of Nations.

By 1921, although Trotsky was still advocating world revolution as a top priority, Lenin and others had begun to realize that such an event, while desirable and inevitable, was not imminent. Here too Lenin recognized the need for compromise, and the emphasis on world revolution was quietly dropped in favor of more traditional diplomatic relations with other countries. Starting with the Treaty of Rapallo with Germany in 1922, Soviet Russia gradually rejoined the world community, a process that climaxed with its admission to the League of Nations in 1934.

FACT: The Treaty of Rapallo contained secret provisions for military cooperation between the two countries. Germany, forbidden to rearm by the Versailles Treaty, obtained the right to use Russian bases for training and testing equipment, in return for which Germany agreed to lend expertise and assist in rebuilding Russia's military industry.

THE RISE OF STALIN

Despite the fact that the Bolshevik Party had always talked in terms of collective leadership, Lenin was unquestionably the acknowledged leader of the Party throughout this revolutionary period. (See Reading 23) While he avoided titles and discouraged flattery, Lenin nonetheless insisted on having his own way, and a combination of political skill and the great respect in which he was held usually resulted in agreement with his position. Hence, a crisis arose when Lenin became seriously ill in 1921, and intensified when he was incapacitated by a series of strokes beginning in 1922. He died as a result of these strokes in

January 1924. (See Reading 24) While the entire leadership of the Party pledged itself at that time to follow Lenin's course and respect the principle of collective leadership, the Party clearly needed a single leader. Even before Lenin died, a power struggle developed to determine his successor. The leading candidate was Leon Trotsky, the charismatic figure who had been Lenin's right-hand man during the October Revolution and commander of the Red Army in the Civil War. Trotsky had weaknesses, however: he disliked routine work, preferred to operate by himself, and was vain and self-centered, qualities that did not endear him to his Party colleagues.

Another candidate was Joseph Stalin. Stalin was in many respects Trotsky's opposite, lacking in charisma, intellectual distinction, and oratorical ability. He had the apparent disadvantage of being a Georgian, not a Russian. And in 1922, Stalin incurred the ailing Lenin's displeasure by being rude to the latter's wife, Krupskaya. (See Reading 25) Stalin had strengths, however. A naturally gifted politician, he used a combination of ideological and practical means to advance his position. He championed the theory of "socialism in one country" to oppose Trotsky's idea that the Soviet Union should concentrate on promoting worldwide revolution. Stalin's theory advocated that a buildup of a Communist base in the Soviet Union should precede efforts toward a world revolution.

When Lenin died in 1924, it was not clear who, if anyone, would be able to assume the powerful position he had established as Party leader. By the end of the 1920s, Joseph Stalin had eliminated other candidates and achieved this position. Here Lenin and his successor are pictured together in 1922.

Stalin maximized his practical advantages as well. Not only was he a member of the influential Politburo, but in 1922 he was named General Secretary of the Party, a position which enabled him to control Party membership, appointments, and promotions. While Trotsky relied on the written and spoken word to gain support, Stalin relied on people who owed him something. He realized that gaining control of the Party apparatus would in turn permit control of the government, the military, and the secret police. Quietly, and with great patience, he became familiar with the inner workings of the Party, and started placing his supporters in key positions. At the same time, he began making alliances with certain Party leaders in order to attack others.

Trotsky was the first victim, in 1925. Denounced by a triumvirate Stalin had formed with Zinoviev and Kamenev, Trotsky was removed, first as army chief, then from his other positions of leadership. Finally, he was exiled from the U.S.S.R. in 1927. The other contenders soon followed, like Trotsky victims of Stalin's determination, political shrewdness, and ruthlessness. (See Readings 26 and 27) By the end of 1927, Stalin was in control of Lenin's Party.

By this time, a decade after their successful coup, the Communist regime had made some notable achievements. They had won a civil war, and created a new state. They had revived a devastated economy through the NEP, and brought both production of goods and standard of living back close to prewar levels. They had reduced class distinctions. They had eliminated political opposition, both inside and outside the Communist Party. They had begun to pull their country out of international isolation. Finally, they had permitted the emergence of a successor to Vladimir Ilyich Lenin. In 1928, however, very few Communists realized the implications of Stalin's emergence. The events of the next decade, under Stalin's leadership, would constitute a revolution that made the events of 1917-1928 pale by comparison.

The following books were helpful in writing this chapter:

Chamberlin, W.H., *The Russian Revolution* (2 vols.), New York: Macmillan, 1935.

Daniels, R.V., *Red October,* New York: Charles Scribner's Sons, 1967.

Daniels, R.V., editor, *The Russian Revolution,* Englewood Cliffs: Prentice-Hall, 1972.

Dmytryshyn, B., *U.S.S.R. A Concise History,* New York: Charles Scribner's Sons, 1978.

Fitzpatrick, S., *The Russian Revolution,* New York: Oxford University Press, 1982.

Thompson, J.M., *Revolutionary Russia, 1917,* New York: Charles Scribner's Sons, 1981.

For students who are interested, we recommend further reading in the sources from which we have taken excerpts as well as the following works:

McNeal, R.H., *The Bolshevik Tradition,* Englewood Cliffs: Prentice-Hall, 1975.
  Short, readable, and incisive biographies of four men who rose to the top of the Soviet regime: Lenin, Stalin, Khrushchev, and Brezhnev.

Moorehead, A., *The Russian Revolution,* New York: Harper and Bros., 1958.
  Not a scholarly work, but probably the most readable account of the events of 1917 and the background to these events.

Reed, J., *Ten Days that Shook the World,* New York: Penguin Books, 1966.
  An American Communist's eyewitness account of the Bolshevik Revolution of 1917. Authentic and unique.

Readings

Chapter Four

List of Readings

1. Initial Disturbances: A Police Account

The February Revolution started with strikes and demonstrations in Petrograd on March 7 (February 23 by the old calendar), as described in the following memorandum sent by the Okhrana (Secret Police) to its precinct superintendents.

On February 23 at 9:00 A.M., the workers of the plants and factories of the Vyborg district went on strike in protest against the shortage of black bread in bakeries and groceries; the strike spread to some plants located in the Petrograd, Rozhdestvenskii, and Liteinyi districts, and in the course of the day 50 industrial enterprises ceased working, with 87,534 men going on strike.

At about 1:00 P.M., the workmen of the Vyborg district, walking out in crowds into the streets and shouting 'Give us bread,' started at the same time to become disorderly in various places, taking with them on the way their comrades who were at work, and stopping tramcars; the demonstrators took away from the tram drivers the keys to the electric motors, which forced 15 tramway trains to quit the lines and retire to the Petrograd tramway yard.

The strikers, who were resolutely chased by police and troops summoned (for this purpose), were dispersed in one place but quickly gathered in other places, showing themselves to be exceptionally stubborn; in the Vyborg district order was restored only toward 7:00 P.M.

2. The Mood in the Streets

One of the first eyewitnesses to record his impressions of the early days of the February Revolution was the Socialist Revolutionary Zenzinov. His descriptions capture the mood of those in the streets and suggest the key role the soldiers would play in these events. The dates are those of the old calendar.

These two days — the 23rd and the 24th — I spent most of my time on the streets. . . I roamed the streets without any plan, turning from one into another, observing the crowds, listening in on conversations. There were more than the usual number of people on the streets; common people predominated. (They were) in an excited state, but not irritated — most of all, one could sense the curiosity of the crowd. It was also evident that the people were not so much residents of these streets as people who had made their way from outlying districts.

Abridged from R.P. Browder and A.F. Kerensky, editors, *The Russian Provisional Government 1917*, Stanford, 1961.

Ibid.

Chains of soldiers were stationed at many points: undoubtedly their duty was not to let the passers-by go any farther, but they performed this duty poorly. I remember how I was detained for a long time by the Moika [a canal in Petrograd] — the soldiers were given strict orders not to let anyone pass through the chain, but the passers-by kept getting into conversations with them, persuading them to let them go through, explaining the necessity for them to go farther, giving reasons that were obviously fabricated — and the soldiers, looking around them to make sure that their superiors did not notice their indulgence, would let (the people) pass. . . In this way I, too, was allowed to pass. From these fleeting conversations it became clear that all these soldiers were for the most part recently mobilized; i.e., only very recently they had been in the same (position) as the crowds around them.

3. The Provisional Government Proclaims the Revolution

On March 16, the Temporary Committee of the Duma appointed a Provisional Government, in effect a cabinet of ministers (of which there were ten), to rule until a permanent form of government could be decided upon. Four days later this Provisional Government issued its first declaration, outlining its objectives and hopes for the future.

Citizens of the Russian State!

A great event has taken place. By the mighty impulse of the Russian people the old order has been overthrown. A new free Russia has been born. The great upheaval crowns many years of struggle.

By the act of October 17, 1905, under pressure of the awakened popular forces, Russia was promised constitutional liberties. However, those promises were not kept. The spokesman of national hopes, the First State Duma, was dissolved. The Second Duma suffered the same fate. And, powerless to crush the national will, the Government decided, by the Act of June 3, 1907, to retract from the people part of the rights to participate in legislative work which had been granted to them. In the course of nine long years, step by step, the people were deprived of all of the rights which they had gained. Once more the country was plunged into an abyss of arbitrary rule and absolutism. All attempts to make the Government listen to reason proved futile, and the great world struggle into which our motherland was drawn by the enemy found it in a state of moral decay, alienated from the people, indifferent to the future of the motherland, and stepped in the infamy of corruption. Neither the heroic efforts of the army, staggering under the crushing burdens of internal chaos, nor the

Ibid.

appeals of the people's representatives who had united in the face of national peril were able to lead the former Emperor and his Government into the path of unity with the people. And when Russia, owing to the illegal and fatal actions of her rulers, was confronted with the gravest disasters, the nation was obliged to take the power into its own hands. The unanimous revolutionary enthusiasm of the people, fully aware of the gravity of the moment, and the determination of the State Duma have created the Provisional Government. And the latter deems it its sacred duty and responsibility to fulfill the people's hopes and lead the country onto the bright path of free civic organization.

The Government believes that the spirit of lofty patriotism, manifested during the struggle of the people against the old regime, will also inspire our valiant soldiers on the field of battle. For its own part, the Government will make every effort to provide our army with everything necessary to bring the war to a victorious conclusion.

The Government will sacredly observe the alliances which bind us to other powers and will unswervingly carry out the agreements entered into with the Allies.

While taking measures to defend the country from the foreign enemy, the Government will, at the same time, deem it to be its primary duty to open a way to the expression of the popular will with regard to the form of government and will convoke the Constituent Assembly within the shortest time possible on the basis of universal, direct, equal, and secret suffrage, also guaranteeing participation in the elections to the gallant defenders of our native land who are now shedding their blood on the fields of battle. The Constituent Assembly will also issue the fundamental laws guaranteeing the country the inalienable rights of justice, equality, and liberty.

Realizing the full gravity of the lack of rights, which oppresses the country and hinders the free creative impulse of the people at a time of grave national upheavals, the Provisional Government deems it necessary to provide the country immediately, even prior to the convocation of the Constituent Assembly, with laws safeguarding civil liberty and equality in order to enable all citizens to apply freely their spiritual forces to creative work for the benefit of the country. The Government will also undertake the enactment of legal provisions to assure all citizens equal participation in the elections of organs of self-government on the basis of universal suffrage.

At this moment of national liberation, the whole country remembers with reverent gratitude those who, in defending their political and religious convictions, fell victims to the vindictive old regime. And the Provisional Government considers it its happy duty to bring back from their exile and imprisonment, with full honors, all those who have suffered for the good of the motherland.

In fulfilling these tasks, the Provisional Government is animated by the belief that it will thus execute the will of the people, and that the whole nation will support it in its honest efforts to ensure the happiness of Russia. This belief inspires it with courage. The Provisional Government sees the only guarantee for the triumph of the new order in the wholehearted support of all of the people.

4. The Petrograd Soviet

The Petrograd Soviet did as the Duma had done, and elected an Executive Committee. It immediately began to assume its "watchdog" function, to make sure that the Provisional Government managed the Revolution properly, and that the interests of the workers (and later, the soldiers and peasantry) were properly represented. The Socialist Revolutionary Sukhanov wrote his impressions of these events, which he witnessed.

...It was already about 11 o'clock [February 28, old calendar] when the Ex. Com. session opened. I have the impression that during these first days its work went on almost uninterruptedly around the clock. But what work it was! They were not meetings, but a frenzied and exhausting obstacle race.

The agenda had been set up, as pointed out above, in relation to the urgent tasks of the moment. But neither at that session nor in general during the days that followed could there be any questions of fulfilling a programme of work.

Every five or ten minutes business was interrupted by 'urgent announcements', or 'emergency reports', 'matters of exceptional importance' which couldn't 'tolerate the slightest delay', and on which the 'fate of the revolution depended', etc. These emergency questions were for the most part raised by the Ex. Com. members themselves, who kept getting some sort of information on the side, or prompted by people who were besieging the Ex. Com. But again and again the petitioners, delegates, and messengers from every possible organization and agency, or simply from the nearby crowds, would themselves burst into the meeting.

In the great majority of cases these emergency matters were not worth a barley-corn. I don't remember what the Ex. Com. did during these hours. I remember only unimaginable hubbub, tension, hunger, and the feeling of irritation at these 'exceptional reports'. There was simply no way of stopping them.

There was no order even in the meeting itself. There was no permanent chairman. Chkheidze, who later performed the chairman's duties almost permanently, didn't do much work in the Ex. Com. during its first days. He was constantly being summoned — either to the Duma Committee or the Soviet sessions or, above all, 'to the people', the constantly-changing crowd standing in front of the Tauride Palace. He spoke practically without stopping both in the Ekaterinskii Hall and in the street, sometimes to workers and sometimes to soldiers. He would scarcely have time to return to the meeting of the Ex. Com. and take his things off before some delegate would burst in with a categorical demand for Chkheidze, sometimes even reinforced by threats — that the mob would break in. And the tired and sleepy old Georgian would get his

Abridged from N.N. Sukhanov, *The Russian Revolution* 1917, New York, 1962.

fur coat on again with a resigned look, put on his hat, and disappear from the Ex. Com.

There was still no permanent secretary, nor were any minutes taken. If they had been taken and preserved, they would not report any 'measures' or 'acts of state' during these hours. They would reflect nothing but chaos and 'emergency reports' about every possible danger and excess we lacked the means to combat. There were accounts of pillage, fires, and pogroms; pogromist Black Hundred† leaflets were brought in — handwritten, alas, and thoroughly illiterate. We gave orders not expecting them to be carried out and sent out detachments without any hope that they would really be formed or do their duty.

I don't remember who presided at this meeting, nor whether there was any chairman at all. . . On the writing-desk of the chairman of the former Finance Committee there appeared from somewhere or other tin mugs of tea with crusts of black bread and other eatables. Someone was looking after us. But there was not much food, or else there was simply no time to get it. A feeling of hunger remains in my memory. . . .

5.   The Revolution as Seen by a Child

Among the many eyewitness accounts of the events of March, 1917 in Petrograd, a particularly interesting one is that of Zinaida Shakhovskoi, who was a child at the time. She was a member of an aristocratic family of some renown, and emigrated with them to Paris after the Revolution, where she eventually became a well-known writer and editor of an influential Russian-language newspaper. The dates are those of the old calendar.

I was ten years old and since September 1916 a pupil at the Empress Catherine Institute for Young Ladies of Nobility, in Petrograd, when the February revolution occured.

Sunday, the 26th of February 1917. In the large white-columned reception hall of the Institute, where once a week the pupils could see their parents (under the stares of two solemn looking Empresses, painted in majesty — Catherine the Great and the Dowager Empress Mariya Fedorovna) the usual crowd of visitors was on this particular day considerably thinner, but no rumors of disquietness had penetrated the walls of the Institute.

As my sister and I took leave of my mother, who was accompanied by my brother Dimitry, in his uniform of the pupils of Alexandrovsky Lyceum, and by my two cousins, one of whom was finishing his studies in the Pavlovsky Military Officers School, I joined my classmates in a small neighboring hall where

Abridged from D. vonMohrenschildt, editor, *The Russian Revolution of 1917,* New York, 1971.

we were allowed to play on Sunday afternoons. There I heard a strange, soon to become familiar, sound: it resembled the dry and regular fall of hail and it was followed by shouting and screams and by the tramping of horseshoes on the pavement. We were even more startled by the hurry with which our mistress in charge, breaking traditional composure, without even bothering to put us in pairs or order us to keep silent, led us to the corridor. At once the grave, somehow monastic atmosphere of the Institute which I found so boring, broke into pandemonium. There were our maids running up and down the stairs, some of them carrying mattresses (as I learned later, to be propped against the windows opening on the quays of Fontanka [a canal in Petrograd]); our janitors, old bemedaled and bearded veterans of the previous war, were hurrying from the entrance hall to the upper floors, where they were never supposed to penetrate. We were shepherded into our classroom overlooking the relative safety of our garden and there our mistresses gave us a summary explanation of what was happening. The unfamiliar word entered my vocabulary: the Revolt, not yet "Revolution."

Of course, the event was beyond our comprehension. The world which I had entered without enthusiasm some months ago, was, in spite of its excellent educational program, remote from reality and nearer the eighteenth century than the twentieth. Over our tight corsets we wore long dresses — green, red or lilac depending on our respective grades — which would have suited the court ladies of Catherine the Great. Our bare arms and ample decolletage were modestly covered by white capes and detachable sleeves. It was a dress which hardly conveyed the idea of the struggle for life.

I must confess, the first day of the February Revolution seemed to us, the seventh-grade pupils, just an exceptionally exciting day which liberated us from the tedious obligation to behave ourselves in a lady-like manner — which meant walking demurely with hands gently crossed over our stomach and making deep reverences when we saw one of our teachers. Discipline was shattered, to our great delight.

While helping other maids to arrange our beds (we were to sleep that night on the floor of our classroom) our young maid Grousha, her arm in a sling, for she was slightly wounded while shutting windows in the great hall, chattered away: "Oh, my dear young ladies, it is terrible what is happening. You see, the crowd thought that they were fired upon from our attic, and they put us under fire. But the police are not here, they are on the roof of Sheremetiev's mansion next door! Oh dear me, what will happen to all of us?! They might well try and burn us during the night." The mysterious "they," who were they exactly? Would "they" roast us during the night? After much speculating on this question, the "young ladies" finally settled down to sleep despite their fears.

The excitement continued during the days that followed as rumors spread that the Pages of the Emperor and the Junkers (student officers) of Pavlovsky Military School would be sent to protect us. The young people of the opposite sex were never, never to be seen outside the great hall! But the awaited defenders didn't come and nobody took the Catherine Institute by assault or fire. . . But there came the day when even we, the youngest of the pupils, became aware that something tragic and final had befallen the Russian Empire and all of us. On March 3, all the pupils and teachers were assembled in the hall as usual for the morning prayers read by one of the highest-ranking pupils. For the first time in about two centuries the prayer for the Tsar and his family was to be omitted, the Emperor having abdicated on the previous day. The girl, who was about 18, stumbled over her words and was unable to pronounce, "Let us pray for the Provisional Government." She started to cry. The teachers and mistresses took to their handkerchiefs and soon the four or five hundred of us were sobbing over something that was lost forever.

The next day the mothers came to take their daughters away; Catherine's Institute was seeing its last days.

Following our mother, my sister Natasha and I stepped out, for good, from the Catherine Institute. I hardly recognized the capital which I had last seen two months ago returning from my winter vacation. All the glamor had left Petrograd; many shops were closed and in front of the others was an unfamiliar sight — long queues were waiting. There were few carriages and no policemen to be seen at the crossings; the streets were full of disorderly soldiers, with a few gloomy civilians hurrying along. Our driver kept saying: "Let's hurry, let's hurry, before the shooting, God forbid, starts again."...

6. Anarchy in the Countryside

In the countryside, disorder increased steadily in the months following the February Revolution, as land-hungry peasants competed, often violently, for what was left of the landlords' estates. By summer, many parts of rural Russia were in a state of complete anarchy, as suggested by the following report in a Petrograd newspaper.

After arriving home, I was elected to the *volost*† committee. In our village there is no order. People live as they did before the Revolution. They make moonshine and sell it for two roubles a bottle. Drunkenness and robbery are on the increase.

The Cossacks who live in the neighbourhood steal from the landholders and peasants and insult the women. They do not even respect the church. In one village the store of the Consumers' Society was looted, and in another the home of a very popular doctor. . . .

With the landlords, it is not as it should be. They have planted sugar-beets, and to harvest them they offer labour one and one-half roubles per day, which is not enough to pay for board.

Abridged from F. Golder, editor, *Documents of Russian History, 1914-1917,* New York, 1927.

Livestock for the army has been bought in the villages at the rate of eleven roubles the *pud.*† It was driven on the land of a certain landowner where many have perished from hunger. . . .

Committees are organized in the villages but have no idea where their authority begins or ends. Can the committee dismiss a worthless priest? Can a landowner sell a piece of timber land without the authorization of the committee? . . . .

The cost of living and profiteering are on the increase. Speculators buy up bread and sell it later for five roubles the *pud*. There are those who have on hand one thousand or more puds of grain and yet buy more for speculative purposes. Merchants hide manufactured goods and allow only a limited amount on the market, for which they charge high prices. There is an abundance of money in the village and, with it, dissipation and debauchery. For the first time in the history of the village we have a house of ill-fame.

The military unit which was sent here to protect, robs the people of their cattle, fowl and bread, and insults the women. . . .

Each year the peasants rented their land from the landowner. This year they went to him as usual and he asked the usual rent. The peasants refused to pay it and, without much bargaining, went home. There they called a meeting and decided to take up the land without paying. They put the ploughs and harrows on their carts and started the field. When they arrived they got into an argument as to the division of the land, because it was not at all the same quality. When they had quarrelled for a time, one of the party proposed that they proceed to the landowner's warehouse, where some good alcohol was kept. They broke into the place, where they found fifty barrels. They drank and drank, but could not drink it all. They became so drunk that they did not know what they were doing and carelessly set the place on fire. Four burned to death; the ninety others escaped. A few days later they returned to the field and once more quarrelled. It ended in a fight in which thirteen were left dead, fifteen were carried off badly injured and, of these, four died.

Soon after that a quarrel started over the rich peasants. In the village there were eighteen farmers who had from twenty-five to thirty *disiatins*† of land. They had a reserve of grain of various kinds. About thirty of the villagers seized this reserve. Another village meeting was called. A few of the more intelligent peasants came out strongly against this act of robbery. It ended in another fight in which three were killed and five badly wounded. One of these peasants, whose son was killed, shook his fist and shouted: 'I will make you pay for my son.'

Three days later one of the village houses caught fire. People came running and asking, 'How did it get on fire?' Someone suggested that the man who a few days ago threatened to get even was the incendiary. The mob started for his place and killed him. When that was done, it was learned that the fire was due to the carelessness of the housewife. On that day a strong wind was blowing straight down the street, and 132 houses were burned. . . .

7. Lenin's Arrival

Lenin, the Bolshevik leader who had been in exile in Switzerland for a decade, was caught by surprise by the events of March 1917. Eager to return to Russia to take part in these events, Lenin accepted a German offer of help, in the form of the famous "sealed train," which brought Lenin, his wife Krupskaya, and a small band of associates to Petrograd's Finland Station on April 16. A reception committee was present, composed chiefly of Bolsheviks, but including the Mensheviks Chkheidze and Skobelev, and the journalist N.N. Sukhanov, who wrote this account of the scene at the Finland Station that night.

The throng in front of the Finland Station blocked the whole square, making movement almost impossible and scarcely letting the trams through. The innumerable red flags were dominated by a magnificient banner embroidered in gold: 'The Central Committee of the R.S. Bolsheviks.'† Troops with bands were drawn up under the red flags near the side entrance, in the former imperial waiting-rooms.

There was a throbbing of many motor-cars. In two or three places the awe-inspiring outlines of armoured cars thrust up from the crowd. And from one of the side-streets there moved out on to the square, startling the mob and cutting through it, a strange monster — a mounted searchlight, which abruptly projected upon the bottomless void of the darkness tremendous strips of the living city, the roofs, many-storeyed houses, columns, wires, tramways, and human figures.

Various delegations that had failed to penetrate into the station had found places on the steps of the main entrance and were vainly trying to retain their composure and keep their places in hand-to-hand struggles with the 'private' public. Lenin's train was expected around 11.

There was a crush inside the station — more delegations, more flags, and sentries at every step demanding special authority for going any further. The title of member of the Executive Committee [of the Soviet], however, appeased the most conscientious watchdogs, and through the mass of discontentedly grumbling people tightly packed together I made my way right through the station to a platform, and towards the Tsar's waiting-room, where a dejected Chkheidze sat, weary of the long wait and reacting sluggishly to Skobelev's witticisms. The whole square was clearly visible through the heavily bolted glass doors of the 'imperial' waiting-room; the scene was extraordinarily impressive. 'Delegates' were enviously clinging to the outside of the windows, and discontented women's voices could be heard: 'Party people have to wait in the street, while they let people inside that nobody ever saw before!'

Abridged from N.N. Sukhanov, *The Russian Revolution 1917,* New York, 1962.

But the indignation was scarcely well-founded: I don't recall seeing any 'public', at all well known in politics, science, or literature, that was not Bolshevik. The parties hadn't sent their official representatives; indeed, of the Soviet people or Executive Committee members, besides the Praesidium,† specially detailed to go, I think there was only myself. In any case there weren't more than three or four people in the 'imperial' rooms besides ourselves, since the local Bolshevik commanders had gone to meet Lenin in Finland. While we were waiting for Lenin at the station, he in the train was already familiarizing himself thoroughly with the state of affairs from 'immediate sources'.

I passed along the platform. There it was even more festive than in the square. Its whole length was lined with people, mostly soldiers ready to 'present A-a-a-r-m-s!' Banners hung across the platform at every step; triumphal arches had been set up, adorned with red and gold; one's eyes were dazzled by every possible welcoming inscription and revolutionary slogan, while at the end of the platform, where the carriage was expected to stop, there was a band, and a group of representatives of the central Bolshevik organizations stood holding flowers.

The Bolsheviks, who shone at organization, and always aimed at emphasizing externals and putting on a good show, had dispensed with any superfluous modesty and were plainly preparing a real triumphal entry. . . .

. . . We [Sukhanov, Skobelev and Chkheidze] waited for a long time, the train was very late.

But at long last it arrived. A thunderous Marseillaise† boomed forth on the platform, and shouts of welcome rang out. We stayed in the imperial waiting-room while the Bolshevik generals exchanged greetings. Then we heard them marching along the platform, under the triumphal arches, to the sound of the band, and between the rows of welcoming troops and workers. The gloomy Chkheidze, and the rest of us after him, got up, went to the middle of the room, and prepared for the meeting. And what a meeting it was, worthy of — more than my wretched pen!

Shliapnikov,† acting as master of ceremonies, appeared in the doorway, portentously hurrying, with the air of a faithful old police chief announcing the Governor's arrival. Without any apparent necessity he kept crying out fussily: 'Please, Comrades, please! Make way there! Make way there! Comrades make way!'

Behind Shliapnikov, at the head of a small cluster of people behind whom the door slammed again at once, Lenin came, or rather ran, into the room. He wore a round cap, his face looked frozen, and there was a magnificent bouquet in his hands. Running to the middle of the room, he stopped in front of Chkheidze as though colliding with a completely unexpected obstacle. And Chkheidze, still glum, pronounced the following 'speech of welcome' with not only the spirit and wording but also the tone of a sermon:

'Comrade Lenin, in the name of the Petersburg Soviet and of the whole Revolution we welcome you to Russia. . . But — we think that the principal task of the revolutionary democracy is now the defense of the Revolution from any encroachments either from within or from without. We consider that what this goal requires is not disunion, but the closing of the democratic ranks. We hope you will pursue these goals together with us.'

Chkheidze stopped speaking. I was dumbfounded with surprise: really, what attitude could be taken to this 'welcome' and to that delicious 'But ———'?

But Lenin plainly knew exactly how to behave. He stood there as though nothing taking place had the slightest connection with him — looking about him, examining the persons round him and even the ceiling of the imperial waiting-room, adjusting his bouquet (rather out of tune with his whole appearance), and then, turning away from the Executive Committee delegation altogether, he made this 'reply':

'Dear Comrades, soldiers, sailors, and workers! I am happy to greet in your persons the victorious Russian revolution, and greet you as the vanguard of the world-wide proletarian army. . . The piratical imperialist war is the beginning of civil war throughout Europe. . . The hour is not far distant when. . . the peoples will turn their arms against their own capitalist exploiters. . . The world-wide Socialist revolution has already dawned. . . Germany is seething. . . . Any day now the whole of European capitalism may crash. The Russian revolution accomplished by you has prepared the way and opened a new epoch. Long live the world-wide Socialist revolution!'

This was really no reply to Chkheidze's 'welcome', and it entirely failed to echo the 'context' of the Russian revolution as accepted by everyone, without distinction, of its witnesses and participants.

It was very interesting! Suddenly, before the eyes of all of us, completely swallowed up by the routine drudgery of the Revolution, there was presented a bright, blinding, exotic beacon, obliterating everything we 'lived by'. Lenin's voice, heard straight from the train, was a 'voice from outside'. There had broken in upon us in the Revolution a note that was not, to be sure, a contradiction, but that was novel, harsh, and somewhat deafening.

Let us admit that essentially Lenin was right a thousand times over. Personally I was convinced that he was quite right, not only in recognizing the beginning of the world-wide Socialist revolution and establishing an unbreakable connection between the World War and the crash of the imperialist system, but in maintaining that we had to steer towards world revolution and evaluate all contemporary historical events in its light. All this was beyond question.

But it was far from enough. It was not enough to acclaim the world-wide Socialist revolution: we had to understand what practical use to make of this idea in our revolutionary policy. If we didn't then the proclamation of the world-wide proletarian revolution would not merely be completely abstract, empty, and futile, but would obscure all the real perspectives and be extremely harmful.

In any case it was all *very* interesting!

The official and public part of the welcome was over. The crowd, burning with impatience, envy, and indignation, was already trying to break through the glass doors from the square. It was noisily and insistently demanding that the newly-arrived leader should come out to it in the street. Shliapnikov again cleared a way for Lenin, shouting: 'Comrades, please! Make way there!'

To another Marseillaise, and to the shouts of the throng of thousands, among the red-and-gold banners illuminated by the searchlight, Lenin went out by the main entrance and was about to get into a closed car, but the crowd absolutely refused to allow this. Lenin clambered on to the bonnet of the car and had to make a speech.

'. . . any part in shameful imperialist slaughter . . . lies and frauds . . . capitalist pirates . . .' was what I could hear, squeezed in the doorway and vainly trying to get out on to the square to hear the first speech 'to the people' of this new star of the first magnitude of our revolutionary horizon. . . .

8. Proclamation of the Military-Revolutionary Committee

Early on the morning of November 6, Kerensky ordered loyal troops to close forcibly the Bolshevik printing press. Believing this to be the first action in a major counter-revolutionary campaign by the Provisional Government, the Military-Revolutionary Committee, which had been set up two days earlier by the Soviets' Central Executive Committee to control the Petrograd garrison, issued an urgent decree, mobilizing forces for the defense of the Revolution.

Soldiers! Workers! Citizens!

The enemies of the people have gone over to the offensive during the night. The Kornilovites at Headquarters are trying to pull cadets and shock battalions in from the outskirts. The Oranienbaum cadets and the shock troops at Tsarskoe Selo† have refused to move. A traitorous blow is being devised against the Petrograd Soviet of Workers' and Soldiers' Deputies. The newspapers *"Rabochi Put"* (Worker's Path) and *"Soldat"* (Soldier) have been closed and the printing plant sealed up. The campaign of the counter-revolutionary plotters is directed *against the All-Russian Congress of Soviets* on the eve of its opening, *against the Constituent Assembly, against the people.* The Petrograd Soviet of Workers' and Soldiers' Deputies is standing up to defend the revolution. The Military-Revolutionary Committee is leading the resistance to the attack of the plotters. The whole garrison and the whole proletariat of Petrograd are ready to deal a crushing blow to the enemies of the people.

The Military-Revolutionary Committee decrees:

1. All regimental company, and crew committees, together with the commissars of the Soviet, and all revolutionary organizations must meet in constant session, and concentrate in their hands all information about the plans and actions of the plotters.

2. Not a single soldier shall become separated from his unit without the permission of the committee.

3. Two representatives from each unit and five from each district soviet shall immediately be sent to the Smolny Institute.†

4. Report all actions of the plotters immediately to the Smolny Institute.

5. All members of the Petrograd Soviet and all delegates to the All-Russian Congress of Soviets are summoned immediately to the Smolny Institute for a special session.

The counter-revolution has raised its criminal head.

All the gains and hopes of the soldiers, workers, and peasants are threatened with great danger. But the forces of the revolution immeasurably surpass the forces of its enemies.

From R.V. Daniels, editor, *The Russian Revolution,* Englewood Cliffs, 1972.

The people's cause is in the firm hands. The plotters will be crushed.

No vacillation or doubts. Firmness, steadfastness, perseverance, decisiveness. Long live the revolution!

9.   The October Revolution: An Eyewitness Account

Around midnight on November 6 armed groups of Bolsheviks began to occupy key points in the city: government offices, public utilities, transportation facilities, etc. This turned out to be an extremely easy task, since the Provisional Government had by then lost its military support and could no longer maintain its authority or public order. The ease of the operation is described by M.M. Lashevich, a Bolshevik in charge of an important segment of the operation.

The Military-Revolutionary Committee decided to act. I was ordered to seize the new state bank, the treasury, the telephone exchange, the telegraph office, and the post office during the night.

On approaching the telephone exchange we captured a patrol of cadets. Forcing our way, we burst into the courtyard of the building, after capturing the armored car at the gate. Cadets started to come running into the courtyard. There was a moment when a clash seemed inevitable, and then it would have been woe to the cadets, for in that box (the courtyard of the telephone exchange) anyone who resisted would have been thrashed. By a stratagem we succeeded in avoiding bloodshed.

Hearing the rattle of rifle bolts, I loudly commanded, "Empty your cartridges." Evidently not realizing who was giving the command, the cadets began to unload their rifles, and the Kexholm Regiment men took advantage of this to push the cadets into groups and surround them. The telephone exchange was taken without a shot.

We succeeded in capturing the state bank and the treasury even more easily. The soldiers of the Semenovsky Regiment who were on guard declared that they too were for the Military-Revolutionary Committee, and would not relinquish their posts, considering this an insulting lack of confidence by the representative of the Military-Revolutionary Committee. To avoid delay we had to agree with this, though to assure their loyalty I nevertheless left some of the sailors and Kexholm men there. At the same time the treasury was occupied by a unit sent there, and we got word of the occupation of the post office and the telegraph office. By eight o'clock (on the morning of the 25th) all the orders of the Military-Revolutionary Committee had been executed.

Ibid.

10. The Fall of the Winter Palace

On the night of November 7, the Winter Palace fell to the Bolsheviks,
after a short siege. This symbolic event was later dramatized in print and on
film, but in actuality it was not particularly difficult or exciting. The following
account is by Maliantovich, Minister of Justice in the Provisional Government,
who was in the Palace at the time.

Suddenly a noise arose somewhere and began to grow, spread and roll
ever nearer. And in its multitude of sounds, fused into a single powerful wave,
we immediately sensed something special, unlike the previous noises — something
final and decisive. It suddenly became clear that the end was coming. . . The
noise rose, swelled, and rapidly swept toward us in a broad wave. . . And poured
into our hearts unbearable anxiety, like a gust of poisoned air. . . It was clear: this
is the onslaught, we are being taken by storm. . . Defense is useless — sacrifices
will be in vain. . . .The door burst open. . . A military cadet ran in, drew himself
up, saluted, his face excited but resolute.

'What are the orders of the Provisonal Government? Defense to the last
man? We are ready to obey the orders of the Provisional Government.'

'No, it is not necessary! It is useless! The picture is clear! We want no
bloodshed! We must surrender,' they all cried in concert, without discussing the
question, merely looking at each other and finding the same feeling and decision in everyone's eyes.

Kishkin came forward. [*Kishkin was a personal friend of Kerensky and*
had been invited to join Kerensky's Coalition Cabinet.] 'If they are here, it means
that the Palace is already occupied.'

'It is occupied. All entrances are blocked. Everyone has surrendered. This
is the only room still under guard. What are the orders of the Provisional
Government?'

'Tell them that we want no bloodshed, that we yield to force, that we
surrender,' said Kishkin.

There was a noise behind the door and it burst open. Like a splinter of
wood thrown out by a wave, a little man flew into the room, pushed in by the
onrushing crowd which poured in after him and, like water, at once spilled into
every corner and filled the room. The little man wore a loose, open coat, a wide
felt hat pushed back on his forehead, over his long, reddish hair, and glasses.
He had a short, trimmed red moustache and a small beard. His short upper
lip rose to his nose when he spoke. The eyes were colourless, the face tired.
He flew in and cried in a sharp, small, insistent voice:

'Where are the members of the Provisional Government?'

Abridged from R. Pethybridge, editor, *Witnesses to the Russian Revolution,* New
York, 1964.

'The Provisional Government is here,' said Konovalov,† remaining seated. 'What do you wish?'

'I inform you, all of you, members of the Provisional Government, that you are under arrest. I an Antonov, chairman of the Military-Revolutionary Committee.'

'The members of the Provisional Government yield to forces and surrender, in order to avoid bloodshed,' said Konovalov.

'To avoid bloodshed! And how much blood have you spilled?' shouted a voice from the mob behind the ring of guards. Many approving exclamations echoed from all sides.

Antonov stopped the outcries.

'Enough, comrades! That's all! we'll straighten that out afterwards. . . . Now we must draw up a protocol. I am going to write it now. I shall ask everyone. . . . But first I request you to surrender all arms in your possession.'

The military surrendered their arms, the rest declared that they carried none.

The room was jammed with soldiers, sailors, Red Guards, some carrying several weapons — a rifle, two revolvers, a sword, two machine-gun ribbons.

When it was learnt that Kerensky had fled, vile oaths were heard from the crowd. Some of the men shouted, inciting the rest to violence:

'These will run off too! . . .Kill them, finish them off, there's no need for protocols! . . .

'Run them through, the sons of bitches! . . . Why waste time with them? They've drunk enough of our blood!' yelled a short sailor, stamping the floor with his rifle — luckily without a bayonet — and looking around. It was almost a call to action. There were sympathetic replies:

'What the devil, comrades! Stick them all on bayonets, make short work of them! . . .'

Antonov raised his head and shouted sharply:

'Comrades, keep calm! All members of the Provisional Government are arrested. They will be imprisoned in the Fortress of St. Peter and St. Paul.† I'll permit no violence. Conduct yourselves calmly. Maintain order! Power is now in your hands. You must maintain order! . . .

11. Maxim Gorky: The Gardener

Descriptions of Russia during the year 1917 customarily tend to emphasize the dramatic and violent elements: urban strife, rural anarchy, military failure, attempted coups. It is well to remember, however, that only a tiny portion of Russia's 170 million people were directly involved in the revolutionary events, and that most remained, at least for a little while longer, untouched by them. This point is eloquently made by the great writer Maxim Gorky.

Abridged from M. Gorky, *Fragments from My Diary,* New York, 1972.

February 1917

MOTOR-CARS, splashing mud against the walls and smothering passers-by, tear rumbling and hooting down the street. They are crowded to overflowing with soldiers and sailors, and bristle with the steel quills of bayonets, like huge hedgehogs running amok. Every now and then there is the crack of a rifle. Revolution! The Russian nation is scurrying about, bewildered with its newly-acquired freedom; it is trying to grasp it, but finds it somewhat elusive.

In the Alexander Park a gardener is engrossed in his solitary work; a thickset man in the fifties. Clumsily and quietly he sweeps away last year's fallen leaves and the litter from paths and flower-beds, and brushes off the freshly fallen snow. He takes not the slightest interest in the bustle that is going on around him, and remains deaf to the screeching of klaxons, the shouts and songs and shots. He does not even see the red flags. I watched him to see if he would look up presently and notice the people running about, the motor-lorries glittering with bayonets. But he bent down over his work and went on with it as stubbornly as a mole. Apparently he is as blind as one also.

March 1917

Along the streets, along the paths in the park, in the direction of the Narodni Dom, hundreds, thousands of soldiers in grey are moving slowly, some of them dragging machine-guns behind them like small iron pigs tied to a string. This is one of the innumerable machine-gun regiments that has just arrived from Oranienbaum.   They say that there are more than ten thousand men in it. They do not know what to do with themselves, and ever since they arrived this morning they have been wandering about the town, looking for lodgings. The passers-by step aside when they meet them, for these men are war-weary, hungry and fierce. Some of them, I noticed, had squatted down by a large, round flower-bed and had scattered their rifles and haversacks over it.

Presently, not hurrying himself in the least, the gardener came up with his broom. He surveyed them angrily:

'What sort of a camping ground do you think you've got here? This is a flower-bed — flowers are going to grow here. You know what flowers are, don't you? Are you all blind? This is the children's playground. Come off it, I say. D'you hear me?'

And the fierce, armed men meekly crawled away from the flower-bed.

6 July 1917

Soldiers in steel helmets, just recalled from the front, are surrounding the Peter and Paul Fortress. They are marching leisurely along the pavements and through the park, dragging their machine-guns behind them, their rifles carelessly dangling from their shoulders. Occasionally one of them calls out good-naturedly to a passer-by:

'Hurry up; there's going to be some shooting!'

The inhabitants are all agog to see the battle and are following the soldiers silently, with fox-like movements, dodging from tree to tree and straining their necks, looking eagerly ahead.

In the Alexander Park flowers are growing at the sides of the paths; the gardener is busying himself among them. He has a clean apron on and carries a spade in his hand. As he walks along he scolds both onlookers and soldiers as though they were a flock of sheep.

'Where are you walking, there? Is that grass made for you to trample on? Isn't there enough room for you on the path?'

A bearded, iron-headed peasant in soldier's uniform, his rifle under his arm, says to the gardener:

'You look out yourself, old boy, or we'll shoot you straight away.'

'Oh, will you? You just try! Fine shot, you are. . .'

'Don't you know there's a war on? There's going to be some fighting.'

'Oh, is there? Well, get on with your fighting, and I'll get on with my job.' 'I'm with you there. Have you got a fag?' Pulling out his pouch from his pocket the gardener grumbled: 'Trampling about where you're not allowed to. . .'

'It's war.'

'What's that got to do with me? Fighting's all very well for them that likes it, and you've got plenty of others to help you; but I'm all alone in this job. You'd better clean that rifle of yours a bit; it's all rusty. . .'

There is a whistle and the soldier, unable to light the cigarette in his lips, puts it hastily in his pocket and runs off between the trees.

The gardener spits after him in disgust and shouts angrily:

'What the devil are you running over the grass for? Isn't there any other road you can go by?'

Autumn, 1917

The gardener walks leisurely along the path, a ladder on his shoulders and a pair of shears in his hand. Every now and then he stops to cut off the dead branches by the side of the path. He has grown thinner — seems almost shrivelled; his clothes hang on him like a sail on a mast on a windless day. The shears snip angrily and creakily as he cuts down the barren wood.

Watching him, I could not help thinking that neither an earthquake nor a flood would prevent him from going on with his work. And if the trumpets of the archangels announcing the day of judgement were not shining brilliantly enough, I am quite certain that he would scold the archangels in precisely the same voice as he scolded the soldier.

'You'd better clean those trumpets of yours a bit, they're all dirty. . . .'

12. John Reed on Lenin

By the 8th of November, the October Revolution was all over; the Bolsheviks controlled the city, and the Provisional Government had gone the way of the Tsars. On that evening, Lenin began the process of constructing a Bolshevik government and planning for the future. The American John Reed, an ardent Communist and supporter of Lenin, was present, and described in dramatic fashion the events of the evening.

...It was just 8:40 p.m. when a thundering wave of cheers announced the entrance of the presidium, with Lenin — great Lenin — among them. A short, stocky figure, with a big head set down in his shoulders, bald and bulging. Little eyes, a snubbish nose, wide, generous mouth and heavy chin; clean-shaven now, but already beginning to bristle with the well-known beard of his past and future. Dressed in shabby clothes, his trousers much too long for him. Unimpressive, to be the idol of a mob, loved and revered as perhaps few leaders in history have been. A strange popular leader — a leader purely by virtue of intellect; colourless, humourless, uncompromising and detached, without picturesque idiosyncrasies — but with the power of explaining profound ideas in simple terms, of analysing a concrete situation. And combined with shrewdness, the greatest intellectual audacity....

...Now Lenin, gripping the edge of the reading stand, letting his little winking eyes travel over the crowd as he stood there waiting, apparently oblivious to the long-rolling ovation, which lasted several minutes. When it finished, he said simply, 'We shall now proceed to construct the Socialist order!' Again that overwhelming human roar.

'The first thing is the adoption of practical measures to realize peace... We shall offer peace to the peoples of all the belligerent countries upon the basis of the Soviet terms — no annexations, no indemnities, and the right of self-determination of peoples. At the same time, according to our promise, we shall publish and repudiate the secret treaties... The question of War and Peace is so clear that I think that I may, without preamble, read the project of a Proclamation to the Peoples of All the Belligerent Countries....'

...His great mouth, seeming to smile, opened wide as he spoke; his voice was hoarse — not unpleasantly so, but as if it had hardened that way after years and years of speaking — and went on monotonously, with the effect of being able to go on forever....

For emphasis he bent forward slightly. No gestures. And before him, a thousand simple faces looking up in intent adoration....

[*Lenin then read the Proclamation.*]

Abridged from J. Reed, *Ten Days that Shook the World,* London, 1966.

...'The Revolution of November 6th and 7th,' he ended, 'has opened the era of the Social Revolution... The labour movement, in the name of peace and Socialism, shall win, and fulfill its destiny...'

There was something quiet and powerful in all this, which stirred the souls of men. It was understandable why people believed when Lenin spoke....

...It was exactly 10:35 when Kamenev† asked all in favour of the Proclamation to hold up their cards. One delegate dared to raise his hand against, but the sudden sharp outburst around him brought it swiftly down... Unanimous.

Suddenly, by common impulse, we found ourselves on our feet, mumbling together into the smooth lifting unison of the *Internationale*.† A grizzled old soldier was sobbing like a child. Alexandra Kollontai† rapidly winked the tears back. The immense sound rolled through the hall, burst windows and doors and soared into the quiet sky. 'The war is ended! The war is ended!' said a young workman near me, his face shining. And when it was over, as we stood there in a kind of awkward hush, someone in the back of the room shouted, 'Comrades! Let us remember those who have died for liberty! So we began to sing the Funeral March, that slow, melancholy and yet triumphant chant, so Russian and so moving. The *Internationale* is an alien air, after all, The Funeral March seemed the very soul of those dark masses whose delegates sat in this hall, building from their obscure visions a new Russia — and perhaps more....

...For this did they lie there, the martyrs of March, in their cold Brotherhood Grave on Mars Field; for this thousands and tens of thousands had died in the prisons, in exile, in Siberian mines. It had not come as they expected it would come, nor as the *intelligentsia* desired it; but it had come — rough, strong, impatient of formulas, contemptuous or sentimentalism; *real*....

Lenin was reading the Decree on Land...

...At two o'clock the Land Decree was put to vote, with only one against and the peasant delegates wild with joy... So plunged the Bolsheviki ahead, irresistible, overriding hesitation and the opposition — the only people in Russia who had a definite programme of action while the others talked for eight long months...

...It was almost seven when we woke the sleeping conductors and motor-men of the street-cars which the Street Railway Workers' Union always kept waiting at Smolny to take the Soviet delegates to their homes. In the crowded car there was less happy hilarity than the night before, I thought. Many looked anxious; perhaps they were saying to themselves, 'Now we are masters, how can we do our will?'...

13. Alexander Blok: The Twelve

The Symbolist poet Alexander Blok attempted to capture the mood and spirit of the October Revolution in his poem The Twelve, *written in January, 1918, from which the following excerpts are taken. Blok's subjects are twelve Red Guards, the paramilitary forces of the Bolsheviks. This revolutionary militia was anarchistic in its outlook and brutal in its actions; to Blok, the Red Guard symbolized the most basic forces unleashed in the events of 1917.*

II

The wind plays up: snow flutters down.
Twelve men are marching through the town.

Their rifle-butts on black slings sway.
Lights left, right, left, wink all the way. . .

Cap tilted, fag drooping, every one
looks like a jailbird on the run.

Freedom, freedom,
down with the cross!

Rat-a-tat-tat!

It's cold, boys, and I'm numb!

Rat-a-tat-tat!

Lights left, right, left, lights all the way. . .
Rifles on their shoulders sway. . .

Keep A Revolutionary Step!
The Relentless Enemy Will Not Stop!

Grip your gun like a man, brother!
Let's have a crack at Holy Russia,
Mother
Russia
with her big, fat arse!
Freedom, freedom! Down with the cross!

Abridged from Alexander Blok, *The Twelve and Other Poems,* J. Stallworthy and P. France, translators, New York, 1970.

III

The lads have all gone to the wars
to serve in the Red Guard —
to serve in the Red Guard —
and risk their hot heads for the cause.

Hell and damnation,
life is such fun
with a ragged greatcoat
and a Jerry gun!

To smoke the nobs out of their holes
we'll light a fire through all the world,
a bloody fire through all the world —
Lord, bless our souls!
● ●

X

Still the storm rages gust upon gust.
What weather! What a storm!
At arm's length you can only just
make out your neighbour's form.

Snow twists into a funnel,
a towering tunnel. . .

'Oh, what a blizzard! . . . Jesus Christ!'
Watch it, Pete, cut out that rot!
You fool, what did Christ and his cross
ever do for the likes of us?
Look at your hands. Aren't they hot
with the blood of the girl you shot?

Keep A Revolutionary Step!
The Enemy Is Near And Won't Let Up!

Forward, and forward again
the working men!

XI

Abusing God's name as they go,
all twelve march onward into snow. . .
prepared for anything,
regretting nothing. . .

Their rifles at the ready
for the unseen enemy
in back streets, side roads
where only snow explodes
its shrapnel, and through quag-
mire drifts where the boots drag. . .

before their eyes
throbs a red flag.

Left, right,
the echo replies.

Keep your eyes skinned
lest the enemy strike!

Into their faces day and night
bellows the wind
without a break. . .

Forward, and forward again
the working men!

14. Dissolution of the Constituent Assembly

The Constituent Assembly was Russia's first, and only, democratically-elected assembly. As such, it truly represented Russia's voters. Of the 703 delegates, 380 were SRs, and only 168 were Bolsheviks. It met on January 18, 1918, with the Bolshevik leaders having already determined to dissolve it if it did not endorse a pro-Bolshevik program. The leader of the SR Party, Victor Chernov, was elected President of the Assembly; the following is his description of the events of that day.

When we, the newly elected members of the Constituent Assembly, entered the Tauride Palace, the seat of the Assembly in Petrograd, on January 18, 1918, we found that the corridors were full of armed guards. They were masters of the building, crude and brazen. At first they did not address us directly, and only exchanged casual observations to the effect that "this guy should get a bayonet between his ribs" or "it wouldn't be bad to put some lead into this one." When we entered the large hall, it was still empty. The Bolshevik deputies had not yet appeared.

The Assembly hall was gradually filled by the deputies. Near the dais were placed armed guards. The public gallery was crowded to overflowing. Here and there glittered rifle muzzles.

At last all the deputies had gathered in a tense atmosphere. The left sector was evidently waiting for something. From our benches rose Deputy Lordkipanidze, who said in a calm, businesslike voice that, according to an old parliamentary custom, the first sitting should be presided over by the senior deputy. The senior was S.P. Shvetsov, an old Socialist Revolutionary (SR).

Abridged from D. vonMohrenschildt, editor, *The Russian Revolution of 1917*, New York, 1971.

As soon as Shvetsov's imposing figure appeared on the dais, somebody gave a signal, and a deafening uproar broke out. The stamping of feet, hammering on the desks and howling made an infernal noise. The public in the gallery and the Bolshevik allies, the Left Socialist Revolutionaries, joined in the tumult. The guards clapped their rifle butts on the floor. From various sides guns were trained on Shvetsov. He took the President's bell, but the tinkling was drowned in the noise. He put it back on the table, and somebody immediately grabbed it and handed it over, like a trophy, to the representative of the Sovnarkom [Council of People's Commissars], Sverdlov. Taking advantage of a moment of comparative silence, Shvetsov managed to pronounce the sacramental phrase: "The session of the Constituent Assembly is open." These words evoked a new din of protest. Shvetsov slowly left the dais and joined us. He was replaced by Sverdlov, who opened the session for the second time, but now in the name of the Soviets, and presented its "platform." This was an ultimatum: we had just to vote Aye or No.

In the election of the Assembly's President, the Bolsheviks presented no candidate of their own. They voted for Maria Spiridonova, nominated by the Left SRs. Later they threw Spiridonova into jail and tormented her until she was on the verge of insanity. But at this moment they wanted to take full advantage of her popularity and reputation as a martyr in the struggle against Tsarism. My nomination as candidate for the Presidency received even greater support than had been expected. Some leftist peasants evidently could not bring themselves to oppose their own *"muzhik* minister." I obtained 244 votes against 150.

I delivered my inauguration address, making vigorous efforts to keep self-control. Every sentence of my speech was met with outcries, some ironical, others spiteful, often buttressed by the brandishing of guns. Bolshevik deputies surged forward to the dais. Conscious that the stronger nerves would win, I was determined not to yield to provocation. I said that the nation had made its choice, that the composition of the Assembly was a living testimony to the people's yearning for Socialism, and that its convention marked the end of the hazy transition period. Land reform, I went on, was a foregone conclusion: the land would be equally accessible to all who wished to till it. The Assembly, I said, would inaugurate an era of active foreign policy directed toward peace.

I finished my speech amidst a cross-fire of interruptions and cries. It was now the turn of the Bolshevik speakers — Skvortsov and Bukharin. During their delivery, our sector was a model of restraint and self-discipline. We maintained a cold, dignified silence. The Bolshevik speeches, as usual, were shrill, clamorous, provocative and rude, but they could not break the icy silence of our majority. As President, I was bound in duty to call them to order for abusive statements. But I know that this was precisely what they expected. Since the armed guards were under their orders, they wanted clashes, incidents and perhaps a brawl. So I remained silent.

The Social Democratic Tseretelli rose to answer the Bolsheviks. They tried to "scare" him by levelling at him a rifle from the gallery and brandishing a gun in front of his face. I had to restore order — but how? Appeals to maintain the dignity of the Constituent Assembly evoked an even greater noise, at times turning into a raving fury. Dybenko and other demagogues called for more and more assaults. Lenin, in the government box, demonstrated his contempt for the Assembly by lounging in his chair and putting on the air of a man who was bored to death. I threatened to clear the gallery of the yelling public. Though this was an empty threat, since the guards were only waiting for the order to "clear" us out of the hall, it proved temporarily effective. Tseretelli's calm and dignified manner helped to restore peace.

There was a grim significance in the outburst that broke loose when a middle-of-the-road deputy, Severtsov-Odoyesky, started to speak Ukrainian. In the Assembly the Bolsheviks did not want to hear any language except Russian. I was compelled to state emphatically that in the new Russia, each nationality had the right to use its own language whenever it pleased.

When it appeared that we refused to vote the Soviet "platform" without discussion, the Bolsheviks walked out of the sitting in a body. They returned to read a declaration charging us with counter-revolution and stating that our fate would be decided by organs which were in charge of such things. Soon after that the Left SRs also made up their minds. Just before the discussion of the land reform started, their representative, I. Z. Steinberg, declared that they were in disagreement with the majority, and left the Assembly.

We knew that the Bolsheviks were in conference, discussing what to do next. I felt sure that we would be arrested. But it was of utmost importance for us to have a chance to say the last word. I declared that the next point on the agenda was the land reform. At this moment somebody pulled at my sleeve.

"You have to finish now. There are orders from the People's Commissar."

Behind me stood a stocky sailor, accompanied by his armed comrades.

"What People's Commissar?"

"We have orders. Anyway, you cannot stay here any longer. The lights will be turned out in a minute. And the guards are tired."

"The members of the Assembly are also tired but cannot rest until they have fulfilled the task entrusted to them by the people — to decide on the land reform and the future form of government."

And leaving the guards no time to collect themselves, I proceeded to read the main paragraphs of the Land Bill, which our party had prepared long ago. But time was running short. Reports and debates had to be omitted. Upon my proposal, the Assembly voted six basic points of the bill. It provided that all land was to be turned into common property, with every tiller possessing equal rights to use it. Amidst incessant shouts: "That's enough! Stop it now! Clear the hall!" the other points of the bill were voted.

Fearing that the lights would be extinguished, somebody managed to procure candles. It was essential that the future form of government be voted upon immediately. Otherwise the Bolsheviks would not fail to charge the Assembly with having left the door open for the restoration of the monarchy. The motion for a republican form of government was carried unanimously.

In the dawn of a foggy and murky morning I declared a recess until noon.

At the exit a palefaced man pushed his way to me and beseeched me in a trembling voice not to use my official car. A bunch of murderers, he said, was waiting for me. He admitted that he was a Bolshevik, but his conscience revolted against this plot.

I left the building, surrounded by a few friends. We saw several men in sailor's uniforms loitering near my car. We decided to walk. We had a long distance to go, and when I arrived home I learned that rumors were in circulation that the Constituent Assembly had dispersed, and that Chernov and Tseretelli had been shot.

At noon several members of the Assembly were sent on reconnaissance. They reported that the door of the Tauride Palace was sealed and guarded by a patrol with machine guns and two pieces of field artillery. Later in the day a decree of the Sovnarkom was published by which the Constituent Assembly was "dissolved."

Thus ended Russia's first and last democratic parliament.

15. Terrorism: the Cheka

With the forcible dissolution of the freely elected Constituent Assembly, the Bolsheviks made it clear that their regime was not to be democratic, and as a result, opposition increased. Defining all opposition as counter-revolutionism, the Bolsheviks in 1918 instituted a policy of terror, implemented by the Cheka.

The head of the Cheka, Felix Dzerzhinsky, himself defined the Cheka's role, in a 1918 interview.

...We stand for organized terror — this should be frankly admitted. Terror is an absolute necessity during times of revolution. Our aim is to fight against the enemies of the Soviet Government and of the new order of life. Among such enemies are our political adversaries, as well as bandits, speculators, and other criminals who undermine the foundations of the Soviet Government. To these we show no mercy. We terrorize the enemies of the Soviet Government in order to stop crime at its inception. . .

We judge quickly. In most cases only a day passes between the apprehension of the criminal and his sentence. But this does not mean that our sentences are groundless. . . When confronted with evidence criminals in almost every case confess; and what argument can have greater weight than a criminal's own confession?...

Abridged from J. Bunyan, *Intervention, Civil War and Communism in Russia, 1918,* Baltimore, 1936.

16. The Cheka in Action

In February, 1918, the following order was issued, to implement the goal announced by Dzerzhinsky.

To All Soviets

. . .The All-Russian Extraordinary Commission to Fight Counter-Revolution, Sabotage, and Speculation asks the (local) Soviets to proceed at once to seek out, arrest, and shoot immediately all members. . . connected in one form or another with counter-revolutionary organizations. . . (1) agents of enemy spies, (2) counter-revolutionary agitators, (3) speculators, (4) organizers of revolts. . . against the Soviet Government, (5) those going to the Don to join the Kaledin-Kornilov band† and the Polish counter-revolutionary legions, (6) buyers and sellers of arms to be used by the counter-revolutionary bourgeoisie — all these are to be shot on the spot. . .when caught red-handed in the act.

The All-Russian Cheka

17. The Civil War

The attitude of the peasants in the years following the Revolution is described in a piece appearing in the newspaper Our Age, *before it was closed down by the Bolsheviks in 1918.*

A DAY IN THE VILLAGE

Colorless, lazy, tedious Riazan† has not changed much since the days of Gogol. The raven continues as of old to clamor from the church steeples. All is quiet in the city except for a dance here and there.

In the *uezds*† it is frightful. The sleepy Russian village has been aroused by Bolshevism and threatens to destroy everything in sight. In the robbing and killing of landlords Riazan *Gubernia*† is notorious . . . conditions are worst in the localities where the deserters and the hidden stills are more numerous. . . .

Father Alexander and I took a walk through the village.

"Take note," said the Father, "of the people's blindness . . . and the use that is being made of it. . . . At the time of the elections (Constituent Assembly) the women came to me to ask how to vote and while doing so kept looking around to see if anyone was listening. Soldiers went from hut to hut telling the

Ibid.

Ibid.

occupants that if they did not vote the Bolshevik ticket their cows, grain, and huts would be taken from them."

While talking we arrived at the schoolhouse. . . . A meeting had been called to hear a lecture on how good the Bolsheviks are and what they would give to the people and . . . why other parties were bad. A soldier was reading from a paper. It was not quite clear who sent him here, whether the Riazan Soviet or an emissary of the People's Commissars. . . .

During the reading there appeared the commissar himself, in soldier's uniform. He walked with a certain assurance, stepped up to the speaker's desk, took off his cap, knocked on the table, and began to talk:

"Comrades! I should like first of all to call your attention to the importance of the period we are living in. It is a time of the freedom of the people, the triumph of the proletariat, and the solution of important problems. . . ."

He spoke rather quickly but not altogether ungrammatically. His speech sounded like an article in *Pravda*, but it was quite evident that he had not assimilated what he had read. He likened Kerensky to a dog whose tail had been cut off but (said that) "it should have been the head." When he talked about the bourgeoisie he became so excited that it seemed as if his eyes would pop out. . . .

I looked at the auditors. They sat there quietly, drinking in everything, believing everything. . . . The village believes him who shouts, beats his breast, and foams at the mouth. The last and loudest speaker has the best chance of carrying his audience with him. But I must return to the speaker of the day.

"Comrades" said the orator, "the time has come when every true peasant and proletarian can say and say loudly: 'Enough! Take the land from the landlords! Go through their bags and pocketbooks!' Do you agree with me, Comrades?"

"We agree!" shouted back the younger men, but the women nudged each other and tried to keep from giggling.

The first speaker was followed by the teacher of the school. He did not know the arts of eloquence, he did not jump up and down, did not fume, and could not get the attention of the audience. . . . His arguments, too, were childish. "The Bolsheviks," he said, "will soon disappear, for how can it be otherwise?" He failed completely.

Father Alexander came next. He had no more than opened his mouth when someone began to make remarks about him.

I left the room and went outside. Three peasants with long beards stood talking, and I approached them.

"How can you listen to such rot, lies, and foolishness?" I remarked.

"Who are you?" asked one.

"One of those city fellows," said another.

"Of course, he does not like to let go of his property," added a third.

The meeting ended and we went home. I spent a miserable night. My room was cold, the baby cried, and the wind howled. . . .

When I awoke in the morning and looked out I noticed a streak of light against the grey sky. Later I learned that it was the flames from one of the manor houses which had been set on fire. . . .

On my way to the station I passed a number of peasant carts, loaded down with furniture, pictures, and a piano. The piano was without its top and rested on its side. A peasant woman was steadying it with one hand and striking the keys with the other. . . .

The train was more than crowded. Every bit of space, including the aisle and the toilet, was occupied. The air was so thick that one almost choked. . . . But even under these conditions a young soldier made a speech. He explained the origin of the bourgeoisie:

"Once upon a time there lived Adam and Eve. They had many children. The children settled in villages and cities. In the cities there grew up 'individuals.' These 'individuals' are people of strong will. They united with the priests, that is to say, with all kinds of clergy, and through this combination the bourgeoisie came into existence. What a bourgeoisie! It has been crushing us and it is about time that we got rid of it. . . . Tolstoy said the same thing. . . ."

I broke in with the question, "What did Tolstoy say?"

He gave me a wicked look of contempt. . . , spat on the floor, and turned his back on me. . . .

Russia has lost herself in the darkness. Lord of Heaven, lead Russia out of the darkness!

18. Isaac Babel: Prishchepa's Vengeance

The horrors of the Civil War also appear in fiction, and nowhere more eloquently than in the short stories of Isaac Babel, a Jew from Odessa who accompanied Budenny, the great Bolshevik General, during the Red Army campaigns against the Poles in 1920-21. The following is one story from his collection Red Cavalry.

I am on my way to Leszniow, where the Divisional Staff is quartered. My companion, as before, is Prishchepa, a young Cossack from the Kuban† — a tireless ruffian who has been turned out of the Communist Party, a future rag-and-bone man, a carefree syphilitic, and a happy-go-lucky fraud. He wears a crimson Circassian coat of fine cloth, and a downy Caucasian hood is thrown back over his shoulders. On our journeys he has told me his story.

A year ago, Prishchepa ran away from the Whites. In revenge, these took his parents as hostages and put them to death. Their property was seized by the neighbors. When the Whites were driven out of the Kuban, Prishchepa returned to his native settlement.

Abridged from I. Babel, *The Collected Stories,* W. Morison, editor and translator, New York, 1955.

It was early morning, daybreak. The peasants' slumber sighed in the acrid stuffiness. Prishchepa hired an official cart and went about the settlement collecting his phonographs, wooden kvass†-jugs, and the towels his mother had embroidered. He went out into the street in a black felt cloak, a curved dagger at his belt. The cart plodded along behind. Prishchepa went from neighbor to neighbor, leaving behind him a trail of blood-stained footprints. In the huts where he found gear that had belonged to his mother, a pipe that had been his father's, he left old women stabbed through and through, dogs hung above the wells, icons defiled with excrement. The inhabitants of the settlement watched his progress sullenly, smoking their pipes. The young Cossacks were scattered over the steppe, keeping the score. And the score mounted up and up — and still the settlement remained silent.

When he had made an end, Prishchepa went back to his despoiled home and arranged the furniture he had taken back in the places he remembered from childhood. Then he sent for vodka, and shutting himself up in the hut, he drank for two whole days and nights, singing, weeping, and hewing the furniture with his Circassian saber.

On the third night the settlement saw smoke rise from Prishchepa's hut. Torn, scorched, staggering, the Cossack led the cow out of the shed, put his revolver in its mouth and fired. The earth smoked beneath him. A blue ring of flame flew out of the chimney and melted away, while in the stall the young bull that had been left behind bellowed piteously. The fire shone as bright as Sunday. Then Prishchepa untied his horse, leaped into the saddle, threw a lock of his hair into the flames, and vanished.

19. Murder of the Royal Family

While ex-Tsar Nicholas and his family were in themselves no threat to the Bolsheviks, their presence constituted a symbol and a possible rallying-point for the more conservative opposition. The Romanovs were moved from Tobolsk to Ekaterinburg, in the Urals, in April 1918. The local soviet was hostile to them from the start, and that hostility increased during July, as the anti-Bolshevik Czech Legion drew closer to Ekaterinburg. Without authorization from higher authority, the locals decided on action. The following is a description by a local workman, who witnessed the events of July 16.

In the evening of July 16th, between 7 and 8 P.M., when the time for my duty had just begun, Commandant Yurovsky [the head of the guard] ordered me to take all the Nagan revolvers from the guards and to bring them to him.

From G.G. Telberg and R. Wilton, *The Last Days of the Romanovs*, New York, 1920.

I took twelve revolvers from the sentries as well as from some other of the guards, and brought them to the commandant's office. Yurovsky said to me: 'We must shoot *them* all tonight, so notify the guards not to be alarmed if they hear shots.' I understood, therefore, that Yurovsky had it in his mind to shoot the whole of the Tsar's family, as well as the doctor and the servants who lived with them, but I did not ask him where or by whom the decision had been made. I must tell you that in accordance with Yurovsky's order the boy who assisted the cook was transferred in the morning to the guardroom (in the Popov house). The lower floor of Ipatiev's house was occupied by the Letts from the Letts Commune, who had taken up their quarters there after Yurovsky was made commandant. They were ten in number. At about ten o'colck in the evening, in accordance with Yurovsky's order, I informed the guards not to be alarmed if they should hear firing. About midnight Yurovsky woke up the Tsar's family. I do not know if he told them the reason they had been awakened and where they were to be taken, but I positively affirm that it was Yurovsky who entered the rooms occupied by the Tsar's family. Yurovsky had not ordered me or Dobrynin to awaken the family. In about an hour the whole of the family, the doctor, the maid and the waiters got up, washed and dressed themselves. Just before Yurovsky went to awaken the family, two members of the Extraordinary Commission [*of the Ekaterinburg Soviet*] arrived at Ipatiev's house. Shortly after one o'clock A.M., the Tsar, the Tsaritsa, their four daughters, the maid, the doctor, the cook and the waiter left their rooms. The Tsar carried the heir in his arms. The Emperor and the heir were dressed in 'gimnasterkas' [soldiers' shirt] and wore caps. The Empress and her daughters were dressed but their heads were uncovered. The Emperor, carrying the heir, preceded them. The Empress, her daughters and the others followed him. Yurovsky, his assistant and the two above-mentioned members of the Extraordinary Commission accompanied them. I was also present. During my presence none of the Tsar's family asked any questions. They did not weep or cry. Having descended the stairs to the first floor, we went out into the court, and from there by the second door (counting from the gate) we entered the ground floor of the house. When the room (which adjoins the store-room with a sealed door) was reached, Yurovsky ordered chairs to be brought, and his assistant brought three chairs. One chair was given to the Emperor, one to the Empress, and the third to the heir. The Empress sat by the wall by the window, near the black pillar of the arch. Behind her stood three of the daughters (I knew their faces very well, because I had seen them every day when they walked in the garden, but I didn't know their names). The heir and the Emperor sat side by side almost in the middle of the room. Doctor Botkin stood behind the heir. The maid, a very tall woman, stood at the left of the door leading to the store-room; by her side stood one of the Tsar's daughters (the fourth). Two servants stood against the wall on the left from the entrance of the room.

The maid carried a pillow. The Tsar's daughters also brought small pillows with them. One pillow was put on the Empress's chair; another on the heir's chair. It seemed as if all of them guessed their fate, but not one of them uttered a single sound. At this moment eleven men entered the room: Yurovsky, his assistant, two members of the Extraordinary Commission, and seven Letts. Yurovsky ordered me to leave, saying: 'Go on to the streets, see if there is anybody there, and wait to see whether the shots have been heard.' I went out to the court, which was enclosed by a fence, but before I got to the street I heard the firing. I returned to the house immediately (only two or three minutes having elapsed), and upon entering the room where the execution had taken place, I saw that all the members of the Tsar's family were lying on the floor with many wounds in their bodies. The blood was running in streams. The doctor, the maid and two waiters had also been shot. When I entered the heir was still alive and moaned a little. Yurovsky went up and fired two or three more times at him. Then the heir was still.

The sight of the murder and the smell of blood made me sick. Before the assassination, when Yurovsky distributed the revolvers, he gave me one but, as I said before, I did not take any part in the murder. After the assassination Yurovsky told me to bring some guards to wash away the blood in the room. On the way to Popov's house I met two of the Senior Guards, Ivan Starkov and Constantin Dobrynin. They were running in the direction of Ipatiev's house. Dobrynin asked me: 'Has Nicholas II been shot?' I answered that Nicholas and the whole of his family had been shot. I brought twelve or fifteen guards back with me to the house. These men carried the dead bodies out to the motor lorry that waited near the entrance and the bodies were placed on stretchers made from bedsheets and shafts of sledges taken from the yard. When they were loaded on the truck they were wrapped in soldiers' clothing. . . The members of the Extraordinary Commission sat on the lorry and the truck drove off. I do not know in what direction the lorry went, neither do I know where the bodies were taken.

20. Victims of the Red Terror

While many targets of the terror were from royal or noble backgrounds, its victims were from all walks of life. Typical of its operation is the following account of a single day's (September 17, 1918) work by the Cheka of the Western Region.

The session took place in the presence of seven members of the Extraordinary Commission and two members of the Central Collegium of the Russian Communist Party.

The following were arraigned:

From J. Bunyan, *Intervention, Civil War and Communism in Russia,* 1918, Baltimore, 1936.

1. Antonevich, S., former (army) officer, an active participant in a counter-revolutionary plot to overthrow Soviet rule. *Decision*: He is to be shot.

2. Gepner, Vladimir, former chief of police of Smolensk. *Decision*: He is to be shot.

3. Korshonboim, former assistant inspector of Smolensk Prison. He flogged political prisoners while holding the position of prison inspector. *Decision*: He is to be turned over to the People's Court and his case is transferred to the Department of Justice.

4. Revknev, I., arrested for serving in the Polish Corps. *Decision*: He is to be released from arrest in view of the fact that he was only a private in the Polish Corps.

5. Sorokin, V., former general and head of the secret police. *Decision*: He is to be shot.

6. Mikhailov, M., a criminal, . . . charged with participation in murders and robberies. *Decision*: He is to be shot.

7. Romanov, Zakhar, former police guard, . . . notorious for cruelty to peasants. *Decision*: He is to be shot.

8. Kondratiuk, G., charged with drunkenness and murder. *Decision*: He is to be transferred to the People's Court.

9. Brazhko, charged with drunkenness and murder. *Decision*: Three months in jail.

10. Toptunov, Leiba, charged with giving a bribe. *Decision*: He is to be released from arrest and to receive his money back.

11. Goncharov, E., Piroga, A., Kozlov, and Egorov, members of the militia, charged with violation of official duties. *Decision*: They are to be released.

12. Dorman, M., former general, involved in the organization of a counter-revolutionary plot against the Soviet Government. *Decision*: He is to be shot.

13. Dorman, Vladimir, son of General Dorman. . . . *Decision*: Being only fifteen years old, he is to be released.

14. Vitkevich, Maria, proprietress of Smolensk, charged with insulting the Soviet Government. *Decision*: She is to be fined ten thousand rubles and freed from arrest upon payment of the fine.

15. Shustov, Evdokim, a store employee, arrested for having a false permit to carry arms. *Decision*: Because he belongs to the proletarian class Shustov is to be released from arrest.

16. Gladyshev, V., former police official of Smolensk. *Decision*:He is to be shot.

17. Filippov. I., Ventov, F., criminals. *Decision*: They are to be shot.

18. Lukstin, A., arrested for delivering 57,000 rubles to a White Guard organization. *Decision*: He is to be shot.

[An additional 36 names follow, of whom 22 are sentenced to be shot.]

Chairman of the Extraordinary
Commission of the Western
Region

21. The Famine of 1921-22

The famine of 1921-22, caused by drought and the ravages of the Civil War, was so devastating that the Soviet government called for outside help. Among those who responded were Quaker relief organizations from the United States. The following account of the situation in Samara, 800 miles southeast of Moscow, is from a report filed by Anna Haines, representative of The American Friends Service Committee in Russia.

I could hear the children crying two blocks away as I approached one of the homes for abandoned children in Samara, the central city of the famine area of Russia. A steady wail that kept up like a moan grew louder as we got nearer. The nurses could do nothing except to go around every morning and separate the babies that were going to die that day; and they went around at different times later and felt them to see if they were cold. In the evening those who had died during the day were gathered together and placed in heaps outside the building. A garbage-cart stopped each night and the baby bodies were loaded in. The garbage-carts stopped in the same way before all of the children's institutions in Samara and the other cities in the Volga region.

Children's homes, which are emptied of dead babies only to be refilled by the constant flow of abandoned children from the country; men and women and young children falling dead on the street from hunger; farm machinery, which in Russia is more precious than human life at the present time, lying scrapped by the roadside and rusting to pieces, tell the story of the extent and horror of the famine which is destroying the lives of 15,000,000 people in the greatest grain belt of Russia.

Though most of us are more familiar with the larger outlines of the Russian famine story, it is still hard to understand the fact that the great Volga Valley, which has always been the granary of Russia, supplying not only its own population, but most of the rest of European Russia and other areas of the world with wheat and rye, is now bare of any grain. Over an area 800 miles long by 500 miles wide there fell during April, May and June of this year—the critical growing months of the grain crop—less than 2.5 inches, the normal being 14 inches, of rain, and the temperatures averaged 12.6 degrees Fahrenheit hotter than the average for the last seventeen years. While 938,000 tons of grain were needed by this area for its own consumption, but 69,000 were produced. Many of the peasants with whom I talked said that all the grain which their land had produced could have been held in their double hands, and this meant rations for a whole family for a year.

It is impossible at the present time to state accurately the death statistics, but the population of the Volga grain area is approximately 20,000,000, and all of

From a report published by The American Friends Service Committee, 1922.

these are vitally affected by the lack of food. We do know, however, that in the children's institutions famine is already making itself felt in dreadful figures. In the institutions for children under three years of age there is a death rate of 90 per cent, and in the homes for older children, those from twelve to fifteen years, there is a death rate of 75 per cent.

A mandate given me by the Commissar of Health, and a working knowledge of the Russian language, enabled me to go to the peasants myself without an interpreter and talk to them personally concerning the conditions under which they were living. I also had the privilege of speaking to the priests, who would be likely to give as opposite statistics from the Soviet figures as truth would allow, because these groups are usually the extreme poles of information in Russia. The members of the co-operative stores also gave valuable information, as they have the best knowledge of the economic situation there today.

We started from Moscow for our trip down into Samara, the largest city affected by the famine. It is situated on the Volga, and is a city of about 300,000 inhabitants, now very much increased in population by the refugees who are constantly pouring in from the country regions. Passing on to Buzuluk, a town formerly containing 20,000 people, now reduced to 12,000 because of the flight of those who could reach Siberia, we traveled out through the country regions.

The steppe ordinarily has no trees; it is a level, slightly rolling plain, with village after village scattered about five or ten miles apart. This fall it looked as though a prairie fire had swept over it. Farms and areas which are usually green or golden with harvest were burned almost black. What grass had grown was only a stunted growth on the surface of the ground. Every few rods as we went along we would scare away the carrion birds which were feasting on the carcasses of the dead horses and dogs that had died along the roadside. There was a continuous stream of refugees going our way, and we passed others going in the opposite direction. They did not much care which way they were going — they were just going to search for food. Some were coming from Uralsk and going to Ufa; some were going from Ufa to Uralsk. One family had passed across the country in June with two horses, small children and a baby, and such household utensils as they could carry. They had been traveling from their home to a place which they had been told contained food. When they reached there they found less food in that town than in their own home, and they were now wandering along the way back, saying that they preferred to die at home rather than in a "foreign land." One horse had died; the one they were using was nothing but a bag of bones. The older children were living upon the rinds of watermelons. Their heads were covered with sores and with flies, and the parents were too listless and tired to care for them.

We entered one of the villages along the wide street which makes up the largest part of a Russian village, with little houses, containing one or two rooms apiece, on either side, and stopped that night at the home of what had been one of the richest peasants in the village. His large wooden house with three rooms was an evidence of his wealth. It was surrounded with barnyards and sheds for stock, all of which were now empty. One of the daughters-in-law said that last year they had twelve horses and six cows. The cows had now all been sold or killed, and all the horses had died but one. The girl showed us the kind of bread the ordinary Russian family is using, and has been using for several months. It was made of grass and leaves and bark which had been ground into flour. There were twelve people in that family, and every day all went out into the countryside for several miles to gather the grass and the leaves and the roots. When this had been ground together the pulp of the hoofs of horses was added to hold it together. That was all this family was living on except soup which was made of horse meat. Later in the evening as the family talked, we learned that they understood that it was not possible for all of them to live until spring.

I talked with the Russian priest and asked if next March would not be the worst month for them. He answered, "No, I think not. This month (September) we will be eating the vegetables and the watermelons and the rinds. In October there will still be the grass, and we can make the grass pancakes. In November, when the snow comes, and we can no longer get anything from the fields, we will still have our little reserve of a few potatoes or a little bit of grass flour. In December people will begin to die, and by the first of the year every bit of the reserve will be gone. In March there will be no one alive in the village."

From all parts of the countryside the abandoned children were being brought daily into the children's homes of the larger towns and cities. These homes, which are hastily prepared as emergency quarters, have no equipment at all. For one of the homes in Samara, a house about six rooms had been taken over in July with the expectation of housing sixty children. At the end of August it contained 400 children. There were thirty-one cups and bowls. There were no sanitary arrangements of any kinds, but the nurses tried to bathe the children and wash as many of the lice from them as possible. But it was of little use, as the same dirty clothing had to be put on them again. There was no attempt at any recreation for the children, nor instruction, because those who had been teachers and caretakers were ill themselves with malaria or dysentery. The children were the most unchildlike babies I have ever seen. They lay perfectly motionless, with lifeless eyes. In the homes for older children the workers would allow them to wander about the streets in the hope of picking up stray bits of garbage as food. But the saddest sights were in the homes for the small babies. These babies were fed the same diet as older children and men and women—the grass bread and the meat soup. They could not digest that food, and it meant simply the question of how many hours the child would live. In one of the homes we visited in Samara the death rate was higher than 90 per cent. It was at these houses that the garbage-cart called daily and, after the bodies were piled in, took them off beyond the city for burial in trenches.

What is the government doing in the face of this appalling disaster? The first thing they concentrated their attention upon was the sending of seed corn into this area. The government realized that even the present famine situation would be as nothing compared to conditions next year if every effort were not given to the planting of seed. It was remarkable to find that the peasants, whose horses were dropping in the field, and whose children were starving, could be seen putting the seed into the ground instead of into their families' mouths. The next most important piece of work it is doing is the attempt to get as many of the people as are not actually needed to plough and plant out of this area into regions where the harvest had been good. It is endeavoring to send all foreigners to the countries of their origin. It is also forming colonies which will settle in Siberia. A group is made up of a bootmaker, a carpenter and other handicraftsmen to form a nucleus about which peasants may be gathered and a new community developed. Several thousands had thus been set out; but while in Siberia they will find wood and possibly grain, there are no materials for building, such as iron, nails or glass; and so the lack of these articles will keep the number who can be sent there relatively small. As many food trains as it is possible to equip from the meager stores at Moscow are being sent into the famine provinces; and food, mostly soup, is fed to the children at railroad junctions. In Samara the government train is feeding 4000 children a day.

Foreign relief has entered. The American Relief Administration will feed 1,250,000 children. But there are more than twelve million men, women and children who will need food as greatly as those who will be fed by this agency. The number of starving people to whom the Quakers will bring food is limited only by the resources which will be at their command. They are now feeding 50,000 children a day, and their organization is complete enough to enable it to expand this feeding to any limit. The people whom the Quakers will save are those who will not be saved by any other agency, and who will surely die before spring unless aid reaches them.

The morning I left Moscow there was printed in "Pravda," the morning newspaper, a simply worded request which had been sent in by a peasant from the famine area who had heard that the people in Moscow were getting a bread ration. He said:

"I come to you from a far country, where the bread and the buckwheat have failed. Only the noisy vultures are busy in the fields where all day the wind whips up the brown dust. Hunger is here. People moan. Their empty bellies swell. The breasts to which the babies turn are dry. You can hear the groans of the people amid the breaking waves of the Volga. You can hear the shower of their tears. You can hear what they cry out, 'Bring help and bring it soon.' "

22. The 1920s: Reduction of Class Distinctions

Of the results of the 1917 Revolution which became apparent during the 1920s, one of the most apparent was the reduction of class distinctions, a social "leveling," here described by the American historian W.H. Chamberlin, writing in 1930.

Two opposed forces are at work in the soul of the present-day Russian; on the one hand is the influence of centuries of semi-Asiatic passivity and deliberation; on the other is Lenin's injunction that Russia must catch up with and outstrip the technical achievements of the leading capitalist countries. Whether Russia ever will acquire the mechanical efficiency of America and Western Europe is a question for the future. In the meantime the rush and roar of modern industrial life seems to recede and subside as one travels from Berlin or some other European capital to Moscow, where there are only a few score taxicabs.

A trip through the provinces is calculated to strengthen rather than change the external impressions which one derives in Moscow. The centralized Soviet political and economic system tends to place a stamp of uniformity on the country. Everywhere the same products of the same state trusts and syndicates; everywhere the same articles in newspapers which differ chiefly in their titles; everywhere the same "weeks" to promote cooperation, health, national defense, or some other object.

Of course, historical, racial, and architectural differences cannot be obliterated overnight. The various cities of the Soviet Union have their distinctive traits, although the element of differentiation is probably less than in the older towns of Europe. . . .

. . . It is only fair to note that the Russian Revolution, while sweeping away even the poor crumbs of civil liberty which existed under the Tsar (a pale and almost powerless parliament, elected on a narrow franchise, a few newspapers which might very cautiously criticize the official viewpoint, etc.), has brought certain social liberties which to the uneducated or scantily educated masses of the people are probably more valuable than the right to vote for rival parties in elections or to write theoretical critical articles. In judging the effect of the absence of civil liberties on the mood of the Russian people it should never be forgotten that the vast majority of these people have not the slightest conception of what these liberties are; that they are not so far removed from the insurgent soldiers who followed the Dekabristi [Decembrists], shouting, "Constantine and Constitutsia!" ("Constantine and a Constitution!") under the impression that "Constitutsia" was Constantine's wife.

What are the social liberties which are associated with the Revolution? First of all, the disappearance of "superior" social classes, based on wealth and

Abridged from W.H. Chamberlin, *Soviet Russia,* Boston, 1930.

birth. The worker does not have to cringe before the "red director"† of the Soviet factory as, in pre-war times, he cringed before the private owner of the factory. He can write letters to the press complaining of conditions in the factory and suggesting changes, something which a worker would scarcely do with impunity even in democratic capitalist countries, where factories are private and not public concerns.

A peasant once remarked to me: "After the Revolution there was more freeedom; I got land." To him freedom meant, not the opportunity to vote for a parliamentary Peasant Party, but the possession of a slice of the landlord's estate. And this identification of land with liberty is a very traditional attitude of mind with the Russian peasantry. It was no accident that one of the revolutionary societies of the nineteenth century called itself "Land and Liberty." It is true that most peasants have not been singing any very loud hymns to liberty since the Communist Party went over to its more radical agrarian policy in the winter of 1927-1928. To the peasant the pressure exerted to make him sell his grain at low fixed prices seems quite as definite an infringement of liberty as the extortion of high rent by the grasping landlord of pre-revolutionary days. But the big landlords have gone forever; it is rather unlikely that the semi-requisitioning methods which have been used in purchasing the peasants' grain during the last two years will last very long.

In general the common man in Russia today has the sense of release, of social liberty, that comes with the disappearances of classes which are visibly above him in wealth and opportunity, culture and social status. When I called on the Soviet governor of an important industrial province, a man who had held high office in the trade-union movement and accompanied a diplomatic delegation to England, I found him in his office wearing the high boots and colorless blouse that constitute part of the distinctive costume of the Russian worker. Walking on the streets or riding on a train he would have been indistinguishable from the textile workers of the province. He certainly represented a different type of official from the decorated "high excellence" who would most probably have held the corresponding post under the Tsar.

Whether the plebeian leveling which characterizes so many fields of Russian social and cultural life is an unmixed blessing is highly debatable. But that it gives to the masses, at least to those of them who have absorbed some of the revolutionary propaganda, a sense of liberty which they did not possess in former times is, I think, undeniable.

23. Bertrand Russell on Lenin

Until he was incapacitated by illness in 1922, Lenin remained the unchallenged leader of the Communist Party, and hence of the new Soviet regime. Of the many descriptions of Lenin, one of the most interesting is that of Bertrand Russell, the great British philosopher, who visited Lenin in 1920. Russell was known for his left-wing political views, but he found Lenin's authoritarianism distasteful.

Soon after my arrival in Moscow I had an hour's conversation with Lenin in English, which he speaks fairly well. An interpreter was present, but his services were scarcely required. Lenin's room is very bare, it contains a big desk, some maps on the walls, two bookcases, and one comfortable chair for visitors, in addition to two and three hard chairs. It is obvious that he has no love of luxury or even comfort. He is very friendly and apparently simple, entirely without a trace of *hauteur*. If one met him without knowing who he was, one would not guess that he is possessed of great power or even that he is in any way eminent. I have never met a personage so destitute of self-importance. He looks at his visitors very closely, and screws up one eye, which seems to increase alarmingly the penetrating power of the other. He laughs a great deal; at first his laugh seems merely friendly and jolly, but gradually I came to feel it rather grim. He is dictatorial, calm, incapable of fear, extraordinarily devoid of self-seeking, an embodied theory. The materialist conception of history, one feels, is his life-blood. He resembles a professor in his desire to have the theory understood and in his fury with those who misunderstand or disagree, as also in his love of expounding. I got the impression that he despises a great many people and is an intellectual aristocrat.

The first question I asked him was as to how far he recognized the peculiarity of English economics and political conditions . . . He does not advocate abstention from Parliamentary contests, but participation with a view to making Parliament obviously contemptible. The reasons which make attempts at violent revolution seem to most of us both improbable and undesirable in this country carry no weight with him, and seem to him mere bourgeois prejudices. When I suggested that whatever is possible in England can be achieved without bloodshed, he waved aside the suggestion as fantastic. I got little impression of knowledge or psychological imagination as regards Great Britain. Indeed the whole tendency of Marxianism is against psychological imagination, since it attributes everything in politics to purely material causes.

I asked him next whether he thought it possible to establish communism firmly and fully in a country containing such a large majority of peasants. He admitted that it was difficult and laughed over the exchange the peasant is com-

Abridged from B. Russell, *The Practice and Theory of Bolshevism*, New York, 1964.

pelled to make, of food for paper; the worthlessness of Russian paper (money) struck him as comic. But he said — what is no doubt true — that things will right themselves when there are goods to offer to the peasant. For this he looks partly to electrification in industry, which, he says, is a technical necessity in Russia, but will take ten years to complete. . . . Of course he looks to the raising of the blockade as the only radical cure; but he was not very hopeful of this being achieved thoroughly or permanently except through revolutions in other countries. Peace between Bolshevik Russia and capitalist countries, he said, must always be insecure; the Entente might be led by weariness and mutual dissensions to conclude peace, but he felt convinced that the peace would be of brief duration. I found in him, as in almost all leading Communists, much less eagerness than existed in our delegation for peace and the raising of the blockade. He believes that nothing of real value can be achieved except through world revolution and the abolition of capitalism; I felt that he regarded the resumption of trade with capitalist countries as a mere palliative of doubtful value. . . .

. . .He said that two years ago neither he nor his colleagues thought they could survive against the hostility of the world. He attributes their survival to the jealousies and divergent interests of the different capitalist nations; also to the power of Bolshevik propaganda. He said that Germans had laughed when the Bolsheviks proposed to combat guns with leaflets, but that the event had proved the leaflets quite as powerful. . . .

I think if I had met him without knowing who he was, I should not have guessed that he was a great man; he struck me as too opinionated and narrowly orthodox. His strength comes, I imagine, from his honesty, courage, and unwavering faith — religicus faith in the Marxian gospel, which takes the place of the Christian martyr's hopes of paradise, except that it is less egotistical. He has as little love of liberty as the Christians, who suffered under Diocletian and retaliated when they acquired power. Perhaps love of liberty is incompatible with wholehearted belief in a panacea for all human ills. If so, I cannot but rejoice in the skeptical temper of the Western world. . . .

24. Vladimir Mayakovsky: Komsomolskaya

Upon his death, Lenin was eulogized in many ways and by many people, beginning what has been called "The Lenin Cult." Among the eulogizers was the poet Mayakovsky, writing in 1924.

> 'Lenin' and 'Death'
> > these words are enemies.
> 'Lenin' and 'Life'
> > are comrades. . . .
> Lenin
> > lived
> Lenin
> > lives
> Lenin
> > will live.

25. Lenin's Testament

With Lenin's illness came the struggle to succeed him as Party leader, a struggle which erupted openly in 1923. Although extremely ill and almost totally incapacitated, Lenin in December 1922 dictated notes expressing his concern about a Party split and his reservations about some of his leading Party colleagues. In this document, called his Testament, *Lenin focused particular attention on Stalin and Trotsky. Early in the next month, he added a postscript, attacking Stalin further, following an incident in which Stalin had been rude to Lenin's wife Krupskaya. Interestingly, this seemingly damning statement by Lenin did not prevent Stalin from succeeding him; Stalin was able to minimize the impact of the* Testament *as the product of a sick man's mind.*

By stability of the Central Committee, of which I spoke above, I mean measures against a split, as far as measures can at all be taken....

...I have in mind stability as a guarantee against a split in the immediate future, and I intend to deal here with a few ideas concerning personal qualities.

I think that from this standpoint the prime factors in the question of stability are such member of the C.C. as Stalin and Trotsky. I think relations between them make up the greater part of the danger of a split. . . .

...Comrade Stalin, having become Secretary-General, has unlimited authority concentrated in his hands, and I am not sure whether he will always

As quoted in N. Tumarkin, *Lenin Lives*, Cambridge, 1983.

Abridged from B. Dmytryshyn, *USSR: A Concise History,* New York, 1978.

be capable of using that authority with sufficient caution. Comrade Trotsky, on the other hand,...is distinguished not only by outstanding ability. He is personally perhaps the most capable man in the present C.C., but he has displayed excessive self-assurance and shown excessive preoccupation with the purely administrative side of the work.

These two qualities of the two outstanding leaders of the present C.C. can inadvertently lead to a split, and if our Party does not take steps to avert this, the split may come unexpectedly....

...Both of these remarks, of course, are made only for the present, on the assumption that both these outstanding and devoted Party workers fail to find an occasion to enhance their knowledge and amend their one-sidedness.

Lenin

December 25, 1922

ADDITION TO THE LETTER OF DECEMBER 24, 1922

Stalin is too rude and this defect, although quite tolerable in our midst and in dealings among us Communists, becomes intolerable in a Secretary-General. That is why I suggest that the comrades think about a way of removing Stalin from that post and appointing another man in his stead who in all other respects differs from Comrade Stalin in having only one advantage, namely, that of being more tolerant, more loyal, more polite and more considerate to the comrades, less capricious, etc. This circumstance may appear to be a negligible detail. But I think that from the standpoint of safeguards against a split and from the standpoint of what I wrote above about the relationship between Stalin and Trotsky it is not a detail, or it is a detail which can assume decisive importance.

26. Stalin: A Lenin Litany

On the eve of Lenin's funeral in January 1924, Stalin delivered a speech that was like a religious catechism, suggesting the possibility that he was assuming the role of high priest of a rapidly-growing Lenin cult.

Departing from us, Comrade Lenin enjoined us to hold high and guard the purity of the great title of member of the Party. We vow to you, Comrade Lenin, that we shall fulfil your behest with honour! . . .

Departing from us, Comrade Lenin enjoined us to guard the unity of our Party as the apple of our eye. We vow to you, Comrade Lenin, that this behest, too, we shall fulfill with honour!...

Abridged from T.H. Rigby, editor, *Stalin,* Englewood Cliffs, 1966.

Departing from us, Comrade Lenin enjoined us to guard and strengthen the dictatorship of the proletariat. We vow to you, Comrade Lenin, that we shall spare no effort to fulfil this behest, too, with honour! . . .

Departing from us, Comrade Lenin enjoined us to strengthen with all our might the alliance of the workers and peasants. We vow to you, Comrade Lenin, that this behest, too, we shall fulfil with honour! . . . .

Departing from us, Comrade Lenin enjoined us to strengthen and extend the union of republics. We vow to you, Comrade Lenin, that this behest, too, we shall fulfil with honour! . . .

Departing from us, Comrade Lenin enjoined us to remain faithful to the principles of the Communist International. We vow to you, Comrade Lenin, that we shall not spare our lives to strengthen and extend the union of the working people of the whole world — the Communist International!

27. Stalin: How to Deal with Opposition

Stalin adroitly and ruthlessly manuvered his way to the top, making use of the Lenin mantle, a shrewd sense, political alliances, the naiveté of his opponents, and above all, his position as Party Secretary. By picturing himself as the chief proponent of Marxist-Leninist ideology, and his opponents as misguided faction-alists, as he here does in a speech to the Fifteenth Party Congress in 1927, Stalin convinced many that the future of the Party lay with him, and with him alone.

From Kamenev's speech it is evident that the opposition does not intend to disarm completely. The opposition's declaration of December 3 indicates the same thing. Evidently, the opposition prefers to be outside the Party. Well, let it be outside the Party. There is nothing terrible, or exceptional, or surprising, in the fact that they prefer to be outside the Party, that they are cutting themselves off from the Party. If you study the history of the Party you will find that always, at certain serious turns taken by our Party, a certain section of the old leaders fell out of the cart of the Bolshevik Party and made room for new people. A turn is dangerous for those who do not sit firmly in the Party cart. Not everybody can keep his balance when a turn is made. You turn the cart — and on looking round you find that somebody has fallen out. (applause)

[There follow examples of Party "turns" in 1903 and 1907-08]

Our Party is a living organism. Like every organism, it undergoes a process of metabolism: the old and obsolete passes away (applause), the new and growing lives and develops (applause). Some go away, both at the top and at the bottom, and lead the cause forward. That is how our Party grew. That is how it will continue to grow.

Ibid.

The same must be said about the present period of our revolution. We are in the period of a turn from the restoration of industry and agriculture to the reconstruction of the entire national economy, to its reconstruction on a new technical basis, when the building of socialism is no longer merely in prospect, but a living, practical matter, which calls for the surrounding of extremely great difficulties of an internal and external character.

You know that this has proved fatal to the leaders of our opposition, who were scared by the new difficulties and intended to turn the Party in the direction of surrender. And if certain leaders, who do not want to sit firmly in the cart, now fall out, it is nothing to be surprised at. It will merely rid the Party of people who are getting in its way and hindering its progress. Evidently, they seriously want to free themselves from our Party cart. Well, if some of the old leaders who are turning into trash intend to fall out of the cart — a good riddance to them! (Stormy and prolonged applause. The whole congress rises and gives Comrade Stalin an ovation.)

Chapter Five

The Soviet Period: 1928 To The Present

Soviet history from 1928 to 1953 was dominated by a single man, Joseph Stalin. The fact that historians refer to Stalinism, Stalin's Russia and the Stalinist system, and often discuss Soviet history since Stalin's death in terms of de-Stalinization is eloquent testimony to this fact. It was he who developed the Soviet system of government that still exists today.

FACT: Stalin's real name was Joseph Dzhugashvili. He was born in what is today Soviet Georgia and, like Lenin, took a revolutionary name. Stalin means man of steel. Stalin spoke Russian with a strong Georgian accent.

By 1927, Stalin had outmaneuvered his political rivals and held firmly the reins of Soviet power. He now put that power to work to bring about a rapid industrialization of Soviet society. This period of industrial transformation is often called the Third Revolution because in many ways it changed the face of the country more than the two revolutions of 1917. Unlike the two earlier revolutions, Stalin's was a revolution from above insofar as it was the government, not the people, which took the initiative.

According to Marx's theory, socialism and communism were possible only in an industrialized country. In 1917, the Bolsheviks had expected the workers of Western Europe to join them in an international revolution. Now Stalin began to argue that it would be possible to take the first step towards communism by building socialism in one country. To do that, the Soviet Union would have to create an industrial base as quickly as possible. Even though the Tsarist economy had begun to grow rapidly before the 1917 Revolution, Russia was quite backward economically compared to Western Europe. About 80% of its population was still isolated in small traditional villages, working the land by primitive and inefficient means. Stalin decided that industrialization, and with it the collectivization of agriculture, was a necessity if the Soviet Union were to survive as a socialist country in a world dominated by capitalist states. As he put it in 1931, "The Soviet Union must march forward so that the world proletariat can look to it as the true fatherland of the working class." And, he added on a more ominous note, "We are fifty or one hundred years behind the advanced countries. We must make good this distance in ten years. Either we do it, or we shall be crushed." The sense of being behind the West that had galvanized the energies of Peter the Great more than two hundred years before also haunted Stalin. As it turned out, precisely ten years later, in June of 1941, Hitler launched Operation Barbarossa, his invasion of the Soviet Union. Historians still debate whether Stalin's policies actually helped the Soviets to be ready for Hitler's attack, or whether the collectivization of agriculture and Stalin's purges in fact reduced the Soviet Union's ability to wage war effectively.

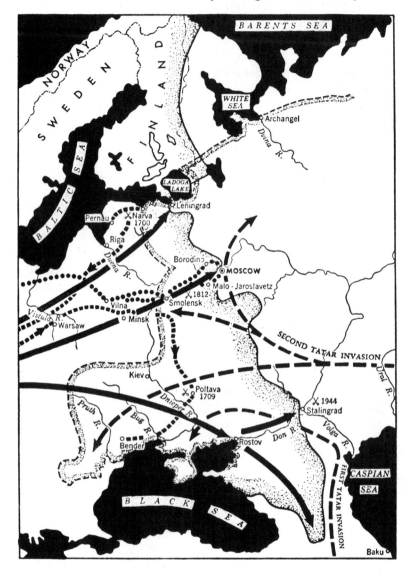

Invasions of Russia

- – – – TATAR INVASION, 13th CENTURY
- EXTENT OF TATAR OCCUPATION
- ······· CHARLES XII, 1701-21
- ●●●●●● NAPOLEON, 1812
- ▬▬▬ HITLER INVASION, 1941
- EXTENT OF GERMAN OCCUPATION, 1941-42

COLLECTIVIZATION AND THE EXCITEMENT OF SOCIALIST CONSTRUCTION

The Fifteenth Communist Party Congress in 1927 authorized the First Five Year Plan. In it, the Soviet government set very ambitious goals for industrial production. The plan called for an end to private property in industry, which had been allowed in small factories and farms during the period of the New Economic Policy, and set a modest goal for the collectivization of agriculture. Collectivization required peasants to give up their small, individual farms and join together to work large tracts of land collectively. They would share ownership of the land and be paid with a share of their joint production.

FACT: By October 1929, 4.1% of peasant households had joined collective farms. By March 1930, 58% of peasants were collectivized. By 1936, 90% of peasants were collectivized.

The government first tried to get the peasants to join collective farms voluntarily. However, few peasants wanted to give up their newly-acquired private farms. The government then introduced an all-out campaign to force them to do what they would not do on their own. The poor and landless peasants were set against their richer neighbors (called *kulaks* by the Party), with promises of sharing the *kulaks'* land and possessions. Young enthusiasts and Party workers from the towns spearheaded what became a second civil war in the countryside. Thousands of peasants who resisted were forcibly sent away to settle unpopulated lands in Kazakhstan and Siberia; others were forced into labor camps. By 1935, over one million exiles had been placed in special settlements to undertake the construction of new enterprises called for in the ambitious economic plan. Recalling this period later during World War II, Stalin confided to Winston Churchill that collectivization had been a terrible struggle, more stressful even than the war.

FACT: It is estimated that between three and seven million people died during the collectivization campaign and the man-made famine that accompanied it. Losses were greatest among Ukrainians and Kazakhs.

Bukharin, one of Stalin's most talented partners in the early stages of socialist construction, observed, "The worst thing about collectivization, which was a horrible example of brutality to innocent and hardworking peasants, was the deep changes it brought to the psychological outlook of those Communists who participated in the campaign...for whom terror was henceforth a normal method of administration." Collectivization led, Bukharin thought, to the dehumanization of the people working in the Party. Stalin, unlike Bukharin, was not troubled by such thoughts. He was determined to bring the peasants under government control regardless of the cost. In the nineteenth century, the peasant, stubborn and resistant to change, had lived his life in his own village and ignored or evaded the wishes of the Tsar's government. Stalin recognized that the stubborn peasant might become a dangerous obstacle to his ambitions. Collectivization put an end to this possibility. (See Reading 2)

Why, it might be asked, was collectivization so important? Why was it pushed through so swiftly? In the view of those who supported it, collectivization was a prerequisite for rapid industrialization. Large agricultural units, they believed, could be farmed more productively by fewer people than could the thousands of small peasants' farms created by the break-up of the *mir* and the landlords' estates. These large farms would make it possible to use modern machinery and also free manpower for industry. Furthermore, the government would be able to collect produce from these farms to trade for the foreign currency necessary to buy industrial equipment from abroad. And finally, the government would find it far easier to control the peasants of Russia, once they were gathered into large groups. Collectivization achieved most of these goals, but it was a success bought at the expense of great human suffering. Livestock were slaughtered and eaten by the owners rather than given to the collective. Production was disrupted and there was a terrible famine in which millions of people died of starvation. Not until Stalin's death in 1953 did the production of food regain its pre-collectivization levels.

Collectivization not only had an enormous cost in human lives, it also left its mark, as Bukharin observed, on the developing style of Soviet administration. The war of 1914, the civil war that followed it, and then the collectivization campaign all helped accustom the new Soviet regime to the use of brutal methods in the service of socialist construction. Lenin himself had taught that the health of the revolution was the highest law. What he meant in effect was that the ends justify the means. Anything that furthered the cause of socialism was permissible. Now Stalin had established himself as the arbiter and last word on what it was that the revolution needed. He had only to say the revolution demanded that he carry out a given policy, regardless of what it cost others, and it was done. His word became law.

The early 1930s were nonetheless a time of rapid industrial growth. As in the 1920s, there was among a large portion of the Soviet population — particularly among Soviet young people — a sense of exhilaration, of new possibilities for themselves personally, and the chance to build a new and better society. The government, which now owned and ran all large factories and other enterprises, set high targets for factory construction and output. Pressure from the central administration to make these targets was intense. Everyone, including women, was expected to work hard to build the socialist future. And work hard they did, under difficult conditions and often with considerable ingenuity. (See Readings 1 and 3)

FACT: During the First Five Year Plan,† which was declared completed after four years, the output of machinery quadrupled and that of oil doubled.

FACT: The number of women in the work force more than doubled between 1928 and 1933, and doubled again by 1940.

In 1935, workers celebrate the 100,000 tractor built at the Kirov factory, so-named in honor of the popular head of the Leningrad Party, S.M. Kirov, who was assassinated in 1934.

Young people worked with enthusiasm to build the foundation of the new industry in such far away places as Magnitogorsk, the new steel center built in the Urals. Electricity was brought to the countryside. (See Reading 4) Education, particularly technical education which bore a direct relation to the regime's economic goals, was widely available. The former peasant, and certainly his son or daughter, could attend night school or the new industrial academies, and look forward to being the foreman of a factory, an engineer or even the manager of a construction project. The contrast between Soviet progress and the Great Depression which was devastating Western Europe and the United States added to the sense that the Soviet Union was on the right track. Though the Soviet standard of living was very low at this time, it did seem to be improving.

Stalin's drive for industrialization was accompanied by a tightening of discipline in all areas of Soviet life. Whereas the revolution of 1917 had been accompanied by ideals of equality and the freedom to experiment with everything from art and literature to education and family relationships, Stalin now introduced tough discipline in school and factory. Factories established sharp wage differentials to encourage workers to get the training necessary to rise in their place of work. Schools were given a dual job: both to achieve literacy and improve technical skills, and to inculcate the values of the new Soviet man. As Stalin put it with characteristic bluntness, education is a weapon in the hands of the man who holds it. It must teach the virtues of hard work, self-discipline, and loyalty to the Communist Party. For Stalin, writers and teachers were to become "engineers of the human soul."

FACT: Literacy as percent of the population

1897	1926	1939	1959	1979
26.3	56.6	89.1	98.5	99.9

The regime also introduced a strict censorship on the media. It required all writers who wanted to be published to follow the canon of Socialist Realism. Socialist Realism required writers to portray heroes as models for behavior, and present situations in which good citizens were rewarded and bad ones suffered. Lenin had introduced the idea that literature must be party-minded,† and serve the state. Now a whole structure of censorship and bureaucracy was developed to make this idea a reality. The regime declared that the job of transforming illiterate, individualistic peasants into cooperative industrial workers was so great that it required the coordinated efforts of everyone, school teachers and artists, radio announcers and writers, as well as political leaders. The result was to put an end to the brilliant creative flowering in the arts that had begun in Russia just before the war. Diaghilev took his Ballet Russe to Paris. The poets Mayakovsky and Mandelshtam, and writers such as Bely, Babel, Pilnyak, Zamiatin and a host of others were either arrested, left the Soviet Union, or committed suicide. Others remained, but, like the poets Akhmatova, Tsvetaeva and Pasternak, were forced "to write for the drawer," that is, to give up all hope of getting their work published.

As Stalin moved to tighten the discipline of society by Party and state, he also centralized power within the Party itself. Lower Party organs were strictly controlled by higher ones, so that a decision made at the top would be carried out throughout the land. Stalin also granted increasing power to the security police organization which he ordered to watch Party and government officials to make sure they were loyal to him. People were encouraged to denounce their neighbors.

FACT: Pavlik Morozov was a small boy who denounced his parents for hoarding grain during the collectivization campaign. The parents were arrested. Shortly after that, the outraged villagers killed the boy. Soviet schools and media then made much of little Pavlik as a martyr to the socialist cause. Children are still urged to imitate him and give their highest loyalty to the state.

The Communist Party Congresses that had brought Party leaders from all over the country together once a year during Lenin's rule met more and more rarely under Stalin. After the 1927 Party Congress, the next meeting was held in 1930, then 1934, 1939 and not again until 1952. The gap between meetings thus grew from three to four, to five, and finally to thirteen years. The Party Central Committee also met rarely. Power was concentrated in the Politburo and, increasingly, in the person of Stalin.

STALIN'S CULT OF PERSONALITY AND THE PURGES

By 1930, Stalin had begun to develop the cult of his own personality. History was rewritten to illustrate Stalin's genius at every turn. Streets, cities, factories, and mountains were named in his honor. Stalin's picture was put up in every school, store, and factory, while newspapers and radios controlled by the Party-state continuously trumpeted the accomplishments of the all-wise leader, the genius Stalin.

The cult of personality both reflected and enhanced Stalin's power. It was soon accompanied, however, by a new and terrible development in Soviet history. In December, 1934, Kirov, the popular head of the Leningrad Party organization, was assassinated. Stalin probably organized this event. In any case, he used it to justify a far-reaching purge of Soviet society, and particularly of the Party. There had been some arrests and accusations of industrial sabotage in the early 1930s, accompanied by public trials that provided scapegoats for the regime. Those put on trial were blamed for making mistakes and causing all the popular suffering during the time of the first rapid industrialization. More often, of course, that suffering was a side effect of a definite government policy, pushing heavy industry rather than consumer goods or agriculture, for example. There had also been arrests and summary executions in the early years of Bolshevik power when the government felt weak and insecure. What now took place was unprecedented in scale. (See Reading 5)

FACT: 1108 of the 1966 delegates to the 17th Communist Party Congress (1934) and 98 of the 139 regular and candidate (non-voting) members elected by that Congress to its Central Committee perished in the purges. Most of them were shot.

If in the 1920s, the Party and security police had dealt harshly with any and all who opposed the Bolsheviks, now the security police turned on the Party itself. The leadership was hardest hit. All past or potential opponents of Stalin were arrested and accused of outlandish plots, such as conspiring with "Judas Trotsky" to murder Stalin and sabotage the country's economy, or plotting with

Germany and Japan to dismember the Soviet Union. In carefully staged, public show trials† that received wide publicity, many of the early Bolshevik leaders such as Kamenev, Zinoviev, and Bukharin confessed to these fictitious crimes after long periods of confinement and torture in prison. Agents of the secret police tracked Trotsky down in Mexico and murdered him there. The purges reached throughout the USSR, into universities and factories, and into towns throughout the Soviet land, striking individuals who had no idea why they were being accused. In some instances, local purges probably served as a means to settle old scores or get rid of a boss who stood in the way of promotion. The purges hit hardest those who had had a measure of responsibility. After purging the Party, the police turned on the army. Three of the top five Soviet military leaders were arrested, including Marshal Tukachevsky, who was widely considered the most brilliant Soviet military strategist. Tukachevsky was accused, tried, and executed for plotting with Japan and Germany to dismember the Soviet Union, activities for which there was absolutely no evidence. Some estimate that as a result of these purges the army lost half of its officer corps. (See Reading 6)

FACT: Estimates are that 8 million people were arrested in the purges, about 5% of the total population. Of these, about 800,000 were executed. Most of the rest were sentenced to labor camps strung out across Siberia. There they joined the vast work force of what the Russian writer Alexander Solzhenitsyn calls the *Gulag Archipelago — gulag* being the acronym for Chief Administration of Corrective Labor Camps.

The purges struck down virtually all of the original Bolshevik leaders. They also removed the revolutionary generation from positions of leadership throughout the country and made way for the young - the Khrushchevs, Brezhnevs and Kosygins. These new men had gained education and quick promotion from the Soviet system, and now rose rapidly to prominent positions. If the purges had this one positive effect, making room for younger, technically trained people in key positions, they also had the pernicious effect of creating fear and suspicion throughout the Soviet population. They created an atmosphere, Stalin's successor Nikita Khrushchev later said, in which no one felt secure and so no one could work well or with confidence.

The reasons why Stalin ordered the purges remain a matter of debate. There is little doubt that he knew what was happening. Of course, there had in fact been opposition to some of his policies, particularly to his methods of collectivization, but by the late 1930s, those who had opposed him had no power. There is also some evidence that there was, in the early 1930s, some quiet, behind-the-scenes opposition to Stalin's increasingly autocratic ways. It seems unlikely, however, that there was serious threat to his authority. From the regime's point of view, the arrests and public trials that followed were useful, in that they gave it the opportunity to blame many of its problems on wilful wrecking and sabotage by a malevolent few. The arrests and trials also helped develop a siege mentality among the population, providing evidence that devious and determined foreign powers were plotting to overthrow the Soviet, socialist state. Such a view of an outside world filled with hostile capitalist states could be used to justify continuous vigilance, sacrifice, and hard work. Nonetheless, it remains hard to understand the reasons for such a large scale attack on the Soviet population. Most historians agree that an important reason for the purges was the growing paranoia of Stalin himself and the deterioration of his mental balance. What is really most remarkable about the purges, however, is that the Stalinist system of government was both willing and able to undertake the destruction of so many innocent people.

WORLD WAR II AND ITS AFTERMATH

At the same time, the late 1930s, the international picture was growing darker and more dangerous for the Soviet Union. After Hitler came to power in Germany in 1933, fear of Germany led the USSR to seek improved relations with the democratic capitalist states. In 1933, it established diplomatic relations with the United States which, until then, had refused to recognize what Americans considered to be a dangerous and uncivilized revolutionary government. In 1934, it entered the League of Nations and, in 1935, signed bilateral agreements with France and Czechoslovakia. In 1935, the Comintern† reversed its policy of requiring foreign Communist Parties to try to undermine democratic governments, and urged them instead to work for a popular front against fascism. By 1935, the Soviets had realized that Fascist Germany, not France or England, posed their greatest threat. In the East, the Comintern supported Chiang Kai-shek and the Chinese Kuomintang against an increasingly militaristic Japan.

While the Soviet Union was continuing to press for alliances and assurances of mutual support from the Western powers, especially Britain and France, it also opened secret negotiations with the Nazis. Stalin was determined to avoid war with Germany at any price. He knew that his country was still backward industrially and militarily, and further weakened by the purges. Nor did he altogether trust the British and French. He feared they might make a deal with Germany against the Soviet Union. On August 23, 1939, Germany and the Soviet Union signed a non-aggression pact. Each agreed not to go to war against the other, and to remain neutral if either side was attacked by a third party. A secret protocol divided up Eastern Europe into spheres of influence. Russia's sphere included the eastern chunk of Poland, Bessarabia (a province of Rumania), Finland, and the independent nations of Estonia and Latvia. Later the Germans added Lithuania to the Soviet sphere. The Ribbentrop Agreement, as this agreement was called in the West, was what Hitler was waiting for. Free now from the danger of war with the USSR, Germany invaded Poland in September. So began what Americans call World War II, and what the Soviets call the Great Patriotic War. The USSR gained peace, at least for a time.

In the summer of 1939, Stalin apparently expected a long war between Germany and the Western allies. As it turned out, the Nazis moved far faster than anyone expected. France fell. Britain retreated to its island fortress. On June 22, 1941, flushed with victory, Hitler turned his panzers eastward against the Soviet Union in what he called Operation Barbarossa.

FACT: Despite warnings from the Allies, the shifting of huge numbers of German troops to the Eastern Front, and frequent flights over Soviet territory by German planes, the Soviet frontiers were barely defended, and some troops were without ammunition on the day of the Nazi attack. The Soviet military had made plans to go on the offensive, should war come, but had made no comprehensive plan of defense.

FACT: Stalin did not appear in public for twelve days after the Nazi attack.

Stalin was stunned, so much so that he was unable even to announce to his people what had happened. He left this unpleasant task to one of his subordinates. For a time, the all-wise, all-knowing leader remained invisible to his people. In the Soviet Union, as in Western Europe, the Germans moved with surprising speed. By December they were set up on the outskirts of Moscow, Leningrad was under blockade, and most of the Soviet Ukraine was under Nazi control.

The situation looked bleak. Not for nineteen long months were the Soviets able to manage their first major victory. Finally, in January of 1943, they stopped the Nazi advance at Stalingrad. In that city, they fought hand to hand in the streets, retreating until they had their backs to the broad Volga River. There, when they could retreat no further, they held. The city was almost totally destroyed, but this heroic and costly struggle proved the turning point of the war. Here, as against Napoleon one hundred thirty-one years before, winter and stubborn bravery helped to secure ultimate victory.

FACT: Over one million people died in the 900-day siege and blockade of Leningrad alone, more than ten times the number of people killed by the atomic bomb dropped on Hiroshima. (See Readings 7 and 8)

FACT: It is estimated that between 15 and 20 million Soviet citizens perished in the war, out of a 1939 population of about 190.5 million, or one out of every ten people. United States war losses were about 400,000, out of a population of close to 132 million. (See Reading 9)

For almost three years, the Soviet Union had to bear the brunt of the Nazi war machine. Although the Americans sent help in the form of vast amounts of equipment and supplies under the lend-lease agreement, the Allies were not able to provide what the Soviets most needed, a diversion of German troops to other fronts. Not until three years after the Nazi invasion of the Soviet Union, in June of 1944, did the Allies land troops on the Normandy beaches. At last they forced the Nazis to fight what the German generals knew they could not win, a two-front war.

In a series of wartime meetings with Churchill and Roosevelt (and after Roosevelt's death with his successor, Harry Truman), Stalin negotiated with his allies first on military matters, and then on the political issues of post-war settlement. During the period that the Soviets were doing most of the fighting and suffering most of the war losses, Stalin held a particularly strong negotiating position. Using this fact and his considerable political skill, Stalin squeezed concessions from the British and Americans. Not only was he treated as an equal partner in all negotiations about the shape of post-war Europe, he also gained the Allies' agreement that there would be friendly states on the Soviet Union's western borders after the war. The historical experience of Polish invasion in the seventeenth century, of Napoleon in the nineteenth century, and the Germans twice in his own century, stiffened Stalin's resolve.

Stalin had a very clear idea about what state could be considered a friendly one: it had to be Communist and amenable to Soviet direction. It seems unlikely that Churchill, Roosevelt, or Truman had any idea that Stalin understood friendly and Communist to be one and the same. They chose to ignore the implications of the Warsaw uprising in the summer of 1944, when Soviet actions foreshadowed events to come. At that time, when the non-Communist Polish underground tried to seize the city from the Nazis, the Russian armies halted their advance at the river Vistula on the outskirts of the city. There they remained while the Nazis systematically wiped out the Polish resistance. When the U.S. Government requested access to air bases on Russian-occupied territories so that they could drop supplies to the beleaguered Poles, Stalin refused. Looking back on this strange decision of Stalin's, it is clear that he was not thinking primarily about the military issue of defeating the Germans and saving Polish lives, but that he was already thinking about who would rule Poland after the war. Nonetheless, the Allied leaders either did not see what Stalin had in mind, or, if they did see, chose not to protest.

At war's end, Soviet troops occupied the vast territory between their own borders and Berlin. In the next few years, taking advantage of this fact, the Soviets supported Communist parties in their bids for power throughout Eastern Europe. The result was that by 1948, they had what they wanted, friendly Communist states on their borders.

FACT: By 1948, Poland, Hungary, Bulgaria, Rumania, Albania, Czechoslovakia, and Yugoslavia all had Communist governments, and all but Yugoslavia were dependent on the Soviet government and subservient to its wishes.

The Soviets called these states "peoples' democracies." The Allies began to call these same states "Soviet satellites," because their policies depended on Soviet power.

Eastern Europe at the End of World War II

▨ Members of The Warsaw Pact

▢ Communist States — not members of the Warsaw Pact

◼ Areas annexed since World War II

FACT: In 1948, the Yugoslav Communist government broke free from Soviet domination. Unlike the Communist Party in other East European countries, the Yugoslav Party had come to power on its own, and its leader, Tito, enjoyed wide popularity.

After the war, the Soviet Union turned inwards to rebuild its devastated economy and to tighten government control of society. During the war, Stalin had relied openly on patriotic appeals, relaxed persecution of the Church, and taken many new people into the Party. Now such measures to increase popularity were no longer necessary. The cult of personality reemerged stronger even than before the war. (See Reading 10)

FACT: Of the new Soviet postage stamps issued in 1950, sixty-two had a picture of Stalin, three had a picture of Lenin, and three others pictured the two men together.

Stalin now opened a campaign against what he called cosmopolitanism, by which he meant influences that were not Russian. Jews in particular were singled out for persecution. The regime took stern measures to cut off contact with the West. The cult of the all-wise, all-knowing, awe-inspiring leader reached new heights. There were even signs in 1952 that Stalin was preparing a new purge.

Stalin's defensive domestic policy was matched by a growing distrust of the outside world. Refusal of American help, notably the Marshall Plan† for postwar reconstruction that was offered originally to the USSR and Eastern Europe as well as to Western Europe, indicated the lengths to which Stalin would go to avoid Western contact. He did not want Europeans to realize how gravely wounded the Soviet Union had been by war, for he feared they might take advantage of that weakness. Rather than cooperating after the war, the former allies, the Soviet Union and the United States, were led by mutual suspicion into an era of competition and antagonism that was called the Cold War. Speaking in Fulton, Missouri in 1946, Winston Churchill remarked that an iron curtain had descended across the continent of Europe, and that those behind it to the east were subject to increasing control from Moscow.

FACT: The iron curtain was not just a figure of speech. The border between most East European countries and Western Europe is still fenced, guarded, and mined in many places. Travel from East to West is greatly restricted.

FACT: The USA dropped an atomic bomb on Hiroshima in 1945. Not until 1949 did the USSR detonate its first atomic bomb. The USA had held a monopoly on this weapon from 1945-1949.

By the end of the 1940s, the allies in war had become enemies in peace. The Western powers saw Soviet domination of Eastern Europe and stubbornness in keeping Germany divided as indications of the Soviet Union's aggressive

Russian and American soldiers meet at the Elbe River, south of Berlin, April 25, 1945.

intentions, and feared the growing power of Communist parties in France and Italy. The Cominform,† a successor organization to the Comintern, set up to coordinate the work of Communist parties all over the world, seemed particularly threatening. The Soviets, for their part, felt weak. They still feared Germany. They still feared invasion from the West, across the unbroken Central European plain. They seemed surprised that the Allies could not see this danger or understand why they needed friendly states in Eastern Europe. The American monopoly on the atomic bomb increased this feeling of vulnerability. Yet the Soviets could not see the Marshall Plan as anything other than an American plot to dominate Western Europe, and build up West Germany.

When, in 1949, the United States joined with Western European states to create the North Atlantic Treaty Organization (NATO) and establish a joint army, the Soviets began to fear possible Western aggression. Six years later the Soviet allies joined forces to form a corresponding military alliance, the Warsaw Pact.

Then, on March 5, 1953, Stalin died.

DE-STALINIZATION AND THE KHRUSHCHEV ERA

Stalin's heirs quickly agreed on one thing: there should be no return to the terror of Stalin's rule. As there was no law or established procedure for choosing Stalin's successor (nor does such a law exist today), the top Party leaders closed ranks and spoke of the need for collective leadership. The dreaded secret police was downgraded in importance and its head, Beria, was shot. Gradually Nikita Khrushchev emerged as the top man. Khrushchev, the son of a simple worker, was one of the men who had risen rapidly into the important positions vacated by victims of the purges, first in the Ukraine and then in Moscow. He had profited from the Stalinist system. Nonetheless he moved away from Stalin's methods. Neither he, nor any of his successors, ruled with the arbitrary, absolute power that Stalin had wielded. They depended instead on the support of the members of the highest Party council, the Politburo.

At the Twentieth Party Congress in 1956, Khrushchev made a now-famous Secret Speech, so-called because it did not appear in the official transcript of the Congress proceedings. It was, however, read out in meetings throughout the Soviet Union.

FACT: All foreigners were barred from this speech (which was given late at night). The speech has never been published in the Soviet Union.

In his Secret Speech, Khrushchev accused Stalin of numerous crimes and brutality against the Soviet people. Khrushchev ushered in a period of reform, or what is called de-Stalinization. (See Readings 11 and 12)

FACT: At this time the name of the city of Stalingrad was changed to Volgograd. Before the Revolution, this city had been called Tsaritsyn.

The Soviet composer, Dimitri Shostakovich, presents the gold medal for first place in the Tchaikovsky piano competition to Van Cliburn. A picture of Tchaikovsky, the great nineteenth century Russian composer, hangs in the background. In 1958, Van Cliburn became the first American ever to win the competition. This seemed particularly significant in a year when Soviet-American relations were beginning to improve.

The Soviet leaders now tried to change many of Stalin's policies and methods, while at the same time maintaining the keystones of his system: Party control, centralized economic planning, collectivized agriculture, a monopoly on the media, and a willingness to use the police to deal with troublemakers if necessary. The Khrushchev regime took steps to improve the standard of living, experimented with loosening political controls on literature, and sought ways to increase the participation of rank and file Party members in responsible positions. Khrushchev also undertook a number of spectacular campaigns, notably his Virgin Lands project to plow and cultivate large tracts of land in Kazakhstan, land previously thought unsuitable for agriculture. He worked for peaceful coexistence with the West, while simultaneously seeking greater influence in the Third World. He sought and held a summit meeting with President Eisenhower, and appeared before the United Nations. (See Reading 13)

Nikita Khrushchev, President Eisenhower, Mrs. Khrushchev and Andrei Gromyko meet the press, September, 1959.

Not all of his projects were successful. De-Stalinization and liberalization at home gave some East European Communist governments the idea they could exercise a bit more independence, too, with the result that the loyalty of Poland and the very existence of Communist control in Hungary were threatened. The Soviets had to send in tanks to crush the Hungarian Revolution in 1956. China slipped out of the Soviet orbit.

FACT: In 1961, the East Germans built a wall between East and West Berlin to stem the tide of refugees from East to West. An estimated two and one-half million people had fled to the West through Berlin between 1945 and 1961. Just before the wall was built, the flood of refugees reached an average of 4000 per day.

Seeking to show his skill in foreign affairs, and reduce the military advantage of the United States, Khrushchev took a gamble. In January of 1959, Fidel Castro had assumed power in Cuba. Soon thereafter, Castro developed close ties with the Soviet Union. The presence of this ally so close to the United States provided Khrushchev with a temptation he could not resist. He decided to install nuclear missiles in Cuba. The result was the Cuban Missile Crisis of 1962, a frightening confrontation with the United States that was resolved only when Khrushchev agreed to dismantle the missile launch pads in return for an American promise not to try to overthrow the pro-Soviet Cuban government of Fidel Castro.

President John F. Kennedy and Nikita Khrushchev meet in Vienna for a summit meeting in June 1961.

Problems at home and abroad led to Khrushchev's downfall. In 1964, the Politburo united against him and Khrushchev was removed from office. For a while Leonid Brezhnev, Aleksei Kosygin, and Nikolai Podgorny formed a collective leadership from which Brezhnev gradually emerged as paramount.

FACT: Unlike Stalin's displaced rivals, who were usually shot, Khrushchev survived to live out his old age and die a peaceful death in 1971.

FACT: In 1967, when the Soviet regime celebrated its 50th anniversary, historians could not mention the men who had led the country for forty of those fifty years: Stalin and Khrushchev were both in disgrace.

These facts alone illustrate the difference between Stalin's way of dealing with disagreement and that of his successors. They also illustrate a continuity in the way in which the Soviet regime deals with unpleasant truths: history is simply rewritten to leave them out.

BREZHNEV AND HIS SUCCESSORS

Since 1964, the Soviet regime has been remarkable for its continuity and stability. There have been no dramatic efforts to make revolution from above, such as the collectivization and industrialization campaigns of the 1920s and early 1930s. There have been no purges similar to those of the middle and late 1930s. Nor have there been rash experiments such as those of Khrushchev who seemed eager to perfect Soviet socialism and recapture the excitement of its early years. On the contrary, the main goal of the Brezhnev regime and its immediate successors, led by Andropov, Chernenko, and now Gorbachev, has been to provide personal and national security, and to perfect the system already in place. The Soviet Union has become a conservative state in the sense that its government no longer seeks to change Soviet society. On the contrary, it seems to fear domestic change and strives to maintain things as they are.

FACT: Between 1965 and 1972, per capita consumption in the Soviet Union rose 5% per year.

FACT: In 1960, 8 out of 100 Soviet families had TV sets; 4 of 100 had a washing machine or a refrigerator. By 1977, 75 of 100 Soviet families had TV sets; 65 of 100 had a washing machine or a refrigerator.

From 1964 until the mid 1970s, the Brezhnev regime succeeded quite well in providing both guns and butter, that is, both a strong military and a steady rise in the standard of living. To do this, it concentrated on developing more efficient management. Education and competence, in addition to political loyalty, became increasingly important as criteria for an important position. Government officials both sought and heeded expert advice. Professional journalists began to publish differing points of view as to how to solve problems, so long as these differences did not touch on politics. Unlike Stalin, his successors no longer equated minor disagreements with disloyalty. In the final decision, of course, the Party decided which debates would be tolerated and who would prevail, but the common practice of the Stalin era in which a Party man frequently overruled the professionals, often without even trying to understand their advice, had come to an end. No longer did virtually everyone fear arrest. In the 1970s and early 1980s, professionals and individual specialists—agronomists, military men, scientists, and factory managers—have had more opportunity to work freely and to influence important decisions than ever before in Soviet history.

At the same time that the Brezhnev regime was pressing for efficient management and listening more closely to its experts, it took a very strict line on unwelcome criticism. Experts were encouraged to criticize economic inefficiency, but no one was allowed to point out basic flaws in Party management or the government. Khrushchev had experimented with looser censorship and had allowed publication in 1962 of Alexander Solzhenitsyn's frank account of life in a Soviet labor camp, *One Day in the Life of Ivan Denisovich*. Nothing of that sort appeared under Brezhnev. Indeed in 1965 the regime arrested two writers, Sinyavsky and Daniel, just for allowing their work to be published abroad. It forced other critics of the regime, among them Alexander Solzhenitsyn, to leave the country.

FACT: When American Congressmen visiting Moscow asked the chief editor of the Soviet Party newspaper *Pravda* (Truth) why Solzhenitsyn had been so harshly treated, the Soviet editor countered by asking what the American government would do to an American writer who slandered Jefferson or Lincoln.

The Brezhnev regime also dealt harshly with other groups of protesters: those who sought more rights for the non-Russian nationalities, religious leaders who sought the right to worship in other than officially approved churches, Jews who sought to emigrate and, of particular interest to those who look for change in the Soviet system, the human rights activists.

FACT: Andrei Sakharov is well-known in the Soviet Union as one of its most brilliant physicists and Father of the Soviet H-Bomb. He was the youngest person ever to be elected a full member of the Soviet Academy of Sciences (the top honor for a scientist). He also received numerous prizes, among them the highest civilian honor in the Soviet Union. Today he lives under house arrest in the provincial town of Gorki, sent there as punishment for his refusal to give up his human rights activities.

The Soviet human rights movement† began when a few Soviet citizens decided to monitor their government to see that it obeyed its own Constitution.

When Soviet citizens were arrested for what they said or wrote, denied the right to an open trial, or stopped from practicing their religion, the human rights activists protested that this was a violation of rights guaranteed by the Soviet Constitution. At first the regime seemed unsure how to deal with this development, but it soon found a solution. The internal police, now called the KGB, began to harass the activists with late-night apartment searches, beatings and warnings. They saw to it that activists and members of their families lost their jobs, and, if this did not work, incarcerated them in labor camps and psychiatric hospitals. Some activists were given a choice between going to labor camps or leaving the country. These protests have mightily embarrassed the Soviet government. The Soviets care about world opinion, and they also want to develop a more secure government of laws. Yet the Party continues to set limits on its writers. It still fears criticism even from loyal Soviet citizens, and ignores its own laws when it feels an important political issue is at stake.

Under the Brezhnev regime, from 1964-1982, the Soviet Union accomplished an age-old dream of the Tsars: it became a world superpower. As a result of its military spending, the Soviet Union now possesses what is, roughly speaking, military parity with its chief rival, the United States. To this extent, it has caught up with the West at last. During this same period, even as the Soviet Union and the United States both rushed to develop more advanced and deadly nuclear weapons, trade between the two countries more than doubled. Both the Soviet and American governments saw an advantage in improving their relations.

FACT: President Nixon visited the Soviet Union in 1972. He was the first American president to visit the USSR while in office.

The first SALT treaty (Strategic Arms Limitation Talks) was also signed in 1972, and negotiations for a second SALT agreement got off to a promising start. To be sure, there were at times strains in the Soviet-American relationship, caused by such events as the Soviet military intervention in Czechoslovakia in 1968, American military involvement in Viet Nam, Soviet support for Cuban troops in Angola, American distaste for Soviet policy towards Eastern Europe, and the continuing conflict in the Middle East. In spite of these problems, however, during the 1970s the desire to maintain a working dialogue prevailed.

FACT: The first use of regular Soviet troops outside of Eastern Europe took place in 1979 when the USSR sent them to Afghanistan.

Soviet-American relations took a turn for the worse when Soviet troops occupied Afghanistan. The U.S. reacted with a boycott of the summer Olympic games held in Moscow, and a refusal to ratify the SALT II agreement. Since then, relations have deteriorated, with accusations by the Soviets against the United States matched by American accusations against the Soviets. In 1984, the

Soviets led their allies in a boycott of the Los Angeles summer Olympic games. Each side remains well aware of the high stakes in the dangerous game they play, and of the need to contain their competition within safe limits acceptable to both. What is hard is to find agreement on what those limits are, for historical experience, conflicting aspirations, and cultural differences continue to breed suspicion and misunderstanding.

The face of the Soviet Union today differs greatly from that of the humiliated empire of 1917. The Soviet Union has become a world power. Its peoples have more access to health-care and education than ever before and are enjoying some of the rewards of industrialization. They look forward now to a period of prosperity. Yet they must also face uncertainty and a period of transition. The generation that has held power for many years, represented by Brezhnev and his immediate successors, Yuri Andropov and Konstantin Chernenko, must inevitably give way to a younger one.

FACT: In 1982, the average age of the members of the Soviet Politburo – the ruling group in the Soviet Union – was 69.

The generation of Mikhail Gorbachev, and the younger men who will soon rule the Soviet Union, did not experience Stalin's purges. They spent their childhood surrounded by the devastation of war, and, as young adults, lived through a period of de-Stalinization. They are more confident, better educated, and more sophisticated than their predecessors. Many of them see flaws in their system, particularly in the economy, that they would like to correct. The future leaders of the USSR are highly nationalistic and eager to gain the recognition and rewards that go with being a superpower. To this new generation, soon, will pass the power and responsibility for directing the policies of the Soviet Union.

The following books were helpful in writing this chapter:

Bialer, S., *Stalin's Successors: Leadership, Stability and Change in the Soviet Union,* Cambridge, England & New York: Cambridge University Press, 1980.

Dmytryshyn, B., *USSR: A Concise History,* New York: Charles Scribner's Sons, 1978.

Hough, J.F. & Fainsod, M., *How the Soviet Union is Governed,* Cambridge, MA & London: Harvard University Press, 1979.

Nove, A., *Stalinism and After,* London: George Allen & Unwin, Ltd., 1975.

Ulam, A., *Expansion and Coexistence,* New York: Praeger, 1974.

For students who are interested, we recommend further reading in the sources from which we have taken excerpts, as well as the following works:

Catchpole, B., *A Map History of Russia,* London: Heineman Educational Books, 1974, 1976.
   Map illustrations and summaries of events written for students.

Conquest, R., *The Great Terror: Stalin's Purges of the Thirties,* New York: Macmillan, 1968, 1973.
   A definitive account of this extraordinary phenomenon.

Fainsod, M., *Smolensk Under Soviet Rule,* New York: Vintage Publishers, 1963.
   This account of daily life in an important province during the 1930s is drawn from captured Soviet archives and gives a unique view of what happened. Now out of print but worth looking for.

Gladkov, F., *Cement,* New York: Frederick Ungar, 1948.
   A novel of the 1920s in the socialist realism mode.

Heller, M. and Nekrich, A., *Utopia in Power: History of the Soviet Union from 1917 to Our Days,* New York: Summit Books, forthcoming in 1984.
   Two outstanding Soviet emigré historians have combined to give detailed insiders' view. Probably suitable only for the more advanced student.

Koestler, A., *Darkness at Noon,* New York: Bantam Books, 1970.
   Fictionalized account of the experience of an Old Bolshevik caught in a purge trial.

Observer, *Message from Moscow,* New York: Vintage Publishers, 1971.
   A British student recounts his life among Moscow students in the 1960s.

Salisbury, H.E., *The 900 Days: The Siege of Leningrad,* New York: 1969.
   Vivid account of the heroism and suffering of the people of Leningrad during World War II.

Solzhenitsyn, A., *One Day in the Life of Ivan Denisovich,* New York: Praeger, 1963.
   A spare and moving account of one day in a Soviet labor camp; his short stories such as "Matryona's House" and "For the Good of the Cause" are also easy to read and highly recommended.

Readings

Chapter Five

List of Readings

1. Mayakovsky: Americans Are Astounded

The poet V. V. Mayakovsky joined the Bolshevik Party when he was fifteen, and enthusiastically participated in the revolution of 1917. He served the new regime with his pen, writing advertising jingles and propaganda verse, as well as poetry and plays, and became the unofficial poet laureate of the Revolution. Gradually he grew disillusioned with what he saw as the reemergence of bourgeois values. He found his own individuality incompatible with the requirements of Socialist Realism and the Stalinist way. Unhappy in his personal life as well, Mayakovsky committed suicide in 1930. This poem illustrates Mayakovsky's popular, breezy style, as well as the Soviet preoccupation with, and ambivalence towards, the United States.

AMERICANS ARE ASTOUNDED

Through horn-rimmed glasses,
                        in their unblinking way,
eyes popping
            from shores afar,
standing on tip-toe
                the U.S.A.
sizes-up
        the U.S.S.R.
What sort of people are they,
                        a strange breed of man,
dabbling in construction
                in that far clime?
They've concocted
                some sort of
                        five-year plan . . .
And want to
        fulfil it
                in four year's time!
You can't measure such
                by the American standard.
Neither dollars
            nor cents
                can procure their seduction,
with all
        their human energy
                        extended,

From *Mayakovsky,* Herbert Marshall, editor and translator, London, 1965.

they work the week round
                         in continuous production.
What sort of people are they?
                         Of what mettle!
To work like that
                 by whom
                         were they scourged?
No sort of lash
              has driven them
                           like cattle—
such steel discipline
                    they themselves
                                  have forged.
Misters,
        you've practised,
                        since ancient history,
work-habits
          with money
                    to buy hard.
So to corpulent misters
                       it's an unsolved mystery,
the roots
        of the zeal
                  of our Communards.
Bourgeoisie,
            astonish
                    at our Communistic shores—
in aeroplanes,
             on tractors,
                         at whatever work task,
your world-famous,
                  streamlined America,
                                     for sure,
we
   shall overtake
                 and surpass.

2. Katya's Account of Collectivization

*What the collectivization campaign meant for much of the Soviet popula-
tion is suggested by this excerpt from the autobiography of Victor Kravchenko.
Here he tells the story of a child from a kulak family deported from a village in
the course of the collectivization campaign. Kulak, the word means "fist" in
Russian, was a pejorative name given to the prosperous farmers. The Bolsheviks
purposefully set the poorer villagers against them, thereby setting up what they
called a class war in the countryside.*

...My cousin Natasha, a Party member who was directing a factory college,
was on the train returning from some business trip. A dirt-crusted, ragged little
girl of ten or eleven, one of the new crop of "wild children," came into the car,
begging for bread in a tremulous, hardly audible voice. The sight was familiar
enough, yet something about the child's pitiful eyes and shriveled features
touched Natasha to the quick. She brought the waif to our house.

"I suppose it was the temperature," Natasha had apologized to mother.
"I couldn't bear the thought of the barefoot, half-naked bit of humanity out in
the cold on a night like this."...

After supper, when mother went to wash the dishes, Katya said, "Auntie,
may I help you?" Carrying the dishes from the table to the kitchen, she seemed
for the first time a normal little girl, a touch of masquerade in her dragging
grown-up gown. Our neighbor, Olga Ivanovna, came in. She was an active
employee of the Regional Party Committee. She not only approved our taking in
the child but offered to share the cost of clothes for her. Suddenly we heard the
girl weeping in the kitchen.

"Let her cry it out," mother said.

But the weeping grew louder until it became hysterical sobbing. In the primordial singsong wail of the peasant she kept repeating, in Ukrainian, "Where's
my mama? Where's my papa? Oh, where's my big brother Valya?" We went into
the kitchen. The girl sat hunched over in a chair, wringing her bony little hands,
tears streaming down her sunken cheeks.

"Please quiet down, Katya darling," mother pleaded. "No one will do
you any harm. You will live with us, we'll get you shoes and clothes, we'll teach
you to read and write. Believe me, I'll be a good mother to you."

The child would not be comforted. She began to tell about herself.

"Don't, little dove, don't. You'll tell us some other time," mother urged.

"I can't," Katya sobbed. "I must tell now. I can't stand not talking. I've
been a whole year without my folks. A whole year! We lived in Pokrovnaya. My
father didn't want to join the *kolkhoz.* † All kinds of people argued with him and

Abridged from Victor Kravchenko, *I Chose Freedom, The Personal and Political Life of
a Soviet Official,* New York, 1946.

took him away and beat him but still he wouldn't go in. They shouted he was a *kulak*† agent.''

"Was your father a *kulak*?" I asked. "Do you know what a '*kulak* agent' means?''

"No, uncle, I don't know what these words mean. Our teacher didn't teach them to us. We had a horse, a cow, a heifer, five sheep, some pigs and a barn. That was all. Every night the constable would come and take papa to the village Soviet. They asked him for grain and didn't believe that he had no more. But it was the truth, I swear it.''—She crossed herself solemnly.—''For a whole week they wouldn't let father sleep and they beat him with sticks and revolvers till he was black and blue and swollen all over.''

When the last...grain had been squeezed out of him, Katya recounted, her father slaughtered a pig. He left a little meat for his family and sold the rest in the city to buy bread. Then he slaughtered the calf. Again "they" began to drag him out every night. They told him that killing livestock without permission was a crime.

"Then one morning about a year ago," Katya went on, "strangers came to the house. One of them was from the G.P.U. [internal police] and the chairman of our Soviet was with him too. Another man wrote in a book everything that was in the house, even the furniture and our clothes and pots and pans. Then wagons arrived and all our things were taken away and the remaining animals were driven to the *kolkhoz*.

"*Mamochka*, my dear little mother, she cried and prayed and fell on her knees and even father and big brother Valya cried and sister Shura. But it did no good. We were told to get dressed and take along some bread and salt pork, onions and potatoes, because we were going on a long journey.''

The memory was too much for Katya. She again burst into wild sobbing. But she insisted on going on with the story:

"They put us all in the old church. There were many other parents and children from our village, all with bundles and all weeping. There we spent the whole night, in the dark, praying and crying, praying and crying. In the morning about thirty families were marched down the road surrounded by militiamen. People on the road made the sign of the cross when they saw us and also started crying.

"At the station there were many other people like us, from other villages. It seemed like thousands. We were all crushed into a stone barn but they wouldn't let my dog, Volchok, come in though he'd followed us all the way down the road. I heard him howling when I was inside in the dark.

"After a while we were let out and driven into cattle cars, long rows of them, but I didn't see Volchok anywhere and the guard kicked me when I asked. As soon as our car was filled up so that there was no room for more, even standing up, it was locked from the outside. We all shrieked and prayed to the Holy Virgin. Then the train started. No one knew where we were going. Some said Siberia but others said no, the Far North or even the hot deserts.

"Near Kharkov my sister Shura and I were allowed out to get some water. Mama gave us some money and a bottle and said to try and buy some milk for our baby brother who was very sick. We begged the guard so long that he let us go out which he said was against his rules. Not far away were some peasant huts so we ran there as fast as our feet would carry us.

"When we told these people who we were they began to cry. They gave us something to eat right away, then filled the bottle with milk and wouldn't take the money. Then we ran back to the station. But we were too late and the train had gone away without us."

Katya interrupted herself again to wail for her mother, father, brothers and sister. Now most of us in the kitchen were weeping with the child. The harder mother tried to soothe Katya, the louder she wept herself. My father looked grim and said nothing. I could see the muscles of his face working convulsively....

We learned to love Katya and she came to feel at home with us. But from time to time, at night, we could hear her smothered sobs and that ancient dirge-like complaint, "Where are you, little mother? Where are you, *papochka?*"

3. John Scott: A Day in Magnitogorsk

A number of idealistic and adventurous young Americans set out to work in Soviet Russia after the Revolution. John Scott was one of them. In this reading he explains why he went and the diverse people he found working together to build a vast industrial complex at Magnitogorsk: Americans on contract, technicians who had been accused of sabotage by the Bolsheviks but now had been pressed into service, Party activists, and the workers themselves, most of them peasants fresh from the villages or the military front.

I left the University of Wisconsin in 1931 to find myself in an America sadly dislocated, an America offering few opportunities for young energy and enthusiasm.

I was smitten with the usual wanderlust. The United States did not seem adequate. I decided to go somewhere else. I had already been in Europe three times. Now I projected more far-flung excursions. Plans for a motor-cycle trip to Alaska, thence by home-made sailboat to Siberia and China came to naught. Where would I get the money to finance the project, and what would I do in China? I looked around New York for a job instead. There were no jobs to be had.

Something seemed to be wrong with America. I began to read extensively about the Soviet Union, and gradually came to the conclusion that the Bolsheviks had found answers to at least some of the questions Americans were asking each

Abridged from John Scott, *Behind the Urals,* Indiana, 1942.

other. I decided to go to Russia to work, study, and to lend a hand in the construction of a society which seemed to be at least one step ahead of the American.

Following wise parental counsel I learned a trade before going to Russia. I went to work as a welder's apprentice in the General Electric plant in Schenectady, and several months later received a welder's certificate.

In due course of time Soviet consular wheels ground out my visa and I entrained for Moscow. For ten days I bounced back and forth between several Soviet organizations, trying to make arrangements for a job. The welding trust was glad to give me work. They needed welders in many places. They were not able to sign me up, however, until the visa department had given me permission to remain in the Soviet Union as a worker. The latter organization could grant such permission only to people with jobs. Neither would put anything in writing.

Finally arrangements were completed, and I started out on the four-day train trip to a place called Magnitogorsk on the eastern slopes of the Ural Mountains.

I was very happy. There was no unemployment in the Soviet Union. The Bolsheviks planned their economy and gave opportunities to young men and women. Furthermore, they had got away from the fetishization of material possessions, which, my good parents had taught me, was one of the basic ills of our American civilization. I saw that most Russians ate only black bread, wore one suit until it disintegrated, and used old newspapers for writing letters and office memoranda, rolling cigarettes, making envelopes, and for various personal functions.

I was about to participate in the construction of this society. I was going to be one of many who cared not to own a second pair of shoes, but who built blast furnaces which were their own. It was September, 1932, and I was twenty years old....

The big whistle on the power house sounded a long, deep, hollow six o'clock. All over the scattered city-camp of Magnitogorsk, workers rolled out of their beds or bunks and dressed in preparation for their day's work.

I climbed out of bed and turned on the light. I could see my breath across the room as I woke my roommate, Kolya. Kolya never heard the whistle. Every morning I had to pound his shoulder for several seconds to arouse him.

We pushed our coarse brown army blankets over the beds and dressed as quickly as we could — I had good American long woolen underwear, fortunately; Kolya wore only cotton shorts and a jersey. We both donned army shirts, padded and quilted cotton pants, similar jackets, heavy scarves, and then ragged sheepskin coats. We thrust our feet into good Russian *'valinkis'* — felt boots coming up to the knee. We did not eat anything. We had nothing on hand except tea and a few potatoes, and there was no time to light a fire in our little homemade iron stove. We locked up and set out for the mill.

It was January, 1933. The temperature was in the neighborhood of thirty-five below. A light powdery snow covered the low spots on the ground. The high spots were bare and hard as iron. A few stars crackled in the sky and some electric lights twinkled on the blast furnaces. Otherwise the world was bleak and cold and almost pitch-dark.

It was two miles to the blast furnaces, over rough ground. There was no wind, so our noses did not freeze. I was always glad when there was no wind in the morning. It was my first winter in Russia and I was not used to the cold.

Down beside the foundation of Blast Furnace No. 4 there was a wooden shanty. It was a simple clapboard structure with a corrugated-iron roof nailed on at random. Its one big room was dominated by an enormous welded iron stove placed equidistant from all the walls, on a plate of half-inch steel. It was not more than half-past six when Kolya and I walked briskly up to the door and pushed it open . . . .

Kolya, the welder's foreman, was twenty-two, big-boned, and broad. There was not much meat on him, and his face had a cadaverous look which was rather common in Magnitogorsk in 1933. His unkempt, sawdust-colored hair was very long, and showed under his fur hat. The sheepskin coat which he wore was ragged from crawling through narrow pipes and worming his way into various odd corners. At every tear the wool came through on the outside and looked like a Polish customs officer's mustache. His hands were calloused and dirty; the soles of the *valinkis* on his feet were none too good. His face and his demeanor were extremely energetic.

The riggers were youngish and had not shaved for several days. Their blue peasant eyes were clear and simple, but their foreheads and cheeks were scarred with frostbite, their hands dirty and gnarled.

'I don't know what we're going to do with our cow,' said a young fellow with a cutting torch stuck in the piece of ragged rope that served him as a belt. He rubbed his chin sorrowfully with the back of his rough hand. His blue peasant eyes were looking through the shanty walls, through the blast-furnace foundation, through the stack of unerected trusses, across two hundred miles of snow-swept steppe back to the little village he had left six months before. 'It took us two weeks to get here,' he said earnestly to a bewhiskered welder sitting next to him, 'walking over the steppe with our bags on our backs and driving that goddam cow — and now she's not giving any milk.'

'What the hell do you feed her?' asked the welder thoughtfully.

'That's just the trouble,' said the young cutter's helper, slapping his knee. 'Here we came all the way to Magnitogorsk because there was bread and work on the new construction, and we find we can't even feed the cow, let alone ourselves. Did you eat in the dining-room this morning?'

'Yeah, I tried to,' said a clean-cut looking fellow; 'only fifty grams of bread and that devilish soup that tastes like it was made of matchsticks.' He shrugged his shoulder and spat on the floor between his knees. 'But then — if we are going to build blast furnaces I suppose we have to eat less for a while.'

'Sure,' said a welder, in broken Russian. 'And do you think it's any better anywhere else? Back in Poland we hadn't had a good meal in years. That's why our whole village walked across the Soviet frontier. It's funny, though, we thought there would be more to eat here than there is.'...

At this point a young, boisterous, athletic-looking burner burst into the room and pushed his way up to the stove. 'Boy, is it cold!' he said, addressing everybody in the room. 'I don't think we should work up on top today. One of the riveters froze to death up there last night. It seems he was off in a bleeder pipe and they didn't find him till this morning.'

'Yeah?' said everybody at once. 'Who was it?'

But nobody knew who it was. It was just one of the thousands of peasants and young workers who had come to Magnitogorsk for a bread card, or because things were tough in the newly collectivized villages, or fired with enthusiasm for Socialist construction.

At about ten o'clock a group assembled in the wooden shanty, far different from that which had been there three hours before. First Syemichkin, the superintendent, arrived. Then came Mr. Harris, the American specialist consultant, with his interpreter; then Tishenko, the burly, sinister prisoner specialist.* They came into the shanty one by one, unbuttoned their coats, warmed their hands, then set to talking over their blueprints. Mr. Harris produced a package of fat 'Kuzbas' cigarettes from the special foreigners' store.** He passed them around with a smile. No one refused. Kolya, who had just come in, got in on it too.

'Well,' said Mr. Harris, through his taciturn interpreter, 'when do you expect to get the rest of the riveting done up on top of No. 3? They were telling me about this new time limit. The whole top is to be finished by the twenty-fifth. That's ten days.'

Tishenko, the chief engineer, convicted of sabotage in the Ramzin trial*** in 1929, sentenced to be shot, sentence commuted, now serving ten years in Magnitogorsk, shrugged his shoulders. He did not speak immediately. He was not a wordy man. He had been responsible engineer for a Belgian company in the Ukraine before the Revolution. He had had a house of his own, played tennis with the British consul, sent his son to Paris to study music. Now he was old. His hair was white. He had heard a great deal of talk since 1917, and had decided that most of it was worthless. He did his job, systematically, without enthusiasm. He liked to think that he was helping to build a strong Russia where life would one day be better than it was for his son in Paris or his sister in London. It certainly wasn't yet, though.

---

*prisoner specialist: one of several thousand engineers and scientists accused of anti-Soviet activities and exiled to outlying places where they held responsible positions working for Soviet industry

**special foreigners' store *(beryozka):* store in USSR where only hard (Western) currency is accepted, mainly used by foreigners

***Ramzin trial: 1930 show trial of Professor Ramzin, accused of sabotaging Soviet industry in collaboration with hostile foreigners

Mr. Harris looked at Tishenko. He understood the older man's position and respected his silence. Still, he was a consulting engineer being paid good American dollars, being supplied with caviar in a country where there was little bread and no sugar, to push Magnitostroi through to completion on time. He pressed the point. And Tishenko finally answered slowly: 'A riveter froze to death last night. Cold and malnutrition. This morning four of the girls we have heating rivets didn't show up. Two of them are pregnant, I think, and it's cold up there. The compressor is working badly.' He stopped, realizing it was all beside the point. If he said that the job would be finished by the twenty-fifth he was a liar and a hypocrite and Mr. Harris would be perfectly aware of it. If he said that it would take longer, he was sabotaging the decision of the Commissar of Heavy Industry. He was already under sentence for sabotage. He looked out of the dusty window. 'It'll take at least a month,' he said....

The door opened and Shevchenko came in. Shevchenko was the great activist among the technical personnel.

His technical knowledge was limited, and his written Russian contained many mistakes. His present job was sectional assistant director of construction. He was responsible to the director and to the party for the fulfillment of construction plans....

We all realized that Shevchenko was a boor and a careerist. But it seemed to take people like that to push the job forward, to overcome the numerous difficulties, to get the workers to work in spite of cold, bad tools, lack of materials, and undernourishment. It took all types to make Magnitogorsk. That was clear.

'Now, Mr. Shevchenko,' said the American, 'orders are orders, but you can't rivet steel with them and you can't heat rivets with them. We must have these things or the job won't be finished by next Christmas. You're an influential man in the party and with the construction administration. It's up to you to get these materials.'

The four men, as heterogeneous a group as one could find — a Cleveland engineer, a prisoner specialist, a Red director, and a young, inexperienced Soviet engineer — sat down around the table to discuss the rest of the points on Mr. Harris's list [of what had to be done]....

EPILOGUE — 1941

The Magnitogorsk I left in early 1938 was producing upward of five thousand tons of steel daily and large quantities of many other useful products. In spite of the purge, the town was still full of rough and earnest young Russians — working, studying, making mistakes and learning, reproducing to the tune of thirty-odd per thousand every year. They were also writing poetry, going to see remarkably good performances of 'Othello,' learning to play violins and tennis. All this out in the middle of a steppe where, ten years before, only a few hundred impoverished herders had lived.

Today, after little more than a decade, Magnitogorsk stands one of the largest metallurgical plants in the world. It produces five thousand tons of pig iron, six to seven thousand tons of steel, more than ten thousand tons of iron ore every day, as well as millions of tons of chemical by-products, structural shapes, steel wire, rods, rails, plates, and strips annually. Furthermore, at the present moment, at least one armament factory previously situated near Leningrad has arrived in Magnitogorsk lock, stock, and barrel, complete with personnel, and is already going into production using Magnitogorsk steel. [Note the year this epilogue was written. The reference is to the Soviet policy of moving whole factories eastward away from the 1941 German advance.]

4.   Zoshchenko: Poverty

A top priority of the early Soviet regime was electrification of the country-side. The slogan of the Party was "Electrification plus Soviet power." Mikhail Zoshchenko, a Soviet satirist born in 1895, depicts here, with consummate skill and humor, the mixed blessing of the advances of industrialization.

Nowadays, brothers, what is the most fashionable word there is, eh?

Nowadays, the most fashionable word that can be is, of course, electrification.

I won't argue that it isn't a matter of immense importance to light up Soviet Russia with electricity. Nevertheless, even this matter has its shady side. I am not saying, comrades, that it costs a lot. It costs nothing more expensive than money. That's not what I'm talking about.

This is what I mean.

I lived, comrades, in a very large house. The whole house was using kerosene. Some had kerosene lamps with, some without a glass, and some had nothing—just a priest's candle flickering away. Real hardship!

And then they started installing electric lights. Soon after the Revolution.

The house delegate [building director] installed them first. Well, he installed and installed. He's a quiet man and doesn't let his tongue give him away. But still he walks a bit strangely, and he's always thoughtfully blowing his nose.

Nevertheless, he doesn't let his tongue give him away.

And then our dear little landlady, Elizaveta Ignat'evna Prokhorov, declares to us that she too wants to put in electric lights in our half-dark apartment.

"Everybody," she says, "is installing them. Even the delegate," she says, "has installed them. Why should we be more backward than other people? All the more so," she says, "since it's economical. Cheaper than kerosene."

You don't say! We too began to install.

From Mikhail Zoshchenko, *Scenes from the Bathhouse,* Ann Arbor, 1973.

We installed them, turned them on—my fathers! Muck and filth all around.

The way it was before, you'd go to work in the morning, come home in the evening, drink a bit of tea, and go to bed. And nothing of this kind was visible as long as you used kerosene. But now when we turned on the lights, we see, here someone's old bedroom slipper lying around, there the wallpaper torn in shreds and hanging down, there a bedbug running away at a trot, trying to save himself from the light, here a rag of who-knows-what, there a gob of spit, here a cigar butt, there a flea hopping.

Holy fathers! You wanted to cry for help. Sad to look on such a spectacle.

Take the couch that stood in our room, for example. I used to think, it's all right, it's a couch. It's a good couch. I often sat on it evenings. And now I was burning electricity—holy fathers! What a couch! Everything's sticking out, hanging down, spilling out from inside. I can't sit down on such a couch—my soul cries out.

So, I think, I don't live very well, do I? Better get out of the house. I begin to develop a negative attitude. My work falls from my hands.

I see the landlady, Elizaveta Ignat'evna, is also going around mournfully, muttering to herself, fussing around in the kitchen.

"What," I ask, "is bothering you, landlady?"

She waves her hand.

"My dear man," she says, "I never thought I was living so badly."

I looked at her fixings—and it really wasn't what you'd call luxurious; in fact, her furniture was painful. And all around, disorder, strewings, litter, rubbish. And all this flooded with bright light and staring you in the eye.

I began coming home kind of depressed.

I come in, I turn on the light, stare at the bulb, and hop into the sack.

After giving it a good deal of thought, I got my pay. I bought some whitewash and started to work. I shook out the bed, killed off the bedbugs, painted over the woodwork, banged the couch back together, decorated, decontaminated—my spirit sings and rejoices.

In general, everything was going well, very well indeed.

But our landlady, Elizaveta Ignat'evna, took another course. She cut the installation wires in her room.

"My dear man," she says, "I don't want to live in the light. I don't want," she says, "my modest circumstances to be lit up for the bedbugs to laugh at."

I begged and argued with her—no good. She held her own.

"I don't want," she says, "to live with that light. I have no money to make repairs."

I tell her: "Why, I'll do the repairs for you myself for next to nothing."

She doesn't want that.

"With those bright lights of yours," she says, "I have to keep busy from morning to night with cleaning and washing. I'll manage," she says, "without the light, as I managed before."

The delegate also tried to convince her. And even quarreled with her. He called her an outmoded *petit bourgeois* [small-minded middle class person]. It didn't work. She refused.

Well, let her have it the way she wants. Personally, I live in the electric light and I am quite satisfied with it.

The way I look at it, the light scratches away all our litter and removes the rubbish.

5. Ginzburg: Into the Whirlwind of the Purges

Stalin's purges led to the arrest and imprisonment of many loyal and devoted Communists. Often those arrested had absolutely no idea why they had been chosen, and believed that "if Stalin only knew" what was happening to them, he would reprimand the local official responsible for it. Eugenia Ginzburg was less naive than this. She was nonetheless devoted to the Communist cause, and has told her story in an unusually well-written and interesting autobiography. This selection begins with a description of the first time she was called in for questioning, shortly after her colleague, an historian named Elvov, had been arrested for misinterpreting the significance of the 1905 revolution in Russia.

The next two years might be called the prelude to that symphony of madness and terror which began for me in February 1937. A few days after Elvov's arrest, a Party meeting was held at the editorial office of *Red Tartary* at which, for the first time, I was accused of what I had *not* done.

I had *not* denounced Elvov as a purveyor of Trotskyist* contraband. I had *not* written a crushing review of the source book on Tartar history he had edited—I had even contributed to it (not that my article, dealing with the nineteenth century, was in any way criticized). I had *not*, even once, attacked him at a public meeting.

My attempts to appeal to common sense were summarily dismissed.

"But I wasn't the only one—no one in the regional committee [of the party] attacked him!"

"Never you mind, each will answer for himself. At the moment it's you we are talking about."

---

*Trotskyist contraband—After Trotsky's ouster by Stalin, connection with him real or fabricated, or possession of his writings was cause for arrest.

Abridged from Eugenia Ginzburg, *Journey into the Whirlwind,* New York, 1967.

"But he was trusted by the regional committee. Communists elected him to the municipal board."

"You should have pointed out that this was wrong. What were you given a university training for, and an academic job?"

"But has it even been proved that he's Trotskyist?"

This naive question provoked an explosion of righteous anger:

"Don't you know he's been arrested? Can you imagine anyone's being arrested unless there's something definite against him?"

All my life I shall remember every detail of that meeting, so notable for me because, for the first time, I came up against that reversal of logic and common sense which never ceased to amaze me in the more than twenty years that followed right up to the Twentieth Party Congress [when Khrushchev gave his Secret Speech. See Reading 11], or at any rate the plenum of September 1953.

During a recess I went off to the editorial office. I wanted a moment to myself to think of what I should do next and how to behave without losing my dignity as a Communist and a human being. My cheeks were burning, and for several minutes I felt as if I should go mad with the pain of being unjustly accused.

The door creaked, and Alexandra Alexandrovna, the office typist, came in. She had done a lot of work for me and we got on well. An elderly, reserved woman who had suffered some kind of disappointment in life, she was devoted to me.

"You're taking this the wrong way, Eugenia Semyonovna. You should admit you're guilty and say you are sorry."

"But I'm not guilty of anything. Why should I lie at a Party meeting?"

"You'll get a reprimand anyway. A political reprimand is a very bad thing. And by not saying you repent you make it worse."

"I won't be a hypocrite. If they do reprimand me, I'll fight till they withdraw it."

She looked at me with her kindly eyes surrounded by a network of wrinkles, and repeated the very words Elvov had said to me at our last meeting:

"You don't understand what's going on. You're heading for a lot of trouble."

Doubtless, if the same thing happened to me today, I would "recant." I almost certainly would, for I too have changed. I am no longer the proud, incorruptible, inflexible being I was then. But in those days this is what I was: proud, incorruptible, inflexible, and no power on earth could have made me join in the orgy of breast-beating and self-criticism that was just beginning.

Large and crowded lecture halls were turned into public confessionals.... Beating their breasts, the "guilty" would lament that they had "shown political short-sightedness" and "lack of vigilance," "compromised with dubious elements," "added grist" to this or that mill, and were tainted with "rotten liberalism."

Many such phrases echoed under the vaulted roofs of public buildings. The press, too, was flooded with contrite articles by Party theorists, frightened out of their wits like rabbits and not attempting to conceal their fear. The power and importance of the NKVD* grew with every day....

(Mrs. Ginzburg began to live in continuous fear of arrest.)

My mind told me that there was absolutely nothing for which I could be arrested. It was true, of course, that in the monstrous accusations which the newspapers daily hurled at "enemies of the people" there was something clearly exaggerated, not quite real. All the same, I thought to myself, there must be something in it, however little — they must at least have voted the wrong way on some occasion or other. I, on the other hand, had never belonged to the opposition, nor had I ever had the slightest doubt as to the rightness of the Party line.

"If they arrested people like you they'd have to lock up the whole Party," my husband encouraged me in my line of reasoning.

Yet, in spite of all these rational arguments, I could not shake off a feeling of approaching disaster. I seemed to be at the center of an iron ring which was all the time contracting and would soon crush me.

The nights were terrifying. But what we were waiting for actually happened in the daytime....

We were in the dining room, my husband, Alyosha, and I. My step-daughter Mayka was out skating. Vasya was in the nursery. I was ironing some laundry. I often felt like doing manual work; it distracted me from my thoughts. Alyosha was having breakfast, and my husband was reading a story by Valeria Gerasimova aloud to him. Suddenly the telephone rang. It sounded as shrill as on that day in December 1934. [Day Kirov was shot]

For a few moments, none of us picked it up. We hated telephone calls in those days. Then my husband said in that unnaturally calm voice he so often used now:

"It must be Lukovnikov. I asked him to call."

He took the receiver, listened, went as white as a sheet, and said even more quietly:

"It's for you, Genia. Vevers, of the NKVD."

Vevers, the head of the NKVD department for special political affairs, could not have been more amiable and charming. His voice burbled on like a brook in spring.

"Good morning, dear comrade. Tell me, how are you fixed for time today?"

"I'm always free now. Why?"

Oh, dear, always free, how depressing. Never mind, these things will pass. So anyway, you'd have time to come and see me for a moment....

[As she went out the door, not to return for many years, her husband said]

"Well, Genia, we'll expect you home for lunch."

---

*Internal police. Its name has changed many times in the course of Soviet history. Today its initials are KGB.

How pathetic he looked, all of a sudden, how his lips trembled! I thought of his assured, masterful tone in the old days, the tone of an old Communist, an experienced Party worker.

"Good-by, Paul dear. We've had a good life together."

I didn't even say "Look after the children." I knew he would not be able to take care of them. He was again trying to comfort me with commonplaces—I could no longer catch what he was saying. I walked quickly toward the reception room, and suddenly heard his broken cry:

"Genia!"

He had the haunted look of a baited animal, of a harried and exhausted human being—it was a look I was to see again and again, *there*....

EPILOGUE

All that this book describes is over and done with. I, and thousands like me, have lived to see the Twentieth and the Twenty-second Party Congress.

In 1937, when this tale begins, I was a little over thirty. Now I am in my fifties. The intervening eighteen years were spent "there."

During those years I experienced many conflicting feelings, but the dominant one was that of amazement. Was all this imaginable—was it really happening, could it be intended? Perhaps it was this very amazement which helped to keep me alive. I was not only a victim, but an observer also. What, I kept saying to myself, will come of this? Can such things just happen and be done with, unattended by retribution?

Many a time, my thoughts were taken off my own sufferings by the keen interest which I felt in the unusual aspects of life and of human nature which unfolded around me. I strove to remember all these things in the hope of recounting them to honest people and true Communists, such as I was sure would listen to me one day.

When I wrote this record, I thought of it as a letter to my grandson. I supposed that by 1980, when he would be twenty years old, these matters might seem remote enough to be safely divulged. How wonderful that I was mistaken, and that the great Leninist truths have again come into their own in our country and Party! Today the people can already be told of the things that have been and shall be no more.

Here, then, is the story of an ordinary Communist woman during the period of the "personality cult."

[Mrs. Ginzburg's book was published in the West in the mid 1960s. It was submitted for publication in the Soviet Union, but, after much discussion, was not published there.]

6.   Stalin's Official History of the Purges

The History of the Communist Party of the Soviet Union was approved by Stalin and published in 1938. It was the official version of Soviet history up to that point. Seventy million copies were printed between 1938 and 1953, and it was used in all schools throughout the Soviet Union. In addition to glorifying Stalin, the History vilifies most of the early Bolshevik leaders who had, by 1938, been arrested and shot in the purges. Those mentioned in this passage, Bukharin, Trotsky, Pyatakov, Zinoviev, Kamenev, Krestinsky et al. were all Old Bolsheviks. There is absolutely no evidence that they plotted against Lenin, betrayed state secrets, or conspired with foreigners. This reading is included less for the facts it recounts than for the tone and language in which these facts are discussed— the tone and language of the purges.

...In 1937, new facts came to light regarding the fiendish crimes of the Bukharin-Trotsky gang. The trial of Pyatakov, Radek and others, the trial of Tukhachevsky, Yakir and others, and, lastly, the trial of Bukharin, Rykov, Krestinsky, Rosengoltz and others, all showed that the Bukharinites and Trotskyites had long ago joined to form a common band of enemies of the people, operating as the "Bloc of Rights and Trotskyites."

The trials showed that these dregs of humanity, in conjunction with the enemies of the people, Trotsky, Zinoviev and Kamenev, had been in conspiracy against Lenin, the Party and the Soviet state ever since the early days of the October Socialist Revolution. The insidious attempts to thwart the Peace of Brest-Litovsk at the beginning of 1918, the plot against Lenin and the conspiracy with the "Left" Socialist-Revolutionaries for the arrest and murder of Lenin, Stalin and Sverdlov in the spring of 1918, the villainous shot that wounded Lenin in the summer of 1918, the revolt of the "Left" Socialist-Revolutionaries in the summer of 1918, the deliberate aggravation of differences in the Party in 1921 with the object of undermining and overthrowing Lenin's leadership from within, the attempts to overthrow the Party leadership during Lenin's illness and after his death, the betrayal of state secrets and the supply of information of an espionage character to foreign espionage services, the vile assassination of Kirov, the acts of wrecking, diversion and explosions, the dastardly murder of Menzhinsky, Kuibyshev and Gorky—all these and similar villainies over a period of twenty years were committed, it transpired, with the participation or under the direction of Trotsky, Zinoviev, Kamenev, Bukharin, Rykov and their henchmen, at the behest of espionage services of bourgeois states.

The trials brought to light the fact that the Trotsky-Bukharin fiends, in obedience to the wishes of their masters—the espionage services of foreign

From Commission of the Central Committee of the C.P.S.U., editor, *History of the Communist Party of the Soviet Union* (Bolshevik), New York, 1939.

states—had set out to destroy the Party and the Soviet state, to undermine the defensive power of the country, to assist foreign military intervention, to prepare the way for the defeat of the Red Army, to bring about the dismemberment of the U.S.S.R., to hand over the Soviet Maritime Region to the Japanese, Soviet Byelorussia to the Poles, and the Soviet Ukraine to the Germans, to destroy the gains of the workers and collective farmers, and to restore capitalist slavery in the U.S.S.R.

These Whiteguard pigmies, whose strength was no more than that of a gnat, apparently flattered themselves that they were the masters of the country, and imagined that it was really in their power to sell or give away the Ukraine, Byelorussia and the Maritime Region.

These Whiteguard insects forgot that the real masters of the Soviet country were the Soviet people, and that the Rykovs, Bukharins, Zinovievs and Kamenevs were only temporary employees of the state, which could at any moment sweep them out from its offices as so much useless rubbish.

These contemptible lackeys of the fascists forgot that the Soviet people had only to move a finger, and not a trace of them would be left.

The Soviet court sentenced the Bukharin-Trotsky fiends to be shot.

The People's Commissariat of Internal Affairs carried out the sentence.

The Soviet people approved the annihilation of the Bukharin-Trotsky gang and passed on to next business....

7.   The Siege of Leningrad

The city of Leningrad had a population of about 2½ million people when it was surrounded by the German advance in September of 1941. It remained surrounded for almost 900 days. Its only supplies had to be dropped by air or, in winter, brought in over an ice road built over Lake Ladoga. During the siege, it is estimated that well over one million people died, mostly from hunger and cold, but also on the front lines and from the German bombardment. This is a Soviet account, published first in the Soviet Union in 1958.

November-December, 1941

...November arrived. Cold, cloudy days and heavy snowfalls replaced the clear, dry days of October. The ground was covered by a thick layer of white that rose in drifts along the streets and boulevards. An icy wind drove powdered snow through the slits of dugouts and shelters, through the broken windows of apartments, hospitals, and stores. Winter came early, snowy, and cold.

The functioning of the city's transportation system deteriorated with each day. Fuel supplies were almost gone, and industry was dying out. Workers and

Abridged from Dmitri Pavlov, *Leningrad 1941: The Blockade,* Chicago, 1965.

employees, quartered in distant parts of the city, had now to walk several kilometers to work, struggling from one end of the city to the other through deep snow. Exhausted at the close of the working day, they could barely make their way home. There they could throw off their clothes and lie down for a short while to stretch their work-heavy legs. Sleep would come instantly, in spite of the cold, but would constantly be interrupted by cramps of the legs or hands. Rising was hard in the morning. Night did not restore the strength or drive away weariness. The fatigue of great temporary exertion will pass off in a single night's rest; but this was weariness that came from the daily exhausting of physical strength. Soon, however, it would be time for work again. Arm, leg, neck, and heart muscles would have to take up their burdens. The brain worked tensely.

The demands on people's strength increased as their nourishment deteriorated. The constant shortage of food, the cold weather and nervous tension wore the workers down. Jokes and laughter ceased; faces grew preoccupied and stern. People were weaker. They moved slowly, stopping often. Rosy cheeks were like a miracle. People looked at the person with surprise and some suspicion. Few people in November paid any attention to the whistle and burst of shells that had shocked them into alertness only a few days before. The thunder of gunfire was like a distant, aimless, hoarse barking. People were deeply absorbed in their joyless thoughts.

The blockade was now fifty-three days old. The most severe economies in food consumption and the delivery of a small quantity of grain across the lake had only resulted in the following meager amounts being on hand on the first of November: flour for fifteen days; cereals for sixteen days; sugar for thirty days; fats for twenty-two days. There was only a very small quantity of meat. The supply of meat products depended almost wholly on the deliveries by air. Out of the whole city, however—although everyone knew that food was scarce, since the rations were being reduced—the actual situation was known to only seven men. Two specially chosen workers recorded the deliveries of food over the lake and air routes (and later over the Ice Road), and these figures and those for food on hand were restricted to a small inner circle, which made it possible to keep the secret of the beleaguered fortress.

The eve of the twenty-fourth anniversary of the October Revolution arrived. [November 7 by revised calendar.] There usually was such a happy fuss and bustle on that evening! Streets and houses would have been ablaze with lights; store windows would delight the eye with their decorations and lavish displays of goods. Fat turkeys, apples, prunes, pastries, thin slices of ham, and a world of other delicacies would lure shoppers. Everywhere, marketing would be going on in lively fashion, as families prepared to spend the holidays with friends. There would have been the noise of happy children excited by the gaiety in the air and the prospect of presents and shows.

In the memorable year of 1941, Leningraders were deprived of pleasure. They had cold, darkness, and the sensation of hunger constantly with them. The sight of the empty shelves in the stores woke a feeling of melancholy in them that was actually painful. The holiday was observed by issuing each child two hundred grams of sour cream and one hundred grams of potato flour. Adults received five salted tomatoes. Nothing more was to be found....

[The Leningraders worked to establish an ice road over Lake Ladoga to bring in supplies and evacuate children and old people. In their desperate need to use the road before the ice was thick enough, they lost many trucks which fell through the ice. Even when the ice road could be used, food and fuel were desperately short.]

Not more than thirty carloads of flour per day were used to feed a population of two and one-half million people. To produce even this much required hard fighting with the enemy and the elements.

The sudden drop by more than one-third in the bread ration had pernicious effects on health. Everyone, dependents especially, began to experience acute hunger. Men and women faded before each others' eyes; they moved slowly; they talked slowly, then an emaciated body would suddenly be lifeless. In those days, death drew itself up to its full stature and loomed menacingly, preparing to reap in masses those who crossed its path, regardless of sex or age.

Cold had settled down to stay in the unheated apartments of the city. Remorselessly it froze the exhausted people. Dystrophy and cold sent 11,085 people to their graves during November, the first to fall under death's scythe being the old men. Their bodies, in contrast to those of women of the same age or young men, offered no resistance at all to acute hunger....

More and more adults and children died every day. First a person's arms and legs grew weak, then his body became numb, the numbness gradually approached the heart, gripped it as in a vise, and then the end came.

Death overtook people anywhere. As he walked along the street, a man might fall and not get up. People would go to bed at home and not rise again. Often death would come suddenly as men worked at their machines.

Since public transportation was not operating, burial was a special problem. The dead were usually carried on sleds without coffins. Two or three relatives or close friends would haul the sled along the seemingly endless streets, often losing strength and abandoning the deceased halfway to the cemetery, leaving to the authorities the task of disposing of the body. Employees of the municipal public services and health service cruised the streets and alleys to pick up the bodies, loading them on trucks. Frozen bodies, drifted over with snow, lined the cemeteries and their approaches. There was not strength enough to dig into the deeply frozen earth. Civil defense crews would blast the ground to make mass graves, into which they would lay tens and sometimes hundreds of bodies without even knowing the names of those they buried.

—May the dead forgive the living who could not, under those desperate conditions, perform the last ceremonies due honest, laborious lives....

There is in Leningrad an Institute of Plant Genetics whose personnel had at one time assembled a rare collection of grain cultures from 118 countries of the world. The work had been done under the direction of Nikolai Ivanovich Vavilov, the famous scientist.* By the beginning of the war, the collection contained more than 100,000 different samples of wheat, rye, corn, rice, and other cereal and bean cultures. A broad study of these flora from all over the world had helped agricultural workers in our country solve a number of important problems.

The war interrupted the creative work of the Institute. Many of its people went to the front, where a number died. The Institute of Plant Genetics (and not only it) dropped from sight in the commotion of the war. The authorities had no time for it, as the workers of the Institute knew; they understood they could do as they pleased with the collection, and no one would hold them responsible if the seed samples disappeared. The members of the Institute, despite the loss of colleagues from their ranks, continued to work, adjusting to circumstances as they arose.

When the enemy was approaching the city, the Institute prepared to evacuate the collection. After having been packed and loaded onto freight cars, the seeds and other scientifically valuable objects finally could not be shipped off because of the blockade. The director of the Institute, I. G. Eichfeld, took steps then to store the samples at the Institute on shelves specially equipped to preserve the seeds. A twenty-four hour watch was kept on them. Every Institute employee took a hand in the watch without exception. They disarmed dozens of incendiary bombs that fell on the roof of the building.

Rats caused a great deal of trouble. The creatures easily got into the empty rooms where the collection was stored, climbed up to the shelves, gnawed through packing, and devoured the seeds.

To protect the collection against the invasion of rats, the seeds were repacked in rat-proof metal boxes and stacked in piles so that they could be under the constant surveillance of the scientists. During the first two months of the blockade, the struggle was chiefly with bombs, rats, and isolated sallies by marauders. More strenuous ordeals were in store for the workers during the famine of November and December, 1941, and the beginning of 1942. This enemy dealt them fearful blows.

In December, Institute employees were often too exhausted to get out of bed, and their work fell to those who could still move about. On one of the coldest days of that dreadful month, the workers heard sorrowful news; their comrade A. Ya. Molibog, the agrometeorologist, had been burned to death in a fire at his home. He had grown so weak from hunger that he could not leave his apartment when it was enveloped in flames. Not long after, the biologist S. A. Egis and

---

*Vavilov (1887-1943?) was Russia's leading plant geneticist and at one time head of the Academy of Agricultural Sciences. He was ousted in 1940 for opposing the theories of T.D. Lysenko and imprisoned. He was "rehabilitated" posthumously.

D. S. Ivanov, the senior scientist in rice culture, died of exhaustion. Twenty-eight other employees of the Institute followed them to the grave from the same cause.

These people all remained interested in the collection to the end. They would smile and their cloudy eyes would brighten when they were told it was still under care and safe....

The proximity to grain and the duty of caring for it in the name of the future while slowly dying of starvation was inhuman torture. But by their solidarity and single-mindedness, the Vavilov collection, which took years to put together, was preserved for science and the future. It cost the lives of many people wholeheartedly devoted to the cause of science but they triumphed over their suffering....

8. A Russian Woman

Quentin Reynolds was a widely-published American correspondent during World War II. The following story of a Russian woman is from one of his dispatches. Stories such as this are still commonly told in the Soviet Union.

At first glance, Uliana looks like almost any middle-aged peasant woman. She sits hunched over a little, the way women do who have spent too many years bending over the soil, coaxing it to yield wheat and corn and potatoes. Until she tells you, you don't know that she bends forward slightly because that eases the pain of a half-healed wound. Until she tells you that she is only thirty-three, you would indeed think of her as just another middle-aged peasant woman....

She was born in the village of Putivl, which is in the soft, lush region of the Ukraine. She had two young sisters, Alexandra and Maria. They were trained as nurses. Uliana herself was a brilliant student and fervent patriot. Her father was postmaster of the village, and he took great pride in the intellectual achievements of young Uliana. So did the rest of the village, for when the old mayor (who had held office for twenty years) died, they elected young Uliana in his place.

In Russia they do not call the head of a community mayor; they call him president of the local soviet; but it means the same thing. She was enrolled as a party member when she was twenty-four, a great honor in the Soviet Union, for there are only two million party members in the whole country. That is one percent of the population. There is a waiting list of more than a million.

As mayor, Uliana settled local disputes over land boundaries, she administered justice, and the village of Putivl was indeed a happy and contented community. And then the German juggernaut rolled through the smooth plains of the Ukraine. Many in the village quite sensibly left, but not Uliana. When the Germans roared into Putivl, Uliana was there, calm and serene, prepared to do her best to make life easier for her fellow villagers.

Abridged from Quentin Reynolds, *The Curtain Rises,* New York, 1944.

But the Germans gave her no chance. They took Uliana and some of the other leading citizens, led them to a near-by monastery, lined them up against a wall and shot them.

"There were eight of us," Uliana told me in a peculiarly detached voice, as though she were telling of something which had happened to someone else. "Three of us, two teachers and I, were women. They marched us to an old monastery. They told us to face the wall and to take off our clothes. By now, of course, I knew that we were going to be shot. The Germans usually make people they are going to shoot or hang take off all their clothes first. It saves them a lot of trouble afterward.

"I undressed slowly, and then the shots came. I still had my stockings and underwear on. Nobody cried out when the shots came. Then I felt something hit me in the side and I fell forward. Things became confused. I half remember being carried into the monastery and down a staircase, then I lost consciousness.

"When I came to, it was dark and there was a weight on me. When my mind began to work, I realized that there were bodies on top of me. Upstairs, soldiers were arguing about the clothes. I could hear them and then I heard someone groaning near me. It was one of the men, a doctor, and he was not dead, though the others were. He cried out to the Germans to come and finish him off, but they didn't hear him. I crawled over to him and said that we should try to get out. We were in the cellar of the monastery."

"How did you get out of there?" I asked.

"When the soldiers left," she continued, "I crawled up the stairs very slowly because my side hurt and I was losing a lot of blood. The doctor followed me. It was night now. We crawled to a farmhouse near by. I couldn't stand up to knock at the door. I lay there, trying to cry out and fearing that the Germans would hear me, but they didn't. The people in the farmhouse took us in. The doctor had a bad wound. He died that night.

"The following night they put me in a wagon, piled hay on top of me and sent me to a farmhouse a few miles away. Each night I would be transferred farther away from my village, farther away from the Germans. Then I reached an unoccupied town which had a hospital. The bullet had gone through my side and had injured my lung, and they didn't think I would live. I did, though, and then when I was better I decided to join the partisans. People in our villages always knew where they could be found."

"Were you expert with a gun?" I asked.

She smiled faintly. "I had never held a gun in my hands before, but I soon learned. We were usually behind the German lines. We kept in touch with the people of the occupied villages. Sometimes we raided these villages. There was a great shortage of salt in the Ukraine. I imagine the Germans sent it back to their country. Once we heard that they had a stock of salt in a certain village. We raided the village, took the salt and distributed it among the people of the neighboring villages. We were well armed, but food, of course, was a problem."

"How would you get food?" I asked her.

"They put me in charge of that," she said. "My wound was giving me trouble and I couldn't go on quick marches. I'd take a few men and lie in wait beside a road. When a convoy of German food trucks came along, we would ambush them and run the loaded trucks back to our headquarters. We shifted headquarters every few nights. We slept by day usually, and fought by night."

"What was the partisans' main job?"

She shrugged her shoulders. "Our main job was to blow up railroads and bridges. We blew up a lot of them, hindering the German advance. They decided to send a good force after us. We heard about it. They sent twenty tanks into the valley where we were, but we outflanked them and blew up five of them with hand grenades. Then we moved somewhere else. We were always on the move."

Uliana lived and fought with the partisans for nearly two years. She doesn't know yet what happened to her mother or to her two younger sisters. She would rather not think about that, she said. Why was she in Moscow? Uliana was a little ashamed of it. Her old wound had given her a lot of trouble, so she had been sent to specialists in the capital. But she would be back with the partisans soon, she said grimly, and then, rather surprisingly, she lost her placidity and became vibrant, alive, dynamic.

"Do your American women know the kinds of beasts we are fighting?" Her eyes flashed now and she no longer bent forward. She no longer looked like a middle-aged peasant woman. She was filled with a righteous hatred of the men who had invaded her country.

"Do they know that every time Germans occupy a village they hang or shoot a group of women just as a lesson to the others?" she said. "As a lesson to make others fall into line and obey them. Their motto is, 'Women and children first.' Yes, first hang the women and starve the children. Have American women ever seen the bodies of children who have starved to death? I have—in many villages of the Ukraine."

Uliana breathed heavily and put her hand to her side. She got up and bowed, and there was a certain majesty about this stocky Russian who couldn't quite stand up straight. She walked out of the room.

9.   Soviet War Losses

Soviet war losses in World War II were about 20 million, out of a population of 191 million in 1939. About one in ten people died during the war. On the following charts, compare the numbers of people who were twenty in 1939 and those who were forty in 1959 and also the numbers of men and women in different age groups in 1959.

The United States lost about 400,000 in World War II. In all its wars, including the Civil War which caused more deaths than any other American conflict, the United States has lost an estimated 1,155,059 people.

Population of the Soviet Union by Age

	1939	1959
0-9	43,574,658	46,362,362
10-15	28,365,849	17,133,406
16-19	13,029,401	14,675,244
20-24	15,785,942	20,343,028
25-29	18,520,257	18,190,129
30-34	15,598,080	18,998,899
35-39	12,957,576	11,590,509
40-44	9,603,495	10,408,095
45-49	7,775,579	12,263,494
50-54	6,635,588	10,446,734
55-59	5,897,046	8,698,854
60-69	8,535,597	11,736,245
70 +	4,461,950	7,971,289
Ages not given	35,872	8,362
Total Population	190,677,890	208,826,650

1959 Census

By Age	Total	Men	Women
0-9	46,362,362	23,608,300	22,754,062
10-19	31,808,650	16,066,487	15,742,163
20-24	20,343,028	10,055,978	10,287,050
25-29	18,190,129	8,916,969	9,273,160
30-34	18,998,899	8,611,011	10,387,888
35-39	11,590,509	4,528,340	7,062,169
40-44	10,408,095	3,998,239	6,409,856
45-49	12,263,494	4,705,764	7,557,730
50-54	10,446,734	4,010,114	6,436,620
55-59	8,698,854	2,905,486	5,793,368
60-69	11,736,245	4,098,922	7,637,323
70-79	6,168,022	2,020,519	4,147,503
80-89	1,578,473	464,794	1,113,679
90-99	203,086	49,940	153,146
100 +	21,708	5,432	16,276
Ages not given	8,362	4,008	4,354
Total	208,826,650	94,050,303	114,776,347

From *Itogi Vsesoyuznoi Naseleniia,* Central Statistics Bureau, Moscow, 1962.

HERE LIE THE PEOPLE OF LENINGRAD.
MEN. WOMEN. CHILDREN.
BESIDE THEM LIE SOLDIERS OF THE RED ARMY
WHO GAVE THEIR LIVES
TO DEFEND YOU, LENINGRAD.
CRADLE OF THE REVOLUTION.
WE CANNOT GIVE ALL THEIR NOBLE NAMES HERE.
THERE ARE SO MANY UNDER THE TIMELESS GUARD OF GRANITE
BUT ALL YOU WHO GAZE ON THESE STONES MUST KNOW:
NO ONE AND NOTHING HAS BEEN FORGOTTEN.

TO THE CITY CAME AN ENEMY CLAD IN IRON AND ARMOUR.
BUT WORKERS, SCHOOLCHILDREN, TEACHERS, MILITIAMEN
ROSE WITH THE ARMY
ALL, AS ONE, DECLARED:
DEATH WILL SOONER FEAR US THAN WE DEATH.
THE COLD, FIERCE AND DARK WINTER OF 1941 — 1942
IS NOT FORGOTTEN.
NOR THE GRIM GUNFIRE.
NOR THE HORRIBLE BOMBING IN 1943.
NOT A SINGLE LIFE, COMRADES, HAS BEEN FORGOTTEN.
UNDER CEASELESS FIRE FROM AIR, LAND, AND SEA
DAILY HEROISM
YOU SET FORTH SIMPLY AND WITH DIGNITY
AND YOU AND YOUR MOTHERLAND
FOUND VICTORY.
BEFORE YOUR IMMORTAL SELVES
LET A GRATEFUL PEOPLE,
THE MOTHERLAND, AND THE HERO-CITY LENINGRAD
ALWAYS LOWER THEIR BANNERS
TO THIS SAD AND HALLOWED GROUND.

Olga Bergholz

The statue of Mother Russia in the Piskariovskoye Memorial Cemetery
outside Leningrad, where those who died in the siege of that city during
World War II lie buried in mass graves.

10. Stalin in the Late 1940s

Milovan Djilas was a leading Yugoslav Communist who fought with the Communist underground against the Nazis, and visited the Soviet Union in 1944, 1945 and again in 1948. In this reading, he describes his impression of Stalin, then at the height of his prestige.

...What could be more exciting for a Communist, one who was coming from war and revolution? To be received by Stalin—this was the greatest possible recognition for the heroism and suffering of our Partisan warriors and our people. In dungeons and in the holocaust of war, and in the no less violent spiritual crises and clashes with the internal and external foes of Communism, Stalin was something more than a leader in battle. He was the incarnation of an idea, transfigured in Communist minds into pure idea, and thereby into something infallible and sinless. Stalin was the victorious battle of today and the brotherhood of the man of tomorrow. I realized that it was by chance that I personally was the first Yugoslav Communist to be received by him. Still, I felt a proud joy that I would be able to tell my comrades about this encounter and say something about it to the Yugoslav fighting men as well....

Suddenly everything that had seemed unpleasant about the USSR disappeared, and all disagreements between ourselves and the Soviet leaders lost their significance and gravity, as if they had never happened. Everything disagreeable vanished before the moving grandeur and beauty of what was happening to me. Of what account was my personal destiny before the greatness of the struggle being waged, and of what importance were our disagreements beside the obvious inevitability of the realization of our idea? . . .

The room was not large, rather long, and devoid of any opulence or decor. But the host was the plainest of all. Stalin was in a marshal's uniform and soft boots, without any medals except a golden star—the Order of Hero of the Soviet Union—on the left side of his breast. In his stance there was nothing artificial or posturing. This was not that majestic Stalin of the photographs or the newsreels—with the stiff, deliberate gait and posture.

He was not quiet for a moment. He toyed with his pipe, which bore the white dot of the English firm Dunhill, or drew circles with a blue pencil around words indicating the main subjects for discussion, which he then crossed out with slanting lines as each part of the discussion was nearing an end, and he kept turning his head this way and that while he fidgeted in his seat.

I was also surprised at something else: he was of very small stature and ungainly build. His torso was short and narrow, while his legs and arms were too long. His left arm and shoulder seemed rather stiff. He had a quite large paunch, and his hair was sparse, though his scalp was not completely bald. His face was

Abridged from Milovan Djilas, *Conversations with Stalin,* New York, 1962.

white, with ruddy cheeks. Later I learned that this coloration, so characteristic of those who sit long in offices, was known as the "Kremlin complexion" in high Soviet circles. . . . Still the head was not a bad one; it had something of the folk, the peasantry, the paterfamilias about it—with those yellow eyes and a mixture of sternness and roguishness.

I was also surprised at his accent. One could tell that he was not a Russian. Nevertheless his Russian vocabulary was rich, and his manner of expression was vivid and plastic, and replete with Russian proverbs and sayings. As I later became convinced, Stalin was well acquainted with Russian literature—though only Russian—but the only real knowledge he had outside of Russian limits was his knowledge of political history.

One thing did not surprise me: Stalin had a sense of humor—a rough humor, self-assured, but not entirely without finesse and depth. His reactions were quick and acute—and conclusive, which did not mean that he did not hear the speaker out, but it was evident that he was no friend of long explanations. Also remarkable was his relation to Molotov. He obviously regarded the latter as a very close associate, as I later confirmed. Molotov was the only member of the Politburo whom Stalin addressed with the familiar pronoun *ty*, which is in itself significant when it is kept in mind that with Russians the polite form *vy* is normal even among very close friends.

The conversation began by Stalin asking us about our impressions of the Soviet Union. I replied: 'We are enthusiastic!' —to which he rejoined: 'And we are not enthusiastic, though we are doing all we can to make things better in Russia.' It is engraved in my memory that Stalin used the term Russia, and not Soviet Union, which meant that he was not only inspiring Russian nationalism but was himself inspired by it and identified himself with it. . . .

I was enthusiastic about this direct, straightforward manner, which I had not till then encountered in Soviet official circles, and particularly not in Soviet propaganda. I felt that I was at the right spot, and moreover with a man who treated realities in a familiar open way. It is hardly necessary to explain that Stalin was like this only among his own men, that is, among Communists of his line who were devoted to him. . . .

[Djilas was later invited to dinner.]

In a spacious and unadorned, though tasteful, dining room the front half of a long table was covered with all kinds of foods on warmed heavy silver platters, as well as beverages and plates and other utensils. Everyone served himself and sat where he wished around the free half of the table. Stalin never sat at the head, but he always sat in the same chair—the first to the left of the head of the table. . . .

Such a dinner usually lasted six or more hours—from ten at night till four or five in the morning. One ate and drank slowly, during a rambling conversation which ranged from stories and anecdotes to the most serious political and even philosophical subjects. Unofficially and in actual fact a significant part of Soviet policy was shaped at these dinners. Besides they were the most frequent and most convenient entertainment and only luxury in Stalin's otherwise monotonous and somber life.

Apparently Stalin's co-workers were used to this manner of working and living—and spent their nights dining with Stalin or with one of their own number. They did not arrive in their offices before noon, and usually stayed in them till late evening. This complicated and made difficult the work of the higher administration, but the latter adapted itself, even the diplomatic corps, insofar as they had contacts with members of the Politburo.

There was no established order according to which members of the Politburo or other high officials attended these dinners. Usually those attended who had some connection with the business of the guest or with current issues. Apparently the circle was narrow, however, and it was an especial honor to be invited to such a dinner. Only Molotov was always present, and I maintain that this was not only because he was a Commissar, that is, Minister for Foreign Affairs, but also because he was in fact Stalin's substitute.

At these dinners the Soviet leaders were at their closest, most intimate with one another. Everyone would tell the news from his bailiwick, whom he had met that day, and what plans he was making. The sumptuous table and considerable, though not immoderate, quantities of alcohol enlivened spirits and intensified the atmosphere of cordiality and informality. An uninstructed visitor might hardly have detected any difference between Stalin and the rest. Yet it existed. His opinion was carefully noted. No one opposed him very hard. It all rather resembled a patriarchal family with a crotchety head whose foibles always caused the home folks to be apprehensive. . .

Stalin took quantities of food that would have been enormous even for a much larger man. . . He drank moderately, most frequently mixing red wine and vodka in little glasses. I never noticed any signs of drunkenness in him, whereas I could not say the same for Molotov, and especially not for Beria [Head of Secret Police] who was practically a drunkard....

It was at these dinners that the destiny of the vast Russian land, of the newly acquired territories, and, to a considerable degree, of the human race was decided....

Thanks to both ideology and methods, personal experience and historical heritage, he [Stalin] regarded as sure only whatever he held in his fist, and everyone beyond the control of his police was a potential enemy....

The world in which the Soviet leaders lived—and that was my world too—was slowly taking on a new appearance to me; horrible unceasing struggle on all sides. Everything was being stripped bare and reduced to strife which changed only in form and in which only the stronger and the more adroit survived. Full of admiration for the Soviet leaders even before this, I now succumbed to a heady enthusiasm for the inexhaustible will and awareness which never left them for a moment. That was a world in which there was no choice other than victory or death....

If we assume the viewpoint of humanity and freedom, history does not know a despot as brutal and as cynical as Stalin was. He was methodical, all-embracing, and total as a criminal. He was one of those rare terrible dogmatists capable of destroying nine tenths of the human race to "make happy" the one tenth.

However, if we wish to determine what Stalin really meant in the history of Communism, then he must for the present be regarded as being, next to Lenin, the most grandiose figure. He did not substantially develop the ideas of Communism, but he championed them and brought them to realization in a society and a state. He did not construct an ideal society—something of the sort is not even possible in the very nature of humans and human society, but he transformed backward Russia into an industrial power and an empire that is ever more resolutely and implacably aspiring to world mastery. . .

. . .Viewed from the standpoint of success and political adroitness, Stalin is hardly surpassed by any statesman of his time. I am, of course, far from thinking that success in political struggles is the only value. . . .All in all, Stalin was a monster who, while adhering to abstract, absolute and fundamentally utopian ideas, in practice recognized, and could recognize, only success—violence, physical and spiritual extermination. However, let us not be unjust toward Stalin! What he wished to accomplish, and even that which he did accomplish, could not be accomplished in any other way. The forces that swept him forward and that he led, with their absolute ideas, could have no other kind of leader but him, given the level of Russian and world relations, nor could they have been served by different methods. The creator of a closed social system, he was at the same time its instrument and, in changed circumstances and all too late, he became its victim. Unsurpassed in violence and crime, Stalin was no less the leader and organizer of a certain social system. Today he rates very low, pilloried for his 'errors,' through which the leaders of that same system intend to redeem both the system and themselves. . . .

11. Khrushchev's Secret Speech

Nikita Khrushchev first publicly criticized Stalin in 1956 at the Twentieth Communist Party Congress. There he revealed what most of his listeners already knew, namely the crimes committed by Stalin, though perhaps the scale of these crimes surprised even those who had helped make them possible. Thereafter it was hard ever again to justify the ruthless tactics Stalin had used. Nonetheless, Khrushchev never attacked Stalin's role in the brutal collectivization of the peasantry, nor his ruthless attack on Trotsky and his other rivals. Khrushchev had no intention of changing the Soviet system of collective and state farms, nor in questioning the basic legitimacy of single party rule.

Stalin acted not through persuasion, explanation, and patient cooperation with people, but by imposing his concepts and demanding absolute submission to his opinion. Whoever opposed this concept or tried to prove his viewpoint, and the correctness of his position—was doomed to removal from the leading collective and to subsequent moral and physical annihilation. This was especially true during the period following the XVIIth Party Congress, when many prominent Party leaders and rank-and-file Party workers, honest and dedicated to the cause of Communism, fell victim to Stalin's despotism.

We must affirm that the Party had fought a serious fight against the Trotskyites, rightists and bourgeois nationalists, and that it disarmed ideologically all the enemies of Leninism. This ideological fight was carried on successfully as a result of which the Party became strengthened and tempered. Here Stalin played a positive role....

Stalin originated the concept "enemy of the people." This term automatically rendered it unnecessary that the ideological errors of a man or men engaged in a controversy be proven; this term made possible the usage of the most cruel repression, violating all norms of revolutionary legality, against anyone who in any way disagreed with Stalin, against those who were only suspected of hostile intent, against those who had bad reputations. This concept, "enemy of the people," actually eliminated the possibility of any kind of ideological fight or the making of one's views known on this or that issue, even those of a practical character. In the main, and in actuality, the only proof of guilt used, against all norms of current legal science, was the "confession" of the accused himself; and, as subsequent probing proved, "confessions" were acquired through physical pressures against the accused.

This led to glaring violations of revolutionary legality, and to the fact that many entirely innocent persons, who in the past had defended the Party line, became victims.

Abridged from "Speech of Nikita Khrushchev Before a Closed Session of the Twentieth Congress of the Communist Party of the Soviet Union on February 25, 1956," Committee Print, Judiciary Committee of the U.S. Senate, 85th Congress, Washington, D.C., 1957.

We must assert that, in regard to those persons who in their time had opposed the Party line, there were often no sufficiently serious reasons for their physical annihilation. The formula, "enemy of the people" was specifically introduced for the purpose of physically annihilating such individuals.

It is a fact that many persons, who were later annihilated as enemies of the Party [were] people [who] had worked with Lenin during his life. Some of these persons had made errors during Lenin's life, but, despite this, Lenin benefited by their work, he corrected them and he did everything possible to retain them in the ranks of the Party; he induced them to follow him....

Stalin, on the other hand, used extreme methods and mass repressions at a time when the revolution was already victorious, when the Soviet state was strengthened, when the exploiting classes were already liquidated and Socialist relations were rooted solidly in all phases of national economy, when our Party was politically consolidated....

The Commission has presented to the Central Committee Presidium lengthy and documented materials pertaining to mass repressions against the delegates to the XVIIth Party Congress and against members of the Central Committee elected at that Congress. These materials have been studied by the Presidium of the Central Committee.

It was determined that of the 139 members and candidates of the Party's Central Committee who were elected at the XVIIth Congress, 98 persons, i.e., 70 percent, were arrested and shot (mostly in 1937—1938). [Indignation in the hall.]

What was the composition of the delegates to the XVIIth Congress? It is known that eighty percent of the voting participants of the XVIIth Congress joined the Party during the years of conspiracy before the Revolution and during the Civil War; this means before 1921. By social origin the basic mass of the delegates to the Congress were workers (60 percent of the voting members).

For this reason, it was inconceivable that a Congress so composed would have elected a Central Committee, a majority of whom would prove to be enemies of the Party. The only reason why 70 percent of Central Committee members and candidates elected at the XVIIth Congress were branded as enemies of the Party and of the people was because honest Communists were slandered, accusations against them were fabricated, and revolutionary legality was gravely undermined.

The same fate met not only the Central Committee members but also the majority of the delegates to the XVIIth Party Congress. Of 1,966 delegates with either voting or advisory rights, 1,108 persons were arrested on charges of anti-revolutionary crimes, i.e., decidedly more than a majority. This very fact shows how absurd, wild and contrary to common sense were the charges of counter-revolutionary crimes made out, as we now see, against a majority of participants at the XVIIth Party Congress. [Indignation in the hall.]

We should recall that the XVIIth Party Congress is historically known as the Congress of Victors. Delegates to the Congress were active participants in the building of our Socialist State; many of them suffered and fought for Party interests during the pre-revolutionary years in the conspiracy and at the Civil War fronts; they fought their enemies valiantly and often nervelessly looked into the face of death. How then can we believe that such people could prove to be "two-faced" and had joined the camps of the enemies of Socialism during the era after the political liquidation of Zinovievites, Trotskyites and rightists and after the great accomplishments of Socialist construction?

This was the result of the abuse of power by Stalin, who began to use mass terror against the Party cadres....

Comrades:

The cult of the individual acquired such monstrous size chiefly because Stalin himself, using all conceivable methods, supported the glorification of his own person. This is supported by numerous facts. One of the most characteristic examples of Stalin's self-glorification and of his lack of even elementary modesty is the edition of his "Short Biography," which was published in 1948.

This book is an expression of the most dissolute flattery, an example of making a man into a godhead, of transforming him into an infallible sage, "the greatest leader," "sublime strategist of all times and nations." Finally no other words could be found with which to lift Stalin up to the heavens.

We need not give here examples of the loathsome adulation filling this book. All we need to add is that they all were approved and edited by Stalin personally and some of them were added in his own handwriting to the draft text of the book.

What did Stalin consider essential to write into this book? Did he want to cool the ardor of his flatterers who were composing his "Short Biography"? No! He marked the very places where he thought that the praise of his services was insufficient.

Here are some examples characterizing Stalin's activity, added in Stalin's own hand:....

"Although he performed his task of leader of the Party and the people with consummate skill and enjoyed the unreserved support of the entire Soviet people, Stalin never allowed his work to be marred by the slightest hint of vanity, conceit, or self-adulation."

Where and when could a leader so praise himself? Is this worthy of a leader of the Marxist-Leninist type? No. Precisely against this did Marx and Engels take such a strong position. This also was always sharply condemned by Vladimir Ilyich Lenin.

In the draft text of his book appeared the following sentence: "Stalin is the Lenin of today." This sentence appeared to Stalin to be too weak, so in his own handwriting he changed it to read: "Stalin is the worthy continuer of Lenin's work, or, as it is said in our Party, Stalin is the Lenin of today." You see how well it is said, not by the Nation but by Stalin himself.

It is possible to give many such self-praising appraisals written into the draft text of that book in Stalin's hand. Especially generously does he endow himself with praises pertaining to his military genius, to his talent for strategy.

I will cite one more insertion made by Stalin concerning the theme of the Stalinist military genius.

"The advanced Soviet science of war received further development," he writes, "at Comrade Stalin's hands. Comrade Stalin elaborated the theory of the permanently operating factors that decide the issue of wars, of active defense and the laws of counter-offensive and offensive, of the co-operation of all services and arms in modern warfare, of the role of big tank masses and air forces in modern war, and of the artillery as the most formidable of the armed services. At the various stages of the war Stalin's genius found the correct solutions that took account of all the circumstances of the situation." [Movement in the hall.]

And further, writes Stalin:

"Stalin's military mastership was displayed both in defense and offense. Comrade Stalin's genius enabled him to divine the enemy's plans and defeat them. The battles in which Comrade Stalin directed the Soviet armies are brilliant examples of operational military skill."

In this manner was Stalin praised as a strategist. Who did this? Stalin himself, not in his role as a strategist but in the role of an author-editor, one of the main creators of his self-adulatory biography.

Such, comrades, are the facts. We should rather say shameful facts.

12. De-Stalinization and the Cult of Lenin

Stalin's reputation in the Soviet Union has risen, fallen, and risen again in the years since his death in 1953. After Khrushchev's revelation of Stalin's crimes, de-Stalinization gained momentum. In 1961, Stalin's tomb was removed from the mausoleum on Red Square in Moscow which housed Lenin's body and, at the 22nd Party Congress that year, his crimes and failings were spelled out in great detail. Historians were urged to reexamine the Soviet past and provide new history books for schools. The city of Stalingrad, the heroic World War II city, was renamed Volgograd. The campaign to discredit Stalin was accompanied by renewed emphasis on the cult of the founder, Vladimir Ilyich Lenin. This new cult is illustrated in Lazurkina's speech to the 22nd Congress presented here.

In the late 1970s, Stalin's star began again to rise. History was again rewritten to credit him with considerable achievement, and the scope and effects of the purges were minimized. The Russian poet Yevtushenko wrote that, in 1973, he was with a group of Soviet young people when one raised a toast to Stalin. He asked if they knew how many people had died in the purges. One eighteen-year-old guessed fifteen to twenty, another two hundred. Only one in the rather large group suggested a figure over two thousand. They were astonished when Yevtushenko told them that the figure should be reckoned in millions rather than thousands. Such is the effect of Soviet censorship and the rewriting of history.

SPEECH BY COMRADE D.A. LAZURKINA, PARTY MEMBER SINCE 1902, LENINGRAD PARTY ORGANIZATION

Comrade delegates! I wholly and fully support the proposals of Comrade Spiridonov and other comrades who have spoken here on removing Stalin's body from the Lenin Mausoleum. *(Stormy applause.)*

In the days of my youth I began my work under the leadership of Vladimir Ilyich Lenin, learned from him and carried out his instructions. *(Applause)...*

Not for a minute—either when I sat in prison for two and a half years or when I was sent to a camp, and later exiled (I spent 17 years in exile)—not once did I blame Stalin. I always fought for Stalin, who was assailed by the prisoners, the exiles and the camp inmates. I would say: "No, it is not possible that Stalin would have permitted what is happening in the Party. This cannot be!" They would argue with me, some would become angry with me, but I stood firm. I had high esteem for Stalin, I knew that he had done great service before 1934, and I defended him.

Comrades! And then I returned completely rehabilitated. I arrived just at the time when the 20th Party Congress was in session. This was the first time I

Abridged from "Speech of D.A. Lazurkina," *Current Soviet Policies IV,* New York, 1962.

learned the hard truth about Stalin. And now at the 22nd Congress, as I hear about the disclosed evil deeds and crimes that were committed in the Party with Stalin's knowledge, I wholly and fully endorse the proposal for the removal of Stalin's remains from the Mausoleum.

We fought to the end. We did not believe there could be such arbitrariness in our Leninist party. We wrote, wrote endlessly. If one were to look through the files of my letters, he could count volumes. I wrote endlessly to Stalin. I wrote to others also, and I wrote to the Party control body [organization responsible for discipline and expulsion of Party members]. But unfortunately, even our Party control was not at the proper level at the time; it yielded to the common fear and also refused to consider our cases.

Such was the atmosphere created by the cult of the individual. And we must root out the remnants of it! It is good that the 20th Party Congress raised this question. It is good that the 22nd Party Congress is uprooting these remnants.

I think that our wonderful Vladimir Ilyich, the most human of humans, should not lie beside someone who, although he did service in the past, before 1934, cannot be next to Lenin.

N.S. Khrushchev.—Right! *(Stormy, prolonged applause.)*

D.A. Lazurkina.—Comrades! . . . The only reason I survived is that Ilyich was in my heart, and I sought his advice, as it were. *(Applause.)* Yesterday I asked Ilyich for advice, and it was as if he stood before me alive and said: "I do not like being next to Stalin, who inflicted so much harm on the Party." *(Stormy, prolonged applause.)*

13. Eisenhower and Khrushchev

As part of the move towards better relations between the United States and the USSR, Khrushchev visited President Eisenhower in 1959. Khrushchev descibes his impressions of Eisenhower and his concerns about the visit in his Memoirs. *These have not yet been published in the Soviet Union, but the tapes of Khrushchev's voice and the transcription of the tapes are at Columbia University. This selection illustrates Khrushchev's suspiciousness towards his host, the degree to which his lack of knowledge of American ways led to misunderstanding, and some of his thinking about arms agreements.*

...The last important event on my visit to the United States was a round of talks with President Eisenhower at Camp David. I've already related how ignorant we had been about Camp David when our embassy first notified us that we were scheduled to go there, how we had thought the President didn't want to receive us in the White House and was discriminating against the Soviet Union by meeting us at some place called Camp David instead. We had been afraid it was like a leper colony. Well, by the time we got to the United States we realized what an honor it was to be invited to Camp David.

Nowadays I sometimes read in the newspaper or hear on the radio that President Nixon has received some foreign guest at the presidential *dacha* [country house] where I met with Eisenhower. For Nixon, Camp David has special significance. It was named after Eisenhower's grandson, who has now grown up and become Nixon's son-in-law by marrying his daughter.

Eisenhower asked me if I would mind flying to Camp David by helicopter since the roads were clogged with traffic. "We'll take off near the White House, and we'll be there in ten minutes," he said. "Besides, you'll get a bird's-eye view of Washington."

Of course I agreed. I was curious to see what Washington looked like from the air. The President's helicopter was a good machine. I think it was made by Sikorsky, a former Russian who ended up in America and made a great contribution to the development of American aviation. As we flew over Washington, the city looked like a table-sized model. Eisenhower pointed out various neighborhoods. At one point we flew over a big green field where he told me he played golf. He asked whether I liked this game. I didn't have the slightest idea what it was all about. He told me it was a very healthy sport.

Leaving the city behind, we began to descend over the forest. There were cars waiting for us when we landed. We drove past some structures resembling the plywood barracks we used to put up for construction workers at building sites; our workers were eaten alive by the bedbugs in those shacks, so we burned them down and built proper dormitories for them.

Abridged from *Khrushchev Remembers,* Strobe Talbott, editor and translator, Boston, 1974.

Eisenhower showed me into the main house. On the outside it looked just like a barracks; but on the inside it was luxuriously decorated, yet at the same time very businesslike—typically American. Everything was sturdily built, clean, and comfortable. I was shown to my private quarters, and the other members of our delegation—Comrade Gromyko [Soviet foreign minister, still in that position in 1984] and the rest—were also settled in nicely.

Eisenhower asked if I like watching movies. I said of course I did, as long as they were good movies.

"What kind of movies do you prefer?" he asked with a smile. Eisenhower's face was always very pleasant when he smiled. "Personally, I like Westerns," he added. "I know they don't have any substance to them and don't require any thought to appreciate, but they always have a lot of fancy tricks. Also, I like horses."

"You know," I told him, "when Stalin was still alive, we used to watch Westerns all the time. When the movie ended, Stalin always denounced it for its ideological content. But the very next day we'd be back in the movie theater watching another Western. I too have a weakness for this sort of film."

"Good. We'll have some Westerns and other movies. I've also invited our navy band to play. Do you mind?"

"Oh, that will be very pleasant. I enjoy music, and I like to look at young faces."

"Fine. They'll play for us at dinnertime."

Whereas we had to dress up for official dinners in Washington, at Camp David we just wore our usual clothes to meals....

In the morning Andrei Andreyevich [Gromyko] and I would get up early and go out for a walk along a secluded path in order to talk things over. We were completely alone—except, of course, for our bodyguards, but they were well trained and kept out of sight. Now, people might ask, "What's this about Khrushchev and Gromyko going out for walks to exchange opinions? Why couldn't they just talk in their rooms?" The answer is perfectly obvious to any statesman. We knew that American intelligence was well equiped with scientific listening devices, and we were simply taking precautions to avoid being overheard. Eisenhower and I were discussing a number of highly sensitive matters of mutual concern, and we knew that the Americans would like to eavesdrop on my confidential deliberations with Gromyko before the working session and get some advance notice of what positions our side would take.

Among the issues still to be discussed were cultural, scientific and economic cooperation....The Americans wanted a much broader exchange of tourists, scientists, and students. They even suggested we send our plant managers for retraining in the U.S. This proposal appealed to us because it would have allowed us to take advantage of their experience and expertise in industrial organization and management. Many of their suggestions were clearly intended to make us open our borders, to increase the flow of people back and forth. They were also trying to pressure me into permitting stores to be opened in the Soviet

Union where our citizens could buy American literature; in exchange they would allow us to open outlets in America where we could sell our books.

But all these issues were of secondary importance. The primary problem before us during our talks at Camp David was disarmament. I could tell just from looking at Eisenhower how anxious he was to reach an agreement which would create conditions eliminating the possibility of war.

"Mr. Khrushchev," he said, "I'm a military man; I've been a soldier all my life. I've fought in more than one war in the past, but I'm not embarrassed to tell you that now I fear war very much. I'd like to do anything I can to help us avoid war. First and foremost I want to come to some sort of agreement with you."

"Mr. President, nobody would be happier than I if we could reach an agreement. But the question is, how?"

We spent the greater part of our talks together trying to answer that question.

It was our side who raised the matter of withdrawing troops from other countries—in other words, eliminating our military bases on foreign territory. This would have meant dismantling both the NATO and Warsaw Pact alliances. The Americans weren't prepared to go this far. They rejected our proposal. Actually, we knew that the conditions for such an agreement were not yet ripe and that our proposal was premature. In fact, our proposal was intended to serve a propagandistic, rather than a realistic, purpose.

The Americans for their part, were willing to accept a ban on the production and testing of nuclear weapons, but only on the condition that international controls were established. Specifically, they insisted on an agreement which would allow both sides to conduct reconnaissance flights over each other's territories. This condition was unacceptable to us at that time. I stress, *at that time*. First, America was in a much stronger position that we were as regards both the number of nuclear weapons it had and also its delivery system. Second, the Americans had us surrounded on all sides with their military bases, including air bases, while our own airplanes couldn't even reach the United States. Third, certain instruments can be mounted on foreign territory to detect atomic testing at a great distance, but, here again, the Americans had an advantage because they had their military installations all around our border. In short, their suggestion for a system of international supervision wasn't fair or equal. Therefore we couldn't accept it.

What you have to remember is that when I faced the problem of disarmament, we lagged significantly behind the U.S. in both warheads and missiles, and the U.S. was out of range for our bombers. We could blast into dust America's allies in Europe and Asia, but America itself—with its huge economic and military potential—was beyond our reach. As long as they had such superiority over us, it was easier for them to determine the most expedient moment to start a war. Remember: we had enemies who believed conflict was inevitable and were in a hurry to finish us off before it was too late. That's why I was convinced that as long as the U.S. held a big advantage over us, we couldn't submit to international disarmament controls. That was my point of view, and I think, at the time, it was correct. Now that I'm in retirement, I still give this whole question serious thought, and I've come to the conclusion that today international controls are possible because they would be truly mutual. An internationally supervised arms ban wouldn't harm our defense capacity now, as it would have then. The situation has changed since I was in the leadership and discussed the problem with Eisenhower....

Chapter Six

The Soviet Union Today

Four characteristics of the Soviet system are basic to the way it functions today. First, the Soviet Union is a Party-state, in the sense that a single political party, the Communist Party of the Soviet Union (CPSU), dominates the government. Second, the Soviet economy is organized according to the principle of state socialism. The state owns all productive enterprises, factories, mines, and farms, sets economic priorities, and both plans and manages the use of resources. The third important characteristic of the Soviet system is that the Party-state seeks to control and organize as much of each person's life as it can. It takes an interest in many aspects of life that in Western countries are considered a private responsibility. These three characteristics are closely related to Marxist-Leninist ideology. The fourth characteristic of the Soviet system, its multinational population and federal form of government, is the legacy of history. Russia, like France and England, expanded and colonized other peoples in the eighteenth and nineteenth centuries. Unlike France and Great Britain, however, which colonized overseas, first in North America and then in Africa and Asia, and were forced ultimately to give up their empires, the Russians colonized their neighbors. The Soviet Union has maintained the unity of the Tsars' land empire.

THE USSR AS A PARTY-STATE

In 1977, the Soviet government approved a new Constitution, its fourth since 1918. The Constitution is not always a good guide, however, for understanding how the Soviet system really works. The Constitution describes the formal structure of government, but does not explain that real power belongs to the Communist Party.

The Soviet Constitution establishes the Soviet Union as a federal state made up of fifteen national republics. It provides for elections in which all citizens over 18 are expected to vote.

FACT: In 1982, 99.8% of those eligible voted in the Soviet elections.

Voters elect local councils called Soviets. Each of the fifteen national republics has an elected national council, or Republic Soviet. At the federal level, there is a Supreme Soviet of the Soviet Union that has the constitutional right to make laws. The Supreme Soviet elects the leaders of both the executive and judicial branches, as well as a Presidium that is empowered to make decisions when the Supreme Soviet is not in session. The Council of Ministers is the top executive body of the state, responsible for running the economy and state-owned enterprises, as well as overseeing the work of the Committee for State Security *(Komitet gosudarstvennoi bezopastnosti—KGB)* or secret police, the Ministries of Defense, Health, and various industries.

The Soviet Constitution also contains a bill of rights that lists many of the same civil rights promised by the U.S. Constitution, as well as rights that the U.S. Constitution does not have, such as the right to work. All rights are granted, however, on condition that they "do not injure the interests of society and the rights of other citizens." If the Party decides that the right to free speech or organization is not in the best interests of society, for example, a person can be arrested and charged with unlawful activity.

One should not assume, therefore, that because the formal institutions of Soviet government resemble those of the United States, that the two systems operate in a similar way.

The Supreme Soviet meets in 1982 to celebrate the 60th Anniversary of the formation of the Soviet Union.

FACT: The Supreme Soviet always confirms proposed legislation. Its decisions are always carefully orchestrated to be unanimous and accompanied by great applause.

FACT: The Supreme Soviet of the USSR, the top federal legislative body, usually meets twice a year for a total of less than ten days. All of its members have other full-time jobs.

From these facts it is clear that the Supreme Soviet cannot make the difficult decisions about all Soviet laws and policies. It should further be noted that in Soviet elections there is only one candidate for each office. There is discussion within the Communist Party about possible nominees ahead of time, but not on election day. Soviet citizens vote, but they do not choose.

The Soviet Constitution also makes no effort to create a separation of powers. There is no independent judiciary, for example, to decide if the government is properly enforcing the laws. Marxism-Leninism teaches that the interests of citizens and their government are one and the same, so there is no need for such a safeguard.

Real power in Soviet society belongs to the Communist Party of the Soviet Union (CPSU), and particularly to those who work full time for the Party, the so-called *Secretariat* and its staff, the *apparat*. The CPSU is the only political party and it is reserved for the elite: only about 9% of the population are members. The Party recruits promising young people to join it. It also sponsors large youth organizations: for young adults, the *Komsomol,* and for children, the Pioneers. These groups hold meetings and organize leisure time activities to bring the Party message to Soviet youth. Membership in the Party is considered a privilege and admission rules are strict. Those who join are expected to serve as examples to others, and to take on extra responsibilities. In return, they get access to scarce consumer goods and the opportunity for the best jobs—all the most important posts in government, top management, the army, and foreign affairs are reserved for Party members. Most journalists, editors and school heads also belong to the Party.

Young Pioneers at school in Leningrad. All Soviet children between the ages of ten and fifteen belong to the Young Pioneers. The red scarf is the Pioneer symbol.

Runners enjoy a crisp winter day.

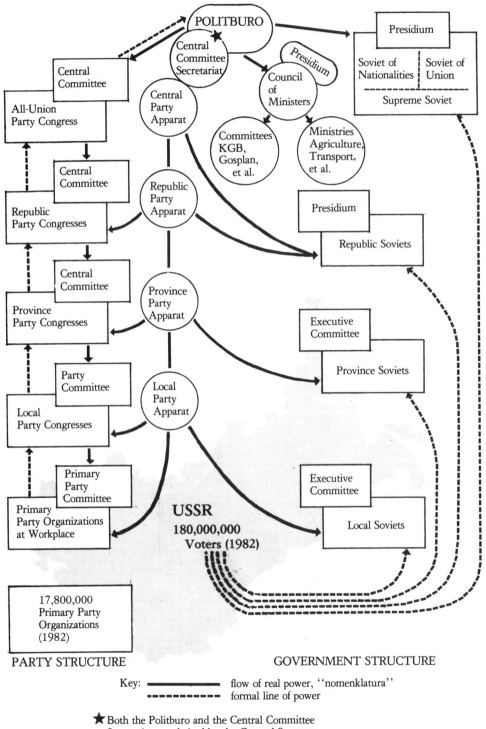

POLITBURO

Presidium

Soviet of Nationalities | Soviet of Union

Supreme Soviet

Central Committee Secretariat ★

Central Committee

Central Party Apparat

Presidium

Council of Ministers

All-Union Party Congress

Committees KGB, Gosplan, et al.

Ministries Agriculture, Transport, et al.

Central Committee

Republic Party Congresses

Republic Party Apparat

Presidium

Republic Soviets

Central Committee

Province Party Congresses

Province Party Apparat

Executive Committee

Province Soviets

Party Committee

Local Party Congresses

Local Party Apparat

Executive Committee

Local Soviets

Primary Party Committee

Primary Party Organizations at Workplace

USSR
180,000,000
Voters (1982)

17,800,000
Primary Party
Organizations
(1982)

PARTY STRUCTURE

GOVERNMENT STRUCTURE

Key: ▬▬▬▬▬▬ flow of real power, "nomenklatura"
    ▬ ▬ ▬ ▬ formal line of power

★ Both the Politburo and the Central Committee Secretariat are chaired by the General Secretary, making him the chief executive of the Party.

The Party is carefully organized in accordance with Lenin's theory of democratic centralism. This means that factions or small groupings within the Party are prohibited. It also means that there are numerous local organizations, or Party cells, in factories and farms, and in offices and institutes throughout the Soviet Union. These local organizations elect representatives to local congresses, and local congresses in turn elect delegates to regional and national congresses. The National Party Congress elects a Central Committee, which, in turn, elects an executive Politburo. In theory, each elected congress elects representatives to the congress above it. This structure makes it seem that power flows upwards, from the rank and file Party members, through their representatives, to the Politburo. The Party seems to be democratic. Despite this appearance, however, in fact *power flows from the top down.* One candidate is selected for each office by Party men at the next level up in the hierarchy. For example, in theory the Central Committee elects the Politburo. In fact, the Politburo decides who will be a candidate for election to the Central Committee. As there is only one candidate for each position, the Politburo in effect selects the Central Committee. Furthermore, higher organizations direct the work of lower ones. Decisions of the Politburo, for example, set guidelines for the Central Committee. While there may be, and often is, discussion before decisions are made, once the decision is taken, further discussion is prohibited. This, too, is an important feature of democratic centralism. The result of this method of organization is great centralization of power in the Politburo. Whatever policy it makes is supposed to be carried out throughout the land without any further discussion.

FACT: The Politburo varies in size, and usually has from 10-16 full, voting members and about 6 candidate (non-voting) members.

The Politburo makes all general policy decisions. This small, exceedingly powerful group meets once or twice each week to discuss and decide important issues. Thursday is its regular meeting day. Once the Politburo has decided on a policy, it is up to the Party Secretariat, and its full-time staff, the *apparat,* to see to it that this policy is carried out. The full-time workers of the Party Secretariat and *apparat* make up a powerful, highly centralized administrative organization that reaches from Moscow throughout the Soviet Union to monitor the work of government, social and economic agencies, and to select or endorse key personnel. The Secretariat is the key administrative organization of the Party-state, and exercises great power throughout the country. Stalin, Khrushchev, Brezhnev, Andropov and Chernenko all served on the Politburo as head of the Secretariat. This post, Party General Secretary, is the single most powerful position in the USSR. The General Secretary usually serves as Presidium or government president as well, but his real power depends on his position at the top of the Party hierarchy.

The role of the Politburo and Secretariat of the CPSU can be summarized quite simply. They maintain a monopoly on ideology and control appointments to all important positions. A monopoly on ideology means that the Party has the last word on what policy should be, and what is right and what is wrong for people in all walks of life. Its position is justified by Marxism-Leninism. Lenin had argued that the Party understood scientific socialism and therefore had the right and obligation to guide the state's march toward Communism. Today this ideological monopoly gives the Party the right to set social goals and establish what is and is not permissible. When different groups in the society disagree, it is up to the Party to find a consensus and set out an authoritative decision. For example, the Party declares whether or not wars between capitalist and socialist states are inevitable, and whether military or consumer spending should take priority. Such decisions then guide policy.

The Party Secretariat also decides who shall hold top positions. It has developed a system called *nomenklatura,* a list of all important jobs. Before anyone can hold one of these jobs—newspaper editor, school superintendent, factory manager, or town governor—he must be approved by the Party Secretariat. By means of *nomenklatura,* the Party makes sure that no one who is not loyal to the Party can hold an influential position.

If the Communist Party makes general policy, selects the people to carry it out, informs the Soviet people of its decisions, and takes responsibility for educating young people in the spirit of socialism, it is up to the Soviet government to put these policies into effect. The government bureaucracy executes Party policy, while the Party Secretariat and its *apparat* watch them carefully to make sure that they do what they are supposed to do. It is because of the powerful position of the Party that the Soviet Union is sometimes called a Party-state.

STATE SOCIALISM: THE SOVIET ECONOMY

Marx and Lenin taught that as long as there was private property, there would be poverty and exploitation. To get rid of it was one of the main goals of the Revolution. Today in the Soviet Union, all land, banks, factories, and businesses are owned and managed by the State. The Soviet economy has been compared to a single giant business corporation that manages a wide variety of industries, but in which all branches must answer to a single boss, the state. There is private property in small things, a house, furniture or clothing, but no private person can hire others to work for him or her, other than to perform a service such as baby-sitting.

The Soviet economy is also characterized by central planning. Central planners strive to organize and coordinate all economic activity to serve the collective interest of the Soviet state and people. This contrasts sharply with a capitalist market economy, such as that in the United States, where independent producers are free to make what they think they can sell.

In keeping with Lenin's teaching about the leading role of the Party, it is the Politburo that determines what the collective interest of the Soviet people is, and decides on broad economic priorities. These general goals are then translated into specific production targets by the State Planning Commission

(Gosplan), and presented in the form of a Five Year Plan. Gosplan sets prices and decides how much will go into investment in new plants and how much into production. The planners collect information from factories and farms, and from mines and power plants all over the Soviet Union. With this information in hand, they set production quotas for each production unit. It is an enormously complicated job. Even with every modern device, including computers, for collecting and storing information, the planners find it hard to manage all the details, and especially to plan for the unexpected — the drought that cuts grain production or reduces available hydro-electric power, or the fire that destroys a plant that was supposed to supply tires to a truck manufacturer. When such events do occur, it is hard for those on the spot to adapt to the new situation quickly and efficiently, because they must get permission to act from so many different organizations.

The manager of a Soviet factory is judged and rewarded for meeting the quota set by the Plan. If he makes hats, for example, he must see to it that the factory produces the number of hats it is supposed to produce according to the Plan. It does not matter to him if the hats are ugly or don't hold their shape. His quota simply requires the right number of hats. Selling them is not his problem. The state stores will have to take whatever he produces — that is part of their Plan. If the factory makes stylish hats that sell well, the manager is paid no more than if it makes ugly hats no one wants. There is no real incentive, then, for quality work, or for innovation. Why risk setting up a new procedure for making hats that might lead to a long term gain but a short term loss if you, the manager, will not benefit from that gain, and will be penalized for the loss? As a result, managers do not innovate or take risks. Much Soviet work is inefficient and of poor quality because of this lack of reward for good work.

FACT: When quotas were set for plate glass factories in square meters of glass, planners found that the plants were fulfilling and over-fulfilling their quotas by making the glass as thin as possible — with the result that new apartment buildings constantly had broken windows.

Soviet planners have been experimenting with better ways to set goals that would encourage innovation and quality workmanship, but so far, they have only tinkered with the system and have not solved this problem.

Soviet agriculture is organized into farms of two types, state farms (the *sovkhoz*) and collective farms (the *kolkhoz*). The preferred type of farm is the state farm which is much larger, and where the workers are employees of the state, paid wages just as if they worked in a factory. The collective farms, the *kolkhozes,* are cooperatives in which the farmers share the profits of the farm. More often than not, the result is that they are paid very little. Most farm families also have small private plots, about one acre in size. On the *kolkhoz,* the large collective fields raise much less per acre than do these tiny private plots, for the farmers seem to work better when they know they will profit directly from what they produce.

FACT: In the late 1970s, private plots, which make up about 3% of the cultivated land, raised at least 12% of the food sold in Soviet markets, in addition to the food eaten by the farmers themselves. Some scholars estimate that as much as 25% of all farm produce is grown on this 3% of the cultivated land.

Soviet farmers travel many miles to sell their privately grown crops, eggs, and milk in special farmers' markets set up in big towns and cities.

FACT: In 1983, a Georgian farmer found it profitable to travel more than 1000 miles by train to Leningrad to sell his fruits and vegetables and fly home. He could get 8 rubles (officially ruble=$1.38) for two big pears in the Leningrad farmers' market.

Although such private enterprise would seem to go against the Soviet theory that stresses the advantages of collective ownership and collective work, the government accepts it because the food is badly needed by the population.

The Soviet people have devised other ways to make up for the inefficiencies of the planners. These activities are called the second economy and are often illegal. Factories barter needed raw materials with one another; there is a brisk secondary rental market in housing in desirable locations; repairmen moonlight for pay, or perhaps barter their work for food, a new shirt, the services of a dentist, or a tutor for a child. These grey areas of economic activity are outside the planners' control but are usually tolerated because they are useful in making the system run. There is also considerable illegal activity that flourishes despite the regime's effort to stop it. Entrepreneurs buy scarce goods, for example, ranging from fashionable clothes that might appear in a store unexpectedly to jeans begged or bought from a foreign tourist, to fruit out of season, or a banned phonograph record. They also steal from the factories in which they work. They then resell these goods for a large profit. It is almost impossible to estimate accurately the size of this second economy, but it probably represents between 5% and 10% of the total Soviet gross national product. (See Reading 5)

FACT: In the Soviet Union in the late 1970s, 12 out of 1000 people owned a car. In the U.S., 448 out of 1000 people owned cars.

Soviet people still live poorly by American standards. In 1983, food rationing was common in the Soviet Union except in the larger cities such as Moscow and Leningrad. Most Soviets live in small houses or crowded apartments, and eat less varied and appetizing food than do most Americans. In 1980, for example, about one fifth of the urban population lived in communal apartments where several families shared a single kitchen and bathroom. Right after the war, this crowding could be explained because many of the cities in the western part of the country were badly damaged by the war. Today poor housing results from the fact that consumer comfort has not been a high priority for Soviet economic planners. Yet compared with the living standards before the

Revolution, when the vast majority of people were illiterate peasants living in villages without electricity, health care, or an adequate diet, the improvement is impressive. Most Soviet peoples saw their living standards rise steadily from the end of World War II until the mid-1970s. Since then this improvement has slowed. On balance, however, the Soviet government has made great strides in providing education, housing, public health, and adequate, if not fancy, food for its people.

FACT: Because the state sets prices, the retail price of milk and eggs in state stores in the USSR did not change between 1962 and 1983. The retail price of beef in state stores, when it is available, is less than half what it costs the state to produce it.

The basic necessities such as simple food, clothing, medical care, public transportation, and lodging are cheap in the Soviet Union, but for most people luxuries are still rare. (See Readings 3 and 4)

Status and pay are not always directly related in the Soviet Union, nor is life style directly related to monetary income.

FACT: The First Secretary of a regional Party committee can get foreign films from Moscow to show his friends, films not available elsewhere because they are thought unsuitable for general distribution.

The elite of Soviet society includes its best artists and athletes, as well as scientists, factory managers, and party leaders. Ballet schools in Moscow and Leningrad continue to train outstanding dancers for the great Soviet ballet companies, the Bolshoi and Kirov.

The special benefits that come with certain important jobs — chauffeur-driven limousines, vacations in state-owned guest houses, a private house *(dacha)* in an exclusive enclave outside the city, shopping privileges in special stores stocked with high quality goods and imported items — are more important than money. They cannot be bought no matter how much money a person has, but are the reward for holding the right sort of elite job. It is estimated that about one million people have access to at least some of these special services. They are the top Party and government officials, and the most successful scientists, writers, athletes, and managers. These favored few live well. They do not stand in lines, ride the crowded buses, or spend their weekends in city parks. Many of them even enjoy the greatest privilege of all, trips abroad.

FACT: In 1978, about 8700 Soviets visited the United States, about 5700 of them on official business. That same year, 100,000 Americans traveled to the USSR, of whom about 5500 were on official business.

The Soviet government takes an unusual attitude towards travel. For many years, those who lived in the countryside, on a state farm or *kolkhoz,* could not travel at all, even within the Soviet Union, without a special permit that was rarely granted. Today, it is still very difficult to get permission to live in Moscow and other big cities such as Kiev. Urban planners do not want their big cities to fill up with the jobless, or other people who will aggravate the already difficult housing situation. Many stories are told about marriages of convenience, in which a man or woman is willing to marry anyone, just so long as the spouse-to-be has a permit to live in Moscow or another desirable city. These are paper marriages only, but they achieve what is most desirable among Soviet Russians: a place at the center of things. As for travel abroad, a Soviet citizen cannot simply send for a passport and buy an air ticket to travel to Western Europe. Special permission must come first, and it is not usually granted unless the trip is an official one. Even influential people are rarely allowed to take their families with them.

Social mobility based on ability has been high in the Soviet Union, provided a person is willing to play along with the Party. Pressure on children to study hard, win academic competitions, and get into the right universities is therefore intense. As in many countries, children of farm or factory workers rarely rise to the top in academic, technical or cultural positions, although they do rise in production jobs and the Party. It is also true that important people in the Soviet Union, as elsewhere, seem to find ways to get their children into the best schools and into good jobs, and so give them a head start on their less-favored peers. Nonetheless, Soviet citizens cannot pass on a large estate or significant sums of money to their children. Limits on private property set by the economic system make that impossible. It is not yet clear whether the Soviet elite will find sure ways to make its position hereditary.

FACT: In 1860, the per capita production of the Russian empire was about 40% of that of the United States. In 1913, it had fallen to 24%; by 1978 Soviet per capita production was estimated to be 50% of that of the United States.

FACT: In 1980 the Soviet GNP was about 60% as large as that of the U.S.

The Soviet economy has made enormous strides since 1913, largely under the present system of state ownership and central economic planning. Economic growth has brought with it a rise in the standard of living. There are, nonetheless, some problems foreseeable in the future. Soviet farmers are not increasing their productivity, and agriculture in general is not keeping up with popular expectations for a better diet. There is evidence that the quality of the Soviet diet has actually declined since the late 1970s. So complex is the planning process that its inefficiencies threaten to hamper future growth in both agriculture and industry. Transportation, too, remains difficult. Without greater decentralization, added autonomy to factories and farms, and a more flexible system of prices and rewards, the Soviet economy will probably not grow as quickly as it has in the past. The very success of the Soviet Union in creating a complex and sophisticated industrial economy now poses to its planners the challenge of creating a correspondingly sophisticated system of planning and management.

THE ORGANIZATION OF SOCIAL LIFE: EDUCATION AND CULTURE

The preamble to the 1977 Soviet Constitution declares that the state has, among its purposes, "to mold the citizen of the Communist society and...to raise the cultural level of the working people." This goal has far-reaching implications for education and culture in the Soviet Union. It influences the way the courts operate and explains Soviet attitudes towards religion. This statement reflects the Soviet government's interest in areas of social activity that in many Western societies are left to the individual. The Soviet government is not satisfied to see to it that its citizens do not bother one another. It expects more than that. It expects its people to work actively for the common good. The job of government is to see to it that they do, and to shape the citizens' thinking and attitudes, as well as their behavior. The goal of the Soviet government is nothing less than to create "the new Soviet man," a new type of person free from greed and selfishness, laziness, and dishonesty, who will be able to create a truly Communist society. (See Reading 6)

Soviet leaders believe that religion is harmful because it prevents people from developing the proper Communist outlook on life. The religious person may obey the laws, but will not accept the Party's claim that it has the final knowledge of what is right and wrong. The religious person is considered by the Soviets to be a half-hearted citizen and one who does not live up to the Soviet ideal. (See Reading 7)

FACT: Although the government has outlawed religious education and discourages religious observance by closing churches and synagogues, a survey published in the late 1960s indicated that 60% of the babies born in the industrial city of Gorki were baptized. Many scholars today believe they see signs of a religious revival in the Soviet Union.

It is important to bear in mind that the Soviets do not believe that the best government is the one that governs least. They do not want to leave individuals free to develop as they choose. On the contrary, they believe that the best government is the one that can organize everyone in an orderly way to work for a common goal, a goal set by the Party. It is for this reason that the Soviet government and Party try to reach into so many corners of Soviet life.

FACT: The manual for teaching two- and three-year olds in nursery schools tells instructors to teach the children to recognize V.I. Lenin in portraits and illustrations.

Two girls at the nursery school at a Moscow factory. To make it possible for Soviet women with young children to work, the Soviet government has established numerous schools and what Americans would call day-care centers.

The Party-state sets all school curricula and emphasizes education for productive work in a socialist society, as well as loyalty to the Soviet government. The Soviets have been very successful in achieving universal literacy and a high level of scientific and technical capability in their citizens.

FACT: The percentage of university-age students in Soviet institutions of higher education is higher than in Great Britain, France or Germany (but not than in the United States).

Many of the values that are stressed in Soviet schools such as self-discipline, industriousness, punctuality, and honesty are stressed in schools in most industrial countries. Soviet schools also teach the importance of collective work and cooperativeness. They do not encourage students to develop individual differences. The new Soviet man is not supposed to be a creative individualist but rather a contributor to the collective.†

The Soviet regime considers history, literature and the arts to be powerful means of education. A short story, for example, should illustrate that a citizen who cheats will be caught and that the one who works selflessly for others will be rewarded. The reader should learn from stories, plays, and paintings that actions that help the collective serve the self as well as others. All media productions, books, films, television, paintings, and even music are carefully screened and censored to make sure that they provide healthy models for Soviet citizens, are easy to understand, and will inspire desirable behavior. It is not enough that literature not criticize the regime in unwanted ways. It must take a further step and encourage what are considered socially useful activities. It is not enough that history be written that does not question the overall benefit of Soviet rule. History must illustrate that Soviet policy has always been consistent and that the Party is always right. (See Reading 8)

FACT: For almost twenty years the Soviet national anthem had no words because its original words mentioned Stalin and therefore had to be changed after the revelation of his crimes. The commission charged to provide new words took twenty years to get the job done.

Today some Soviet writers and artists continue to write and work in their own styles, even if they know that the official censor will not allow their work to be published. Sometimes they turn to *samizdat*, literally translated "to publish oneself." Writers type and duplicate what they have written and circulate it privately among friends. Human rights activists continue to push the regime to grant to Soviet citizens, notably to writers, cultural minorities, and religious believers, the freedom of speech and assembly promised by the Soviet Constitution. These persistent and brave men and women are called dissidents, because they dissent from official views and do not agree with the Party line. They are willing to risk KGB harassment, arrest and even long prison terms for their beliefs and actions. (See Reading 9)

It may seem odd that a state inspired by the writings of **Karl Marx**, who taught that ideas are a smoke screen to hide economic interests, should now consider ideas so powerful and so important. Some governments do not care very much what books are published because they do not think writers are significant. Not so in the Soviet Union. Great Soviet writers such as Alexander Solzhenitsyn or Boris Pasternak come under fire not only when they point out shortcomings in the regime, but even if they suggest that there are basic human questions that have not yet been answered, or if they portray people with religious or humanitarian views in a sympathetic manner. The Soviet regime attributes great power and importance to its writers, and yet it finds it cannot tolerate some of its most gifted ones. This is one of the many paradoxes of the Soviet system.

THE MULTINATIONAL STATE: THE SOVIET NATIONALITIES

The Soviet Union today is home to peoples of many different nationalities. They live in a multinational federal state made up of fifteen socialist republics. Each of these republics is homeland to a people of a different language and background, and each of these peoples has a proud culture and history of its own. Unlike the United States, which also contains peoples of many different national origins, the Soviet peoples still live in their historic homelands. They did not leave their land voluntarily to go to a new country as did those who emigrated to the United States. Rather the Russian state expanded its control over its diverse neighbors who then became part of the Tsars' empire and later of the Soviet Union.

Four men from Azerbaidjan gather for sociability, tea, and backgammon. Azerbaidjan, Georgia, and Armenia together comprise the Transcaucasian Republics of the USSR. Each of the peoples has its own distinct ethnic traditions; traditions very different from those of the Slavs.

There is a built-in tension in Soviet policy towards its nationalities. On the one hand, the Soviet Constitution grants important rights to the national republics, much more autonomy than is granted to the American states by the federal constitution of the United States. Soviet republics have many rights of self-government, as well as the legal right to secede from the Union of Soviet Socialist Republics. In fact, however, their autonomy is strictly limited and their policies determined by the Party.

FACT: The Ukrainian and Belorussian Republics of the Soviet Union both have seats in the United Nations. Stalin wanted all the Soviet republics to be represented there, but finally agreed to this as a compromise.

On the other hand, the central government uses all the resources at its command, most particularly the Communist Party, which is highly centralized and controlled from Moscow, to see to it that its non-Russian peoples develop a loyalty to the Soviet government.

FACT: Russians made up 52% of the Soviet population in 1979, but held 67% of the seats on the Central Committee of the Party. The Slavs (Russians, Ukrainians and Belorussians) were 72% of the population in 1979, but held 86% of the Central Committee seats in 1981.

FACT: In non-Russian republics, the First Secretary of the Party, the top post, is held by a member of the local nationality. The Second Secretary, the person who holds primary responsibility for job appointments (administers the *nomenklatura*), is usually a Russian, and always a Slav.

The Folk Arts continue to play a prominent role in the Soviet Union.

Soviet policy towards the non-Russian nationalities seeks to maintain a delicate balance between making allowances for the reality of cultural differences and exercising central control. The central government recognizes the need to use national languages, and encourages the performance of the traditional arts of each people. National languages are also used in schools. In Uzbekistan, for example, a native child will usually enter a school in which Uzbek is the language of instruction. Soon the child will begin to learn Russian as a second language, because the Soviets believe that all of their peoples must be able to communicate with one another if they are to feel a part of a single state, and the Russian language seems to be the logical choice for this purpose. If a native child, or the child's parents, is eager to have a career of great importance, mastery of the Russian language is essential. On the other hand, some members of the non-Russian nationalities consider such emphasis on the Russian language a threat to the survival and development of their own national cultures. They also object to the fact that the Russian child growing up in a non-Russian republic rarely learns the local language.

As the non-Russian peoples have become better educated and have taken an increasingly active part in managing local affairs, they have grown more determined to shape their own national destinies within the Soviet state. Some of them look with hostility on the Russians whom they consider interfering outsiders. They resent the fact that Russians hold many influential positions in the non-Russian republics and make important decisions. Others believe their peoples have benefited greatly from Soviet rule. The situation varies from republic to republic, but most national republic leaders agree that they want a strong voice in running their own republics. To satisfy this demand without giving up central economic planning and political control presents a great challenge to the Soviet government.

THE SOVIET UNION IN THE WORLD TODAY

The Soviet Union has achieved what it has long sought, a position as a world superpower and a rough military parity with the United States. To this extent it has attained the dream of Peter the Great: to catch up with the West, at least militarily. This accomplishment has cost dear in terms of economic investment in the military rather than in consumer goods. During the 1960s and 1970s, continuous economic growth made it possible to satisfy demands for both guns and butter, that is both to provide for a rise in the standard of living and a big military build-up. As a result, the Soviets were able to close what had been a large gap between their military capabilities and those of the United States. The probability that future economic growth will be far smaller means that it will be increasingly difficult for the Soviets to continue such large military investments without pinching the consumer economy. This situation will force difficult choices on the Soviet leadership.

   The Soviet Union's overriding foreign policy goal is to avoid a nuclear confrontation with the United States. Knowledge of the devastation of World War II is still a fresh memory, kept alive by frequent references to it in government publications and by war monuments that dominate public squares and fields throughout the nation. Peace for the Soviets, however, does not mean friendship and trust, but does require adequate communication and sufficient agreement to avoid military confrontation. The Soviets will probably continue to try to extend their influence. They expect their position in the world to improve. The heritage of Marxist-Leninist ideology, notably the idea that history is on the side of socialism, pervades the thinking of Soviet leaders. They believe that there exist in Africa, Asia, and Latin America societies that are eager to move away from what the Soviets call capitalist imperialism towards socialism. In these areas the Soviets welcome change and are quite willing to support those opposed to the *status quo.* Today they can and do offer military as well as moral support to possible Third World allies. Yet the Soviets seek this influence in the Third World cautiously, anxious to avoid a direct confrontation with the United States. This policy poses difficulties at times. They find that the United States reacts angrily to Cuban activities in Africa and Latin America, for the U.S. makes little distinction between Soviet and Cuban activities there. Furthermore, the United States interprets any Soviet involvement with Latin American reformers as a threat to American interests. As it has done on occasion since the Monroe Doctrine was originally invoked in the 1820s, the U.S. generally intervenes to protect those interests. In this way, Third World countries seeking to change and reorder their own societies find that they have become embroiled in superpower politics. In some cases the Soviets have miscalculated the effects of their actions in the Third World on the Soviet-American relationship. It seems probable, for example, that they did not expect the United States to react so strongly against their move into Afghanistan. Each of the superpowers walks a narrow line, trying to promote its own interests and influence without getting into direct conflict with the other. It is a dangerous game. (See Readings 12, 13, and 14)

   Even if they believe that historical forces are on their side in the Third World, however, the Soviets have had to look with new eyes on relations with their fellow socialist states in Eastern Europe. There they have been unable to turn reluctant satellites into enthusiastic allies. The outpouring of support for Lech Walesa, the Polish labor leader who tried in the early 1980s to organize the Solidarity Labor movement as a force independent from the Polish Communist Party, confirmed what the Soviets no doubt knew: most Communist East European regimes have not achieved real popularity with their people. It seems that the more closely the Soviets try to control their East European allies, the more unpopular East European governments become with their own people. The peoples of Eastern Europe are often restless under Soviet control and threaten to burst out in opposition movements such as Solidarity.

FACT: The Soviets have twice had to use troops to put down national political movements in Eastern Europe that had broad popular support: in Hungary in 1956 and in Czechoslovakia in 1968.

The Soviet Union today is a world power, far more confident of its position and capabilities than it was even fifteen years ago. It seeks to expand its influence in the Third World, while at the same time maintaining a dialogue with the United States in order to avoid disagreements or misunderstandings that could lead to war. Here, the Soviets believe, they have an area of common interest with the United States. Insofar as economic problems make the arms race more and more costly for the Soviets, since they can no longer support both a continuing large scale military buildup and a steady rise in the standard of living, it seems likely that they would welcome a slowing of the arms race. The Soviets are determined, nonetheless, to maintain the present military balance with the United States. The Soviets also continue to face challenges in their relations with those countries that were once their most docile allies: the states of Eastern Europe and China. Of those fellow Communist states, China presents the greatest worry. The prospect of the world's most populous country as a hostile neighbor, particularly if it should ally with the United States and Japan, conjures up a nightmare of encirclement that blunts the Soviets' general optimism about its future in world affairs.

PROBLEMS AND PROSPECTS

The Soviet leaders can look with satisfaction on what they have achieved. Yet they also have their share of problems. Like other large industrial nations, the Soviet Union has a problem with young people who challenge the world of their parents. There, this often takes the form of cynicism about Marxism-Leninism and the Party, and a fascination with Western culture, clothes, and rock music. (See Reading 11) More and more Soviet citizens are primarily interested in personal advancement, and their own well being, rather than in building Communism. Their enthusiasm for building a new kind of society has waned. The Soviet system of state ownership and central planning now seems to be having a demoralizing effect on the work force. Many workers are putting more and more of their energies into the second economy, turning up late for work, or simply avoiding all their problems by turning to drink.

FACT: From 1970 to 1979, the population of the Soviet Union grew by 9%; the production of hard liquor grew 33%, and that of wine 49%.

No matter how hard the KGB works to crush the various dissident movements, a few individuals persist in criticizing the regime, in writing their idiosyncratic poetry, or in worshipping their God. There is, too, the ever present question of the non-Russian nationalities. Today, at the very time that Russian

Celebration of May 1, International Workers Day, at Red Square in Moscow.

elites are growing more and more overtly nationalistic, the relative number of Russians in the Soviet Union is declining. The Russian birthrate is far lower than that of the peoples of Central Asia and some other nationalities. To date, Moscow has been very effective in maintaining its delicate balance between central control and local autonomy, but this situation requires continuous attention. The fact that the Soviet economy is no longer growing rapidly makes all these problems a bit harder to solve, for it means less investment for all the national republics, as well as fewer consumer goods for the work force, or less money for the military to keep up the arms race with the United States. In times of scarcity, quarrels over benefits grow more bitter.

The Brezhnev regime managed to prevent any of these problems from rocking the boat, mostly by avoiding changes whenever possible. But life does not wait. It seems unlikely that Brezhnev's successors can continue this immobility without risking real difficulties. Neither Andropov nor Chernenko was able to push through any major new policy. What Gorbachev can accomplish remains to be seen. Brezhnev's heirs have inherited a basically stable system, but their country, like others, faces serious challenges in the 1980s.

FROM RUSSIA TO USSR

As they look back at the history of the Soviet Union since 1917, historians often discuss the question of continuity and change. How much does the Soviet Union today differ from Tsarist Russia? How many of its cultural and political traditions have been carried on, at least among the Russians? It is impossible to answer this question once and for all, but the effort to answer it provides a good way to review the Russian and Soviet past.

Those who stress continuity between the Russian past and the Soviet present see many things that have not changed. They point out that the Soviet Union, like the Tsar's empire, is highly centralized, militaristic, authoritarian, and dominated by the Russians. They point out that censorship and a secret police existed under the Tsars, as they do today, that opposition is often interpreted as disloyalty or even treason, and that the law is a weak reed when the winds of political expediency begin to blow. The government today, even more than that of the past, tries to control both the political and spiritual life of its people. Holy Russia may be no more, but Marxist ideology, like the Christian Orthodoxy of old, serves the state as the single approved guide for spiritual life. Marxism-Leninism now helps to reinforce such traditional Russian attitudes as devotion to the group and distrust of individuals who are different. Disorder and disagreement are still feared as a danger to group survival, and home and family prized as a refuge from the state.

The Soviet Union, like the Empire before it, extends its reach when it is strong, and keeps ever present the memory that when weak, it has suffered terribly from the invasions of its neighbors. Its leaders still look upon their Western neighbors with a mixture of fear and admiration. Soviet elites, not unlike their

Russsian counterparts of old, are torn between a desire to imitate the West and be accepted as its equal, and a desire to prove that Soviet socialism is morally superior to American and European capitalism.

Historians who stress change, however, point out that Holy Russia and its peasant village society have been transformed. The Soviet Union of today is a modern superpower, industrial, urban, literate, highly nationalistic, and militarily stronger than its neighbors. Its elite no longer speaks a language different from that of the people, as did the French-and German-speaking courts of the eighteenth and nineteenth century Tsars. On the contrary, the government expends great energy on mobilizing the Soviet peoples to support a coordinated state policy and assuring them that their interests and those of the state are identical. Unlike the Tsar's government, which had neither the desire nor the capacity to transform society, the Soviet Party-state has tried to create a new type of man. This Party-state, with its capacity to direct the work of all types of social groups, from the elite to the poorest farm worker, and from the villages near Moscow to the cities of Uzbekistan, has created a relationship between the leaders and the led that is qualitatively different from anything achieved by the Tsars. While the institutions of censorship and secret police existed under the Tsars, the wide scope of today's censorship and the ubiquitous presence of the KGB represent a qualitative change.

There is yet a third school of thought that sees continuity not between Soviet Russia and the Westward-looking court and elites of the eighteenth and nineteenth centuries, but between Soviet attitudes and behaviors and those of the village and court of Old Russia. These historians argue that Lenin's genius for organization and Stalin's ruthless use of force closed Peter the Great's window on the West, rooted up the Western-looking *intelligentsia,* and set Russia on a course that combines certain traits of early Russian society with a totally new type of political and social organization: that of the Party-state.

To draw up a true balance sheet of continuity and change is, of course, impossible. There is no doubt that the Tsar's empire has been transformed. It is just as sure that many Soviet attitudes and patterns of behavior, especially those that puzzle outsiders most, are akin to those of traditional Russia. As in all countries, long experience determines what most people fear and what they want, what seems familiar and acceptable and what seems alien or frightening, as well as what makes a government feel secure or threatened. The habits of centuries do not change overnight or on command. They are acquired over a long period of time as part of a particular historical experience, and their roots go deep. It is true that the Soviet regime has made an attempt to change those habits that in scale and comprehensiveness is virtually unprecedented in history. Nonetheless, it has had to build on the traditions of the Russian empire even as it has tried to change them. New Soviet institutions and attitudes have combined with those of the Russian empire in such a way that the experience of that empire, those peoples, and that landscape lives on today in the outlook of the peoples of the Soviet Union.

In addition to books used in Chapter 5, the following books were helpful in writing this chapter:

Carrère d'Encausse, H., *Confiscated Power: How Soviet Russia Really Works,* translated by George Holoch, New York: Harper & Row, 1982.

Lane, D., *Politics and Society in the USSR,* New York: New York University Press, 1978.

For students who are interested, we recommend further reading in the sources from which we have taken excerpts, as well as the following works:

American Association for the Advancement of Slavic Studies, *Current Digest of the Soviet Press,* 1314 Kinnear Rd., Columbus, Ohio 43212.
    Useful for students are its periodic compilations of representative articles from the Soviet press, most recently, *The USSR Today,* 1982, which includes a copy of the Constitution, and a "Who's Who in the Politburo," and *Soviet Foreign Policy Today* (1983).

Bronfenbrenner, Y., *Two Worlds of Childhood: US and USSR,* New York: Russell Sage Foundation, 1970.
    Compares schooling and education in USA and USSR.

Cracraft, J., editor, *The Soviet Union Today,* Chicago: University of Chicago Press, 1983.
    Short essays, most of which appeared in *The Bulletin of the Atomic Scientists,* on various aspects of contemporary Soviet society, from dissent to the economy, religion and nationalities.

Cox, A.M., *Russian Roulette: The Superpower Game,* New York: Quadrangle/Times Books, 1982.
    Sensible account of Soviet-American relations today.

Dornberg, J., *The Soviet Union Today,* New York: Dial Press, 1976.
    A *Newsweek* correspondent has written this highly readable book to be accessible to middle and high school students.

Gerhart, G., *The Russian's World: Life and Language,* New York: Harcourt Brace and Jovanovich, 1971.
    Intended for language teachers, this book has Russian words interspersed in the text and is not to be read through, but may be consulted for interesting details: how Russian names are formed, plot plan of apartments, sketches of Russian clothing over the centuries.

Gruliow, L., *Moscow,* Amsterdam: Time-Life Books, 1977.
    Gruliow knows Moscow well. Photographs and text about the life of the city.

Hollander, P., *Soviet and American Society: A Comparison,* New York: Oxford, 1970, University of Chicago Press, 1978.
    American scholar who grew up in Hungary reflects on two societies.

Rubenstein, J. *Soviet Dissidents, Their Struggle for Human Rights,* Boston: Beacon Press, 1980.
    A factual summary by Amnesty International activist.

Sivachev, N. and Yakovlev., N., *Russia and the United States: U.S.-Soviet Relations from the Soviet Point of View,* translated by Olga Adler Titelbaum, Chicago: University of Chicago Press, 1979.
Survey of Russian-American Relations by two Soviet historians.

Shipler, D.K., *Russia: Broken Idols, Solemn Dreams,* New York: Times Books, 1983.
Up-to-date account of daily life, with perceptive analysis.

Smith, H., *The Russians,* New York: Quadrangle, The New York Times Book Co., 1976.
Daily life by the correspondent of the *New York Times.*

Starr, S.F., *Red and Hot: The Fate of Jazz in Soviet Society,* Cambridge, England and New York: Oxford University Press, 1983.
Readable, pioneering work on popular culture.

Whitney, T., editor, *The Young Russians,* New York: Macmillan Press, 1972.
Ten short stories by Russian authors about Russian teenage life.

Readings

Chapter Six

List of Readings

1. A Day in the Country

Muscovites continue to hold a deep love for the country. Their dream, and the reality for the privileged few, is to own a country house (dacha), outside the city. To visit it with friends to feast and drink is a favorite way to spend the weekend. The fact that the guests and hosts described here have foreign goods is a further indication of the fact that they are both fashionable and privileged by Muscovite standards. Andrea Lee, a young American writer, describes the country, first in the fall and then in the spring.

...Pasternak † has described this weather perfectly. "On such days," he writes, "the sky is incredibly high, and through the transparent pillar of air between it and the earth there moves an icy, dark-blue radiance coming from the north." The suggestion of winter in the word "north" is correct: there is an intense, almost perilous feeling to this short northern fall, as if the first snow (which my friends have predicted for the end of this month) were already bearing down. Even now, it's quite cold once you're out of the strong sunlight. Running, I can feel the shadows of the trees on my back.

Today the woods were full of people. There were old women in black coats and gray shawls sifting the fallen leaves with long sticks as they looked for mushrooms. (These accessible woods are usually picked clean.) In the distance was the university orchard, an unkempt clearing full of tall pale grass and stunted fruit trees. Here I saw an old man helping an old woman to climb up; she rattled her stick among the branches, and he gathered the tumbling fruit into a large basket. I passed mothers and fathers whose small children were already extravagantly bundled up in scarves and waterproof suits; many of the families carried bouquets of huge yellow maple leaves, which all Russians seem to gather at this time of year. (Leaf collecting amounts to a craze here. I recently came across the old woman attendant in the library cloakroom pressing leaves with an iron to decorate her windows. And in all my friends' apartments summer flowers have been replaced by vases of leaves.)...

[On an early spring weekend, the author and her Russian friends Seryozha and Anya] got off the train at one of the small concrete rural stations where there is usually an ice cream kiosk, a postcard stand, and a tiny old woman selling sunflower seeds from a sack. We walked toward the *dacha* settlement through a rough green field where several goats were tethered. It was one of those fantastically lush May days that the devious Russian spring looses suddenly upon the countryside. The sun was strong, and the air—raw and stinging through April—felt like a new element: superbuoyant, caressing. The fields that just a few weeks earlier had been seas of mud dotted with gray heaps of melting ice were now shaggy with buttercups; far off we could see bluish pinewoods checkered

Abridged from Andrea Lee, *Russian Journal,* New York, 1979.

with the light green of young birch foliage. All around us walked families bound for the settlement, their newly bared arms already reddening in the sun. Everyone was lugging big bundles of gardening tools, provisions, and tomato seedlings. A tall stoop-shouldered youth passed us, carrying a wicker basket from which chicks peeped feebly; from time to time he lifted the cover and peered inside with such an expression of dull-witted solicitude that Seryozha began to giggle. "Village idiot, village idiot!" he whispered, poking Anya. "Look at his ears!" An old woman, still wearing a winter head shawl and bowed beneath the weight of a huge green rucksack, stared hard at me and at Seryozha's black-market clothes. "Look at the foreigners," she said to her companions.

At the *dacha,* everyone was very fashionable, with foreign jeans and American catch phrases like "Okay" and "Forget it." The woman who owned the place was rumored — like half the people in Moscow — to be part Jewish and to be planning to emigrate to New York. Her name was Svetlana; she was an anxious-looking, fresh-faced brunette of thirty, faintly stout, who used cosmetics with the skill of an American secretary. With considerable pride she motioned us to a table on which stood several bottles of Chianti and a few cans of California almonds. "Darling Aldo brought these to me from the diplomatic store,"* she said. Aldo was an Italian businessman, short and bald, with a shy grin and a pair of enormous sinewy arms. Svetlana was obviously thrilled at being able to achieve what for a Moscow hostess is the utmost in chic: to display several foreigners at a private gathering. Besides Aldo and Lyubov Alekseyevna, there was a thin, surly artist named Volodya; a plump Ukrainian poet with protruding cheeks that nearly hid his tiny gray eyes; a plain girl who was a friend of Lyubov Alekseyevna and whom she addressed as Olya; and two villainous-looking old women, painted, penciled, and dyed, who worked for Mosfilm.

As soon as he could, Seryozha dragged me out into the side yard. "I won't stay," he whispered frantically. "Let's leave, please! My second cousin has a *dacha* around here. We could catch a bus right down the road." ...

The three of us walked through the yard — past a nettle patch, an outhouse whose open door revealed an interior papered with British and American cigarette ads, a rusted bicycle, an ancient wooden arbor, and a caved-in greenhouse — to a small, weedy pond. The banks of the pond were thick with buttercups, and a strong swampy smell rose from the water. "Careful," said Seryozha, taking a finicky step backward. Anya squealed as her new shoes got wet. Over the back fence, which was just beyond the pond, we could see into the yards of other *dachas* — all big, flimsy wooden houses like the one behind us, most with the same herringbone pattern of boards, painted gray or blue or dark green. In some gardens, stunted apple trees still held a few white blossoms; in the fall, I knew, they would produce the small, gnarled, half-wild apples that friends are always pressing upon you, fruit which is always unexpectedly sweet and juicy. There

---

*Special store for diplomats. Such stores accept only foreign currency and have many goods not available in regular stores.

were people in all the yards: children playing, men and women gardening or drawing water from wells. In the yard directly in front of us, two middle-aged men and a woman were sunbathing comfortably in their underwear on newspapers spread out on the grass. Dragonflies and water striders zigzagged across the pond and the sky slowly turned hazy. I dreamily watched the teeming life in the back yards and the pond, and thought about the long, slow, cold months that had gone before. How suddenly everything had changed! My shoulders were still compensating for the weight of a sheepskin coat.

Anya said, "My uncle had a *dacha* near here. The same kind of place: big, creaky, buried in pines. We had a good time there when we were little. But he sold it. Most *dachas* are a nuisance—no plumbing, no insulation. And it gets boring, summer after summer, with nothing to do but eat raspberries and gossip."...

2. The Public Bath

The public bath in Soviet Russia is a place to enjoy oneself and socialize, just as it was before the Revolution.

...There is nothing imported about a Russian bath. Russians have been cleaning themselves for centuries with a combination of intense heat, birch leaves and cold water. Every village has a bath, every city has a number of them. The village version is a simple wooden hut with a stove, but in the cities the bath is an elaborate institution. The grandest of all are the 19th-century Sundonovski Baths in Moscow.

Sundonovski built his establishment at the bottom of a hill on a side street a long block from Kuznetski Most, the most fashionable street of shops in pre-revolutionary Moscow. He put up a three-story building a block long, built in the style of 19th-century Moscow—stucco-fronted neo-classical, with rows and rows of large windows. Sundonovski's name is no longer advertised, but everyone still uses it to describe the old building, which has changed very little (and not at all for the better) since 1917.

Sundonovski divided the baths into three classes, a distinction that survives, though the word "class" has been replaced by "department."

The present management (the city of Moscow) demonstrates less concern for the preservation of the old building than the Sundonovski family undoubtedly did, but there is still something grand about the first-class facilities on the second floor.

One senses the grandeur on the circular marble stairway that leads to them. An imposing chandelier and multi-colored, carved ceilings mark the way. The

Abridged from Robert Kaiser, *Russia: The People and the Power,* New York, 1976.

first rooms are paneled in warm, dark wood, and divided into cubicles. Naked men, some wrapped in white sheets, lounge on upholstered seats, some drinking beer, most smoking and talking. (Smoking and drinking are both forbidden by the posted regulations.) They are resting between sessions in the hot room, the shower room or the pool. This last is a Roman monument, Olympic size, surrounded by Corinthian columns and marble walls. The intricate tile floors that Sundonovski selected a century ago are still in place, though whenever a fault appears the repair work is done in a contemporary orange tile that distorts the beautiful old patterns.

According to published descriptions of the baths at the turn of the century, they were then a bastion of luxurious hedonism. A large staff of underpaid boys did the bidding of a wealthy clientele, fetching refreshment, scrubbing and massaging, pressing suits and shining boots. It isn't like that now, though elderly men in white smocks will press a suit or fetch some beer or a bottle of vodka. And the feeling one gets lounging around the baths of a Friday morning must still approximate the pleasurable sense of self-indulgence that made the establishment so popular before 1917.

The bath attracts all kinds of clients. A group of distinguished professors from the Academy of Sciences* likes to spend most of Saturday there. They come to the first-class section with a good supply of vodka and Armenian brandy, salami, smoked fish and loaves of bread, which they consume—between visits to the hot room and the pool. Their neighbors may be scruffy laborers who come to the bath once a week to dislodge the grime they absorb on the job. Many of the bathers come at the same time on the same day every week, creating societies of friends who have been steaming, drowning and caressing themselves together for years. . . .

The atmosphere in the baths is something like that of a locker room, but it isn't a place to dress and undress for some other activity—it *is* the activity. The sheet and pillowcase one gets (for 13 kopeks) to wrap around the body and put under the seat make the clients look like Romans in a B movie. The fact that no one has any clothes on seems to reduce the barriers between people. Conversation is easy.

The talk covers every conceivable subject. Jokes are a favorite pastime. The Friday-morning crowd could spend most of the morning chewing dry smoked fish, drinking beer and telling jokes. . . .

Most of one's time at the baths is spent on the benches in a series of interludes separating the main business. From the benches in the third-class section the bathers pass through a heavy door into the showering and scrubbing room, a long hall, perhaps 100 feet by 30, lined with marble slabs arranged like beds in a hospital ward. The ceiling of this hall is held up by ancient girders which have been eaten away by rust for decades in the steamy atmosphere, but somehow

---

*Leading organization of Soviet research in the natural and social sciences to which most successful researchers belong.

continue to bear the weight. Men lie asleep on the marble slabs, lounge on them, massage themselves or each other, scrub from head to toe with great mountains of soapsuds. At the end of each marble platform two ancient spigots with smooth wooden handles dispense hot or cold water. Above some of them are shower heads that make it possible to lie under a stream of water for extended periods. Some men fall asleep this way.

The hot room opens off the far end of this hall. It is relatively small, perhaps 25 feet square, on two levels. Just inside the door the heat is strong but not intense. To really feel it one must walk up the tiled steps to the second level, where the old physics lesson about heat rising comes to life. Here the real zealots stand for 20 or 30 minutes, some dressed in little peaked caps and gloves. The head is most sensitive to the heat. The hands start to burn as they collide with the hot air when one whacks himself (or his neighbor) with bunches of leaves. The whacking is meant to open the pores and promote circulation. Serious bathers keep hitting themselves until the leaves come off the dried branches, so the floor is covered with slippery leaves.

The assembled company can never agree on the temperature in the hot room. The fanatics always think it is "weak," and toss small quantities of water onto the big bricks which—made red hot by a gas fire—heat the room. The water creates a fine steam which raises the temperature.

The only unpleasant moments in the bath are the inevitable arguments in the hot room about the temperature. The pretensions to expertise are quite remarkable; at any time there are at least two or three people in the hot room who confidently explain that they know exactly what is best for everyone, what the history of the Russian bath is, why the heat should be higher or lower or unchanged. These experts never agree with each other. Usually, whoever wants it hotter prevails, because he can himself continue tossing water onto the bricks when the others have stopped doing so. Finally it gets too hot for everyone, and there is a stampede of bare bodies down the stairs from the second level.

3.   Moscow Women

Most Soviet women have full-time jobs. They work for personal satisfaction and also out of financial necessity. These 1978 interviews with Moscow women done by two Swedish women provide a glimpse of how Soviet families live. They underline the effects of the continuing housing shortage and the difficulty of combining work and family life.

. . .Lida is a short, solid woman, pale and without makeup. She has a boyish haircut and is wearing a faded sweater past its prime, brown slacks of coarse wool, and heavy shoes. She looks tired and worn.

Tell us about yourself.

I'm already thirty-one years old. Some years ago I started to work as a chambermaid. I work between nine and six.

What did you do before?

I worked on geological expeditions, traveling all over the country. During summers I worked outdoors the whole time, and in winter I lived in a small room on the site. We made geological charts and did a lot of other things. Sometimes the work was very heavy, but I enjoyed it a lot. I kept on meeting new people, going to new places. It was an interesting life. But you get tired of that, too. I wanted to have children, and I had to create another life for myself, so I got a job in Moscow.

How do you live now?

I have a room in a communal apartment.* Of course I'd like to have a place of my own, but there's absolutely no chance of that. It's a fairly large room — 15 square meters. Only my son and I live there.

Before that I lived with my mother. But there's a law here that states that single parents have a right to a single room, so after a while I got this one.

Do you have your son in a day-care center?

No, he's only two and a half, so he's in a nursery. He spends the entire week there. I leave him on Monday morning and pick him up on Friday evening.

Is he happy there?

Yes, he likes it a lot. There are toys, other children, things that a kid needs.The staff is good and caring. But of course it's hard to see so little of

---

*Soviet experts estimate that 20-25% of the population live in communal apartments where several families share bathroom and kitchen.

Abridged from C. Hansson and Karen Liden, *Moscow Women,* New York, 1983.

him. I miss him. He spends his days with strangers, and when he comes home he seems to want to be back with them. People who aren't even related to him seem closer to him than I am.

He doesn't behave like a real son; sometimes he uses the polite form of address with me.* But in general things are all right. I'd never be able to bring him home every day.

What time do you come home from work?

I don't leave work until six, which means that the earliest I get home is at seven. At least three times a week I have to stop and shop on the way home, and since that's the time the crowds are the worst, it often takes at least an hour. Most of the time I don't get home until eight.

Do you manage to have any free time?

Hardly. I have to cook and wash and do things like that at night. But I do have a couple of hobbies. One is the theater. I'm part of an amateur group. It consists of people who are interested in the theater, both students and workers. We rehearse four times a week—Monday, Wednesday, and Saturday nights and all of Sunday. When we're about to perform we work as much as we can bear. Right now we're working on a piece by Mayakovsky.** It's a lot of fun.

My second hobby is sculpting in wood. I collect pieces of wood in the forest and sculpt figures out of them. I usually do that late at night...[In answer to the question as to whether or not she was divorced, Lida answered, "I was never married. I wanted to have a child, not a family. I'm not the kind of woman who fits easily into a marriage."]

[Lyuba]

I'm an artist, thirty-two years old. I was married once before and have a son from that marriage. I was twenty-one when we got married, and I already had the baby. We were divorced when I was twenty-five. Now I'm married for the second time—six months ago.

A lot of people get divorced very early here. Why do you think that's so?

We know so little about life when we marry; we become independent so late. Almost without exception young people are dependent on their parents to help out economically. The money problem becomes especially acute if a couple has a child and the woman has to stop working. Here a family can't possibly live on one salary. Never! Well, perhaps two people can live on the man's salary, but with a child it's impossible. And it almost never happens that a young person

---

*The Russian language has both a polite and an informal form of address, unlike English. Family members normally use the informal form.

**Vladimir Mayakovsky (1893-1930), leading Russian Futurist poet. See Reading 1, Chapter 5.

can have her own apartment which she can take care of herself. Newly married couples have to wait a long time to get their own apartment and have to live with their parents in the meantime. If the parents have means, they can buy into a cooperative and the young people can move in after a year or two. But sometimes they have to live with their parents for ten years, or perhaps all their lives.

Very often young people divorce just after they've moved away from their parents. Before they moved they were still like children, and only when they start living by themselves do they notice that they're very different from each other and that they can't live together. Or if the parents don't like their daughter-in-law or son-in-law, there always seems to be a way of making the children divorce....

[Nadezhda Pavolovna, 48, is a university professor and Party member. She has done well. Like many successful American women, she does not think there are special obstacles to a women's success.]

Your profession has obviously always been very important to you.

Definitely! When I was fifteen I never thought of just having children and a home and a husband. Never! I felt that kind of thinking was beneath a woman's dignity. I had a long correspondence with my future husband about woman's role in society. How I let myself go in those letters! My husband confessed several years later that he was more interested in the way I ended the letters than in the whole women's debate. But I took the whole thing very seriously!

Is work still the most important thing for you?

The most important thing for me is...our country. Of course there are people who express their dissatisfaction nowadays with...well, politics. But they underline even more clearly what this country, what the Soviet Union has done for me. When I compare my life with Mama's...then I know. Everything I've attempted has seemed to be so easy. My studies went smoothly, my career also. It was probably the right place, the right time, the right profession.

But the children...I was often sad that I didn't have more.

Tears come to her eyes, but she quickly composes herself while she blows her nose. "This ought not to be taped!" she laughs. Then she cries again and says, "My third child was stillborn."

Her daughter consoles her, and Nadezhda Pavolovna is soon laughing again and saying to her daughter, "Hurry up so that I can be a grandmother instead!" We laugh together and then move on to a completely different question.

What does equality between men and women mean to you?

My own situation is one of total equality. If one of us does a particular chore in our home, the other will reciprocate some other time. But heavy physical work is hard for a woman, so my husband takes care of the furnace. It's a dirty job and...it isn't my cup of tea. I always do the laundry. That's the way we've divided up the chores.

I think that all this talk about equality is something they invented in big cities. There it can obviously become a gigantic problem for a couple to decide who is going to clean an apartment floor which consists of a few pitiful square meters. Our house is ten by twelve meters, and there's never a question about who's going to clean the floors. I do that. My husband makes the fires. He digs up the garden. I do the planting....

[Natasha and Yura are students with a small child.]

I'll be twenty-two in May. Right after attending school in Sverdlovsk in the Urals, I came to the University of Moscow. That was four years ago. I'm a student at the faculty of law and will graduate this year. I specialize in criminal law. At first I was interested only in juvenile crime, but gradually I've become interested in all forms of crime. I'm especially interested in the social context of crime.

What does your husband do?

He's majoring in mathematics. We'll graduate at the same time, and then we'll be moving to Akademgorodok.*

Have you lived here since you got married?

No. Actually, we could have had a room at the university. Neither Yura nor I have relatives in Moscow, so we really don't have any place to live here. We lived at the university until we got married, and it wouldn't have been too difficult to get a room in a two-room apartment there. That would have meant a small private room with shower, toilet, and coat closet shared with the neighbors, and a large communal kitchen—there's one on every floor. But we were tired of living in student rooms. There are always people milling around. And then it was a question of finances. Neither he nor I get much help from home.

Mama is a pediatrician, but she doesn't make terribly much—no more than 120 rubles per month, or maybe 130 if she works overtime at night. She sends me money, but I try to make her stop. Basically, we live on what we earn....[At the official exchange rate, .8 ruble = $1.00]

But there are several people living in the apartment, aren't there?

Of course. We considered this when we chose Yura's job. We found a spot where we had friends—some of our classmates live here too—Yura's brother

---

*A suburb of Novosibirsk in Siberia, where the Siberian section of the Soviet Union's Academy of Science is located. Akademgorodok is populated almost exclusively by scholars and students who work at the university. The standard of education and research is considered very high.

and one of his friends. The three of them arranged to live together. It has its good and bad sides, since I'm the only woman—the others aren't married, so I end up doing the cooking for everybody.

Of course they help with the shopping, but it's still a lot of work. On the other hand it's nice to be the only woman in the kitchen. I can iron and wash and cook when I want to, and there aren't any conflicts. In communal kitchens there are often four women scurrying around, and that creates problems. So in a way I'm lucky.

How long have you lived here?

Not very long. Before this Yura worked as a superintendent in another place. But we were only given an apartment in the basement and it wasn't very suitable for small children. When the baby was really little, things worked out well because we had a small yard where we could put his carriage. But the room was too small and the corridor so drafty that he couldn't play there, and I couldn't keep him in his bed and playpen all day. But we had warm water, and that made things much easier.

You don't have any hot water here?

No, and no bathroom. It's a big problem. I have to heat water for the dishes and the wash. Fortunately there's a public bath not far from here that we use. But we bathe the baby at home and have to heat the water. And the kitchen! Sometimes I visit one of Yura's brothers who lives in a new suburb, and I bathe the baby there. They have a bathroom and a kitchen that are tiny but clean and bright—they're completely white. But this place is horrible!

Where is the baby during the day?

He's with us—as he's always been. Since we don't have anyone else to take care of him, we take turns.

Right before he was born I went home to my mother. I ended up staying there for three months. Because he wasn't very strong and had a little trouble eating when he was born, we don't want to put him in a nursery yet.

Will he go later?

Yes, next year.

Do you think most people think nurseries are a good solution?

No, for the most part people place children in them out of necessity. There are some good ones, especially those connected to factories and institutions; there you don't have to worry about your children. But for the most part nurseries are very bad; the staff is usually very inexperienced and untrained, and turnover is constant. They get minimal wages, the job is taxing, and the groups are far too large—twelve to fifteen children per adult. The children are constantly catching cold because they're always running around in wet diapers. If we were paid for the whole year after having a baby, most women would probably take advantage of it....

4. Shortages

This article speaks for itself.

MOSCOW — Clear plastic wrap. Bouillon cubes. Large paper tissues. Rice Crispies. Credit cards. Checkbooks. Secondhand furniture shops. Carbon paper. Copying machines. Videotape cassettes....

Telephone books listing individuals rather than government offices. Decent spark plugs. Night cream and other cosmetics. Hardware stores. Automatic clothes washers. Clothes dryers. Film for 35-mm cameras that comes in its own cassette, ready to be loaded. Chests of drawers....

Clean, comfortable coffee bars. Clean hotel rooms. Meat and fruit all year round. A wide choice of cars, quickly available. Direct-dial telephones to the rest of the world. Real estate agents. Ice cream in more than two or three flavors. Deep freezes....

These are just some of the everyday bits and pieces of modern life that Americans and Europeans and Japanese take for granted, that the privileged elite here has had some access to, but that the average Soviet citizen just does not see.

They are the price of the SS-20 missile, of the T-72 battle tank, of keeping 4 million men under arms, of equaling the United States in nuclear and conventional forces, of one-party control.

Well, well, you say. Many of the items are frivolous anyway. Americans don't really need them. Why should Russians?

Yet Westerners still seem to think Soviet people live as they do — oh, a bit poorer, perhaps, but of course they have credit cards, don't they? I mean, doesn't everyone?

No, they don't. Outside of the military forces, life has an old-fashioned, turn-of-the-century air here. Branches of the one and only state bank have inkwells and nib pens, even in Moscow.

It is comfort and convenience that people here lack.

They do have some things, of course. Apartments are below Western standards, but the rent is cheap. One friend pays 17 rubles and 62 kopecks ($26.50) for a three-room apartment about half an hour by subway from the city center. He pays 4 rubles ($6) more a month for heat (through radiators) and electricity, and 2 more rubles a month for telephone ($3); after that, all calls are free within

David Willis, "Shortages: Where Telephone Books and Tinfoil are Luxuries," in "Soviet Memorandum," *The Christian Science Monitor,* March, 1981.

the city. That amounts to $35.50 a month for housing, or 14 percent of the average wage here of about $240 a month.

Almost always, however, both husband and wife work, so it is only about 7 percent of combined income.

And the state spends huge sums to keep basic food prices down: more than $40 billion a year. Bread, meat, cheese, sugar, butter, and most fish prices have not changed for more than a decade.

The catch is that quality is also low. People don't spend the money they have because they say there's nothing interesting to buy. Many keep their cash in mattresses or in old socks rather than entrusting it to the state bank. When people do go out to buy a touch of class, they find it is just the fancy items that have risen in price. Carpets, for instance, shot up 50 percent in January 1977, then another 50 percent in July 1979.

A favorite device is to put out a new item, or an old one with a new label, and charge a higher price for it. Officially, "inflation" doesn't exist here. But the cost of living goes up steadily. If Russians decide the poor-quality food in the state stores isn't good enough and shop instead at the 6,500 farmers' markets around the country [where produce of the private plots is sold] they say they have little money left over for anything else. Market prices can be five times as high as state prices, or more.

"You can get tinfoil," says one Muscovite defensively. "You can get decorative candles, from the Baltic states. You can get tiny packets of *kukuruznyie khlopya* (corn flakes), but we don't eat them much, and when we do, we take them dry, from the box. You have to know where to look, where to go. You have to stand in line. You have to buy now: Later it will have gone. I even saw lemons the other day—imagine! I would have joined the line, but it was very long and I was in a hurry. . . .

That last comment is pure Soviet, heard everywhere.

People also cannot get large bank loans. A friend and her intellectual husband were suddenly told late in 1980 that their long-pending application to buy a car had risen to the top of the list and had been granted. Joy—but despair, too—set in: Where could they lay their hands on the 8,700 rubles ($13,000) required for their four-cylinder Russian-made subcompact? If they didn't hurry, they would lose their turn.

They did it the Russian, developing-country way. The wife sat down in the morning and began telephoning all her friends and asking for loans. By the end of the day she had raised the money. "And now we must keep track of who wants it back in a week, who in a month, who in six months, who in a year, who can wait indefinitely," she said.

The only Moscow telephone book was published in 1978 in a limited edition of 170,000 and lists only offices and state stores, not individuals. "Most people don't need a phone book anyway," says a party-supporting acquaintance. "What would they use it for?"

Cramped housing creates and intensifies social frictions. Almost everyone lives in an apartment—generally with one, two, or three rooms, a tiny kitchen, and even smaller bathroom. Housing is assigned by the state: No one can simply move at will, unless he is a top party official. Millions of new units are built each year, but they hardly dent the shortage.

Unofficial swapping of houses is a part of many lives — deals within deals, two rooms high up in one outlying building for two rooms low in another closer in.

Deals, often struck on street corners, must be registered with the authorities. People involved must prove they have permission to live in the city; the stamp "Moscow" in an internal passport is most highly prized. Shops are better stocked here. There's more to do.

To get a "Moscow" stamp, many a man from out-of-town pays a Moscow girl to go through a wedding ceremony. Once he is registered as the Spouse of a Muscovite, he leaves her and goes his own way. Both profit. "And it happens more often than you might think," says a friend.

The party elite lives in well-built, brown-brick apartment houses tucked away on inner-city streets and guarded by police. The rest of the population struggles as best it can.

Up to 30 percent of all housing in downtown Moscow and Leningrad remains communal. I shall never forget the first time I visited one. In a Western capital, the street would have been high-rent, chic, sought-after, close to shops and theaters, fashionable.

In Moscow, beyond the usual litter and debris in the lobby, the ancient elevator clanked to an upper floor. My friend put a finger on his lips. I was not to speak, in case someone heard I was not Russian. In the dim light of a 25-watt bulb, he opened a tall door and we stepped into a long corridor, also dim. Seven doors along the right-hand wall, three along the left. Behind each of the seven doors a separate family: 23 people in all. All shared the one bathroom, one toilet, one kitchen.

The bathroom was a disaster: tub dirty and leaning wearily to the right, no shower curtain, grimy floor, cracked gray tiles, single weak bulb suspended from the ceiling, no shade. Seven zinc tubs hung from seven pegs on the wall — for washing clothes.

The room our friends lived in was tall and long, but shabby. Whenever they visited their parents, who had a small apartment in a new building about half an hour away by metro, they refused to eat, on principle: "We can take care of ourselves." But they gratefully ran baths and luxuriated in the hot water without someone constantly banging on the door to get in.

"What do you do here," I asked, "if you don't feel well, or if you are in a hurry in the morning? If you need the bathroom?"

"We do what all Russia does," was the simple reply.

"We wait."

5.   Car Owners' Woes

The Soviet press often carries articles about problems that need to be remedied: pilfering from factories, alcoholism, absenteeism and other inefficiencies. This article is quite typical. It is particularly interesting in its suggestion that there may be a place for private initiative in the solution to this problem. The article also indicates how and why the so-called second economy flourishes.

Soviet Editors' Note. — Numerous readers have written us in response to the newspaper's Aug. 7 article, "Who Will Fix Automotive Service?" We invited a number of specialists to participate in a round-table discussion of this topic.

Question. — Letters to the editors cite numerous cases of poor performance on the part of automotive service stations. What more needs to be done to improve automotive service in our country?

A. Krutko, Deputy Director of the Moscow Administration for Combating the Embezzlement of Socialist Property and Speculation. — Law violations at automotive service stations have become too widespread. For example, we are presently prosecuting cases of large-scale bribe taking at the Zhiguli Automotive Service Center on the Warsaw Highway in Moscow. Cheating of car owners is also widespread. We have one such case in which car owners were cheated out of more than 5,000 rubles, altogether. Furthermore, the people who are supposed to be auditing to ensure that billing is correct are sometimes themselves involved in thefts. We have also uncovered cases of large-scale thefts from automotive manufacturers. The situation at the Leninist Young Communist League Automotive Plant is especially disturbing.

S. Petrachenkov, general director of Mosavtotekhobsluzhivaniye [the Moscow Automotive Service Association]. — We realize the need for close contacts between automotive service and the agencies charged with combating the embezzlement of socialist property and speculation. One thing that worries us are the auto mechanics who take small bribes or cheat customers out of a ruble or two here and there, but whose offenses are too small to warrant criminal prosecution. There are no legal grounds for firing such people, either. About the only way to punish them would be to deprive them of bonuses, but that wouldn't be any deterrent — they take enough extra money from customers in a week to make up two monthly bonuses. So we are virtually helpless to stop these widespread abuses.

Yu. N. Yagunov, deputy general director of the Moscow Leninist Young Communist League Automotive Plant. — Of course, an effective punishment must be found for such abuses, but it's also necessary to institute effective incentives, so that the amount of money an auto mechanic legally earns is directly proportionate to the quality of work he does.

Abridged from V. Petrov and V. Yakovlev, *Sovetskaya Rossia,* October, 1981, "Once Again About Automotive Service," *Current Digest of the Soviet Press,* Vol. 33, No. 52.

Q. — What about the fact that it's often the customers themselves who give auto mechanics the opportunity to earn money illegally, "on the side"?

S. N. Vinokurov, Director of Rosavtotekhobsluzhivaniye [the Russian Republic Automotive Service Association]. — Considering how much time it normally takes private motorists to get their cars repaired, it's no wonder that they're willing to pay extra money to get the job done more quickly. For example, we recently calculated that a private motorist in Lipetsk Province spends an average of 60 hours just to get one repair performed on his car.

Q. — There's a statistic showing that only four out of every 10 cars that require repairs are repaired at state service stations. If we assume that one private motorist in 10 may do his own car work, that leaves five out of 10 repairs to be done by mechanics working "on the side" — either on state time and at state service stations, or after work but using state materials. Aside from the issue of criminal lawbreaking, don't these enterprising private mechanics constitute an untapped reserve for improving automotive service?

R. Kislyuk, the Volga Automotive Plant's deputy general director for automotive service. — In Hungary, where auto mechanics are allowed to do private work, they buy their own parts and pay income tax to the state. Establishing a similar practice in our country would create healthy competition for state service stations and stimulate them to provide better service.

S. Vinokurov. — Incidentally, this form of service is already being introduced in the Baltic republics.

Q. — What radical steps can be taken to improve state automotive service?

R. Kislyuk. — The reason that illegal practices in automotive service have come to constitute a whole system of their own is that car production is simply outstripping the growth in state automotive service. To provide normal service to all private motorists we would need twice our present service capacity. To keep up with the current production of Zhigulis alone, we should be opening eight new service bays a day, but we are having great difficulty opening even two.

The Volga Automotive Plant's experience demonstrates that the establishment of large specialized service stations with direct ties to auto manufacturers is one way to make service more efficient. Right now the fact that Soyuzavtotekhobsluzhivaniye [the All-Union Automotive Service Association] acts as a middleman between service stations and manufacturers greatly slows the process by which the stations obtain spare parts and makes it impossible for us to know which parts and how many each station needs. In addition to specialization, we need to computerize the inventorying and distribution of spare parts. For a long time now there has been talk of setting up an Auto Service Automated Management System, but so far only five of the 50 computers that are needed for this purpose have been installed....

6.   The Soviet People's Court

The People's Courts in the Soviet Union judge petty offenders. Judges often seem to base their decisions on the character of the defendant as well as on the crime committed. Notice the way the judge suggests the witness should have taken more responsibility for a fellow-worker and the lecture about proper behavior and morality.

...Soviet trials begin with a short biography of the accused.

A Russian judge would think it silly to deal with Ivan Ivanov, a stranger off the street. Who is this fellow? What is his record at work? In the courts? What about his personal and family background? And so, information about the character and history of the defendant—information which is usually kept secret in English and American courts until guilt or innocence has been decided—is sought and aired at the outset.

[In this case Kondakov has been accused of stealing a pair of galoshes from the place where he works. The judge is questioning a witness.]

"What do you remember about this case? Tell the court everything you know."

"What do I remember? Not very much. I remember it happened on the night shift, sometime in early October—"

"The night of October 11-12?"

"That's right. Kondakov"—she glances in his direction and smiles at him—"arrived about twenty minutes late for work. It was quite clear that he had been drinking. He was pretty drunk. He kept on getting up from his table—I worked next to him—and singing the first stanzas of folk songs. And getting up to congratulate us, I don't know for what. Ordinarily he was a quiet sort.

"Well at about three-thirty he announced loudly that he was going to the bathroom. Of course, I paid no attention. But a few minutes later there was a commotion in the next shop. Everyone ran out—I did too. There he was with the galoshes. He had stuffed them under his coat and the guard noticed it. Well, that's all I know. The police came and took him away. He seemed confused. Embarrassed. He kept saying, "I never stole a thing in my life.""

"Did he swear?"

"Not while I was there. He just muttered to himself, sort of."

"Was he stealing shoes before this incident?"

"I don't know, I have no idea, I don't think so."

"Why do you think he committed this act?"

"I haven't the faintest idea. He was quite drunk."

"But not so drunk that he didn't know he was stealing?"

"I can't say. I don't think so."

Abridged from George Feifer, *Justice in Moscow,* New York, 1964.

"Was he often drunk at work?"

"Not often."

"But he *has* been drunk; did you know he was warned about that?"

"Yes, I knew."

"What can you tell us about his character?"

"He was all right. Decent. I never had any unpleasantness with him."

"But you know that he had 'unpleasantness' with the administration."

"Yes."

"Did you know that he was fired from other jobs and arrested for petty hooliganism [undesirable behavior, juvenile delinquency]?"

"No."

"You didn't know that. Perhaps you ought to have interested yourself in your neighbor. Well, what kind of man was he at work? Did you expect that he might steal? What can you say about his working habits?"

"He wasn't a bad worker. Or unusually good, either. He did his share. I'd call him normal."

"You mean that a normal worker is late and absent and drunk on the job?"

"Uh, he worked well—"

"Worked well! He *stole* well. What about the reprimands he kept getting?"

"During the last couple of months, he worked very hard. I don't think he had any reprimands."

"If you don't count thieving."

"I think he was trying to—"

"Such people have got to be taken under control, they have got to be shown. He drinks, he fails to appear at work, he creates scandals—and now look where he ended. The logical end; he didn't want to heed the warnings. Well, we have a job to do; the people of Moscow need shoes and the Red Hero is trying to supply them. We don't have to put up with people who deliberately stand in the way."

The judge puts back her glasses.

"Now is there anything else you would like to add? Can you tell us anything more about his intentions?"

"I don't know anything more. It was a surprise to me."

The judge turns to the assessors. "Have you any questions?"

They shake their heads, No.

[Kondakov got one year hard labor.]

[In another case, the defendant is a Soviet go-getter, an entrepreneur whose deals are illegal. He is from Azerbaidjan, but is being tried in Moscow where he has illegally taken up residence.]

Articles 147 and 198: Swindling and Violation of Passport Regulations. The defendant, a skinny, dark, itinerant Azerbaijanian born in Baku, grins uncontrollably. . . .

He has admitted guilt on both charges. The swindling was attempted in a local *rinok* (an open market where collective farmers are permitted to sell produce from their private plots). With a fellow Azerbaijanian he worked a variation of an old confidence game, known in both the East and West as the "pocket-book drop," on a dashing Uzbek soldier on leave in Moscow. Promising to split the contents of a wallet they supposedly found, the two accomplices enticed the victim to part with his own fortune of sixty-three rubles. . . .

The second charge is illegal residence in Moscow: the accused has no *propiska* (a residence permit, issued by the police). This permission, which is stamped in the citizen's (internal) passport, is required in the major Soviet cities—Moscow, Leningrad, Kiev—and in the coastal strip along the Black Sea and in other popular areas. A Soviet citizen cannot simply take up residence in these areas as he could, for instance, in Irkutsk. For a newcomer, permission to stay usually depends upon his having a job which would entitle him to a *propiska;* but for most jobs—to complete the vicious cycle—possession of the *propiska* is a prerequisite. The purpose is to deter migration to already overcrowded cities. Thus, the Azerbaijanian, having no steady job, has no legal right to live in Moscow; he has been warned four times during the past two years about his being there.

The judge is a ponderous man who plays with his words and his fingers. "Young man, you have got to get a job, you have got to find yourself an honest place in our socialist society. And you cannot do it in Moscow. Do you understand that you are living at the expense of society? Young man, you are a piece of fungus. You have done nothing with your life but practice the bourgeois creed of getting something for nothing. Why didn't you go back to your homeland and work, like a Soviet man?"

Grinning, the skinny defendant asks for mercy. He knows that he must be punished, of course; he understands that he did wrong—but could the court please make it as light as possible? You see, he has a sick mother in Baku, he has asthma, and he has a burning desire to reform. . . .

But the sentence is four years in a labor colony, strict regime. The Azerbaijanian is stunned; the grin becomes a mouth agape, then a grimace of hatred. . . .

Four youths stole three rolls of tar paper from their factory: three years each. A drunk sneaked a mirror from a grammar school on Election Day: two years. A sober man took the windshield wipers and mirror from a parked car: one year. An obviously imbecilic old lush insisted on annoying strangers at a metro station: one year. A waitress had been pouring each glass of wine a few drops short and taking home a bottle a fortnight for herself: two years. A man rolled a drunk for his greasy jacket and scruffy shoes: one year. The punishments are astonishingly severe. . . .

7. New Soviet Rituals

The Soviet regime has made every effort to discourage religious practice, including the creation of new Soviet rituals to replace the old, religious ones. The results are discussed in this 1983 article from the New York Times.

KIEV, U.S.S.R. — Religion, Karl Marx said, is the opium of the people, so it seems only logical that his heirs, in their struggle against it, would turn to substitute drugs.

The Ukraine has led the way. More than any other Soviet republic, it has instituted elaborate "socialist rites" for life's milestones ranging from birth through marriage and death.

No simple civic ceremonies these. At any of a chain of Palaces of Festive Events throughout Kiev and the Ukraine, women in long gowns and glittering chains of office are ready to perform the new rituals at altar-like tables flanked by a white bust of Lenin and accompanied by appropriate music from an organ or full choir. An "eternal flame" burns in an adjacent room, from which celebrants can ignite their hand-held torches, and a government corporation, Svyato, provides whatever services are needed. Administrators of the new rituals insist that they neither derive from religious rites nor were intended to replace them.

"Religious ceremonies are withering away by themselves," said Galina N. Menzheres, a Kiev Deputy Mayor who serves as chairman of the Commission on the Composition and Implementation of New Rites. "People needed new ceremonies to mark major occasions, and we looked to folklore and national customs to find what had been confirmed by experience. Then we looked at contemporary life and selected what people wanted."

The evolution of rites has been part of a Soviet effort to transfer to the state some of the symbolic and ceremonial functions of the church. But the new rites often seem pale imitations and even parodies of what they were meant to supplant.

The Ceremonial Registration of the Newborn, for example, has taken liberally from Christian baptism. Godparents have been replaced by "invited parents," candles and torches are lighted from an "eternal flame," and in lieu of a baptismal cross the infant receives a "name star" symbolizing the Great October Socialist Revolution, the official name of the Bolshevik Revolution of Nov. 7, 1917–Oct. 25, according to the Julian calendar then used.

As the robed woman places the star around a child's neck, she exhorts the parents:

"Let this star light the path of your son as the Star of October lights the path for the whole world."

From Serge Schmemann, "New Soviet Rituals Seek to Replace Church's," *New York Times,* March 15, 1983.

The high point of the rite is "Name-giving." With the child in the hands of the invited parents, the officiant declaims:

"By an act of government of the Ukrainian S.S.R., the child of the Popov family, born March 1, 1983, will bear the name Ivan, Ivan Ivanovich Popov, and his rights as a member of the great family of Soviet peoples, as a citizen of the U.S.S.R., are confirmed."

The name — embodying first name, patronymic and family name — and the date of birth are fictional. But the text is from an officially approved manual.

More Than Master of Ceremonies

The officiant is more than a master of ceremonies. The title, "obryadovy starosta" (ceremonial elder), is borrowed from the title of a church warden.

Most of the officiants are women and their winter dress is a fur-trimmed cape and floor-length gown, with the badge of office hung round the neck on a broad chain. As citizens pass through life, they may return to the Palace of Festive Events to celebrate the first day and last day of school; receipt of an internal passport, or identity document, at the age of 16; the first job, symbolizing "entry into the working class;" marriage, induction into the army, golden anniversary and death.

The most popular of the ceremonies is the wedding. Lyudmila P. Ponomarev, an adviser to the Kiev city administration on festivals and ceremonies, said that virtually all marriages in Kiev were now being performed with the new rites. Last year, on its 1500th anniversary, the city opened a modern new Central Palace of Festive Events, whose enormous output of marriages is accompanied by the latest word in socialist symbolism and equipment.

On the recent tour, couples were observed on the lower level waiting their turn to fill out forms, consult with a counselor and browse in the Svyato salon for anything from rental wedding gowns to leased cars outfitted with ribbons, twinned rings and dolls. On the upper level, wedding parties awaited the big moment to piped-in music.

Among them were Ivan Karmash and his fiancee, Tatyana Samchuk, and 20 relatives and friends. When it was their turn, they paraded into the hall, and a choir in the gallery burst into a Ukrainian song, "Look Upon Your Bride, Your Wish, Your Fate."

At the end of the airy hall stood the officiant, Viktoriya K. Galintsovskaya, next to a ceremonial table and an enormous white bust of Lenin. For 15 minutes, Mrs. Galintsovskaya led the couple through a deep bow to their parents, the donning of wedding bands and a ritualized signing of the marriage certificate, with the robed woman pointing out the spaces to write in with a carved, wand-like pointer. The 12-member choir, accompanied by two *banduras,* Ukrainian folk instruments, offered a total of six songs, including the patriotic Soviet stand-by, "How Broad Is My Beloved Land."

Mix of Sermon and Exhortation

The text was a mix of emotional sermonizing and patriotic exhortation, with stress on the omnipresence and beneficence of the Soviet state.

"You have given your hand to each other at a happy time," Mrs. Galint-sovskaya intoned, "under the peaceful sky of the motherland of the Soviet people, led by the party of Lenin along the bright path to the Communist future."

At the end, she reminded the newlyweds of their "obligation to raise children as worthy, industrious citizens of our motherland."

The fee was 13.50 rubles ($19) apart from whatever clothes the newlyweds rented or the feast they laid out.

Mrs. Ponomarev, the city adviser, said Kiev seemed to be leading the way in instituting the rites in part because it has been working on them for almost 20 years and has established a broad network of ceremonial halls, services and practitioners.

No Figures on Church Attendance

Although there seemed to be no reason to doubt her assertion that all weddings and 60 to 80 percent of infant registrations in Kiev were now being performed with the new rites, it was difficult to gauge how effective they have been in supplanting religious ceremonies. The Orthodox Church keeps no figures on church attendance, much less on baptisms and weddings, and the Government places serious hurdles in the way of religious observances.

The formal campaign to institutionalize the rites began about a decade after Stalin's death in 1953. The first Soviet Conference on Socialist Rituals was held in May 1964, and the early years of Leonid I. Brezhnev's tenure was marked by the introduction of special days dedicated to various occupations, such as Geologists' Day on April 3 or Truck Drivers' Day on Oct. 30.

But attempts to replace the symbols and traditions of Holy Russia have been a feature of Soviet life almost from the outset. The iconography of the church has found its imitations in portraits of Lenin and other Soviet heroes. Foods once associated with church feasts, like the sweet Easter cake known as *kulich,* have found their way into secular usage, in this case as spring cake.

10 Commandments Replaced

Even the 10 Commandments have found their counterpart in the Moral code of the builders of Communism, adopted by the party's 22nd congress in 1961. The central tenet is that "man is to man a friend, comrade and brother."

But some discordant reviews have emerged. The Moscow daily Sovetskaya Rossiya cited a poll in which 90 percent of those questioned said the rites were needed, but 50 percent said they did not achieve their purpose.

Svetlana Stepunin, writing in the paper, said one problem was that the new rites were being created for the less cultivated levels of society.

"It seems to me," she wrote, "that these modern rites will reach the level expected of them when they become works of art, aimed at the most discriminating taste."

Her proposal was to form an institute in Moscow where ethnographers, historians, folklorists, philosophers, writers and musicians would join to create model rites, "uniting word and music, true to national tradition."

8. Polyakov: Fireman Prokhorchuk

This short story was published in Moscow in 1953, the year of Stalin's death. It pokes fun at the severity of censorship under Stalin. While censors in the Soviet Union have become more sophisticated in the years since then, they continue to monitor everything that is published in the Soviet Union. This is possible because all publishing houses are owned by the state. The only way to escape the censor is to publish things yourself (the Russian word for this is samizdat, *which means self-publishing) by typing out a manuscript and circulating it illegally.*

THE STORY OF A STORY OR FIREMAN PROKHORCHUK

(The action takes place in the editorial offices of a Soviet magazine. A woman writer—a beginner—shyly enters the editor's office.)

She: Pardon me...Please excuse me...You're the editor of the magazine, aren't you?

He: That's right.

She: My name is Krapivina. I've written a little short story for your magazine.

He: All right, leave it here.

She: I was wondering whether I couldn't get your opinion of it right away. If you'll permit me, I'll read it to you. It won't take more than three or four minutes. May I?

He: All right, read it.

She: It is entitled "A Noble Deed." *(She begins to read.)*

It was the dead of night—three o'clock. Everybody in the town was asleep. Not a single electric light was burning. It was dark and quiet. But suddenly a gory tongue of flame shot out of the fourth-floor window of a large grey house. "Help!" someone shouted. "We're on fire!" This was the voice of a careless tenant who, when he went to bed, had forgotten to switch off the electric hot-plate, the cause of the fire. Both the fire and the tenant were darting around the room. The siren of a fire engine wailed. Firemen jumped down from the engine and dashed into the house. The room where the tenant was darting around was a sea of flames. Fireman Prokhorchuk, a middle-aged Ukrainian with large black mustachios, stopped in front of the door. The fireman stood and thought. Suddenly he rushed into the room, pulled the smoldering tenant out and aimed his extinguisher at the flames. The fire was put out, thanks to the daring of Prokhorchuk. Fire Chief Gorbushin approached him, "Good boy, Prokhorchuk," he said, "you've acted according to regulations!" Whereupon the fire chief smiled and added: "You haven't noticed it, but your right mustachio is aflame." Prokhorchuk smiled and aimed a jet at his mustachio. It was dawning.

Vladimir Polyakov, "The Story of a Story, or Fireman Prokhorchuk," translated by A. MacAndrew, *Partisan Review,* Volume 28, Summer, 1961.

He: The story isn't bad. The title's suitable too: "A Noble Deed." But there are some passages in it that must be revised. You see, it's a shame when a story is good and you come across things that are different from what you'd wish. Let's see, how does it start, your story?

She: It was the dead of night—three o'clock. Everybody in the town was asleep...

He: No good at all. It implies that the police are asleep and those on watch are asleep, and...No, won't do at all. It indicates a lack of vigilance. That passage must be changed. Better write it like this: It was the dead of night—three o'clock. No one in the town was asleep.

She: But that's impossible, it's night time and people do sleep.

He: Yes, I suppose you're right. Then let's have it this way: Everybody in the town was asleep but at his post.

She: Asleep at their posts?

He: No, that's complete nonsense. Better write: Some people slept while others kept a sharp lookout. What comes next?

She: Not a single electric light was burning.

He: What's this? Sounds as if, in our country, we make bulbs that don't work?

She: But it's night. They were turned off.

He: It could reflect on our bulbs. Delete it! If they aren't lit, what need is there to mention them?

She: *(reading on)* But suddenly a gory tongue of flame shot out of the fourth-floor window of a large grey house. "Help!" someone shouted, "we're on fire!"

He: What's that, panic?

She: Yes.

He: And it is your opinion that panic ought to be publicized in the columns of our periodicals?

She: No, of course not. But this is fiction...a creative work. I'm describing a fire.

He: And you portray a man who spreads panic instead of a civic-minded citizen? If I were you I'd replace that cry of "help" by some more rallying cry.

She: For instance?

He: For instance, say..."We don't give a damn! We shall put it out!" someone shouted. "Nothing to worry about, there's no fire."

She: What do you mean, "there's no fire" when there is a fire?

He: No, "there's no fire" in the sense of "we shall put it out, nothing to worry about."

She: It's impossible.

He: It's possible. And then, you could do away with the cry.

She: *(reads on)* This was the voice of the careless tenant who, when he went to bed, had forgotten to switch off the electric hot-plate.

He: The what tenant?

She: Careless.

He: Do you think that carelessness should be popularized in the columns of our periodicals? I shouldn't think so. And then why did you write that he forgot to switch off the electric hot-plate? Is that an appropriate example to set for the education of the readers?

She: I didn't intend to use it educationally, but without the hot-plate, there'd have been no fire.

He: And would we be much worse off?

She: No, better, of course.

He: Well then, that's how you should have written it. Away with the hot-plate and then you won't have to mention the fire. Go on, read, how does it go after that? Come straight to the portrayal of the fireman.

She: Fireman Prokhorchuk, a middle-aged Ukrainian...

He: That's nicely caught.

She: ...with large black mustachios, stopped in front of the door. The fireman stood there and thought.

He: Bad. A fireman mustn't think. He must put the fire out without thinking.

She: But it is a fine point in the story.

He: In a story it may be a fine point but not in a fireman. Then also, since we have no fire, there's no need to drag the fireman into the house.

She: But then, what about his dialogue with the fire chief?

He: Let them talk in the fire house. How does the dialogue go?

She: *(reads)* Fire Chief Gorbushin approached him. "Good boy, Prokhorchuk," he said, "you've acted according to regulations!" Whereupon the fire chief smiled and added: "You haven't noticed it, but your right mustachio is aflame." Prokhorchuk smiled and aimed a jet at his mustachio. It was dawning.

He: Why must you have that?

She: What?

He: The burning mustachio.

She: I put it in for the humor of the thing. The man was so absorbed in his work that he didn't notice that his mustache was ablaze.

He: Believe me, you should delete it. Since there's no fire, the house isn't burning and there's no need to burn any mustachios.

She: And what about the element of laughter?

He: There'll be laughter all right. When do people laugh? When things are good for them. And isn't it good that there's no fire? It's very good. And so everybody will laugh. Read what you have now.

She: *(reading)* "A Noble Deed." It was the dead of night—three o'clock. Some people slept while others kept a sharp lookout. From the fourth floor window of a large grey house somebody shouted: "We are not on fire!" "Good boy, Prokhorchuk!" said Fire Chief Gorbushin to fireman Prokhorchuk, a middle-aged Ukrainian with large black mustachios, "you're following the regulations." Prokhorchuk smiled and aimed a jet of water at his mustachio. It was dawning.

He: There we have a good piece of writing! Now it can be published!

9. Bukovsky: Dissenters and the KGB

Vladimir Bukovsky was an ardent human rights activist in the USSR, one of those who insisted that he be treated according to Soviet law and the Soviet Constitution. After a number of years in Soviet prisons and psychiatric hospitals, he emigrated to the United States and published a memoir. In this section of it, he recalls his questioning by a KGB agent, illustrating the dilemma these legal protesters cause for the Soviet regime. He describes the camaraderie that springs up between Soviet citizens even when they are on opposite sides of the fence. He also explains why it is that the regime resorts to psychiatric diagnoses and hospitalization for Soviet dissidents. Bukovsky speaks first in this conversation with his KGB investigator.

"...I am a citizen of the USSR."

"What opinions do you hold?"

"What does that have to do with my case? I hope you're not holding me in jail for my opinions?"

"Do you admit your guilt?"

"How can I answer that when I don't understand the charges? Tell me."

Under the law they were obliged to explain them to me....

To begin with, of course, they wouldn't give me any copies of the criminal codes. I received a visit from the Lefortovo Prison governor, Colonel Petrenko with his shaggy gray eyebrows sticking out from under a Caucasian fur cap. "It's not allowed."

All right. I wrote another sheaf of complaints and threatened a hunger strike. No more than two days went by before Colonel Petrenko put himself to the trouble of coming to see me again, saying almost tearfully: "We haven't got any codes, we've turned the whole library upside down. All I've got is my own copy, with a dedication from Semichastny. What do you want me to do — give you that?"

I took not only his presentation copy, autographed by the then chairman of the KGB, but also a copy of the Criminal Procedure Code, complete with commentaries, and a whole pile of assorted legal literature. The only thing they couldn't find was a copy of the Constitution. But I was adamant and on the fourth day, puffing and blowing, the deputy governor, Lieutenant Colonel Stepanov, came running in with one.

"Here you are, I've brought you the Constitution," he said in his comical provincial accent. "But it's for the Russian Republic, I couldn't find one for the USSR. Still, they're both the same. Bought it myself. Cost three Kopecks. Never mind, we'll settle up later."

Abridged from Vladimir Bukovsky, *To Build a Castle,* translated by Michael Scammell, New York, 1977.

Petrenko and I became the best of friends. He would come to my cell, make an effort to knit his shaggy brows into a stern frown beneath his fur cap, gaze thoughtfully at my empty shelves, and ask: "Why haven't you got any food?"

"I've eaten it all. It's all gone."

"When is your next parcel due?"

"Not for a while yet. In a month."

"Write an application. I'll allow you an extra one." And then he would leave.

He himself was a former investigator and now, reading my endless complaints, he could see clearly that the investigation had run up a blind alley. There was nothing to charge me with.

Meanwhile I was devouring the criminal codes as if they were detective novels, memorizing them like multiplication tables, and was discovering to my amazement how many rights I really had. And I started to make the fullest use of those rights.

Now I openly made fun of my investigators, deluged them with complaints, and forced them to write out my statements ten times in a row.

It was summer, the heat was killing, and my investigators sweated away, dreaming of shady woods. "Vladimir Konstantinovich! Surely that's enough? How many more times can it be copied?"

Around the middle of summer they came up against a total dead end and started a new investigation under Article 70.* But this time they began with caution and stealth, not telling me the new charges. What a hope! The law's the law. Tell me the charges and then ask your questions. Another stream of complaints from me: illegal investigation! Criminals! Put them on trial!...

Finally the case ground to a complete halt and there was nothing more to talk about. My investigator started calling me in just for the sake of it, for a chat. With all the squabbling going on, neither of us had noticed how friendly we had become, and now he found it boring if he let a day go by without arguing with me over something or other. He himself lived in the provinces, in Yaroslavl, and like all provincials was ashamed of how badly informed he was. "Well, tell me about one of your books. What about that book by Djilas that you were charged with in 1963?** What sort of a whatsit was it?"

"Do you mean to say they don't let you read them either? Don't they trust you either?"

"Not likely. All you get to read in my job is what you turn up in the searches. And back in Yaroslavl, there's nothing to find. Total darkness."

He listened with rapt attention, like people listening to a lecture in a planetarium: "Is there life on Mars?" I told him everything I could remember from the books I had read in *samizdat* — let him take it all back to his Yaroslavl

---

*The Article that forbids "agitation or propaganda carried on for the purpose of subverting or weakening the Soviet regime." Dissidents are often charged with its violation.

**Djilas, a Yugoslav, wrote *The New Class,* suggesting that there was a new privileged group in the USSR. It was banned in the USSR. Another book by Djilas is excerpted in Chapter Five.

and tell his friends. They were human beings, after all, and dying to hear something new.

In some ways he quite appealed to me—tall, with a broad forehead and a frank, open face. He didn't care for our case or the role he had been assigned to play in it. Our farewell was even touching....

It was a matter of fact that most of the participants in the movement, with their precisely formulated civil-rights position and refusal to accept Soviet reality, were peculiarly vulnerable to psychiatric repression. I could easily imagine Lunts* rubbing his hands and croaking: "Tell me, why won't you acknowledge your guilt?"

And all the legal formulations and references to articles in the Code, constitutional freedoms, and the absence of intent, that is, the entire arsenal of the citizen's rights position, devastating as it was to the investigation, would backfire on you, for it offered an irrefutable syndrome:

You don't acknowledge your guilt? Therefore you don't understand the criminal nature of your actions, therefore you cannot answer for them.

You keep talking about the Constitution and the laws, but what normal man takes Soviet laws seriously? You are living in an unreal world of your own invention, you react inadequately to the world around you.

Do you put the blame for your conflict with society on society? What do you mean, the whole of society is wrong? A typical madman's logic.

You had no intent? That means that you are incapable of understanding the consequences of your actions. You didn't even understand that you were certain to be arrested.

"Very well," croaks Lunts. "If you consider yourself to be in the right, why do you refuse to give evidence during the investigation?"

And again you haven't a leg to stand on—your morbid suspicion and distrustfulness are too plain.

"Why have you been doing all these things? What were you hoping to achieve?" None of us expected any practical results—that wasn't the aim of our actions—but from the point of view of common sense, such behavior was pure madness.

As before, this procedure worked very well with the Marxists—they had an obvious reforming mania, an overvalued idea of saving mankind. With the believers it was even simpler, as it had always been, and with the poets—a clear case of schizophrenia.

The theoretical "scientific" base had long since been prepared. In the conditions of socialism, according to the assertions of the country's leading psychiatrists, there were no social causes of criminality; therefore, any antilegal act was *ipso facto* a mental aberration. Under socialism there is no contradiction between society's goals and man's conscience. Existence determines consciousness, hence there is no such thing as a nonsocialist consciousness.

*Chief of Department Four, the political department, at Serbsky Institute of Forensic Psychiatry.

But the psychiatric method had now been worked out in much greater detail. First of all in the form of that old, tried and true diagnosis: *paranoidal development of the personality.* (The following quotations are from Professors Pechernikov and Kosachev of the Serbsky Institute.)

"Most frequently, ideas about a 'struggle for truth and justice' are formed by personalities with a paranoid structure."

"Litigiously paranoid states come into being as a result of psychologically traumatic circumstances affecting the subject's interests and are stamped by feelings that the individual's legal rights have been infringed."

"A characteristic feature of overvalued ideas is the patient's conviction of his own rectitude, an obsession with asserting his 'trampled' rights, and the significance of these feelings for the patient's personality. They tend to exploit judicial proceedings as a platform for making speeches and appeals."

And, of course, complaints about persecution by the KGB, being searched and followed, telephone tapping, the opening of letters, and dismissal from work were pure persecution manias. The more open and public your position, the more obvious your insanity....

There was one more incident that attracted attention to psychiatric repressions, and that was the forcible hospitalization of the well-known scientist Zhores Medvedev.* The Soviet academic world was up in arms—the repressions had reached their very doorstep. The most prominent scientists in the Soviet Union led the campaign for his release.

It was all right for Zhores Medvedev, he was well-enough known in the scientific world. But what could be done for the workman Borisov, the bricklayer Gershuni, the students Novodvorskaya and Iofe, or the stage designer Victor Kuznetsov? For them there was no prospect of academicians raising hell with the Central Committee or the world community of scientists threatening a scientific boycott. According to our information, there were hundreds of little-known individuals being held in psychiatric prisons for political reasons. Who would take up the struggle on their behalf?...

---

*Zhores Medvedev, a prominent Soviet biologist and twin brother of the historian Roy Medvedev, was forcibly committed to a mental hospital in June 1970. As the result of a worldwide campaign of protest he was released after nineteen days. He now lives in England.

10. The Joke: Social Commentary Soviet-Style

Vladimir Bukovsky, author of an autobiographical journey through the Gulag Archipelago, To Build a Castle *(New York: Viking Press, 1977) and an incisive commentator on the Soviet world, has suggested that someone ought to put up a monument to the political joke. It is a form of creative expression that is particularly enjoyed in the Soviet Union where people lack a free press. These jokes often express people's opinion of events and are told and retold, embroidered, refurbished and brought out for new occasions. What follows is just a small sampling of the thousands of jokes told throughout the Soviet Union.*

Stalin Jokes

A Party activist was making his periodic check-up on the farms in his district. He stopped a peasant in his field, and asked about the potato crop. "There has never been a crop to equal this, thanks to the glorious plan of our leaders," the peasant answered. "If we were to place all our potatoes in a pile, they would stretch to the very feet of God." The activist became angry: "You know there is no God." "Ah," said the peasant, "But there are no potatoes either."

Some time ago, an American and a Russian were discussing the merits of their leaders. The Americans said that Herbert Hoover was a greater man than Stalin, because he put into effect Prohibition, and taught the Americans not to drink. "That's nothing," replied the boastful Russian, "Stalin taught us not to eat."

Khrushchev Jokes

Khrushchev often talked of the fact that the USSR would soon catch up and surpass the United States. The following story was told: A Moscow class was studying the United States and the teacher asked a student: "Iurii, what is the United States like?" Iurii replied, as he had been taught: "the United States is a capitalist country which has millions of people unemployed and starving." And now, continued the teacher, "What is the goal of the Soviet Union?" Iurii answered, "to catch up with the United States."

Khrushchev also spoke of the fact that soon the Soviet people would enter the era of true socialism: Two Soviet citizens were talking about how near they were to socialism. One observed, "The Party told me that socialism is on the horizon. I wasn't sure what the word "horizon" meant, so I looked it up in the dictionary. I now see what they meant. The horizon is an imaginary line which moves further away from you as you approach it."

Retold by Janet Vaillant

From the Brezhnev Era

After the successful Apollo-Soyuz joint Soviet-American space flight, Brezhnev called in the cosmonauts to congratulate them. Then he continued: "The Americans are winning the space race. We must accomplish something to surpass them. They have landed someone on the moon, so we in the Politburo have decided to send you to land on the sun." The cosmonauts let out a groan, "But Comrade Brezhnev, we'll be burned alive!" "Fools, do you think we haven't thought of that problem? Don't worry. We've planned it so that you can complete your landing at night."

A Short Course in Soviet History

Lenin, Stalin, Khrushchev and Brezhnev found themselves together on a train speeding across Siberia. It abruptly stopped. Lenin said, "don't worry," and stepped out to talk with the engineers, raised the consciousness of the driver, and the train began to move forward again. Unfortunately it soon stopped again. This time, Stalin stepped forward, went up to the driver, and shot him. Once again, the train began to move slowly forward. But once again it stopped. It was Khrushchev's turn. He went up to the engine, talked the situation over with the men in it, and came up with a solution: everyone was to get out of the train, pull up the track over which they had passed, and lay new track ahead of the train so that it would be able to go forward. Alas, this proved only a "harebrained scheme" and temporary solution, for the train halted once more. Comrade Brezhnev talked the situation over with his advisors, and hit on a final solution: he ordered that the shades be pulled down in the railroad car in which they were riding, and that everyone pretend that the train was still moving forward.

Jokes That Continue To Be Told Today

It is well-known that workers often steal material from the factories where they work. Every day a Russian worker left his factory pushing a wheelbarrow full of straw. Every day, the guard halted him and searched carefully through the straw, but he found nothing. After several months of this, the guard said to the worker, "I am being transferred far away from here, so you can talk freely to me now. What have you been stealing?" "Wheelbarrows," confessed the worker.

A man walking down a Moscow street spat on the curb. A voice behind him whispered, "Please, this is no place to talk politics."

On election day, a group of workers were escorted to the polls by a Party activist, handed an envelope, and told to put it into the ballot box. One worker was curious so he opened his envelope to see what was inside. "What are you doing?" called out the Activist. "I'd just like to find out for whom I'm voting," answered the worker. "You fool—don't you know that this is a secret ballot?"

Two old friends were talking on a Moscow street. "Tell me Ivan, you are a wise man, do you think that there will be a war?" "Certainly not," replied his friend Sergei, "but there will be such a struggle for peace that not a stone will be left standing."

In the year 2001, a boy asks his grandfather: "Grandfather, what does the word 'queue' mean?" "Well, my boy, back in 1975 there wasn't enough meat for everyone, so people had to wait in queues, one behind the other, to buy a piece of meat. Does that explain it to you?" "Yes," replied the boy, "But what does the word 'meat' mean?"

A husband came home and found his wife in the arms of another man. He was understandably furious. "You wretch," he shouted, "This is how you spend your afternoon, when all the good wives are out at the corner store standing in line to get the lemons which have just come in."

What is the tallest building in Moscow? The Lubianka (KGB building). From there, you can see Magadan, Siberia.

11. Young People: Articles from the Soviet Press

The Soviets go to great lengths to discourage Western influences, especially among young people. Nonetheless, young people in Moscow and smaller cities as well, are fascinated by Western music, covet Western jeans, and even like to intersperse English words in their conversation. This is the subject of the following two articles that appeared recently in the Soviet press. Note the moralizing tone and style of Soviet journalese.

IS SLANG REALLY SO INNOCUOUS?

...Slang words don't hurt a language so long as they are only sprinkled through it and are merely elements of stylistic diversity or a means of making a joke or creating irony. But when a secondary- or high-school student's language is totally crammed with slang words, when a young person virtually loses the ability to express his or her thoughts in any other fashion, the situation becomes very depressing indeed....

There is one aspect of the current young people's slang that gives cause for particular concern and worry.

Abridged from M. Gorbanevsky, "Is Slang Really So Innocuous" *Komsomolskaya Pravda,* November, 1981. *Current Digest of the Soviet Press,* Vol. 33, No. 47.

That is the English-language slang of secondary- and higher-school students. . . .Sometimes it seems that some of the young people talking among themselves are strangers from some distant planet and are speaking an unintelligible language. But they are even more like strangers from the hinterlands of some sort of Michigan, Texas or California with their endless strings of distorted English words like *leibl* (label) and *batton* (button), *voch* (watch) and *beg* (bag), *fazer* (father) and *seishn* (session). . .*flex* (flat) and *stripovy* (striped), *spikat* (speak) and *ringanut* (ring up). . .

All this "richness" is to be found in the speech of high-school students and upper-grade pupils, mainly those from large cities and certain social strata. . . .

Obviously, in time many of the young people will undergo a reevaluation of their values and will realize the vulgarity of the "Americanized" words and other kinds of slang that appeal to them now. But how long will it be before this reevaluation takes place? In the meantime they may lose their sense of the beauty, richness, picturesqueness and melodiousness of their native language, and their speech may become totally impoverished.

Proper mastery of the Russian language, knowledge of all its riches and treasures, and a protective attitude toward the language—all of this is linked in the directest fashion to the concept of patriotism. . . .

Therefore, I would like to ask: Is English-language slang really so innocuous? . . .

To combat [slang], a specific set of efficacious measures is needed. In all likelihood these should include: improvement of Russian language instruction in the upper grades of secondary school (this problem has long been urgent), the introduction of instruction in Russian language style and the grammatical accuracy of speech in the ninth and tenth grades, specific explanatory work with the teachers and instructors trained to give such instruction, the publication of popular literature in mass editions (although a good deal has already been done here) and active distribution of it through Young Communist League committees in secondary and higher schools, and more effective participation in the effort to improve the language standards of radio and television. . . .

WHO IS YOUR IDOL?

Leningrad—. . .A 10th-year student came up to me one day after a lecture and, literally puffed up with pride, said that he knew the names of 160 foreign musical groups by heart. . . .[But] to my surprise, it turned out that this "connoisseur" of pop music had not heard the songs of Dean Reed, Pete Seeger and other artists that are popular among the world's progressive youth and was totally unfamiliar with John Lennon's song: "Give Peace a Chance," Paul

Abridged from V. Lisovsky, "Who Is Your Idol?" *Izvestia,* January 1982, *Current Digest of the Soviet Press,* Vol. 34, No. 3.

McCartney's "Give Ireland Back to the Irish" and Ringo Starr's "Silent Homecoming." But the budding scholar had heard more than enough about the scandals and drunken adventures of his idols....

Some young people, especially if nature has not endowed them with a musical ear, are readily convinced (taking their cue from someone else, of course) that "if it's Western music, it must be good." But after all, groups in the West also differ. Even in the West, normal people have long since recoiled from the racket created by certain pop groups....

For a total of 200 hours a day, 37 foreign radio stations send hostile broadcasts to the Soviet Union. The broadcasts that are aimed at young people in socialist countries have a special "sound." However, stories about the accomplishments of groups and artists are always supplemented with doses of anti-Sovietism and advertise the advantages of the "Western way of life." They are gambling on the mindless credulity and political naivete of some of our young people. Ideological opponents will resort to anything to exert a corrupting influence on the minds of Soviet people, especially young men and women. They lure them with half-truths and hard-to-verify myths. They use suggestive repetition of information, utilize the "bandwagon" effect, lavish false praise, juggle ideas and advertise vulgar happiness. Sports, fashion and the latest music serve as the background for this ideological influence. In order to lend the reported information a "scientific basis," it is often presented as the result of various types of pseudosociological studies....

Ideological subversion against socialism calls for the active foisting of reactionary ideas on people, for the purpose of arousing discontent and distrust in communist ideals and instilling a consumer ideology. That's why it's important to make every young person understand that the unthinking "hit" is terribly tasteless, and that talented performers are often used to divert young people in the West from serious social problems....

WOMEN'S SKI-TEAM COACH JAILED FOR SMUGGLING JEANS

Customs officials at Moscow's Sheremetyevo Airport noticed that the returning Alpine ski team's equipment included eight cardboard boxes without any name tags or identifying marks. At first Gera Sergeyevich Abramishvili, trainer of the combined women's team, claimed that the boxes contained cargo to be delivered to the USSR State Committee for Physical Culture and Sports. Upon opening them, however, customs officials found 50 pairs of denim blue jeans, 160 pairs of blue velour trousers, several pairs of children's trousers and 470 grams of mohair yarn, worth a total of 14,262 rubles and 60 kopeks.

The Volgograd Borough People's Court sentenced G.S. Abramishvili to six years' deprivation of freedom, with confiscation of all his property.

From V. Verstova, "Women's Ski Coach Jailed for Smuggling Jeans," *Sovetskaya Rossia,* May, 1983. *Current Digest of the Soviet Press,* Vol. 35, No. 25.

12. Ex-Soldier Sentenced to Death as CIA Spy

This Soviet newspaper account of a Soviet citizen recruited to spy for the CIA illustrates the connections made by Soviet officialdom between life style and bad deeds. It also provides an example of model behavior by a loyal Soviet mother, and the way in which the Soviets like to keep their people aware of the persistence and ubiquitousness of the CIA. The exhibition referred to is one of the official industrial exhibitions mounted by the US in the USSR, with young American Russian-speaking guides. They are often very popular with Soviet citizens.

No matter what tricks our enemies use, their path is everywhere reliably blocked by the Soviet Chekists—counterintelligence agents who vigilantly guard the security of the socialist homeland....

There are a good many examples of this. Here is one, involving the exposure of the American spy Kalinin.

This happened recently. Kalinin unexpectedly came within the purview of the American intelligence service.

A tall, sullen young man with shifty eyes was wandering around an American exhibition in Moscow. Now and then he looked around warily. Seizing a moment when no other visitors were nearby, Kalinin quickly went up to an American guide and said:

"I'm interested in life in the States. Have you got something I could read on this subject? It would be better if it were in Russian. I'd appreciate it as a gift."

"Don't talk so loud," the American warned. "I can give you some books and magazines, but not until tomorrow."

"That won't do," Kalinin replied. "I'm just passing through Moscow after being discharged from the Army. Tomorrow morning I'll be home in Leningrad."

Hearing the word "discharged" and measuring Kalinin with a glance, the guide said:

"This evening then, perhaps, but not here—in the city."

The meeting took place at the appointed time. The guide brought along two American Embassy staff members. They invited Kalinin to ride along to their "Moscow home" for the literature about America.

After driving Kalinin all over the city in an Embassy car, the Americans took him to the US Embassy building. For a reception? No, for processing as a spy.

This task was begun at once by Embassy staff members—or, more precisely, CIA staff members disguised as diplomats. The young man proved to be

Abridged from M. Stepichev, "Caught Red-Handed: The CIA in the Service of the Enemies of Detente and Peace," *Pravda,* March, 1983, *Current Digest of the Soviet Press,* Vol. 34, No. 1.

talkative and pliable. Little by little, he began to tell what he knew about military units and their location and about combat equipment and to give the addresses of colleagues and the names of commanding officers.

A morally unstable person who felt that he had been bypassed for promotion while in the service, Kalinin began to utter various fabrications about our reality. His personal injuries and failures had shut his eyes to life around him.

The experienced intelligence officers sensed this. They began to pay much closer attention to Kalinin.

"You're one of us, young man," said an American, slapping him on the shoulder. "In time, you'll be rich. All you have to do is carry out a few assignments—and we'll open a bank account for you in the US."

This was the beginning of Kalinin's criminal path. He was instructed to gather classified information about Leningrad enterprises. He was given money and a souvenir—a ballpoint pen autographed by the US President. However, the Americans didn't part with him at this point. Kalinin remained in the Embassy building. "Diplomats" trained him in cryptography, the use of communications devices and the transmission of materials....

Late the following night, Kalinin was secretly driven in a diplomatic car, hidden under a rug, from the Embassy building to the Smolensk subway station. That same night he left for Leningrad, where he soon got a job at a defense industry enterprise and began to gather information that the CIA agents demanded he procure.

All this became known later, during the investigation of Kalinin's case. For the time being, the Chekists had only scattered facts and their suspicions. It had not escaped their attention that a visitor at the American exhibition had persistently tried to establish contact with foreigners. The KGB [State Security Committee] had also noticed an American guide talking with a tall, sullen young man with shifty eyes. And then the question arose: What made this fellow hang around the exhibition for three days? Was it only curiosity?

This was the beginning of an operation, one of many that do credit to staff members of the state security agencies.

With the help of exhibition personnel, a rough portrait of this man was reconstructed. It later became known that the visitor had been in the capital for just a few days. Then, as if on a radar screen, the threads crossed at the place where Kalinin had stayed while in Moscow, after which his tracks led to the banks of the Neva [Leningrad, where his mother lived].

After her son [Kalinin] returned from the Army, Vera Aleksandrovna literally had not one moment of peace. For three months Vladimir worked nowhere, had himself a good time, and listened to foreign radio stations. Several times his mother indignantly told him that the Western radio voices told lies and pleaded with him to get those foolish ideas out of his head, but the son did as he pleased, praising the Western way of life....

Relatives and acquaintances supported the mother and upbraided Kalinin, but he, acting nervously and rudely, told them to be quiet. Kalinin took the slanderous, poisonous broadcasts of the foreign stations Radio Liberty, Voice of America and Deutsche Welle at face value.

Once Kalinin received a letter from Moscow. He was out of the city at the time. Reading the letter, his mother was amazed: The address was written in her son's hand, but the letter itself was in someone else's handwriting. How could that be? The text was strange, too. "Do Ninochka's teeth still bother her? Are you going to Nevsky Prospect?" Vera Aleksandrovna sensed that something wasn't quite right about all this.

Soon Kalinin received another strange letter. In the morning, the Mother saw her son ironing his trousers. Then he put them aside and began ironing the letter. Why? The mother's heart sank; she sensed that something was wrong with her son. After Valdimir had left the house, his mother looked at the coded letter.

"My son has gotten into some kind of dirty business," Vera Aleksandrovna decided. Having copied this letter, which she didn't understand but whose text alarmed her, she invited her friend Nadezhda Petrovna to come over.

"Nadyusha, look what Volodka just received."

The mother was ill at the time, so it was decided that Nadezhda Petrovna would go to the state security agencies, tell them everything and ask what to do next. The security officials listened carefully to Nadezhda Petrovna and thanked her.

At this point, the Chekists already knew something about Kalinin that his mother didn't yet know.

Vera Aleksandrovna's health grew worse, and in a few days she was taken to the hospital. At that time, Kalinin, having obtained by deceit a short-term leave of absence from the enterprise where he worked, told everyone he was going to Gatchina but instead took a plane to Moscow to pick up an espionage container that had been secreted for him by CIA intelligence agents.

In the evening Kalinin, after walking past the telephone booths near the Belorussian Railway Terminal several times, at 11:05 p.m. took a magnetic container from the cache. Then he tried to get away, but he was detained by operational personnel. The container was found to hold code pads, carbon paper for use in coding messages, and covering letters designed for mailing espionage reports to dummy addresses abroad....

Exposed by incontrovertible evidence of the crimes he had committed, he was forced to describe his espionage work and ties with CIA representatives. He fully admitted that he was guilty of the gravest crime against the homeland— espionage.

There was a mountain of evidence against him: CIA intelligence instructions, code pads, cryptography devices, information prepared for transmission to the American intelligence service, packets of money, passes and blank forms he had stolen at the enterprise.

The investigators could see, as on a screen, the whole insipid and spiritually bankrupt life of a person who had sold the holy of holies—his people.

At the same time, the investigation showed that, whatever mask the enemy may hide under, he will inevitably be uncovered and disarmed. Soviet people know this, and our foes sense it....

The USSR Supreme Court's Military Collegium sentenced V. Kalinin to the supreme penalty—death by shooting....

13. A Soviet View of U.S. Policy

Academician G. Arbatov, the author of this official assessment of U.S. policy, is the leading Soviet expert on the United States. Pravda *(the word means truth in Russian), is the daily newspaper of the Communist Party. The article was published in March, 1983. The tone and substance of this article illustrates the kind of information available to the Soviet public. It can be compared with George Kennan's account in Reading 14.*

The fact that the Reagan Administration has reached the midpoint of its term in office with poor results is, generally speaking, disputed by no one except the President himself and his entourage....

[After detailing the ways in which President Reagan's domestic policy has failed, Arbatov turns to foreign affairs.]

For, whatever US interests we take—economic, domestic-policy, military, foreign-policy, even Reagan's electoral interests—everywhere common sense requires the normalization of the international situation and an end to the arms race. But, alas, many people have long suspected that common sense is now the least of the factors by which American foreign policy is guided. Apart from certain political shifts in the country—quite a bit has been written about them— this seems, to some extent, to be linked to the present administration's unique style and way of thinking and acting.

For example, a good deal has been written about the provincialism of many of the people on the Reagan "team." This is true—not, of course, in the sense that they lack a capital-city gloss, but the fact is that these people have very often lived, built their careers and worked in isolation from the main problems of the country and of the world as a whole, away from the main roads of history and politics. The nature of Washington policy can't help but be affected by how poorly informed, and sometimes downright thickheaded, many of those who are currently making this policy are. Don't forget how some nominees for high posts couldn't answer the most elementary questions when they were before Congress for confirmation. And remember the embarrassing situations that have occurred at press conferences held by prominent Washington officials and in their conversations with foreign leaders.

Abridged from G. Arbatov, "The United States: Will There Be Changes?" *Pravda,* March, 1983, *Current Digest of the Soviet Press,* Vol. 35, No. 11.

Much has also been written about the fact that in and around the US government there are now grouped (as advisers) an unusual number of "specialists" in strategy and military policy who hold such extreme views that many of them have in fact been deemed in need of medical assistance.

If to this one adds the administration's political extremism, many of the sources of the present US leaders' striking isolation from reality, which has distinguished their policy so far, will become understandable. This policy is based on distorted ideas about the world and its problems, about countries and about America itself....

In the first place, as politicians many of these people are pure products of propaganda, and very second-rate propaganda at that. Their current prophets, ... are fanatical anticommunists, loudmouths who aren't capable of understanding the complexity of today's world. And sometimes the American leaders derive their wisdom from even more out-of-the-way "thinkers."

In his first major foreign-policy speech, in May 1981, President Reagan told the cadets at the West Point Military Academy that the nation should put its faith not in parchment and paper (i.e., in treaties and agreements) but in weapons. In this connection, he referred to the books "The Treaty Trap" and "Survival and Peace in the Nuclear Age," by one Laurence Beilenson. Journalists rushed out to hunt up this new political prophet. He turned out to be an 82-year-old retired lawyer, a bosom buddy of Reagan's from the time when (even before the ill-famed Senator J. McCarthy emerged on the political stage) both of them had harassed the "Reds" in Hollywood. When Beilenson was located by journalists, this hale and hearty old man told them that nuclear war is inevitable, that "we must overthrow all Communist governments" and that all those who are prepared to fight the Communists should be "openly" offered money ("I call it 'foreign aid for freedom,' you call it subversion — it's all the same")....

Having been molded politically and spiritually by such odious propaganda, many people who are now in the top echelons of power in America perceive the world, emerging problems and events and politics itself in purely propagandistic concepts. I have in mind not only the blind and absolutely implacable hatred of the Soviet Union that a number of American leaders have, and not only the extremely noisy and mendacious propaganda campaigns that they are constantly launching.

I'm also talking about the fact that events displeasing to the US rulers are quite often perceived as the results of someone's malicious propaganda. And the response to these events naturally, comes in the form of another propaganda campaign.

An example of this approach is Washington's appraisal of the antiwar movement in Europe (and then in the US, too) as the result of Moscow's propaganda intrigues. An effort was promptly launched to expose these propaganda "intrigues." When it became clear that this wouldn't help, Washington agreed to arms limitation talks. But attempts were made to reduce these talks to propaganda, too. If anyone had any doubts on this score, they were dispelled by

Reagan's nominee for the post of Director of the Arms Control and Disarmament Agency, K. Adelman, who candidly said: "The arms limitation talks are just a trick, one we simply had to use in order to calm the American people and our European allies."

Should it come as any surprise that the US proposals at the arms limitation talks are designed to produce an impression on an unsophisticated public (just look at the words they use—"'zero option,'" the acronym START for the strategic arms talks, the name Corpus Christi for a new nuclear submarine, Peacekeeper for a nuclear missile) and, at the same time, be obviously unacceptable to the Soviet Union)...

Since our striving for detente, lasting peace and disarmament remains unchanging, we will be reliable partners in any honest talks and agreements that have these aims in view. But we know very well that peace accords are not achieved by begging and that one has to wage a stubborn and skillful struggle for them, because aggressive circles will not abandon their plans unless they encounter a resolute—very resolute—rebuff.

The fits of anti-Soviet hysteria that follow one after another also prevent us from believing that the policy of Washington's current rulers may change for the better. Frenzied calls are being made for crusades, statements that smack not only of the cold war but sometimes of outright medievalism. And all this is covered up by hypocritical talk about faith and God, about morality, eternal good and eternal evil.

As time goes on, it's becoming clearer that the US administration not only constantly starts confrontations, but, because of its isolation from the realities of the world, starts them in places that are very inconvenient and very disadvantageous for it. Who can seriously see it as the foremost defender of democracy, civil liberties and trade union rights when both the past and the present of many people now in Washington completely refute this?...

A great deal is changing now in the world, and in America. People can't continue living under the growing threat of universal death, and they don't want to . Therefore, they are questioning not individual postulates of the US's peace-endangering nuclear policy and strategy but its very foundations. They want not words but deeds, concrete deeds capable of removing the threat of a catastrophe that is hanging over the world.

14. An American View of Soviet Policy

George F. Kennan, scholar, diplomat and former ambassador to the Soviet Union, is one of America's leading experts on the U.S.S.R. (His great uncle, also George Kennan, is the author of Reading 13, Chapter Three.) Kennan believes that Americans tend to exaggerate and oversimplify when thinking and talking about the Soviet Union. He urges a more reasoned approach, based on serious study of Soviet society.

"Take but degree away, untune that string
And, hark! what discord follows...."

Troilus and Cressida

These deeply perceptive words by Shakespeare have their relevance to a sizable section of United States opinion, official and private, on the Soviet Union.

It is not that there is no truth in many of the things that people say and believe about the Russians; it is rather that what they say and believe involves a great deal of exaggeration and oversimplification. And this is serious, because there are times when exaggeration and oversimplification, being harder than falsehood to spot, can be fully as pernicious.

We are told that the official Soviet outlook is one of total cynicism and power-hungry opportunism. Is this view wrong? Not entirely. But it is over-drawn. The way in which the outlooks of the present Soviet leaders, tempered as these outlooks are by the discipline of long political experience and respon-sibility, relate to the sanguine ruthlessness of the pure Leninist doctrine as conceived some sixty years ago in the heat of the revolutionary struggle is complicated. There is traditional lip service to established doctrine; there is also considerable inner detachment.

The Soviet leadership, we are told, is fanatically devoted to the early achievement of world revolution. Is this allegation wrong? Partly, and it is cer-tainly misleading. It ignores the distinction between what Soviet Communists think would be ideally desirable and what they see as necessary or possible to try to achieve at the present moment. It also ignores the distinction between what they claim they believe will ultimately occur and what they actually intend to bring about by their own actions.

We hear much about the menacing scale of Soviet military programs and the resulting tilting of the arms balance in our disfavor. Wrong? Again, not entirely, but often exaggerated. Part of this view rests on "worst-case" calcula-tions, particularly regarding conventional armaments. Often, it ignores our own contribution to the adversely developing balance—by our unrestrained inflation and by the various unnecessary deficiencies of our conventional forces. Much

From the Op. Ed article, *New York Times,* February 18, 1981.

of it is corrupted by the fundamental error of measuring armaments, weapon for weapon, against another country's armaments instead of against one's own needs, as though the needs of any two great countries were identical and any statistical disparity between their arsenals was a mark of somebody's superiority or inferiority.

We hear of the menace of Soviet expansionism or "adventures" in the Third World. Is this all wrong? No, not all. The Soviet presence in Cuba, in which we should never have tacitly acquiesced in the first place, is not indefinitely compatible with our vital interests. Soviet collaboration with, and support for, Colonel Muammar el-Qaddafi, the Libyan leader, is a signal disservice to the stability of the Near East. The occupation of Afghanistan has created serious international complications. Yet in general, such Soviet efforts have not been very successful. The Soviet Union's position in the Third World is actually weaker than it was years ago, before the disruption of Moscow's relationships with Peking, Cairo, and Jakarta. And the methods by which Moscow recently has been trying to gain influence in the Third World, primarily the dispatch of arms and military advisers, resemble too closely our own for us to indulge gracefully in transports of moral indignation.

It is alleged that the Soviet leaders never respect international agreements. Right? Mainly not. Their record in the fulfillment of clear and specific written obligations, especially those that avoid questions of motivation and simply state precisely what each side will do and when, has not been bad at all. Vague assurances of high-minded general purpose, on the other hand, such as those embedded in the Helsinki agreements, are viewed by them with the same cynicism they attribute to the other party who signs such documents.

It is asserted that no useful collaboration with the Soviet Union is possible. True? Not really. There is indeed an extensive area within which what we would consider normal and intimate relations are not possible, their being precluded by Soviet ideological commitments, procedural habits, and other oddities, not to mention a few of our own. But there is another area, admittedly limited, involving certain forms of travel, trade, scholarly exchange, and collaboration in cultural and other nonpolitical fields, where things are different. And it is important that this area not be neglected, for interaction of this sort, in addition to increasing our knowledge and understanding of Soviet society, serves as an indispensable cushion, absorbing some of the shock of the misunderstandings and conflicts that may occur in other fields.

In a relationship of such immense importance as the Soviet-American one, there should be no room for such extremisms and oversimplifications. Not only do they produce their counterparts on the other side, but they confuse us. They cause us to see as totally unsolvable a problem that is only partly so.

Soviet society is made up of human beings like ourselves. Because it is human, it is complex. It is not, as many of the oversimplifications would suggest, a static, unchanging phenomenon. It too evolves, and the direction in which it evolves is influenced to some degree by our vision of it and our treatment of it.

What is needed on our part is not an effort to prove our own virtue by dramatizing Soviet iniquities, but rather a serious effort to study Soviet society in all its complexity and to form realistic, sophisticated judgments about the nature and dimensions of the problem it presents for us. If we do this, there is no reason to suppose that the conflicts of interest that divide these two great countries, so different in geography, in history, and in tradition, should lead to the sort of disastrous climax that modern weapons, most tragically, now make possible.

ACKNOWLEDGMENTS

The authors, publishers, museums, libraries and photographers who supplied the readings and illustrations are thanked for their cooperation and are listed below. If in any case the acknowledgment proves to be inadequate, the authors apologize. In no case is such inadequacy intentional, and if any owner of copyright who has remained untraced will communicate with the publishers, the required acknowledgment will be made in future editions of the book.

"Impressions of a Modern Visitor" abridged from *Russians as People,* ©1960 by Wright Miller. Reprinted by permission of the publisher, E.P. Dutton, Inc.

"Life in the New Siberia" reprinted from *The Siberians* by Farley Mowat, ©1970 by Farley Mowat, Limited. By permission of Little, Brown and Company in association with the Atlantic Monthly Press.

"Life in Novgorod," "The Lay of Igor's Campaign," "The Sack of Riazan," and "The Time of Troubles" abridged from *Medieval Russia's Epics, Chronicles and Tales,* ©1963 by Serge A. Zenkovsky. Reprinted by permission of the publisher, E.P. Dutton, Inc.

"The Tsar and His Powers" reprinted from *The Travels of Olearius in Seventeenth Century Russia,* translated and edited by Samuel H. Baron, with the permission of the publishers, Stanford University Press, ©1967 by the Board of Trustees of the Leland Stanford Junior University.

"The Maiden Tsar" reprinted from *Russian Fairy Tales* by Alexander Afanas'ev, translated by Norbert Guterman. ©1945 by Pantheon Books, Inc. and renewed 1975 by Random House, Inc. Reprinted by permission of Pantheon Books, a Division of Random House, Inc.

"Seventeenth Century Moscow" and "The Building of St. Petersburg" reprinted by permission of Faber and Faber Ltd. from *Palmyra of the North: The First Days of St. Petersburg* by Christopher Marsden.

"Nikolai Gogol: Nevsky Avenue" excerpted from "The Overcoat" from *Tales of Good and Evil* by Nikolai Gogol. Translation ©1956 by David Magarshack. Reprinted by permission of Doubleday and Company, Inc.

"Alexander Herzen: Thoughts on the Peasant Community" reprinted from *Mind of Modern Russia: Historical and Political Thought of Russia's Great Age,* edited by Hans Kohn. ©1955 by the Trustees of Rutgers College in New Jersey. Copyright renewed 1983.

"Ivan Turgenev: The Nihilist" reprinted from *Fathers and Sons* by Ivan Turgenev, translated by Barbara Makanowitsky. ©1959 by Bantam Books, Inc. By permission of Bantam Books, Inc., all rights reserved.

"Sergei Witte: A Proposal for Russia's Industrialization" reprinted from "A Secret Memorandum of Sergei Witte on the Industrialization of Imperial Russia" in *Journal of Modern History,* Vol. 26, March, 1954. ©1954 by The University of Chicago Press.

"The Potemkin Mutiny" reprinted from *The Potemkin Mutiny* by Richard Hough. ©1960 by Richard Hough. Reprinted by permission of Pantheon Books, a Division of Random House, Inc.

Additional acknowledgments are as follows:

Lloyd Berry and Robert Crummey, editors, *Rude and Barbarous Kingdom,* ©1968, The University of Wisconsin Press; Lubomyr Hajda, "Ethnic Groups According to 1979 Census," ©1981 by Lubomyr Hajda; Samuel Cross, translator, "The Primary Chronicle," *Harvard Studies in Philology and Literature,* Vol. XII, ©1930 by the President and Fellows of Harvard College, reprinted by permission of the Harvard University Press; Edward L. Keenan, "Russian Political Culture," ©1975 by Edward L. Keenan; Peter Putnam, editor, *Seven Britons in Imperial Russia, 1698-1812,* ©1952, ©renewed 1980 by Princeton University Press, excerpt pages 38-9 reprinted by permission of Princeton University Press; Walter Arndt, translator, *Alexander Pushkin: Collected Narrative and Lyrical Poetry,* ©1984 by Ardis Publishers; Phillip Longworth, *The Three Empresses,* ©1972 by Constable & Co., Ltd,; Nicolas Berdyaev, *The Origin of Russian Communism,* ©1960, University of Michigan Press; G. Vernadsky, *et al,* translators, *A Source Book For Russian History, Vol. 3,* ©1972, Yale University Press; Henri Troyat, *La Vie Quotidienne en Russie au Temps du Dernier Tsar (Daily Life in Russia Under the Last Tsar),* ©1959, 1961 by Hachette; "Circular of the Petrograd Military-Revolutionary Committee" from the book *The Russian Revolution,* edited by Robert V. Daniels, ©1972 by Prentice-Hall, Inc., by permission of the author; From *Witnesses to the Russian Revolution,* by R. Pethybridge. ©1967. Published by Citadel Press, a division of Lyle Stuart, Inc.; From *Fragments from My Diary* by M. Gorky, New York: Praeger Publishers, 1972, reprinted by permission; John Reed, *Ten Days That Shook the World,* ©1966, Penguin Books; Alexander Blok, *The Twelve and Other Poems,* translated by John Stallworthy and Peter France, ©1970 by Methuen and Co.; J. Bunyan, *Intervention, Civil War and Communism in Russia, 1918,* ©1936 by The Johns Hopkins University Press; Anna Haines, "Famine in Russia," 1922, by permission of the American Friends Service Committee; N. Tumarkin, *Lenin Lives!,* ©1983, Harvard University Press; Basil Dmytryshyn, from *USSR: A Concise History,* ©1965, 1971, 1978 Charles Scribner's Sons, reprinted with the permission of Charles Scribner's Sons; Herbert Marshall, translator and editor, *Mayakovsky,* ©1965, Dobson Books Ltd.; Victor Kravchenko from *I Chose Freedom,* ©1946 Victor Kravchenko, copyright renewed 1974, reprinted with the permission of Charles Scribner's Sons; John Scott, *Behind the Urals,* ©1942, The Indiana University Press; Mikhail Zoshchenko, *Scenes from the Bathhouse,* ©1973, The University of Michigan Press; International Publishers Co., Inc., "History of the Communist Party of the Soviet Union (Bolshevik) Short Course," 1939; Columbia University Press, "Current Soviet Policies IV," 1962; Robert G. Kaiser, from *Russia: The People and the Power,* ©1976 Robert G. Kaiser, reprinted with the permission of Atheneum Publishers; David K. Willis, "Soviet Memorandum," Jan. 14, 1981, reprinted by permission from *The Christian Science Monitor,* ©1981 The Christian Science Publishing Society, all rights reserved; *Current Digest of the Soviet Press;* George Feifer, *Justice in Moscow,* ©1964 by George Feifer, reprinted by permission of Literistic, Ltd.; Serge Schmemann, "New Soviet Rituals Seek to Replace Church's" ©1983 by the *New York Times* Company, reprinted by permission; Vladimir Bukovsky, *To Build a Castle,* ©1977, Viking Press; George F. Kennan, "A Risky U.S. Equation," published in *The New York Times,* reprinted by permission of Harriet Wasserman Literary Agency, Inc. ©1981 by George F. Kennan.

ILLUSTRATION ACKNOWLEDGMENTS

William Craft Brumfield, 13, 45, 70
Dow Jones & Co., Inc., *Photo Source: Lael Morgan,* 2
John F. Kennedy Library, Boston, Massachusetts, 246
MacClancy Collection, 158, 164 (left), 178
New York Public Library, 8, 28, 76, 99, 164 (right), 172
John Richards II, 279
Sovfoto, 233
Soviet and East European Language and Area Center Program, Harvard University,
    228, 245, 297, 303, 306, 308, 309, 313
U.S. Army Photo, 242-243
Victoria and Albert Museum, London, England, 43

Glossary

Antichrist (also seen anti-Christ). In Christian tradition, a Satanic force who misleads his followers with a claim to be the true Christ. The world ends in battle between followers of Christ and those of the Antichrist.

Apparat. The organization of full-time workers for the Communist Party. The individual is called an apparatchik.

Artel. A cooperative association of Russian craftsmen.

Autocrat. Ivan III was the first Russian ruler to assume this title formally, in the late fifteenth century. At that time, it meant a ruler independent of any foreign power. His successor Ivan IV interpreted it to mean the unlimited (and arbitrary) power of the monarch over his people, and this interpretation became traditional with later Tsars.

Avant-garde. A French phrase meaning "in the forefront," often applied to artists, musicians and writers who are considered to be ahead of their time.

Black Hundreds. Reactionary political groups of the early twentieth century who supported autocracy and anti-Semitism. Under the slogan "Save Russia," they organized pogroms against Jews and terroristic activities against liberal and radical groups. Nicholas II publicly thanked them for their support.

Bourgeois. A member of the bourgeoisie, or property-owning middle class, comprised of businessmen on the one hand, and professional people (doctors, lawyers, professors) on the other. A capitalist.

Bourgeois nationalist. Pejorative term given by Bolsheviks, and later the Communist Party, to anyone who seems to put local interests above those of the Party or the centralized Soviet government.

Boyar. A member of the privileged aristocratic class, summoned to advise the princes of Kievan Rus'.

Collective. Group. In Soviet language, the collective is the source of real value— be it the collective of factory, school, or nation. Individuals are expected always to serve the interests of the collective.

Cominform. The Communist Information Bureau, established in 1947 to encourage cooperation among the East European Communist parties.

Comintern. The Communist International. Established in 1919 as an organization to coordinate activities of Communist parties around the world, in fact directed from Moscow. Abolished in 1943 as a gesture of Allied solidarity.

Commune (mir). The peasant community of Imperial Russia. The mir regulated its own internal affairs and was collectively responsible for paying its taxes.

Constantinople. Capital of the Byzantine Empire from the fourth century. The city fell to the Turks in the fifteenth century. They renamed it Istanbul, although Europeans continued to refer to it as Constantinople.

Cossack. Frontiersman and warrior. Cossacks lived in free, democratic communities on the border of Poland, the Ukraine and Russia, with the Islamic world. Subjugated by the Tsars in the late eighteenth century, they later served in special fighting units.

Democratic centralism. The principle of Communist Party organization developed by Lenin according to which factions within the Party are outlawed, and all decisions of higher organizations are binding on lower ones. Once a decision is taken, it must be carried out without further discussion.

Democratic Socialism. In Soviet usage, a term first used by Lenin to describe socialism which has been corrupted by liberal, bourgeois principles and is therefore both wrong and dangerous.

Disiatin (dessiatine). A Russian unit of land area equal to 2.7 acres.

Dissident. Person in the Soviet Union who earns the disfavor of the Soviet regime. Soviet dissidents famous in the West include people of very different views such as Solzhenitsyn and Sakharov.

Druzhina. Russian collective noun that means "friends." Prince's retinue or bodyguard in Kievan Rus'.

Duma. Word means "thought" or thinking, and by extension advice or counsel. In the early twentieth century the Tsar created an elected State Council called the Duma.

Five Year Plan. Soviet planners usually set economic plans for five year intervals.

Fortress of St. Peter and St. Paul. In Imperial Russia, the chief prison for political offenders.

"Gendarme of Europe." "Gendarme" is the French word for policeman. After 1815, the more reactionary European rulers assumed the duty of policing the continent in order to rid it of revolutionary activity.

German Quarter. That section of Moscow in which, at the time of Peter the Great, most foreigners lived, so-called because Germans were the most numerous and prominent among the foreigners.

Gosplan. The state planning commission in the Soviet Union. It designs central economic plans.

Human rights movement. A movement by a small number of Soviet citizens to pressure the Soviet regime to honor its own Constitution and laws.

Internationale. The anthem of The International Workingmen's Association.

Kaledin-Kornilov Band. Kaledin, a Cossack leader, and Kornilov, commander of the Russian army during much of 1917, were both early opponents of the Bolsheviks following the October Revolution.

Kamenev. Lev Kamenev was one of the most important Bolshevik leaders in 1917.

Kolkhoz. A Soviet collective farm. All land is owned by the collective — the people who live on the farm. Workers are paid a share of the common produce.

Kollontai, Alexandra. One of the leading female Bolsheviks in 1917, and an outspoken feminist.

Komsomol. The Young Communist League. A selective organization for promising Soviet youth between the ages of 14 and 28.

Konovalov. A Minister of the Provisional Government in the fall of 1917.

Kuban. A region in the south of Russia, just to the north of the Caucasus Mountains.

Kulak. Word means "fist" in Russian. Name given to prosperous peasants by the Soviet regime. During the collectivization campaign, poor peasants were encouraged to dispossess the "kulaks," who were often accused of hoarding grain they did not have, and either forced into collectives or exiled to Siberia.

Kvass. A fermented beverage popular in Russia.

Marseillaise. The French national anthem, which had originated in the revolution of 1789, and which was later used by revolutionary groups throughout the world.

Marshall Plan. Named for General George C. Marshall. A program of economic aid to war-torn Europe, initiated in 1947 by the Truman Administration. It was offered also to the USSR, but Stalin refused it.

Nevsky Prospekt. The premier avenue of St. Petersburg. See Reading 8.

Nomenklatura. A list of important positions for which Party approval is needed before a person can be appointed.

Pan-Slav. The nineteenth century movement that sought to unite all Slavic peoples for political and cultural ends under the leadership of Russia.

Party-minded. Keeping the goals of the Communist Party in mind as a standard for thought and action.

Party-state. A term sometimes used to describe the Soviet state system. Party and state institutions are virtually fused, with the Party playing the leading role.

Pasternak. Boris Pasternak, 1890-1960, author of the novel *Dr. Zhivago,* and an outstanding poet of the Soviet period. He received the Nobel Prize for literature in 1957, but was forced to renounce it.

Peoples Democracy. Term used by Soviets to describe those countries of Eastern Europe with Communist Party rule. These same countries are often called "Soviet satellites" by Americans.

Peterhof. Location of one of the great imperial palaces on the Gulf of Finland a short distance from St. Petersburg.

Pioneers. In the USSR, the organization for young people aged 10 to 15.

Pise. A building material, somewhat akin to stucco.

Pogrom. An organized persecution and/or attack on a minority group, often the Jews.

Politburo. The small executive committee of the Communist Party Central Committee. The most powerful group in the Soviet Union.

Presidium. An executive committee, as for example the Presidium of the Supreme Soviet, which is elected by the Supreme Soviet and serves as its executive committee. In 1917, the term referred to the small group of men who were most influential in the Petrograd Soviet's leadership.

Pud (pood). A Russian unit of weight, equal to about 36 pounds.

"Red Director." The state-appointed factory manager of the 1920s.

Revolutionary legality. The principle of law that follows Lenin's precept that "the health of the Revolution is the highest law."

Riazan. A region in Russia southeast of Moscow, on the Volga River.

R.S. Bolsheviks. Russian Soviet Bolsheviks, as Lenin's party was known at the time.

Ruble. The basic monetary unit in Russia since the fourteenth century. Today the official Soviet exchange rate is $1.00 U.S. for about .80 ruble.

Russification. A program, begun in the Imperial Period, to promote Russian culture and the use of the Russian language in non-Russian parts of the Empire.

Samizdat. Literally, self-publishing. A term that is used for typed or mimeographed manuscripts, circulated among friends, which cannot pass state censorship.

Satellite. Term given by Western observers to those countries of Eastern Europe that have Communist Party governments and follow the directives of the Soviet Union.

Scientific Socialism. Soviet term, used by Lenin to indicate the proper form of socialism that is in accord with the laws of history.

Secretariat of the Central Committee. A small, centralized organization of full-time Party workers that directs the work of the Party apparat and Soviet society as a whole.

Serfdom. The institutionalized arrangement in which most Russian serfs were, until 1861, bound to a landlord's estate and prohibited from moving by a decree dating from 1649.

Shliapnikov. A.G. Shliapnikov was an early member and leader of the Bolshevik Party.

Show trials. In the 1920s and 1930s, public trials of so-called spies and saboteurs received wide publicity and were used to explain present hardships, warn others, and justify the need for discipline and vigilance.

Slavophiles. Group of nineteenth century Russians who believed that Russia had unique qualities that made it basically different from Western Europe, and that these qualities should be preserved.

Smolny Institute. A former girls' school in St. Petersburg, Smolny became the headquarters for the defense of Petrograd in 1917. The Military-Revolutionary Committee of the Petrograd Soviet was housed there.

Socialist realism. A literary principle introduced by Stalin, whereby literature must portray the world as the Party wishes it to be, and provide instructive and easily understandable models for readers.

Soviet. Russian word for council. Today elected councils at all levels of the government of the USSR are known as soviets.

Sovkhoz. A Soviet state farm. All land is owned by the state and the workers of the land are paid salary.

State socialism. An economic system in which all property is owned by the state.

Steppe. The prairie grasslands of the southern portions of the Soviet Union.

Supreme Soviet. The top elected government council, charged by the Soviet Constitution with the making of laws.

Taiga. The great forests of northern Russia, consisting largely of coniferous trees but including some deciduous species such as birch and aspen as well.

Tsarskoye selo. "Tsar's Village," site of one of the Tsar's palaces fifteen miles south of St. Petersburg.

Tundra. A region of cold desert in extreme northern and southern latitudes, including much of northern Siberia, characterized by poor soil and limited plant life.

Uezd. An administrative district in imperial Russia roughly equivalent to a county.

Vanguard Party. The term used by Lenin to refer to his party, which is ahead of the working class in its understanding of the revolutionary process.

Veche. Town council, a universal institution in Old Russia, particularly important in early Novgorod and Pskov.

Volost. The smallest administrative division in rural imperial Russia, comprising several villages.

INDEX

THE ROMANOV DYNASTY

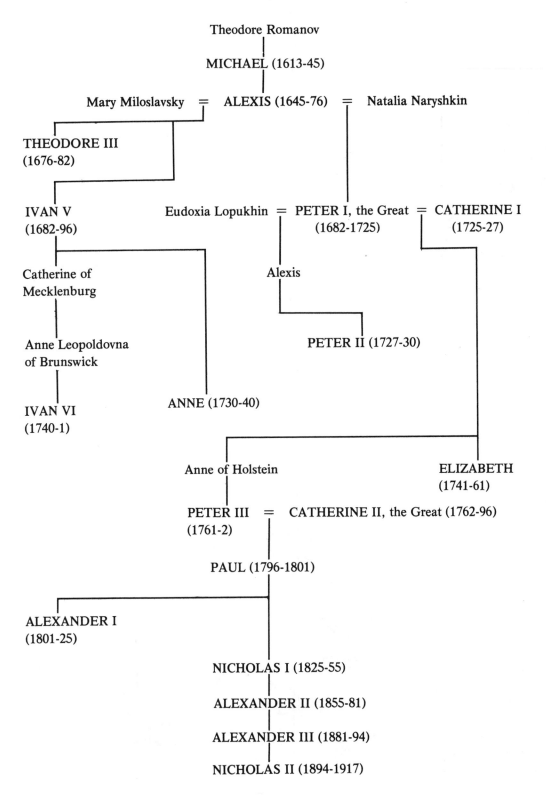

Theodore Romanov

MICHAEL (1613-45)

Mary Miloslavsky = ALEXIS (1645-76) = Natalia Naryshkin

THEODORE III
(1676-82)

IVAN V
(1682-96)

Eudoxia Lopukhin = PETER I, the Great = CATHERINE I
(1682-1725) (1725-27)

Catherine of
Mecklenburg

Alexis

Anne Leopoldovna
of Brunswick

PETER II (1727-30)

IVAN VI
(1740-1)

ANNE (1730-40)

Anne of Holstein

ELIZABETH
(1741-61)

PETER III = CATHERINE II, the Great (1762-96)
(1761-2)

PAUL (1796-1801)

ALEXANDER I
(1801-25)

NICHOLAS I (1825-55)

ALEXANDER II (1855-81)

ALEXANDER III (1881-94)

NICHOLAS II (1894-1917)

Chronology of Russian and Soviet History

With Significant Western Dates as Reference

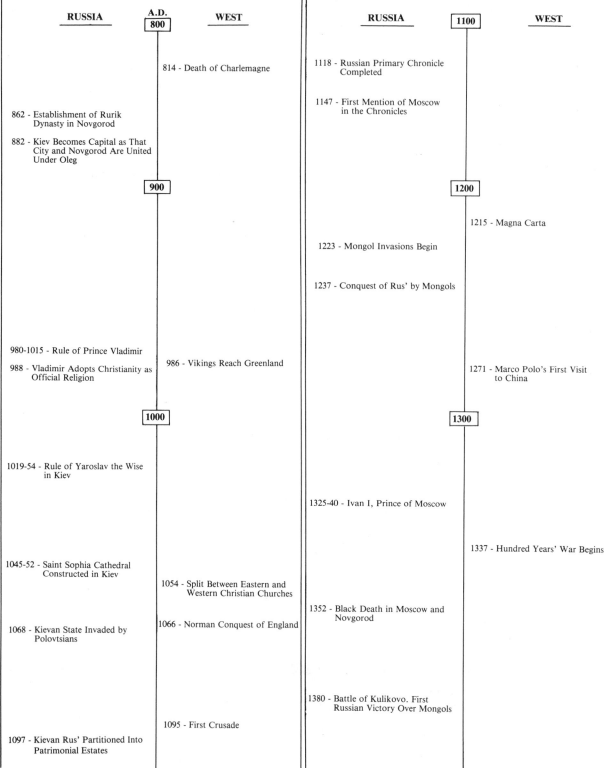

RUSSIA	A.D. 800	WEST

814 - Death of Charlemagne

862 - Establishment of Rurik Dynasty in Novgorod

882 - Kiev Becomes Capital as That City and Novgorod Are United Under Oleg

900

980-1015 - Rule of Prince Vladimir

988 - Vladimir Adopts Christianity as Official Religion

986 - Vikings Reach Greenland

1000

1019-54 - Rule of Yaroslav the Wise in Kiev

1045-52 - Saint Sophia Cathedral Constructed in Kiev

1054 - Split Between Eastern and Western Christian Churches

1066 - Norman Conquest of England

1068 - Kievan State Invaded by Polovtsians

1095 - First Crusade

1097 - Kievan Rus' Partitioned Into Patrimonial Estates

RUSSIA	1100	WEST

1118 - Russian Primary Chronicle Completed

1147 - First Mention of Moscow in the Chronicles

1200

1215 - Magna Carta

1223 - Mongol Invasions Begin

1237 - Conquest of Rus' by Mongols

1271 - Marco Polo's First Visit to China

1300

1325-40 - Ivan I, Prince of Moscow

1337 - Hundred Years' War Begins

1352 - Black Death in Moscow and Novgorod

1380 - Battle of Kulikovo. First Russian Victory Over Mongols

RUSSIA	**1400**	WEST
		1453 - Constantinople Falls to Ottoman Turks
1462-1505 - Rule of Ivan III, the Great		
1480 - Mongol Rule Overthrown By Ivan III		
1487 - Novgorod *Veche* Bell Removed to Moscow		
		1492 - Columbus Discovers America

RUSSIA	**1500**	WEST
1533-84 - Rule of Ivan IV, the Terrible		1517 - Martin Luther's 95 Theses. Beginning of Protestant Reformation
1547 - Ivan IV Assumes Title of Tsar		
1553 - The Englishman Richard Chancellor Discovers Sea Route to Russia Around North Cape		
		1562-1603 - Reign of Elizabeth I in England
1565-84 - Ivan IV's Reign of Terror		
1587-98 - Boris Godunov Acts as Regent		
		1588 - Spanish Armada
1598-1613 - "Time of Troubles"		

RUSSIA	**1600**	WEST
		1607 - Founding of Jamestown
1613 - Michael Romanov Named Tsar. Beginning of Romanov Dynasty		
		1618-48 - Thirty Years' War in Central Europe
		1620 - Pilgrims Found Plymouth
1637 - First Russian Explorers Reach Pacific Ocean		
1649 - Decree Issued Tying Serfs to Land		
1650 - Town of Okhotsk in Eastern Siberia Founded		
		1661 - Louis XIV Takes Throne in France
		1688 - England's "Glorious Revolution"
1689 - Peter the Great Becomes Tsar		
1697-98 - The "Grand Embassy"		

RUSSIA	**1700**	WEST
1707 - St. Petersburg Replaces Moscow as Capital		
1709 - Battle of Poltava. Decisive Victory Over Sweden		
1721 - Great Northern War With Sweden Ends		
1725 - Death of Peter the Great		
1741-62 - Rule of Empress Elizabeth		
1762 - Catherine the Great Gains Throne by Coup d'Etat		
1773 - Pugachev Rebellion		
1785 - Charter of the Nobility		1776 - American Declaration of Independence
1795 - Final Partition of Poland		1789 - French Revolution Begins
1796 - Death of Catherine the Great		

RUSSIA	**1800**	WEST
1801 - Alexander I Becomes Tsar		1803 - Louisiana Purchase
1812 - Napoleon Invades Russia and is Repulsed		1815 - Battle of Waterloo. Exile of Napoleon
1825 - Alexander Succeeded by Nicholas I. Decembrist Revolt		
1837 - First Russian Railroad		
1854-56 - Crimean War v. France and England		1848 - Marx Publishes *Communist Manifesto*
1855-81 - Rule of Alexander II		
1861 - Emancipation of Serfs		1861 - U.S. Purchases Alaska
		1861-65 - U.S. Civil War
1881-94 - Rule of Alexander III		1871 - Bismarck Unites Germany
1891 - Trans-Siberian Railway Begun		
1894-1917 - Rule of Nicholas II		1898 - Spanish-American War

RUSSIA	**1900**	WEST
1903 - Lenin Forms Bolshevik Party		
1904-05 - Russo-Japanese War		
1905 - Year of Revolutionary Violence		
1914-18 - World War I		
1917 - Russian Revolution. End of Romanov Dynasty. Bolsheviks Take Power		1917 - U.S. Enters World War I
		1918 - U.S. and Other Countries Intervene in Russian Civil War
1918-21 - Civil War		
1924 - Death of Lenin		
1928-53 - Rule by Joseph Stalin		
1936-39 - The Purges		1933 - U.S. Recognizes U.S.S.R.
1941-45 - The Great Patriotic War		
1956-64 - Khrushchev in Power		1941-45 - U.S. in World War II
1960 - Sino-Soviet Split		1950-53 - Korean War
1964-82 - Brezhnev in Power		1961 - Berlin Wall
1974 - Solzhenitsyn Expelled From USSR		1962 - Cuban Missile Crisis
		1962-75 - Viet Nam War
1979 - SALT II Agreement		
1979 - Invasion of Afghanistan		1977 - U.S. & U.S.S.R. Sign SALT I Agreement
1982-84 - Yuri Andropov in Power		
1984 - Chernenko in Power		
1985 - Gorbachev Assumes Control		